CRITICAL REFLECTIONS ON THE COLD WAR

Number Two:
Presidential Rhetoric Series
Martin J. Medhurst, General Editor

In association with
The Center for Presidential Studies
George Bush School of Government and Public Service

CRITICAL REFLECTIONS ON THE COLD WAR

Linking Rhetoric and History

EDITED BY

MARTIN J. MEDHURST AND H. W. BRANDS

Texas A&M University Press
College Station

First edition

∞ The paper used in this book meets the minimum requirements
of the American National Standard for Permanence
of Paper for Printed Library Materials, Z39.48-1984.
Binding materials have been chosen for durability.

Library of Congress Cataloging-in-Publication Data

Critical reflections on the Cold War : Linking rhetoric and history / edited by Martin J. Medhurst and H. W. Brands.—1st ed.

p. cm.—(Presidential rhetoric series ; no. 2)

Includes bibliographical references and index.

ISBN 0-89096-943-4 (alk. paper)

1. United States—Foreign relations—1945–1989. 2. Cold War. 3. United States—Foreign relations—Soviet Union. 4. Soviet Union—Foreign relations—United States. 5. Rhetoric—Political aspects—United States—History—20th century. I. Medhurst, Martin J. II. Brands, H. W. III. Series.

E840.C75 2000
327.73047—dc21

00-021236

To

Abbott Washburn

In recognition of his distinguished public service—

before, during, and after the Cold War

Contents

Acknowledgments

The essays appearing in this book were first presented at the fourth annual conference on presidential rhetoric held at Texas A&M University's George Bush Presidential Conference Center, March 5–8, 1998. The annual conferences are sponsored by the Center for Presidential Studies in the Bush School of Government and Public Service. The editors gratefully acknowledge the assistance of Center Director George C. Edwards III, the departments of speech communication and history at Texas A&M, the Office of the Vice President for Research and Associate Provost for Graduate Studies, and the unflagging support of Linda and Herman Giesen of Dallas, Texas.

Special thanks must go to the conference planning committee composed of James Arnt Aune, Vannesa Bowles Beasley, Leroy G. Dorsey, Tarla Rai Peterson, Enrique D. Rigsby, and Kurt Ritter. Without the able assistance of graduate students Amy Melissa Tilton and Darren Pierson, and the cheerful aid of administrative assistant Colleen Hoffman, we could not have succeeded. We are especially grateful to the many scholars who chaired panels or served as respondents to the papers. Their critical commentary was the basis for many fruitful discussions. We also want to thank Dr. David Alsobrook, director of the George Bush Presidential Library, for his stimulating luncheon talk and his personally guided tour of the Bush Library holdings.

Finally, we must express our sincere appreciation to Dr. Walt W. Rostow, national security adviser to Lyndon Johnson, Ambassador Abbott Washburn, cofounder of the Crusade for Freedom, and Mr. James Olson, Central Intelligence Agency agent-in-residence and former chief of counterintelligence at Langley, for participating in a special panel on "The Production and Dissemination of Cold War Propaganda." Our thanks also go to C-SPAN for covering that very illuminating discussion.

CRITICAL REFLECTIONS ON THE COLD WAR

Introduction

The Rhetorical Construction of History

MARTIN J. MEDHURST

In this history I have made use of set speeches, some of which were delivered just before and others during the war. I have found it difficult to remember the precise words used in the speeches which I listened to myself and my various informants have experienced the same difficulty; so my method has been, while keeping as closely as possible to the general sense of the words that were actually used, to make the speaker say what, in my opinion, were called for by each situation.

—Thucydides, *History of the Peloponnesian War,* vol. 1

Since the moment Thucydides penned his account of the Peloponnesian War, history and rhetoric have been inextricably linked. At one level, it is easy to understand how an ancient historian, writing mostly from exile and with only intermittent recourse to primary sources, "invented" the speeches that he put into the mouths of his historical characters. At a deeper level, however, this act of "invention"—the creation or discovery of speech materials—becomes more complex, for Thucydides, following the rhetorical handbooks of his day, utilized a method that allowed him to recover the "truth" about the Peloponnesian War even as the objective facts faded from memory.

For Thucydides, as for his near contemporaries Gorgias and Isocrates, rhetoric provided a method for the discovery of truth in those situations where factors such as time, distance, memory, lack of records, competing interpretations, and differences in judgment precluded certain knowledge. Aristotle, recognizing the contingent nature of the art, later defined rhetoric as "the ability, in each [particular] case, to see the available means of persuasion."[1] In the case of Thucydides, one of his goals was clearly to construct an account of the war that would be persuasive to his readers. To accomplish this goal, he turned to the art of rhetoric. What he found in that art was a systematic approach to the construction of character (*ethos*), an inventory of human emotions (*pathos*), and a checklist of rational appeals (*logos*). He also found advice—precepts—concerning how various types of people think and act—a sort of typology of human motivation, along with numerous maxims and cultural truisms ready-made for adaptation to particular circumstances. With these tools in hand, as well as firsthand knowledge of the Greek city-states, their inhabitants, their policies, and their proclivities, Thucydides wrote a book that is still read and admired some twenty-four hundred years later.

Still, one might contend that Thucydides was not "really" writing history. History—good, scientific, objective history—is about what really happened, not what some ancient historian thought happened or what he imagined might have happened. Such ancient authors may have been good storytellers, but they were not equipped with the modern tools of historiography and thus could not have hoped to distinguish between what really happened and the happenings that were rhetorically constructed in their books.

This distinction between the real and the apparently real or rhetorical is at least as old as Plato, who distinguished between the ideal forms of knowledge and the mere shadows or appearances of reality that were the sorry lot of most humans. Reality, Plato taught, resided at the level of the archetype—ideal, eternal, immutable—which was accessible to human consciousness only through an act of mind; that is, through dialectical inquiry whereby one reasons, through a logical process of systematic elimination of options, to a final, certain conclusion. This kind of conclusion, Plato holds, is the only kind of knowledge worthy of the name, and the only entree to reality. Anything less than knowledge (*episteme*) secured through dialectical analysis is not knowledge at all but mere opinion (*doxa*), which for Plato constituted the realm of rhetoric, particularly as practiced by the Sophists of his own day.[2]

The dialectical pairs of knowledge/opinion and reality/appearance provide the structure for Plato's universe, and in one form or another they have structured "modern" scientific thought ever since. The most popular manifestation of this way of thinking is, of course, the distinction between rhetoric and reality—between the real and the false or fake. Such a move is predicated on two assumptions: (1) that there is a reality apart from human sensory perception, and (2) that some people are better able to recognize and apprehend that reality than are others. Both assumptions, I shall argue, are problematic. More to the point, the essays that follow in this volume will demonstrate that the common distinction between rhetoric and reality is, in fact, unsustainable. Why? Because if there is a reality above or outside of human perception, we cannot know it, being creatures of limited symbolic capacities. All of what we call knowledge is symbolically mediated.

If we have no access to a reality outside of the human capacity to think, feel, see, touch, taste, smell, and hear, then we are left with humans as they are—"symbol-making, symbol-using, symbol-misusing" creatures.[3] If there is no external referent for determining what is real or good or true or beautiful, then there is only humanity awash in a sea of symbols, language foremost among them. This is not, of course, a new insight. The ancient Sophists, contemporaries of Thucydides, clearly understood this principle, and it seems clear that Thucydides's propensity for pairing opposed speeches reflected the teachings of Protagoras and the rhetorical doctrine of *dissoi logoi,* or two-sided arguments.[4]

In the contemporary field of rhetorical studies, Robert L. Scott, Barry Brummett, Thomas Farrell, Richard B. Gregg, Richard A. Cherwitz, and James Hikins, among others, have articulated various perspectives on the relationship of rhetoric to human knowing—the branch of philosophy known as epistemology.[5] For Scott, rhetoric "is a way of knowing; it is epistemic."[6] According to this view, rhetoric does not simply convey or make persuasive some truth already discovered or preexistent; instead, rhetoric is the human activity by which truths come into being through the process of argumentation and debate.

In the field of history, Hayden White, Alan Megill, J. H. Hexter, Hans Kellner, and Nancy Streuver, among others, have explored the rhetorical nature of historical investigation.[7] According to White:

> in his efforts to reconstruct "what happened" in any given period of history, the historian inevitably must include in his narrative an account of some event or complex of events for which the facts that would permit a plausible explanation of its occurrence are lacking. And this means that the historian must "interpret" his materials by filling in the gaps in his information on inferential or speculative grounds. A historical narrative is thus necessarily a mixture of adequately and inadequately explained events, a congeries of established and inferred facts, at once a representation that is an interpretation and an interpretation that passes for an explanation of the whole process mirrored in the narrative.[8]

The noted rhetorician David Zarefsky agrees. "The historian cannot recount *all* of 'what happened,' and the historian's view of 'what happened' is influenced by his or her own perspective. Facts do not speak; they must be spoken for. Historical scholarship is an interaction between the scholar and the historical record. Necessarily, then, it is interpretive. Regarding the selection of some historical materials and not others, it is well to remember Burke's dictum that a reflection of reality is also a selection and a deflection."[9]

In short, one cannot escape or avoid the rhetorical, because rhetorical is precisely what we human beings are. Rhetoric is one of humanity's defining characteristics, as Isocrates taught long ago. So whether we call ourselves historians, rhetoricians, philosophers, literary critics, or political scientists, the fact remains that we are all creatures who are made by language—giving ourselves labels and then imbuing those labels with meaning—and who, in turn, use language to make and remake the world around us. To paraphrase Kenneth Burke, we are the language-created language creators.

Even granting that all of the above may be true, what has it to do with the Cold War? To begin, the very term "Cold War" is a rhetorical construction. As Robert L. Scott notes in his 1990 introductory essay to *Cold War Rhetoric:* "once in our reflective consciousness the term seems strange, even inappropriate. Can a war be cold? If so, it is an oxymoron expressing some degree of ambivalence. Even the most vigorous of cold warriors, those completely convinced of the diabolical nature and intentions of their nation's adversaries, are ambivalent; that is, their words and actions have thus far stopped short, and stopping short is essential to the meaning of cold war. Ambivalence is built into the concept."[10]

Thus, Cold War is, itself, a rhetorical construction. This does not, of course, make the Cold War any less real or less significant for being rhetorical. To the contrary, we know that the Cold War involved matters of the greatest importance—even, in some cases, life and death—and an entire political culture was spawned, the effects of which linger even to this day. But this is so precisely *because* the Cold War was rhetorical in nature. As Lynn Boyd Hinds and Theodore Otto Windt, Jr., observe: "we argue about what events signify, which actions were important, and what understanding of each is more prudent and reasonable. When we begin to argue about meaning, we are engaged in constructing reality. Insofar as people believe these meanings, a reality is created upon which people act. It is in this sense that we believe political rhetoric creates political reality, structures belief systems, and provides the fundamental bases for decisions."[11]

To clarify, I am not arguing that the Cold War was nothing but rhetoric; I am arguing that even in its most material manifestations—armaments, armies, air forces, agreements, et cetera—rhetorical dimensions were necessarily present. I am further arguing that to understand those rhetorical dimensions is to gain a new way of thinking about the Cold War, a way that can provide important insights not readily attained by other approaches. Of course, the best way to demonstrate that claim is to engage in the act of rhetorical criticism, which is precisely what the authors do in this volume.

Five noted diplomatic historians—Norman A. Graebner, Frank Costigliola, H. W. Brands, Randall Bennett Woods, and Robert J. McMahon—join with five noted scholars from rhetorical studies—Robert P. Newman, Shawn J. Parry-Giles, J. Michael Hogan, Rachel L. Holloway, and Robert L. Ivie—to explore selected aspects of Cold War discourse. The essays are intentionally eclectic with respect to both objects of investigation and critical method, with chapters ranging from analysis of single speeches, to reassessment of once-secret documents, to revelation of public programs that spanned several administrations, to critique of specific language strategies. Each essay is provocative by itself. Taken together, however, these ten chapters accomplish three goals: (1) they provide new insights into some of the fundamental rhetorical texts of the Cold War; (2) they illustrate how different scholars can understand and utilize rhetorical precepts; and (3) they create new ways of "knowing."

It will become immediately clear that not all of the authors understand rhetoric in the same way. Norman Graebner, for example, tends to equate rhetoric with myth and thus laments its influence on the unfolding of the Cold War. Graebner often comes close to contrasting rhetoric to reality, as though our understanding of reality might exist apart from rhetorical construction. Graebner argues that "As a purely verbal formulation, however, a doctrine may quickly assume a doubtful relationship to reality and, by the very power of its appeal, become exceedingly dangerous." Reality, under this view, exists somehow apart from the verbal formulations used to encompass that reality. Yet, as David Zarefsky observes, "Rhetoric is not different from reality; it is a set of choices that invite us to see one reality rather than another." [12]

Graebner is highly critical of the choices that American policy makers enacted during the course of the Cold War. He argues that these choices did not comport with reality. Yet many of the best minds in America made those choices, presumably on the basis of analysis and interpretation of the evidence at hand. That we today can see flaws in the Munich analogy and the domino theory simply underscores the point: reality did not change, only our ability to read and interpret that reality—a reality *that was our own construction in the first place.* By reading and interpreting differently, we have come to understand and judge the past in new ways. Furthermore, the fact that scholars still contest portions of Graebner's analysis illustrates that there is no single, monolithic view of reality out there waiting to be discovered, but only various interpretations competing in the marketplace of ideas for acceptance. The coin of this marketplace is none other than rhetorical discourse.

Cold War rhetoric was not, of course, limited to discourse produced by Americans. In chapter 2, Frank Costigliola examines the speech given by Joseph Stalin on February 9, 1946, and the interpretations of that speech by American opinion leaders. Costigliola raises several issues that are central to rhetorical analysis: the role of memory, the often disparate purposes of speakers and listeners, the centrality of context in interpretation, the nature of multiple audiences, and the linguistic choices made by both speakers and listener-interpreters.

Costigliola writes: "Both the United States and the Soviet Union, categorizing each other as aggressive and in planning for the worst contingency, revealed an inability to escape the traumatic memory of Hitler's belligerence. Nor could the two nations escape the memory of their prewar resentment." Memory is central to all acts of historical interpretation. The ways in which memories, especially public memories, are formed, maintained, and used is the subject of much recent scholarship.[13] One thing seems clear: we remember purposefully—in line with some interest or goal or commitment. Public memory is selective, focusing on those elements that comprise a usable past for the culture. Rhetoric plays a role, both in the formation of public memory and in its articulation, reconstruction, and rearticulation over time. Stalin clearly understood this principle and thus sought to use rhetorical discourse to reconstruct the past for Soviet citizens. However, in bringing myth and memory to bear for his own political purposes, Stalin may have overlooked an equally important rhetorical precept: different people remember differently.

What may have been an attempt, according to Costigliola, to rhetorically reconstruct a Soviet past for Soviet citizens was clearly understood by some in the West as an attempt to intimidate and challenge. Thus, in the context of Soviet domestic politics, the speech could be read as intended to bolster and reinforce the regime. The same speech, read in the context of postwar geopolitics, could also be interpreted as a menacing boast, prefiguring a race for military hegemony. The context shared by an interpretive community thus becomes the dominant factor in the meaning and significance attached to a communication. Because communities remember differently, they also interpret differently, activating different sociological, psychological, and contextual cues in the process of meaning construction.

In the context of an emerging Cold War, Stalin's use of the phrase "insured against any eventuality" could easily be read in several different ways. That it was construed by many in the West as a virtual declaration of war says more about the assumptions of the interpretive community than it does about the language itself. As Costigliola notes, "much depended on who was interpreting the speech and with what preconceptions." The ability of interpreters such as Walter Lippmann to use their own rhetoric to "frame" audience interpretations points to yet another aspect of symbol use in the modern world: Most communication is mediated—through newspapers, television, radio, the Internet. Audiences respond to issues as *framed* by the media, which provide further context, interpretive cues, and memory traces.

In chapter 3, Robert P. Newman examines some of the rhetorical dimensions of NSC-68, a once top-secret document. Newman is concerned with the rhetorical construction of the document and the clues such construction might hold for analysis of authorial motives, particularly the motives of the principal author, Paul H. Nitze. Newman argues that the government policy of secrecy concerning NSC-68 was a large factor in the document's ability to wield such rhetorical power.

Newman challenges many of the myths concerning NSC-68, including the view that it served as a blueprint for the Cold War. In doing so, he offers both a critique and an interpretation. Newman's critique is straightforward: Nitze's interpretations of the facts concerning U.S.-Soviet relations at the beginning of 1950 were wrong. They were so wrongheaded, Newman holds, that Nitze must have been "hallucinating." Furthermore, Nitze's own anti-Soviet ideology caused him to interpret facts and opinions that challenged NSC-68 as, instead, evidence of agreement with its premises and conclusions.

Newman persistently questions how Nitze could claim to know certain things, such as: "How did Nitze know Russia and our allies would interpret a no-first-use pledge this way?" He is acutely aware that claims to such knowledge demand support—be it theoretical, experiential, or empirical. Yet Newman finds no such support for Nitze's statements, concluding that Nitze substituted his own ideological *beliefs* for knowledge of the facts. Newman is on strong ground as far as he goes, but perhaps he does not go far enough. Is it ever possible to have "knowledge of the facts" in any pure, pristine form? Newman implies that such knowledge is now available to him and to us as readers—and that it was also available to Nitze in 1950, if only he had opened his eyes to see and his mind to understand. But is that really the case? Does not any claim to knowledge presuppose some position—ideological, geographical, political, socioeconomic, religious, racial, gender—from which that knowledge is constructed? Do not all interpreters function within a particular constellation of spatial-temporal-ideological forces that impel or predispose (if they do not determine) what "counts" as meaningful or significant?

One can agree with Newman that Nitze willfully misinterpreted and misreported the views of others without holding that there was one right, true, and perfect way to convey the situation surrounding the construction of NSC-68. After all, *any construal of the situation,* however arrived at, however composed, and however delivered would have been a construal by *someone* (or some group), and thus subject to all the normal limitations of symbol-using creatures. Newman's appeal to the counterevidence, reason, history, documents, and memories is well taken, but it cannot be definitive because in matters of human symbol usage there is no neutral or transcendent place from which to render final judgment. There are only interpretations—some stronger and some weaker, to be sure—based on argument and evidence, which seems from the standpoint of the interpreter and his or her interlocutors to be "right" or "accurate" or "useful" at the moment of interpretation.

Rhetorical analysis must necessarily, then, concern itself with a large number of factors—touching, at a minimum, on matters of philosophy, psychology, sociology, and language behavior. At one level, Newman seems clearly to understand this, picturing Dean Acheson and Nitze as interpreting the world "through their Chicken Little lenses." By contrast, others, viewing the world through different lenses, construed that world differently. Yet, for all his insight, Newman is insistent that the author of NSC-68 created "not security, but insecurity." Perhaps. But that, too, is a matter of definition and interpretation inasmuch as one person's security may be another's insecurity.

In chapter 4, Shawn Parry-Giles describes the evolution of U.S. government propaganda from a "journalistic paradigm" (propaganda as news) to what she calls a "military paradigm" (propaganda as weapon). Part of this evolution involved questions of control, content, and responsibility: who would run the propaganda program, what would be its mission, where would it be located on the organizational chart, and who would be responsible for both its content and its operation? The question of goals and purposes was, of course, implicated in the movement from one paradigm to the other.

The establishment of the Psychological Strategy Board (PSB) in 1951 signaled the completion of a "progression toward centralizing propaganda strategy in the White House, reducing congressional input, and militarizing communication strategies." Starting with the "Campaign of Truth" in April, 1950, U.S. propaganda efforts took on an increasing tone of crisis, marked by the adoption of "the language of all-out warfare." What was the metaphor of war in April became the fact of war in June, as North Korean forces crossed the 38th parallel. From that moment on, according to Parry-Giles, there was no questioning of the suitability of propaganda as a necessary instrument of war.

The Eisenhower administration took the existing military paradigm of propaganda and fine-tuned it through creation of the U.S. Information Agency (USIA) and the Operations Coordinating Board (OCB). That Eisenhower used public rhetoric to mask Cold War propaganda motives is now well established. Parry-Giles explores the first of Ike's public campaigns—"The Chance for Peace"—which clearly illustrates the ways in which "propaganda camouflages rhetorical motives." Even so, to this day some prominent students of the Eisenhower presidency continue to believe that the Chance for Peace campaign was a sincere attempt to establish a *modus vivendi* with the Soviet Union.[14] Parry-Giles's analysis, as well as other sources, suggests otherwise.[15]

"Peace" was the rhetorical token under whose cover Eisenhower waged war—psychological, economic, geopolitical, cultural warfare. Parry-Giles illustrates this, and in so doing underscores the view that Eisenhower was a skilled practitioner of the art who understood rhetoric and used it as "a weapon with which to wage Cold War."[16] Although he personally disliked the term propaganda, Eisenhower never hesitated to employ it when he thought it could serve his broader purposes.

Rhetoric as propaganda is an important subject because it reminds us, as no other activity can, that what we think we know is not necessarily the case. When rhetoricians use language to intentionally deceive, mislead, obfuscate, or dissemble, the ability to interpret goals, motives, and true intentions—never perfect in the best of all possible worlds—becomes even more difficult. Parry-Giles urges the examination of both public and private sources as a partial antidote to misunderstanding and misinterpretation. Vigilance and a "hermeneutics of suspicion" are at a premium in a rhetorical world. It is either that or Plato's solution: banish the orators (along with the poets and musicians) from the republic.

J. Michael Hogan investigates another dimension of rhetoric as propaganda in chapter 5. Focusing on George Gallup and the use of public opinion polling during the Cold War, Hogan demonstrates how the new communication sciences were enlisted (or, in the case of Gallup, volunteered) for service in the fight against communism. Hogan pictures Gallup as a cold warrior who "'naively' believed in the 'natural' superiority of democracy" and who was, at times, "barely less 'hysterical' about communism than Joseph McCarthy himself."

For Gallup and other social scientists, the public opinion poll was a way to find out what people were thinking about, what they believed and disbelieved, what they feared, and what solutions they favored. Armed with such knowledge, professional cold warriors such as James Lambie, C. D. Jackson, and Abbott Washburn could fashion political discourse with specific goals and specific target audiences in mind. On the strength of such polls, they believed that they knew what their audiences were thinking and how best to appeal to them.

Such early attempts to use public opinion polling to shape political discourse and decision making were, for the most part, unsuccessful. That did not, of course, stop such usage. Today, Bill Clinton never gives a major speech without first taking a series of polls. Unlike Eisenhower—who did not hesitate to override the counsel of his advisers and who, as Hogan clearly shows, did not follow the specific approach that his poll-reading prognosticators crafted—today's political leaders appear to live or die by the latest poll. But can Bill Clinton, for all his sophistication in the science of political communication, really be said to "know" the American people—their values, their hopes, their desires—better than, say, Harry Truman or Dwight Eisenhower?

Coming to grips with history *as it is being lived* is no easy thing to master. Choosing to construct Cold War policy from what George Gallup discovers from his polling is one thing; relying on the years of experience of a George Kennan or a Charles "Chip" Bohlen is something else entirely—as is relying on one's own intuition, something Eisenhower seemed to do frequently. How one tries to encompass the world in which one lives is an important topic of investigation. For Gallup, knowledge appears to be synonymous with information or facts. Yet knowing the facts and knowing how to interpret them and use them are different things. The Greeks called the first *episteme;* the second they called *phronesis.* In politics, as in life, knowing the wise thing to *do* is more important than simply knowing. The actional dimension—acting in history in order to make history—has always been central to the rhetorical tradition. Knowledge is important only to the extent that it helps one make wise decisions in particular circumstances.

In chapter 6, H. W. Brands defends the proposition that "the Cold War in fact provided significant impetus for some of the most important liberal reforms of the postwar era." These include expansion of social security coverage and massive federal aid to education (Eisenhower), executive intervention in the nation's economy and expansion of the space program (Kennedy), and extension of voting rights and waging a war on poverty (Johnson). Brands links all of these programs and more to one or more dimensions of the Cold War:

the need to keep up with the Soviets (space), to present a good public image to the world (race relations), to maintain America's technological superiority (aid to education), to demonstrate how the capitalist system outperforms a command economy (tax cuts and investment incentives). Paradoxically, many of the most important success stories for American liberalism between 1953 and 1969 came about, at least in part, because of Cold War imperatives.

Brands demonstrates how Eisenhower, Kennedy, and Johnson each rhetorically constructed the need for these domestic improvements and how each utilized the Soviet threat or the demands of the Cold War as rationales for action. Such rhetorical linkages were a proven way to secure passage of even the most difficult pieces of legislation. As long as the Cold War was going relatively well, this rhetorical strategy proved effective. However, when the context changed, so, too, did the fortunes of domestic liberalism. Brands argues that by tying domestic reforms so closely to the Cold War consensus, liberals opened themselves to counterattack when that consensus dissolved in the jungles of Vietnam.

Brands's argument is provocative in and of itself. However, it points to an even larger lesson about rhetoric and history: that successful rhetoric both draws from and responds to the historical situation; that as that situation changes, the rhetoric must also change if it is to be effective; that rhetorical strategies employed over long periods of time—decades in the case of the Cold War—linger long after the original impetus has dissipated; and that to miss the change in audience beliefs, values, and predispositions is to be left talking a language that no longer communicates a message capable of moving an audience to action. In these ways, rhetoric and history move in syncopation with one another.

In chapter 7, Randall Bennett Woods examines the role of J. William Fulbright (D-Arkansas) in the rise and fall of Cold War internationalism. As H. W. Brands finds the influence of the Cold War suffusing domestic liberalism, so Woods finds liberalism at the heart of Cold War foreign policy. Fulbright's role in the liberal internationalist consensus was central. Consequently, when Fulbright broke ranks—starting in 1964 with his speech "Old Myths and New Realities," and culminating with the 1966 Senate Foreign Relations Committee hearings on Vietnam—the consensus was no more. As Woods notes, by 1966 Fulbright had come to believe that "the war represented nothing less than the perversion of the very liberal internationalism he and Lyndon Johnson had been espousing."

Woods describes the peculiar mixture of motives that led to Fulbright's final break with the Johnson White House. Just as he came to reject the ideology of liberal internationalism, so, too, did Fulbright reject the rhetorical discourse associated with that ideology:

> Our national vocabulary is full of "self-evident truths" not only about "life, liberty, and happiness," but about a vast number of personal and public issues, including the cold war. It has become one of the "self-evident truths" of the postwar era that just as the President resides in Washington and the Pope in Rome, the devil resides immutably in Moscow. We have come to regard the Kremlin as the permanent seat of his power and we have grown almost comfortable with a menace which, though unspeakably evil, has had the redeeming virtues of consistency, predictability, and familiarity. Now the Devil has betrayed us by travelling abroad and worse still, by dispersing himself, turning up now here, now there, and in many places at once, with a devilish disregard for the laboriously constructed frontiers of ideology.[17]

As Woods notes, Fulbright was acutely sensitive to the rhetorical forms associated with Johnson's defense of his Vietnam policies. Consequently, Fulbright rejected both the policies and the rhetorical forms that were used to articulate, defend, and justify them. "The president was using liberal internationalist arguments to mobilize and sustain support for the war," Woods writes, "and thus it was these arguments that would have to be discredited."

What Woods does not say is that by discrediting the administration's arguments, Fulbright necessarily had also to challenge the values, presuppositions, and self-images implicit in those arguments. Not just Johnson's policies but who we were as Americans was called into question. If we were not "defenders of liberty," then what were we? If the United States was not "helping the South Vietnamese to defend their democratic form of government," then what kind of government were we defending? If we had no motive other than to "preserve freedom so that the Vietnamese can live in peace," then why were the Vietnamese not rushing to join our side? Fulbright's exposure of these fissures in the American self-concept led, eventually, to a loss of faith in President Johnson and, ultimately, to a discrediting of the liberal ideology, both at home and abroad.

In chapter 8, Rachel L. Holloway investigates another dimension of liberal ideology: faith in technological progress. Focusing on the selling of the Strategic Defense Initiative (SDI) by President Reagan, Holloway isolates an argumentative form that she calls "the technological sublime." Reagan utilized this form of argumentation, she holds, to overcome opposition from the scientific establishment and move the American public toward acceptance of the need for an SDI program. "By splitting the scientific community rhetorically into those who were living in a past of 'expertise' and those with the courage and vision to create a future transformed by defensive weapons," Holloway argues, "Reagan reaffirmed American belief in technical solutions to problems."

Holloway emphasizes the ways in which rhetoric, science, and politics were inextricably intertwined during the debate over SDI. Both sides marshaled arguments, enlisted proponents, presented evidence and testimony, and claimed that the bulk of scientific/technological knowledge supported their cause. Both sides used rhetoric; both appealed to history. But Reagan did more. He took the arguments on behalf of SDI and placed them "within a broader notion of American destiny," thus giving them a transcendent meaning and purpose. "History," Reagan told the American people, "asks us once again to be a force for good in the world." No longer would these weapons serve the cause of war and death; through technological progress married to the will to think creatively, such weapons would themselves become the guarantors of peace.

By placing SDI proponents within the forward movement of history and calling upon the rhetorical form of the technological sublime, Reagan was able to convince the American people that continued reliance on the theory of Mutually Assured Destruction (MAD) really was mad and that there was a better way. Apparently he convinced the Soviet leaders, too, for they began to divert more of their defense budget into SDI-type research. Whether this was a major factor contributing to the Soviet Union's implosion in 1991 is still hotly debated, but the efficacy of the technological sublime as an argumentative form seems clear.

In chapter 9, Robert J. McMahon isolates what ancient rhetoricians called a *topos*—a topic that provides a rich resource for building arguments across speakers, eras, or ideologies. From Truman through Bush, from the opening days of the Cold War through the fall of the Berlin Wall, from Democrats and Republicans alike, the *topos* of "by helping others, we help ourselves" was employed to great rhetorical effect. Why was such a line of argument repeatedly called upon? Quite simply because it was useful. It condensed, in one brief span, the basic myth of America's founding. As McMahon observes: "Ever since the era of the founding fathers, the nation's statesmen have simply taken for granted that what was best for the United States was best for the world as a whole."

The expression of this sentiment in presidential discourse has been remarkably consistent over the decades and has served both to create and sustain a narrative of self-understanding and self-identity. It is a story we tell to ourselves about ourselves—and for the most part we tend to believe it. And why not? It casts America in the heroic role of savior, symbolically transforming what might, at one level, be viewed as self-serving, nationalistic policies into other-directed, universalistic actions. As McMahon puts it, "U.S. chief executives have always depicted the United States as the noble and courageous guardian not just of American interests, but of the world's."

Such a conceit presupposes, of course, that we know what is in the best interests of the "Other." We assume that their interests are the same as our own and then act to ensure that our interests will prevail, holding all the while that we are really acting for the good of the entire world. Although McMahon does not explicitly say so, it is clear that such an assumption ignores a host of inconvenient facts: that most of the world is yellow, brown, or black and not white; that free-enterprise capitalism was, until quite recently, the exception rather than the rule; that very few countries had two hundred years of democratic traditions and institutions to draw upon; that our notions of freedom (primarily freedom *to* worship, assemble, petition the government, etc.) were often quite different from others' notions of freedom (primarily freedom *from* hunger, poverty, violence, disease, etc.). While it is easy to see how this argumentative topic worked for us, it is more difficult—though equally important—to perceive the myriad ways in which it may have worked against us as a form of self-deception and an expression of national hubris.

Robert L. Ivie also urges us to reconsider part of this ongoing narrative. In chapter 10, Ivie examines what America's leaders seem to signify by their application of the term democracy to the post–Cold War world. Focusing primarily on Bill Clinton's foreign policy rhetoric, Ivie argues that "the rhetoric of democracy . . . is a powerful vehicle for carrying the legacy of America's global struggle and enlarged fear of hostile aliens into present representations of post–Cold War provocations, opportunities, and responsibilities." Ivie holds that our traditional representations of democracy are inadequate to the global political life of the twenty-first century.

The problem, as Ivie sees it, is that our political imagination has been restricted by our uncritical acceptance of our own rhetorical construction of democracy, a construction that privileges free-enterprise capitalism and republicanism. Such a construction—limiting, as it does, our ability to understand both ourselves and others—needs to be rhetorically reconstructed to serve the needs of globalism as different nations struggle toward their own definitions, policies, and practices. The first step in such a rhetorical reconstruction is to become aware of our own language choices and the narratives and assumptions embedded in those choices.

Ivie's examination of Clinton's foreign policy rhetoric reveals a consistent message that "conveys the sense of tenuous times, fragility, instability, uncertainty, the compensatory need for control, and thus the fear of democracy itself." The president's words, Ivie holds, "are a national repository of democratic anxiety." Furthermore, Clinton's use of the term *democracy* "is sufficiently obtuse to disguise the fact that 'democracy' is a contested term." By rehabilitating democracy, Ivie points to a new kind of rhetorical republic, one based on "addressing audiences, developing strategies of identification, and transacting agreements through public persuasion." In such a republic, rhetoric "exercises democracy and strengthens it by courting and befriending the otherwise threatening Other wherever and whenever possible." Under such a conceptualization, rhetoric becomes more than just the means of conducting democracy; it is *constitutive* of democracy.[18]

Ivie's position parallels closely the distinction between rhetoric as a mere conveyor of previously established truth and rhetoric as a cocreator of truths. As students of the Cold War, we are constantly tempted to think of history as past fact—simply as the way things were. Of course that is a naive view, both of what history is and of how we come to know it—and to make it. Our constructions may be better informed, more theoretically sophisticated, and more conceptually elegant than those of Thucydides, but they are constructions nonetheless. Both historians and rhetoricians are engaged in making (*poesis*), not merely recording or reporting. The multiple ways in which those rhetorical constructions of history take place is the subject of this book.

Notes

1. Aristotle, *On Rhetoric,* trans. George A. Kennedy (New York: Oxford University Press, 1991), 36.

2. For Plato's views concerning the relationship of rhetoric to knowledge see his dialogues "Gorgias" and "Phaedrus" in *Plato: The Collected Dialogues,* ed. Edith Hamilton and Huntington Cairns (Princeton, N.J.: Princeton University Press, 1961), 229–307, 475–525.

3. Kenneth Burke, "Definition of Man," in *Language as Symbolic Action* (Berkeley: University of California Press, 1966), 3–24.

4. See Edward Schiappa, *Protagoras and Logos: A Study in Greek Philosophy and Rhetoric* (Columbia: University of South Carolina Press, 1991), 89–102; "Dissoi Logoi or Dialexeis," in *The Older Sophists,* ed. Rosamond Kent Sprague (Columbia: University of South Carolina Press, 1972), 279–93.

5. See, for example, Robert L. Scott, "On Viewing Rhetoric as Epistemic," *Central States Speech Journal* 18 (1967): 9–17; Barry Brummett, "Some Implications of 'Process' or 'Intersubjectivity': Postmodern Rhetoric," *Philosophy and Rhetoric* 9 (1976): 21–51; Thomas B. Farrell, "Knowledge, Consensus, and Rhetorical Theory," *Quarterly Journal of Speech* 62 (1976): 1–14; Richard B. Gregg, *Symbolic Inducement and Knowing: A Study in the Foundations of Rhetoric* (Columbia: University

of South Carolina Press, 1984); Richard A. Cherwitz, "Viewing Rhetoric as a 'Way of Knowing': An Attenuation of the Epistemological Claims of the 'New Rhetoric,'" *Southern Speech Communication Journal* 42 (1977): 207–19; Richard A. Cherwitz and James W. Hikins, *Communication and Knowledge: An Investigation in Rhetorical Epistemology* (Columbia: University of South Carolina Press, 1986). For an overview of various positions see Richard A. Cherwitz, ed., *Rhetoric and Philosophy* (Hillsdale, N.J.: Lawrence Erlbaum, 1990).

6. Scott, "On Viewing Rhetoric as Epistemic," 9.

7. See, for example, Hayden White, *Metahistory: The Historical Imagination in Nineteenth-Century Europe* (Baltimore: Johns Hopkins University Press, 1973); Alan Megill and Donald N. McCloskey, "The Rhetoric of History," in *The Rhetoric of the Human Sciences: Language and Argument in Scholarship and Public Affairs,* ed. John S. Nelson, Alan Megill, and Donald N. McCloskey (Madison: University of Wisconsin Press, 1987), 221–38; J. H. Hexter, "The Rhetoric of History," in *Doing History* (Bloomington: Indiana University Press, 1971), 15–76; Hans Kellner, *Language and Historical Representation: Getting the Story Crooked* (Madison: University of Wisconsin Press, 1989); Nancy S. Struever, "Historical Discourse," in *Handbook of Discourse Analysis,* vol. 1, *Disciplines of Discourse,* ed. Teun A. van Dijk (London: Academic Press, 1985), 249–71.

8. Hayden White, *Tropics of Discourse: Essays in Cultural Criticism* (Baltimore: Johns Hopkins University Press, 1978), 51.

9. David Zarefsky, "Four Senses of Rhetorical History," in *Doing Rhetorical History: Concepts and Cases,* ed. Kathleen J. Turner (Tuscaloosa: University of Alabama Press, 1998), 20–21.

10. Robert L. Scott, "Cold War and Rhetoric: Conceptually and Critically," in *Cold War Rhetoric: Strategy, Metaphor, and Ideology,* by Martin J. Medhurst, Robert L. Ivie, Philip Wander, and Robert L. Scott, rev. ed. (East Lansing: Michigan State University Press, 1997), 4.

11. Lynn Boyd Hinds and Theodore Otto Windt, Jr., *The Cold War as Rhetoric: The Beginnings, 1945–1950* (New York: Praeger, 1991), xx.

12. David Zarefsky, "The Rhetorical Cold War: A Response to Professor Norman A. Graebner" (paper presented at the keynote session of the fourth annual Conference on Presidential Rhetoric, Texas A&M University, Mar. 5, 1998).

13. See, for example, Michael Kammen, *Mystic Chords of Memory: The Transformation of Tradition in American Culture* (New York: Knopf, 1991); John Bodnar, *Remaking America: Public Memory, Commemoration, and Patriotism in the Twentieth Century* (Princeton, N.J.: Princeton University Press, 1992); John R. Gillis, *Commemorations: The Politics of National Identity* (Princeton, N.J.: Princeton University Press, 1994); Carole Blair, Marsha S. Jeppeson, and Enrico Pucci, Jr., "Public Memorializing in Postmodernity: The Vietnam Veterans Memorial as Prototype," *Quarterly Journal of Speech* 77 (1991): 263–88; Stephen H. Browne, "Reading, Rhetoric, and the Texture of Public Memory," *Quarterly Journal of Speech* 81 (1995): 237–50; Barbie Zelizer, "Reading the Past Against the Grain: The Shape of Memory Studies," *Critical Studies in Mass Communication* 12 (1995): 214–39; Bryan Hubbard and Marouf A. Hasian, Jr., "Atomic Memories of the *Enola Gay:* Strategies of Remembrance at the National Air and Space Museum," *Rhetoric & Public Affairs* 1 (1998): 363–85; Bradford Vivian, "The Art of Forgetting: John W. Draper and the Rhetorical Dimensions of History," *Rhetoric & Public Affairs* 2 (1999): 551–72.

14. See, for example, Stephen E. Ambrose, *Eisenhower,* vol. 2, *The President* (New York: Simon and Schuster, 1984), 149.

15. See, for example, Robert L. Ivie, "Dwight D. Eisenhower's 'Chance for Peace': Quest or Crusade?" *Rhetoric & Public Affairs* 1 (1998): 227–43; Martin J. Medhurst, *Dwight D. Eisenhower: Strategic Communicator* (Westport, Conn.: Greenwood, 1993), 71–96.

16. Martin J. Medhurst, "Introduction," in *Eisenhower's War of Words: Rhetoric and Leadership*, ed. Martin J. Medhurst (East Lansing: Michigan State University Press, 1994), 1.

17. J. William Fulbright, "Old Myths and New Realities," in *Old Myths and New Realities and Other Commentaries* (New York: Random House, 1964), 7.

18. See also, Robert L. Ivie, "Democratic Deliberation in a Rhetorical Republic," *Quarterly Journal of Speech* 84 (1998): 491–505.

CHAPTER ONE

Myth and Reality

America's Rhetorical Cold War

NORMAN A. GRAEBNER

Throughout its forty-year history the American Cold War was fundamentally a rhetorical exercise. It emerged and thrived on images of impending global disaster. The nuclear arsenals symbolized the long Soviet-American rivalry, but they never reflected any clash of interests whose resolution demanded a resort to such levels of violence. No issue that divided the two superpowers was worth an hour of nuclear war, even of conventional war. Through forty years of recurrent high tension and mutual recrimination, the United States and the Soviet Union, inhibited by fears of mutual destruction as well as the limited nature of the issues that divided them, did not approach a decision for war. The Cuban missile crisis of October, 1962, was no clear exception. Never did the country's role as special defender of the free world monopolize its interests or activities. Despite the trillions that the country expended on defending itself and much of the world, the Cold War, for most Americans, remained an abstraction, acknowledged but not understood. It levied few impositions on the vast majority who lived through it—confident, untouched, and secure—conscious only of the unprecedented opportunities that the long experience provided.

For some Americans the euphoria of victory and peace in 1945 evaporated quickly. That the Soviet Union's total victory over Germany had upset the historic European balance of power mattered little to Americans who had lauded the Soviets for their costly and necessary contributions to Allied successes. But for a small minority of U.S. officials and writers who had been conditioned to distrust the Kremlin, the continued Soviet occupation of Eastern Europe merely enhanced that country's strategic position in the Balkans and rendered bordering regions vulnerable to further Soviet expansion.[1] It required only the Kremlin's postwar demands on Iran and Turkey to unleash visions of Soviet military expansion reminiscent of the Italian, German, and Japanese aggressions that so recently had brought war to the world. Joseph and Stewart Alsop, writing in the May 20, 1946, issue of *Life*, defined the emerging Soviet threat in Hitlerian terms: "Already Poland, the Baltic States, Rumania, Bulgaria, Yugoslavia and Albania are behind the Iron Curtain. Huge armies hold Hungary and half of Germany and Austria. Czechoslovakia and Greece are encircled. . . . In the Middle East the Soviets are driving southward. Iran is in danger of being reduced to puppethood; Turkey and Iraq are threatened. Finally, in the Far East, the Kuriles and half of Korea are occupied and Manchuria has been stripped and left in condition to be transformed at will into another Azerbaijan. The process still goes on. One . . . must also wonder whether they will ultimately be satisfied with less than dominion over Europe and Asia."[2]

Responding to Soviet pressures on Turkey for a new Straits settlement in August, 1946, Acting Secretary of State Dean Acheson and the Joint Chiefs of Staff (JCS), with advice from State Department experts, prepared a memorandum on Turkey for the president. The memorandum, signed by Acheson, Navy Secretary James Forrestal, and Secretary of War Robert Patterson, warned: "If the Soviet Union succeeds in its objective of obtaining control over Turkey, it will be extremely difficult, if not impossible, to prevent the Soviet Union from obtaining control over Greece and over the whole Near and Middle East . . . [including] the territory lying between the Mediterranean and India. When the Soviet Union has once obtained full mastery of this territory . . . it will be in a much stronger position to obtain its objectives in India and China."[3]

Such rhetorical portrayals of Soviet territorial ambitions far exceeded Soviet military capabilities and intentions. Stalin was no Napoleon or Hitler. The Kremlin had already demonstrated its extreme reluctance to confront the West militarily along its Iranian and Turkish borders, where its strategic advantage was profound. Confronted by the predictable resistance of the non-Soviet world, Kremlin leaders understood that any military venture would end in disaster. Indeed, U.S. officials concluded as early as 1946 that the Soviet Union had no intention of embarking on a career of military aggression. That conviction, however, scarcely constrained the country's burgeoning insecurities.

At issue in the growing fear and distrust of the Soviet Union was not the American dislike of Communism or the size and power of the Soviet armed forces. American citizens overwhelmingly loathed Communism as inimical to Western principles of liberal democracy. But for most the ideological foundations of the Soviet state were not an American concern. What seized the country's emerging anti-Communist elite was the fear that the real Soviet danger, one that rendered military aggression irrelevant, lay in the limitless promise of Soviet ideological expansion. Soviet rhetoric had long predicted Communism's ultimate conquest of the world. For those Americans who took the Soviet rhetoric seriously, the Soviet Union, as the self-assigned leader of world Communism, possessed the power and will to incite or support Communist-led revolutions everywhere, imposing on them its influence, if not its direct control. Ideological expansionism, assuring future Soviet triumphs without war, transcended the limited possibilities and high costs of military adventurism by enabling the Soviet Union to extend its presence over vast distances without military force. It mattered little whether Soviet troops or even Soviet officials were present at all. The alleged capacity to expand far beyond the reach of its armies seemed to transform the Soviet Union into an international phenomenon of unprecedented expansive power. The immediate danger to Western security lay in the chaotic economic, social, and political conditions that prevailed throughout much of postwar Eurasia, offering unlimited opportunities for Soviet ideological exploitation. The doubtful validity of liberal ideas and capitalist institutions in a revolutionary environment suggested that much of the world's resources might still escape the West and fall into the Kremlin's clutches.

As early as 1946 anti-Communist writers and spokesmen detected few limits to the Kremlin's external needs and ambitions. George F. Kennan's famed "Long Telegram" of February attributed the Kremlin's insatiable designs on the United States to a paranoia that demanded the destruction of all competing power. "We have here," he warned, "a force committed fanatically to the belief that with the United States there can be no permanent modus vivendi, that it is desirable and necessary that the internal harmony of our society be disrupted, our traditional way of life destroyed, the international authority of our state broken, if Soviet power is to be secure."[4] Kennan's analysis created a sensation in official Washington, especially among those who shared the burgeoning fears of Soviet expansionism. Taking his cue from the Long Telegram, State Department official H. Freeman Matthews observed in April that, for the Kremlin, "the Soviet and non-Soviet systems [could not] exist in the world side by side." Writing for *Life* magazine, foreign policy expert John Foster Dulles warned the country in June that the Soviets intended "to have governments everywhere which accept[ed] the doctrine of the Soviet Communist Party." The achievement of that goal, he acknowledged, would give the Soviet Union world hegemony. Also that year, former ambassador William C. Bullitt averred, "As conquest of the earth for Communism is the objective of the Soviet government, no nation lies outside the scope of its ambitions."[5] A report on the Soviet danger by Clark Clifford and George Elsey, presented to the president in September, 1946, reflected the broad convictions of Washington insiders: "The key to understanding of current Soviet policy," the report concluded,

". . . is the realization that Soviet leaders adhere to the Marxian theory of ultimate destruction of capitalist states by communist states."[6]

The Doctrine of Anti-Communism

Such graphic depictions of impending doom transformed anti-Communism into a seductive national doctrine that created and sustained the country's Cold War mentality. Rhetoric, when encompassing a doctrine, can have enormous influence over the minds and behavior of individuals and nations. As a purely verbal formulation, however, a doctrine may quickly assume a doubtful relationship to reality and, by the very power of its appeal, become exceedingly dangerous. Even as early as 1946 the promise and reality of coexistence questioned the doctrine's essential validity. It was either coexistence or war, and few Americans and Soviets favored war. Perhaps no writer warned more tellingly against doctrines, with their adherence to images, than did William Graham Sumner, the noted Yale sociologist, early in the century:

> Doctrines are the most frightful tyrants to which men ever are subject, because doctrines get inside of a man's own reason and betray him against himself. Civilized men have done their fiercest fighting for doctrines. . . . What are they all? Nothing but rhetoric and phantasms. Doctrines are always vague; it would ruin a doctrine to define it, because then it could be analyzed, tested, criticised, and verified; but nothing ought to be tolerated which cannot be so tested. . . . A doctrine is an act of faith . . . an abstract principle; it is necessarily absolute in its scope and abstruse in is terms. . . . It is never true, because it is absolute, and the affairs of men are all conditioned and relative. . . . [J]ust think what an abomination in statecraft an abstract doctrine must be. Any politician or editor can, at any moment, put a new extension on it. The people acquiesce in the doctrine and applaud it because they hear the politicians and editors repeat it, and the politicians and editors repeat it because they think it is popular. So it grows.[7]

America's Cold War anti-Communist doctrine, with the pervading fears that it evoked, was no exception. It quickly revealed the malleable quality of verbal images and their vulnerability to distortions, stereotypes, political commitments and ambitions, fears rational and irrational, and demands and expectations however unachievable or threatening to other national interests. Anti-Communism's central assumption was the threatening power of Soviet ideological expansionism. But ideology was no expansive force. Nationalism and the demands for self-determination served as a universal defense against Soviet ideological expansionism. Without access to external military support that mattered, Communist power struggles, invariably indigenous, always succeeded or failed on their own. No Communist regime would war on sentiments of patriotism and national allegiance or compromise its country's sovereignty to serve the Kremlin's interests. Therefore, any alleged Communist threat to global security would fall below the threshold of an American military response. If the Soviet Union would not expand militarily and could not expand ideologically, how was it to conquer anything? Possessing no expansive power other than military force, the Kremlin, relying on generally risk-free policies, gained nothing territorially, or even politically, throughout the decades of Cold War.

Anti-Communism not only overstated the Soviet danger but also, in the process, created undesirable consequences that were never intended. The exaggerated fears compelled the United States to finance an excessive military arsenal dominated by thousands of nuclear-tipped warheads, and to engage in covert operations designed to overthrow sovereign governments declared to be pro-Soviet. By embracing any regime, however reprehensible, that professed anti-Communism, the U.S. government repeatedly violated its own ideals of democracy and self-determination. Anti-Communism defined dangers so universally, yet so capriciously, that it often prevented the creation of genuine policy. Any purposeful crusade against alleged Communist dangers would require the destruction of governments and embrace global objectives beyond the capacity, effectiveness, or relevance of U.S. military power. Finally, anti-Communism's boundless rhetorical fears, demands, and aspirations left little room for the day-to-day decisions required for successful coexistence—the inescapable condition required by the interests of humanity. Constrained by such limitations, Washington never pursued a genuine anti-Communist program. It never made a serious attempt to free Eastern Europe, China, the Soviet Union, or any other region of the globe from Communist control. Indeed, what perpetuated the decades of laudable superpower coexistence was the decision of successive administrations to abjure the dictates of ideology and pursue the limited goals of containment, with their acceptance and defense of the status quo where it mattered, as well as their studied avoidance of direct and unnecessary conflict with the Soviet Union.

The Truman Doctrine

In framing the Truman Doctrine's defense of Greece and Turkey in February and March, 1947, U.S. officials defined the Soviet danger not in terms of specific and limited national objectives, but with rhetorical, anti-Communist perceptions of the Kremlin's limitless power to expand without reference to any historic restraints. With no clear evidence of Soviet designs on Greece, President Truman presented his case to Congress and the nation: "It is necessary only to glance at a map to realize that the survival and integrity of the Greek nation are of grave importance in a much wider situation. If Greece should fall under the control of an armed minority, the effect upon its neighbor, Turkey, would be immediate and serious. Confusion and disorder might well spread throughout the entire Middle East. Moreover, the disappearance of Greece as an independent state would have a profound effect upon those countries in Europe whose peoples are struggling against great difficulties to maintain their freedom and their independence while they repair the damage of war."[8]

This widely repeated rationale for the defense of Greece and Turkey established the Munich syndrome as the guiding principle in meeting the Soviet challenge. Greece and Turkey had become symbols of the status quo; their fall, like that of Austria, the Sudetenland, and Czechoslovakia after 1938, would, the president advised, "undermine the foundations of international peace and hence the security of the United States."[9]

Others quickly embellished the requirement that the country take a stand on Greece and Turkey. Will Clayton, undersecretary of state for economic affairs, repeated the warning: "If Greece and then Turkey succumbs, the whole Middle East will be lost. France may then capitulate to the Communists. As France goes, so Western Europe and North Africa will go."[10] Senator Arthur Vandenberg of Michigan accepted the administration's prescription uncritically. He warned in a letter dated March 12: "Greece must be helped or Greece sinks permanently into the Communist order. Turkey inevitably follows. Then comes the chain reaction which might sweep from the Dardenelles to the China Sea. . . . I can only say that I think [our new American policy] . . . is worth trying as an alternative to another 'Munich' and perhaps another war." Senator Walter George of Georgia, after a briefing from the U.S. ambassador to Turkey, declared that the aid bill was essential to stop further Soviet expansion. "If unchecked," he said, "Russia will inevitably overrun Europe, extend herself into Asia and perhaps South America. . . . [T]his process may go on for a full century."[11] The Soviet refusal to press their alleged ambitions in Greece, Turkey, and Iran seemed to verify the assumptions of the Munich paradigm: that firm resistance to aggression prevented war. For countless Americans the burgeoning domino theory—and the concurrent need to resist—became a self-evident truth. Yet the concept of falling dominoes had no precedent in history. Territorial expansion had always rested on naked military force.

To base policy vis-à-vis the Soviet Union on the Munich syndrome was a misreading of the past and an application of metaphors, images, and historical analogies without any examination of their applicability. Nowhere did the Munich rhetoric of 1947 correspond to the realities of 1938. What the West faced at Munich was open German aggression on a massive scale. German forces already occupied Austria. Huge Nazi armies stood poised to mass along Germany's borders with Czechoslovakia and Poland, preparatory to invasion and war. But in 1947 no Soviet forces awaited orders to advance against a neighboring state. Indeed, the rhetorical references to Munich, designed to rationalize the defense of Greece and Turkey, never contemplated Soviet military aggression; nor did they advocate any crash program to prepare the West for war. They described threats reaching across Europe, the Middle East, south Asia, and Africa encompassing territories hundreds, even thousands, of miles from Soviet territory, with no reference to the means whereby the Soviets intended to expand anywhere. Furthermore, those who described the Kremlin's territorial objectives never seemed to agree on what they were. What mattered to them were the Soviet Union's apparently limitless power and determination to expand and the dangers they conveyed. The Munich analogy, along with its domino theory counterpart, provided a necessary rhetorical extension to anti-Communist doctrine. The verbal images of the Kremlin's unprecedented capacity to expand indefinitely through the exploitation of successive gains, always unhampered by historic restraints, found their necessary rationale in the power of Soviet ideology to conquer and absorb.

Western Superiority and Global Insecurity

American portrayals of Soviet territorial ambitions beyond Greece and Turkey far exceeded what the Kremlin could achieve peacefully or afford at the price of war. Moreover, the rhetorical depictions of the Soviet Union's expansive power took no measure of the West's economic, political, and diplomatic predominance.

During the two years that followed congressional approval of the Truman Doctrine, the Western powers achieved an unbroken succession of diplomatic triumphs that demonstrated their total superiority. The sometimes astonishing successes began in 1948 with the elimination of Communists from the French government. Although the French Communists never revealed any affinity for Soviet causes, U.S. officials feared that a French Communist victory at the polls would carry that country into the Soviet orbit and endanger Western interests in Europe, Africa, and the eastern Mediterranean.[12] Similarly, Washington's varied economic pressures and electioneering efforts in Italy paid off in the

April, 1948, election that brought a new government, free of Communists and Socialists, into power. In June, Marshal Tito, Yugoslavia's staunch Communist leader, broke with the Kremlin to demonstrate that Communism could not erode the power of nationalism and that Kremlin control extended only as far as the reach of Soviet armies.

During subsequent months, America's varied policies aimed at the containment of Soviet power emerged victorious. In Greece the U.S.-supported government finally eliminated the Communist-led insurgency in August, 1949, driving the surviving guerrillas into Albania. President Truman proclaimed victory on November 28.[13] Meanwhile, U.S. officers organized and modernized the Turkish army, vastly improved the country's military capabilities with shipments of equipment and aircraft, and constructed new roads and airstrips. Even greater triumphs came with the passage of the Marshall Plan in 1948, which set Western Europe on a course of unparalleled economic growth. In May, 1949, Stalin lifted the Berlin blockade, instituted a year earlier to prevent the unification of Germany's three western zones. A month later the Paris Foreign Ministers Conference announced the formation of the Federal Republic of Germany, an achievement long opposed by the Kremlin.[14] Finally, in April, 1949, twelve Western countries formed a North Atlantic alliance to underwrite the stability and security of Western Europe.[15]

Washington, amply supported by the European powers, gained the full spectrum of its immediate objectives consistently, even overwhelmingly, because Europe's postwar challenges gave the economic supremacy of the United States a special relevance. With Europe in ruins and the Soviet Union reeling from near disaster, America's economic superiority was absolute. The war had rained destruction on every major power of Europe and Asia, destroying countless cities, factories, and rail lines. By contrast, the United States, with its many accumulating elements of power, had escaped unscathed. Its undamaged industrial capacity now matched that of the rest of the industrialized world. Its technological superiority was so obvious that the world assumed its existence and set out to acquire or copy American products. During the immediate postwar years the United States reached the highest point of world power achieved by any nation in modern times.[16] Abroad, the United States gained its marvelous triumphs where it mattered: the economic rehabilitation of Western Europe and Japan, the promotion of international trade and investment, and the maintenance of a defense structure that underwrote the containment effort and played an essential role in Europe's postwar political development and burgeoning confidence. These contributions to the world's unprecedented security and prosperity were the essence of the nation's postwar international achievement. By 1949, the Soviet Union faced the greatest manifestation of opposing power in the peacetime history of the world. The persistent Soviet retreats were evidence enough that Europe's balance of forces had turned against it.[17]

However, Western superiority on the international scene offered reassurance only to those who measured the Soviet danger by Soviet behavior and comparative levels of economic and military power. For American anti-Communists, whose central concern was Soviet ideological expansionism, the Soviet threat to Western security was only emerging. By 1948 the official American worldview could detect no visible limits to Soviet expansionism—which now embraced the entire globe. The National Security Council's (NSC) study, NSC-7, dated March 30, 1948, defined the Kremlin's challenge in precisely such terms. "The ultimate objective of Soviet-directed world communism," the document averred, "is the domination of the world. To this end, Soviet-directed world communism employs against its victims in opportunistic coordination the complementary instruments of Soviet aggressive pressure from without and militant revolutionary subversion from within." With its control of international Communism, NSC-7 continued, the Soviet Union had engaged the United States in a struggle for power "in which our national security is at stake and from which we cannot withdraw short of national suicide."[18] The more pervading NSC-20/4, approved by the president on November 24, 1948, defined the danger in similar terms: "Communist ideology and Soviet behavior clearly demonstrate that the ultimate objective of the leaders of the U.S.S.R. is the domination of the world."[19]

Designed specifically to kindle the nation's insecurities, NSC-68, written in April, 1950, comprised the final and most elaborate attempt of the Truman Cold War elite to arrive at a definition of national defense policy. This document, like its predecessors, described the danger of Soviet expansion in global, limitless terms. It concluded that the U.S.S.R., "unlike previous aspirants to hegemony, is animated by a new fanatic faith, antithetical to our own, and seeks to impose its absolute authority over the rest of the world." For the Soviets, conflict had become endemic, waged through violent and nonviolent means in accordance with the dictates of expediency. "The issues that face us," NSC-68 continued, "are momentous, involving the fulfillment or destruction not only of the Republic but of civilization itself." Defeat at the hands of the Soviets would be total.[20] Faced with such a determined enemy, diplomacy was scarcely promising.

Still, neither NSC-68 nor any of its predecessors offered a response commensurate with the rhetoric of fear. None of them anticipated the necessity of force to counteract the dangers. The authors of NSC-20/4 averred that the United States could achieve the goal of promoting the gradual retraction of Soviet power and influence, until they ceased to be threatening, simply by placing massive political and economic strain on the Soviet imperial structure.[21] Such ill-defined means for victory defied effective policy implementation. Similarly, NSC-68 assumed that the United States, with "calculated and gradual coercion," could unleash the forces of destruction within the Soviet Empire itself. In its need to limit Soviet ambitions, the United States could anticipate support within the Soviet Union. "If we can make the Russian people our allies in this enterprise," NSC-68 predicted, "we will obviously have made our task easier and victory more certain." In the process of inducing change, the United States would avoid, insofar as possible, any direct challenge to Soviet prestige and "keep open the possibility for the U.S.S.R. to retreat before pressure with a minimum loss of face."[22] However grave the dangers portrayed by this most terrifying of documents, their elimination required neither risk nor war.

The Essential Cold War: East Asia

The rhetorical suppositions of a global Soviet challenge would ultimately find their chief affirmation not in Europe, where the Soviets made no advances, but in east Asia. Whereas in Eastern Europe the West faced an unmovable Soviet occupation, in east Asia the Soviet Union had neither conquering nor occupying armies. Any proclaimed Soviet expansion there could result only from the Kremlin's power to command and exploit local Communist-led revolutions. In attributing to the Soviet Union the capacity to pursue a career of global conquest across Asia and elsewhere without the presence of armed forces, U.S. officials by midcentury could at last demonstrate the Soviet Union's limitless power to expand through ideological affinities alone. However, Washington's responses never conformed to the dangers so perceived. Every Communist movement in postwar Asia was indigenous and defiant of Soviet control; it therefore presented no danger to Western security precise enough to permit the creation of effective countermeasures. Never would the United States confront the Kremlin directly or militarily over any alleged Soviet-backed Communist aggression outside Europe.

What underwrote U.S. fears of Soviet expansion across east Asia was the overwhelming conviction, anchored to a troubling rhetoric, that the powerful Communist movements in China and Indochina were totally under Moscow's command. John Moors Cabot, U.S. consul general in Shanghai, warned as early as February, 1948, that if the Communists succeeded in gaining control of

China they would "install in China a tyranny as subservient to Russia and a terror as brutal as Tito's."[23] Despite the absence of Soviet forces in east Asia, a State Department memorandum of October, 1948, prepared by the department's China experts, concluded that Soviet policy was designed to install Soviet control and predominance in China as firmly "as in the satellite countries behind the Iron Curtain."[24] Secretary Dean Acheson, in the China white paper's letter of transmittal, again presumed that China had fallen victim to Kremlin control. "The Communist leaders," he concluded, "have foresworn their Chinese heritage and have publicly announced their subservience to a foreign power, Russia."[25]

Mao Zedong's final triumph in China in late 1949 demonstrated graphically the alleged expansive might of Soviet ideology because it appeared to place what remained of east and Southeast Asia in danger of Soviet conquest. Ambassador Edwin F. Stanton, writing from Bangkok, Thailand, warned Washington that Soviet pressures, unless countered effectively, would cause "*the whole of Southeast Asia [to] fall a victim to the Communist advance, thus coming under Russian domination without any military effort on the part of Russia.*"[26] This presumption of the Kremlin's capacity to conquer without military force quickly exposed Washington's deepest fears. National Security Council study NSC-48/1 described fully the terrible consequence of events in China: "The extension of Communist authority in China represents a grievous political defeat for us; if southeast Asia also is swept by communism we shall have suffered a major political rout the repercussions of which will be felt throughout the rest of the world, especially in the Middle-East and in then critically exposed Australia."[27] To the NSC, the Soviet Union, through its alleged control of China, had become an Asiatic power of the first order, "with expanding influence and interests extending throughout continental Asia and into the Pacific."[28] Such presumptions of expanding Soviet authority in Asia discounted totally the countering resistance of nationalism, with its single-minded quest for self-determination in Asian affairs.

This denial of nationalism as the driving force in China's Communist triumph inaugurated the debate over Titoism as a program for freeing China from Soviet control through a variety of special inducements. At issue in a Titoist policy was the presumed power of the United States to break a binding Moscow-Beijing relationship, one under Kremlin control.[29] The Yugloslav experience provided no precedent for that presumption; the Moscow-Yugoslav relationship was not binding. Tito's easy assertion of Yugoslav independence demonstrated the force of nationalism and the limits of Soviet power. If the Kremlin could establish no forcible control over neighboring Communist-led

Yugoslavia, it was not clear how it could do so over a Communist government in a huge, distant, self-centered, sovereign, historically antagonistic, and highly nationalistic country such as China, especially without a huge bureaucracy backed by an overpowering army. The Chinese Communist Party was indigenous, both organizationally and ideologically; it owed little or nothing to the Soviets for its success.[30] China, unoccupied by Soviet forces, remained free to pursue its external relations in accordance with its own interests.

Long convinced that the Kremlin would exploit any opportunity to advance its influence across Asia, U.S. officials attributed the North Korean invasion of South Korea in late June, 1950, to Soviet expansionism. The president declared that the attack on Korea "makes it plain beyond all doubt that Communism has passed beyond the use of subversion to conquer independent nations and will now use armed invasion and war."[31] The generally unquestioned presumption that the Kremlin had designs on broad areas of the Pacific recalled the Munich paradigm. For Truman, the North Korean attack, unless challenged, meant a third world war. "My thoughts," he wrote, "kept coming back to the 1930s—to Manchuria-Ethiopia-the Rhineland-Austria-and finally to Munich. If the Republic of Korea was allowed to go under, some other country would be next, and then another, just like in the 1930s."[32] Presidential candidate Dwight D. Eisenhower also saw the U.S. response to the North Korean invasion as an attempt to prevent World War III. He declared on October 24, 1952: "World War II should have taught us all one lesson: To vacillate, to hesitate, to appease—even by merely betraying unsteady purpose—is to feed a dictator's appetite for conquest and to invite war itself."[33] For Truman and Eisenhower alike, the Kremlin, unless confronted with counterforce, would topple dominoes into another world war.

Still, the American war effort never contemplated war against the Soviets, even when official U.S. rhetoric attributed the Chinese entry into the war in November, 1950, to Soviet influence and ambition. Acheson warned the country in a nationwide radio address on November 29: "Those who control the Soviet Union and the international Communist movement have made clear their fundamental design. It is to hold and solidify their power over the people and territories within their reach." The following day Truman declared: "We hope that the Chinese people will not continue to be forced or deceived into serving the ends of Russian colonial policy in Asia."[34] Even the *New York Times* proclaimed on December 8: "The Chinese Communist dictatorship will eventually go down in history as the men who sold out their country to the foreigners, in this case the Russians, rather than as those who rescued China from foreign 'imperialism.'"[35]

Thereafter Washington continued to dwell on the alleged Chinese subservience to Kremlin direction. The president reminded the American people in his State of the Union message of January, 1951: "Our men are fighting . . . because they know, as we do, that the aggression in Korea is part of the attempt of the Russian Communist dictatorship to take over the world, step by step."[36] It was left for John Foster Dulles to carry the full might of Soviet influence in the Far East to its ultimate conceptualization. "By the test of conception, birth, nurture, and obedience," he informed a New York audience in May, "the Mao Tse-tung regime is a creature of the Moscow Politburo, and it is on behalf of Moscow, not of China, that it is destroying the friendship of the Chinese people toward the United States."[37] Not even such graphic suppositions of Soviet control over vast regions of Asia, threatening the world's balance of power, produced any direct confrontation with the Kremlin.

It was the doubtful application of the Munich syndrome to the struggle for Vietnam that rendered Saigon's victory essential for Western security in east Asia and the Pacific. The domino theory, applied to the Vietnam War, served as a dramatic warning that a peripheral contest could, if not resolved, become one of pivotal importance. Eisenhower offered such terrifying imagery to a press conference in April, 1954, by warning that if one knocked over the first domino in a row of dominoes, the last would fall very quickly and create a disintegration of profound significance. The loss of Indochina, he warned, would lead to the possible loss "of Burma, of Thailand, of the Peninsula, and Indonesia." From that geographical advantage the Communists could "turn the island defense chain of Japan, Formosa, of the Philippines and . . . threaten Australia and New Zealand."[38] General Douglas MacArthur similarly warned the country against any appeasement of aggression in Vietnam: "The Communist threat is a global one. Its successful advance in one sector threatens the destruction of every other sector. You cannot appease or otherwise surrender to Communism in Asia without simultaneously undermining our efforts to halt its advance in Europe."[39] John F. Kennedy evoked the same imagery in June, 1956, when he instructed the Senate that Vietnam was "the cornerstone of the Free World in Southeast Asia, the keystone to the arch, the finger in the dike." If the red tide swept across Vietnam, he warned, it would engulf "Burma, Thailand, India, Japan, the Philippines, and obviously Laos and Cambodia."[40] In an address at Gettysburg College in April, 1959, Eisenhower warned those who doubted the wisdom of the ever-broadening U.S. commitment to the Saigon regime: "Strategically, South Vietnam's capture by the Communists . . . would set in motion a crumbling process that could, as it progressed, have grave consequences for us and for freedom."[41]

Even as President Lyndon B. Johnson contemplated the Americanization of the war during the early months of 1965, the imagery of falling dominoes assured the necessary congressional and public support for the mounting death and destruction. That imagery always centered on the Munich tragedy and the need to prevent further aggression and another world war by turning back the Communist enemy. Addressing the American Society of International Law in April, Secretary of State Dean Rusk asserted that "surely we have learned over the past three decades that the acceptance of aggression leads only to a sure catastrophe. Surely we have learned that the aggressor must face the consequences of his action and be saved from the frightful miscalculation that brings all to ruin."[42] Senator Henry Jackson (D-Washington) reminded Americans that "our sacrifices in this dirty war in little Vietnam will make a dirtier and bigger war less likely." Thomas J. Dodd of Connecticut warned the Senate: "The situation in Vietnam today bears many resemblances to the situation just before Munich. . . . We are again confronted by an incorrigible aggressor, fanatically committed to the destruction of the free world, whose agreements are as worthless as Hitler's. If we fail to draw the line in Viet-Nam, in short, we may find ourselves compelled to draw a defense line as far back as Seattle and Alaska."[43] For the JCS, the war against South Vietnam was "part of a major campaign to extend Communist control beyond the periphery of the Sino-Soviet bloc. . . . It is, in fact, a planned phase in the Communist timetable for world domination."[44]

Unfortunately the Munich syndrome, with its exaggerated images of Communist expansion far beyond Vietnam, uninhibited by the costs, risks, and limitations of military conflict, determined the manner that official anti-Communist rhetoric perceived the Soviet danger. The predictions of Soviet expansion never proved valid because the Soviets had no intention of fighting in Southeast Asia. Moreover, the domino theory never recognized the power of nationalism or the individuality of nations that rendered all Southeast Asia countries resistant to external encroachments. Thus no Washington official could define the enemy that, having acquired Saigon, would thereafter spread Communist aggression across east Asia and the Pacific. If Moscow and Beijing were the enemy, then fighting Hanoi was irrelevant. If Hanoi's defeat assured the peace and stability of Asia, as U.S. policy presumed, what was the meaning of falling dominoes? Hanoi, driven by its conception of self determination, possessed the power to unite Vietnam; it possessed neither the power nor the intention to expand across Asia and the Pacific. It was not strange that criticism of America's Vietnam involvement kept pace with official efforts to escalate the costs and the importance of the struggle. The unleashing of huge quantities of destruction against a jungle population on the Asian mainland challenged both the credulity and the moral sensibilities of millions of Americans for whom the Soviet Union posed no threat to Southeast Asia—or any other Third World region. Yet the concept of falling dominoes underwrote the later fears of Communist expansionism in such countries as Angola, Afghanistan, Nicaragua, El Salvador, and Grenada.

The Cold War: A Golden Age

Despite America's long, dramatic rhetorical portrayal of the alleged expansive power of Soviet Communism, the actual danger posed by the Soviet Union remained so imprecise that no Washington official cared to define it. Rhetorically, the Soviet threat was global, but with the exception of bordering Afghanistan, nowhere—not in Europe, the Middle East, Asia, Africa, or Latin America—did the Soviets reveal any ambition or interest of sufficient importance to merit resorting to military force or a showdown with the United States. Nowhere did the Kremlin threaten direct military aggression against any region regarded vital to the security of the United States or its Western allies. Monstrous weapons were tested often, but they remained unused. Even the occasional encounters remained provisional, usually conducted by alleged proxies whose interests were always indigenous. In 1983 George Kennan reminded a Washington audience of the absence of any perceptible dangers in the continuing, costly, divisive Soviet-American conflict. "There are no considerations of policy—no aspirations, no ambitions, no anxieties, no defensive impulses," he said, "that could justify the continuation of this dreadful situation."[45] Some analysts saw similarities between the world of the 1980s and that of 1914, with the leading powers arming for a war that nobody wanted and quarreling over issues that few considered critical.

What ultimately symbolized the limited role of the U.S.-Soviet conflict in world politics was its failure to dominate the behavior and outlook of international society or discourage the material progress that characterized the postwar era. Common interests in trade, investment, and other forms of international activity governed international life far more than did the fears of Soviet aggression and war. The flourishing of world commerce after midcentury was totally without precedent. Soviet-American expenditures for military preparedness scarcely touched the world's rapidly accumulating achievements in business and architecture. By most standards of human progress, the forty years of Cold War were the most pervading, most prosperous golden age in history. The prodigious investment of human and physical resources assumed a fundamental international security, one that, despite the recurrence of limited aggression and war, permitted the evolution of the complex, dynamic, technology-driven civilization that emerged during the age of Cold War. Peoples and governments assumed that the varied forces underwriting international stability were dominant enough, whatever the official state of U.S.-Soviet relations, to sustain the material gains of the age, symbolized graphically by the changing skyline of every major city of the Western world. Even as the perennial Cold War rhetoric argued insistently that the country and the world were in danger of global Communist conquest, every modern nation built with the confidence that its civilization was secure, and none more so than the United States itself.

Notes

1. For examples of early predictions of Soviet expansionism, with the concomitant danger of war, see Joseph C. Grew, *Turbulent Era: A Diplomatic Record of Forty Years, 1904–1945*, ed. Walter Johnson (Boston: Houghton Mifflin, 1952), 2:1446; Mark Ethridge's memorandum on Bulgaria and Rumania, Dec. 7, 1945, *Foreign Relations of the United States, Diplomatic Papers* (hereafter *FRUS*), *1945*, vol. 5 (Washington, D.C.: GPO, 1967), 637; John D. Hickerson to James Byrnes, Dec. 10, 1945, *FRUS, 1945*, vol. 4 (Washington, D.C.: GPO, 1968), 407; Joint Chiefs of Staff quoted in Melvyn P. Leffler, *A Preponderance of Power* (Stanford, Calif.: Stanford University Press, 1992), 50.

2. Joseph and Stewart Alsop, "Tragedy of Liberalism," *Life*, May 20, 1946, 69.

3. Edwin G. Wilson to Byrnes, Mar. 18, 1946, *FRUS, 1946*, vol. 7 (Washington, D.C.: GPO, 1969), 818–19; George Lewis Jones to Loy Henderson, Aug. 9, 1946, *FRUS, 1946*, 7:830; Acheson to Byrnes, Aug. 15, 1946, *FRUS, 1946*, 7:840–41.

4. For Kennan's "Long Telegram" of Feb. 22, 1946, see George F. Kennan, *Memoirs: 1925–1950* (Boston: Little, Brown, 1967), 547–59.

5. On the fears of Matthews and other U.S. officials see John Lewis Gaddis, *The United States and the Origins of the Cold War* (New York: Columbia University Press, 1972), 319; John Foster Dulles, "Thoughts on Soviet Foreign Policy and What To Do About It," *Life*, June 3, 1946, 113–26, and June 10, 1946, 119–20 (quotation, 119); William C. Bullitt, *The Great Globe Itself: A Preface to World Affairs* (New York: Scribner's Sons, 1946), 100–102, 175.

6. The Clifford-Elsey Report, "American Relations with the Soviet Union," in Arthur Krock, *Memoirs. Sixty Years on the Firing Line* (New York: Funk and Wagnalls, 1968), 427, 431.

7. William Graham Sumner, "War," in *Essays of William Graham Sumner*, ed. Albert Galloway Keller and Maurice R. Davie (New Haven, Conn.: Yale University Press, 1934), 1:169–73; Norman A. Graebner, ed., *Ideas and Diplomacy: Readings in the Intellectual Tradition of American Foreign Policy* (New York: Oxford University Press, 1964), 259–60.

8. Harry S. Truman's message to Congress, Mar. 12, 1947, Department of State *Bulletin* 16 (Mar. 23, 1947): 536.

9. Ibid.

10. Frederick J. Dobney, ed., *Selected Papers of Will Clayton* (Baltimore: Johns Hopkins Press, 1971), 199.

11. Arthur Vandenberg to R. F. Moffett, Mar. 12, 1947, in *The Private Papers of Senator Vandenberg,* ed. Arthur H. Vandenberg, Jr., and Joe Alex Morris (Boston: Houghton Mifflin, 1952), 342; Walter George quoted in Richard J. Barnet, *Intervention and Revolution: The United States in the Third World* (New York: World Publishing, 1968), 123.

12. For the uncertain and ultimately failed relationship between the Soviet Union and the French Communist Party see Alfred J. Rieber, *Stalin and the French Communist Party, 1941–1947* (New York: Columbia University Press, 1962), 309–30.

13. Howard Jones, *"A New Kind of War": America's Global Strategy and the Truman Doctrine in Greece* (New York: Oxford University Press, 1989), 191–226.

14. For the negotiations leading to the establishment of the Federal Republic of Germany in Mar.–Apr., 1949, see *FRUS, 1949,* vol. 3 (Washington, D.C.: GPO, 1974), 156–77; Acheson to George W. Perkins, Oct. 19, 1949, *FRUS, 1949,* vol. 4 (Washington, D.C.: GPO, 1975), 469–70.

15. Norman A. Graebner, "The United States and NATO: Ends Without Means," in *America as a World Power: A Realist Appraisal from Wilson to Reagan* (Wilmington, Del.: Scholarly Resources, 1984), 149–50.

16. For America's economic predominance see Harold J. Laski, "America—1947," *The Nation,* Dec. 13, 1947, 641; Robert Payne quoted in *Newsweek,* Jan. 11, 1993, p.36; Haynes Johnson, "The War That Remade America," *Washington Post National Weekly Edition,* Aug. 14–20, 1995, 9.

17. For a critical evaluation of the Soviet system and the postwar attitudes of Soviet citizens toward it see Nina Tumarkin, "The Great Patriotic War as Myth and Memory," *Atlantic Monthly,* June, 1991, 26–44. Edward Crankshaw discusses the failure of the Soviet system in "Russia's Power: Not Ideas but Force," *New York Times Magazine,* June 3, 1951, 29–30.

18. "Report by the National Security Council on the Position of the United States with Respect to Soviet-Directed World Communism" (NSC-7), Mar. 30, 1948, *FRUS, 1948,* vol. 1, pt. 2 (Washington, D.C.: GPO, 1976), 546.

19. "U.S. Objectives with Respect to the USSR to Counter Soviet Threats to U.S. Security" (NSC-20/4), in *Containment: Documents on American Policy and Strategy, 1945–1950,* ed. Thomas H. Etzold and John Lewis Gaddis (New York: Columbia University Press, 1978), 204.

20. Joseph M. Siracusa, "NSC-68: United States Objectives and Programs for National Security, Apr. 14, 1950," in *Into the Dark House: American Diplomacy and the Ideological Origins of the Cold War* (Claremont, Calif.: Regina Books, 1998), 213.

21. NSC-20/4, in *Containment,* ed. Etzold and Gaddis, 209–10.

22. NSC-68 in Siracusa, *Into the Dark House,* 217, 227.

23. Cabot to W. Walton Butterworth, Feb. 6, 1948, *FRUS, 1948,* vol. 8 (Washington, D.C.: GPO, 1973), 468.

24. Memorandum prepared by the research division of the Department of State, enclosed with Acting Secretary of State to Certain Diplomatic and Consular Offices, Oct. 13, 1948, *FRUS, 1948,* vol. 1, pt. 2, 643.

25. Letter of Transmittal, July 30, 1949, *United States Relations with China, With Special Reference to the Period 1944–1949* (Washington, D.C.: GPO, 1949), xvi, xvii.

26. Stanton to Secretary of State, June 14, 1949, *FRUS, 1949,* vol. 8 (Washington, D.C.: GPO, 1975), 50–51. Emphasis added.

27. NSC-48/1, Dec. 23, 1949, in *Containment,* ed. Etzold and Gaddis, 259

28. Ibid., 253.

29. For accounts of U.S. intentions to produce rifts in Sino-Soviet relations see Gordon H. Chang, *Friends and Enemies: The United States, China, and the Soviet Union, 1948–1972* (Stanford, Calif.: Stanford University Press, 1990), 19–41; John Lewis Gaddis, "Dividing Adversaries: The

United States and International Communism, 1945–1958," in *The Long Peace: Inquiries into the History of the Cold War* (New York: Oxford University Press, 1987), 147–94; David A. Mayers, *Cracking the Monolith: United States Policy Against the Sino-Soviet Alliance, 1947–1955* (Baton Rouge: Louisiana State University Press, 1986), 33–150.

30. The State Department's Policy Planning Staff concluded as early as September, 1948, that China's future rested with the Chinese. See "U.S. Policy Toward China" (PPS 39), Sept. 7, 1948, *FRUS, 1948*, 8:146–55.

31. Harry S. Truman, "Truman's Statement on the Situation in Korea, June 27, 1950," in *Public Papers of the Presidents of the United States* (hereafter *Public Papers*), *1950* (Washington, D.C.: GPO, 1965), 492.

32. Louis W. Koenig, ed., *The Truman Administration, Its Principles and Practice* (New York: New York University Press, 1956), 286; Goran Rystad, *Prisoners of the Past? The Munich Syndrome and Makers of American Foreign Policy in the Cold War Era* (Lund, Sweden: CWK Gleerup, 1982), 35.

33. Aaron Singer, ed., *Campaign Speeches of American Presidential Candidates, 1928–1972* (New York: Ungar, 1976), 245.

34. Acheson's speech in Cleveland, Nov. 29, 1950, Department of State *Bulletin* 23 (Dec. 18, 1950): 964; Truman's statement to the press, Nov. 30, 1950, Department of State *Bulletin* 23 (Dec. 11, 1950): 925–26.

35. For further assumptions of Soviet dominance of China see "Minutes, Truman-Attlee meeting," Dec. 7, 1950, *FRUS, 1950*, vol. 7 (Washington, D.C.: GPO, 1976), 1456; Norman A. Graebner, *Cold War Diplomacy: American Foreign Policy, 1945–1975* (New York: D. Van Nostrand, 1977), 52.

36. Harry S. Truman, "Annual Message on the State of the Union," Jan. 8, 1951, in *Public Papers, 1951* (Washington, D.C.: GPO, 1965), 7.

37. Dulles's address before the China Institute of New York, May 18, 1951, Department of State *Bulletin* 24 (May 28, 1951): 844.

38. Eisenhower's news conference for Apr. 7, 1954, in *Public Papers, 1954* (Washington, D.C.: GPO, 1960), 383.

39. See MacArthur's speech to Congress, Apr. 4, 1954, *Reminiscences* (Greenwich, Conn.: Fawcett, 1965), 400.

40. Kennedy quoted in Rystad, *Prisoners of the Past?* 40.

41. Eisenhower's speech at Gettysburg College, Apr. 4, 1959, Department of State *Bulletin* 40 (Apr. 27, 1959): 580–81.

42. Rusk's address to the American Society of International Law, Apr. 13, 1965, Department of State *Bulletin* 52 (May 10, 1965): 699.

43. Thomas J. Dodd's speech in the Senate, Feb. 23, 1965, *Congressional Record*, 89th Cong., 1st sess., vol. 111, pt. 3, 3350.

44. Department of Defense, *United States–Vietnam Relations, 1945–1967* (Washington, D.C.: GPO, 1971), 2:664.

45. Kennan quoted in Norman A. Graebner, "The Soviet-American Conflict: A Strange Phenomenon," *Virginia Quarterly Review* 60 (1984): 569.

CHAPTER TWO

The Creation of Memory and Myth

Stalin's 1946 Election Speech and the Soviet Threat

FRANK COSTIGLIOLA

One of the most famous and most emotional rhetorical statements associated with the Cold War was William Douglas's labeling of Joseph Stalin's February 9, 1946 speech as "The Declaration of World War III." [1] Douglas's language expressed shock and disappointment. Disseminated by Navy Secretary James Forrestal, Douglas's comment helped delegitimate a policy of trying to compromise with Moscow. The remark meant that Stalin had, in effect, declared war on his allies only six months after the terrible suffering of World War II and in defiance of widespread aspirations for peace through the United Nations. Furthermore, Stalin's rhetoric seemed part of a pattern of Soviet brutality and repression in Eastern Europe. Recording Douglas's comment in his diary in capital letters, Forrestal welcomed evidence for his contention that the Soviet Union posed a menace to the postwar peace. A few days later, Forrestal copied in his diary the entirety of Moscow chargé George Kennan's famous Long Telegram, another emotion-provoking statement that depicted the Soviet Union as a penetrating, almost inhuman force that had to be contained.[2]

Although the third world war supposedly declared on February 9 never occurred, what did begin on that date, many policy makers and scholars would later conclude, was the so-called Cold War. This essay moves beyond previous discussions of Stalin's speech through close reading of the speech's language and rhetorical structure and through analysis of Stalin's objectives in terms of the production of memory and myth. It explores the contrast between the rhetorical structure of Stalin's speech—an internally directed statement that sought to reshape the Soviet people's memory of World War II—and the perception by influential Americans such as State Department officials and Walter Lippmann that the speech signaled a dangerous challenge. A close reading of Stalin's speech and its reception in the United States illustrates how the Cold War became the dominant paradigm—that is, the interpretive lens—for viewing relations between the Soviet Union and the United States.[3] The predominance of a metaphor based on war to explain relations between two nations that, despite fundamental disagreements, determined to avoid war with each other, also signified the post–World War II legacy of Adolf Hitler. Both the United States and Soviet Union, in categorizing each other as aggressive and in planning for the worst contingency, revealed an inability to escape the traumatic memory of Hitler's belligerence. Nor could the two nations escape the memory of their prewar resentment. Although scholars today cannot—and should not—overlook the memory of Stalin's notorious purges and exterminations within the Soviet bloc, they also need to look anew at how emotion and language helped exaggerate the threat to the West posed by Stalin and other Soviet leaders.[4]

In 1945–46 both Americans and Soviets struggled to make sense from—and to impose meanings upon—swirling events. General Dwight D. Eisenhower observed "great confusion" in Washington.[5] There was also uncertainty in the Soviet Union. During the war, many non-Russian nationalities had sided with the Germans, the Communist Party had had to loosen its grip, the military had gained prestige relative to the party, masses of soldiers had joined the party with little ideological indoctrination, and soldiers had encountered the lures of foreign lands and ideas. An anti-Soviet guerrilla war still raged in western Ukraine.[6] Such ferment undermined the ideological control imposed by the terrible purges of the 1930s. Soviet leaders tried to reimpose ideological control by creating from the experience of World War II a simplified, usable meaning that emphasized the central role of Communist ideology as interpreted by Joseph Stalin. Many U.S. leaders and opinion makers attached to this ideological speech their own simplified, usable meaning that portrayed the Soviets as a menace. The widespread acceptance of these respective usable meanings in the Soviet Union and in the United States marked the victory of certitude, clarity, and simplicity over ambivalence, ambiguity, and confusion.

Two aspects of Stalin's speech troubled American commentators most. The first was expressed by a banner headline in the *New York Times:* "STALIN SETS A HUGE OUTPUT NEAR OURS IN 5-YEAR PLAN; EXPECTS TO LEAD IN SCIENCE Seeks Production Rise to 'Guarantee Against Any Eventuality.'"[7] Kennan pinpointed the second troubling aspect: Stalin's "straight Marxist interpretation" of the two world wars "as the inevitable result of the development of the world economic and political forces on the basis of monopoly capitalism."[8] A British official commented that because capitalism "is still the nearest thing to a universal religion in the United States," Americans resented Stalin's "strong denunciation of so cherished a creed."[9] One did not have to denounce capitalism, however, to believe that Germany in World War I and Germany, Japan, and Italy in World War II had gone to war to gain a larger share of global wealth, territory, and markets. After Stalin asserted in his speech that World War II had been "the inevitable result" of economic competition under world capitalism, he qualified that claim of inevitability by stating that the dissatisfied capitalist nations "usually" resorted to force. More important, however, he complimented the motives of the Western powers and departed from a strict Marxist interpretation by declaring that World War II "assumed from the very beginning"—that is, before the entry of the Soviet Union—"an anti-Fascist liberating character having also as one of its aims the reestablishment of democratic liberties."[10] In the speech, Stalin neither claimed nor hinted that differences between capitalism and Communism would lead to the Communist states' attacking the capitalist states or that war between Communist and capitalist states was inevitable. Yet some Americans interpreted the speech as predicting an attack.

Despite its Marxist emphasis, the speech focused on nation states rather than on international classes or revolution. Although blaming the capitalist system for spawning wars, Stalin also condemned the destruction of "bourgeois democratic liberties" and the "sovereignty and freedom" of non-Communist nations by the Axis. While reemphasizing the Marxist ideology that had been downplayed during the war, Stalin's speech retained the wartime distinction between capitalist enemies and capitalist allies. At the end of this overtly Marxist introduction, the speech returned to the non-Marxist classification system that had justified the wartime alliance, when the Soviets had formed, in Stalin's words an "anti-Fascist coalition" with "the United States of America, Great Britain and other freedom-loving countries."[11]

Did this ambivalent speech indicate a Soviet threat? By signaling the reversal of wartime liberalizing trends and Soviet determination to maintain a prickly, ideological, isolated independence, the address disappointed and antagonized many Americans. Already angered by Soviet actions in Eastern Europe and in Iran and by Soviet refusal to join the World Bank and International Monetary Fund (IMF), opinion makers such as the *New York Times* exaggerated the challenge posed by Stalin's speech. Such exaggeration intensified emotions and thus helped form the self-perpetuating discourse of the Soviet menace.

After discussing the systemic problems of capitalism in just five paragraphs of his speech, Stalin devoted fifty-two paragraphs (out of the total of seventy-seven paragraphs of printed text) to what was for him a pressing political need: reshaping the Soviet people's memory of World War II and the 1930s. The war had exposed Soviet vulnerabilities. Although Stalin later assumed the exalted rank of generalissimo, he had initially been shocked into near-paralysis by the success of the German invasion. "Lenin left us a state and we have turned it to shit!" he had said with despair.[12] He also reportedly considered surrendering to Hitler a vast portion of Soviet territory in exchange for peace.[13] Many Ukrainians and other nationalities initially greeted the Nazi invaders as liberators, and captured Red Army soldiers fought with the German-supported General Vlaslov.[14] Later, as they drove the Germans back, millions of Soviet soldiers had been exposed to the higher living standards of eastern and central Europe, where peasant homes had such comparative luxuries as wooden floors.

By 1946 the Soviet leadership had aggravated its nationalities problem by annexing additional territories inhabited by non-Russians. Kennan reported that there was "genuine concern in Moscow over [the] lack of enthusiasm for [the] Soviet system in newly acquired areas."[15] Similar nationalist dissent had undermined czarist rule. Faced with this unhappy past, Stalin needed a usable, mythologized history that could reconfigure popular memory and so legitimate Soviet rule. In February, 1946, Soviet leaders attempted such myth production by staging an elaborate ceremony for the first election to the Supreme Soviet since 1937.

While Western observers understandably ridiculed this "election" because it did not encompass Western-style choice, most of them also missed the significance of what Kennan observed as the "unparalleled pomp and circumstances" surrounding the election ritual.[16] An observer described the "gigantic campaign of ideological re-indoctrination . . . through all the resources of the press, radio, cinema and oral agitation."[17] Another observer noted that the "countless banners and slogans" gave election day "the appearance of a major public holiday."[18]

This ideological pageant constituted what we might term a memory project from above. It was an effort to establish myths that would justify the brutality of the forced collectivization, industrialization, and purges of the 1930s; erase memories of the nearly fatal defeats and divisions of World War II; and justify the future rule of the Communist Party. In a command society, a command election was neither a contradiction nor something of which to be ashamed. As Foreign Minister Vyacheslav Molotov told voters on February 6, the election was "a test" of the public "attitude . . . towards the leadership of the Communist Party and towards the policy of the Soviet Government." With pride rather than irony, he said that the leaders "have grounds to look forward with confidence" to the election results.[19] For the Soviets, the election was a staged show in which their foreknowledge and control of the outcome only enhanced the significance of the reaffirmation ceremony. In other words, their very success in repressing alternative voices, which in Western eyes invalidated the election, constituted instead in the Soviet view evidence of having imposed a legitimating unanimity.[20]

Much of the language in Stalin's election speech at the Bolshoi Theater constituted what we might term "truth dicta." A truth dictum is language that tries to attach specific meanings to events. Stalin habitually signaled such truth dicta—especially the more dubious ones that amounted to assertions of faith—with declarations such as, "it would be incorrect to think," "everybody now recognizes," "as is well known," "it would be a mistake to think."[21] However, the very language of such declarations betrayed a measure of doubt about the truth dictum, and the declarations inadvertently pointed to viewpoints that remained alternatives even if "incorrect."[22]

Stalin devoted most of his speech to two intertwined tasks: elucidating the three "conclusions" that the Soviet people should draw from the military victory and justifying the Communist Party's collectivization and industrialization policies before the war. His conclusions tried to refute arguments that the Soviet system was, in Stalin's words, "a risky experiment, doomed to failure . . . a house of cards"; that the Soviet multinational state was a fragile, "artificial structure"; and that the Red Army "would fall to pieces like a colossus with feet of clay."[23] The detailed attention that Stalin paid to these charges—and the graphic metaphors of dissolution that he used to depict them—indicate that he viewed the breakup of the Soviet Union as a serious danger against which the population, particularly non-Russians, had to be thoroughly indoctrinated.

The logical thrust in this, the core of Stalin's speech, was to transfer the truth value of the indisputable military victory to shakier propositions about the viability of the Soviet social system and the Soviet multinational state. In an explicit assertion of meaning, Stalin said that "victory means, first of all, that our Soviet social system . . . has proved its complete vitality." Note his quest for certitude—not just vitality but "complete vitality." He claimed, moreover, that the Soviet system was "better" than any other system.[24] After having asked the Soviet people to fight for patriotism during the war, he now told them that "the war has shown that the Soviet social system is a truly popular system."[25] In promulgating this myth Stalin still had to attribute to someone or something the doubts about the Soviet system. Hence the locating of criticism in "the foreign press"—which situated the scapegoat safely outside the Soviet fold and yet did not impugn the governments of the wartime allies.[26]

Stalin also dwelt on the enormous problem that forty-five years later would tear apart the Soviet Union: divisive nationalism. In the second of his "conclusions," the dictator seemed compelled to cite predictions, again attributed to "the foreign press," that "the disintegration of the Soviet Union is inevitable, that the Soviet Union would meet the fate of Austro-Hungary."[27] His language is evidence of his determination to make people believe that "the war has proved" such predictions false. He asserted this alleged proof nine times in six consecutive sentences.[28] Such repetition amounted to a kind of liturgy, an attempted inculcation of faith that the war had proven the Soviet Union a viable, indeed superior, multinational state. Stalin's reference to the war was, however, a dangerous move because the war had in fact revealed wholesale ethnic rebellion. Trying to reshape this memory—to fashion a myth usable for the future—the dictator had little to work with aside from Soviet ideology. Asserting a "truth" based not on the perceived experiences of millions of Soviet citizens but rather on a memory in the process of being mythologized, Stalin emphasized that the Soviet Union would avoid "national mistrust and national animosity" because those problems had "a bourgeois foundation." He claimed that the Soviet system, in contrast, "promotes friendship and fraternal collaboration between the peoples of our state."[29]

Although the final lesson from the war—that "our Red Army had won"—was the least disputable of the three conclusions, Stalin mentioned it last and downplayed its significance. The dictator was chipping away at the prestige gained by the military at the expense of the Communist Party. In creating the mythology of his first two conclusions, Stalin had used the language of certitude: "victory means" and "the war has shown."[30] In his third conclusion, however, he introduced a note of ambiguity with the formulation that "our victory implies that it was the Soviet armed forces that won."[31] Stalin's first two conclusions were myths spun from shaky evidence and shaky logic. His third conclusion, however, was based on the solid evidence of military victory.

What, then, were the implications the Soviet leader drew from this military success? Did he in effect or by implication declare World War III? To be sure, Stalin derided prewar foreign criticisms of the Soviet army, and he proudly listed sixteen major victories. He did not mention America's generous lend-lease aid program, and although he acknowledged that "we, together with our allies were the victors," his discussion of fighting focused on the Red Army.[32] Yet Stalin drew relatively modest and nonbellicose implications from the victory. In contrast to his ideologically driven claims for the superiority of the Soviet social and multinational systems, he argued "that the Red Army is a first-class army, which could teach others quite a lot."[33] This was boastful language, but neither inaccurate nor denying that other nations also could have a first-class army—or a first-class navy, air force, and atomic bombs, none of which the Soviets had. Stalin did not use this discussion of military victory as a take-off point to detail further military needs and plans. Nor, at this crucial juncture of his speech, did he allude to future military conflict and competition. Instead, he returned to his preoccupation with internal, ideological issues.

After informing the Soviet people "how we understand" the victory, Stalin made a sharp turn in logic. He inadvertently signaled the difficulty and dubiety of that turn with three consecutive truth declarations. He asserted that "it would be a mistake," "it would be no less erroneous," and "it would be even more erroneous" to think that the Soviet Union could have achieved victory without the Communist Party's five-year plans, collectivization, and industrialization—and the purges that accompanied that forced development.[34] In twenty-five statistic-filled paragraphs, Stalin compared the Soviet Union's productive capacity not with that of the West but with that of czarist Russia. Recalling the humiliation of Russian inadequacy in World War I when "one rifle was issued for every three soldiers," Stalin itemized the Soviet Union's massive production in World War II.[35] From this contrast, Stalin wanted the Soviet people to derive the meaning that their suffering and sacrifices had all been necessary for the military victory.

After justifying his kind of Soviet rule, Stalin devoted five paragraphs—out of the speech's seventy-seven—to the future. He mentioned first that "the rationing system will be abolished, special attention will be focused on expanding the production of goods for mass consumption, on raising the standard of life of the working people."[36] Thus his first stated priority was neither military production nor heavy industry, but rather the civilian economy and increased living standards, which had plummeted during the war. Second, he stressed devoting additional resources to science, asserting that "our scientists will be able not only to overtake but also in the very near future to surpass the achievements of science" abroad. As in other statements where Stalin made dubious claims, he inadvertently signaled the shakiness of this claim by prefacing the sentence with the declaration "I have no doubt."[37] Stalin's reference to science probably meant atomic bomb research. Two weeks earlier he had told the head of the Soviet atomic bomb project to spare no expense in quickly building a bomb.[38] As to the mood of this speech, note that Stalin referred explicitly to science—he mentioned neither atomic weaponry nor military competition nor an atomic arms race.[39]

Stalin did stress plans for "a new mighty upsurge of [the] national economy"—the threefold production increase over prewar levels of heavy industry that the *New York Times* featured in its headline. He called for the production, after three or more five-year plans, of "50,000,000 tons of pig iron per year,

60,000,000 tons of steel, 500,000,000 tons of coal and 60,000,000 tons of oil."[40] "Only under such conditions"—that is, with the improvement in living standard, science, and heavy industry—"will our country be insured against any eventuality."[41]

What can we say about this development program, which some Western observers interpreted as preparation for war? First, the language "insured against any eventuality" lent itself to sinister interpretation because of its vagueness. Did "any eventuality" mean a Soviet-launched war? Although the *New York Times* and much of the American press interpreted the Russian word as "eventuality," the British embassy in Moscow rendered the word as "hazards" and as "accidents," and recent studies have translated it as "contingencies."[42] In view of the Soviet experience with invasions in 1941, in 1914, and during the Russian civil war, economic and scientific development to insure against any "hazards," "accidents," "contingencies," or "eventuality" seems more precautionary than belligerent. Second, although ambitious, the plan for heavy industry called for a threefold increase over a long time span: from 1940 to 1960 or beyond that if more than three five-year plans were required. Some of that capacity had already been achieved in World War II. Third, although the *New York Times* headline warned that Stalin's output goals were "near ours," the *Times*'s own figures cited U.S. production in 1944 of 61 million tons of pig iron and 90 million tons of steel, both of which well exceeded Stalin's 1960 projections. Fourth, given the devastation of the Soviet Union and given the overall effort by the United States to encourage world production, such goals announced by any other nation would have been interpreted as normal, welcome evidence of progress.

The *New York Times*'s representation of Stalin's projected production figures as "near ours" expressed what would become a Cold War tendency to interpret actions taken by the Soviets for internal or autonomous reasons as actions referring directly to the United States.[43] Although Stalin bragged about future Soviet production without trying to reassure Western observers, some of those observers, such as the *New York Times,* escalated the tension further by interpreting the bragging as an overt challenge.[44] The headline may also have stemmed from a measure of insecurity about American capitalism's ability to compete on a peacetime basis with a planned economy.

Although most American analysis of the speech ended with the section on industrial growth, the speech itself returned to Stalin's concern with Communist Party issues. Stalin concluded with a discussion of party organization that took up five paragraphs—the same number devoted to plans for industrial growth.

In sum, the emphasis and rhetorical strategy in Stalin's speech point to the purpose of mythologizing prewar and wartime experiences to create a common, usable memory that would legitimate continued Communist Party rule. Such myth production achieved partial success. For the generations that survived the "Great Patriotic War," the Soviet Union's victory stood out as one of the few justifications for the Soviet system. Yet even this affirmation of Soviet ideology was undercut by persistent nationalism: consider the very language of the name "Great Patriotic War." Nonetheless, memory of the war as a mythologized "Great Past" became more vital as the "Great Future" of true communism receded into the distant future, and as the revelation of Stalin's crimes darkened the achievements of the 1930s. Some observers have argued that the Soviet Union itself lasted only so long as the World War II generation stayed in power.[45]

Stalin's address had a mixed impact on the Americans and British; much depended on who was interpreting the speech and with what preconceptions. In an after-dinner talk in which Truman was boasting to a largely female audience about his familiarity with Churchill and Stalin at Potsdam, the president lightly remarked, "Well, you know we always have to demagogue a little, before elections."[46] In Britain, the Foreign Office observed that although the speech "received relatively little attention in this country . . . [it] had such a strong effect in the United States." British diplomats in the United States described that effect as physical and as not completely rational: "an electric shock on the nerves" and "the biggest fluttering of the dovecotes."[47] Although reflecting habitual British condescension, these metaphors also pointed to the emotionalism in the American reaction. Emotions are embodied thoughts—that is, thoughts that are suffused with a pressing, bodily sense that "this event, policy, or development is important to me personally and engages my feelings." When emotions are engaged—when, metaphorically, nerves are shocked or one is fluttering about—there can be a greater tendency to make snap judgments, to cut through ambiguity and ambivalence with a simplifying, clarifying conclusion. The British observed that the Americans reacted to Stalin's speech with a "clarification and unification of American attitudes towards Russia."[48]

Although many Americans interpreted Stalin's speech in ways that "clarified" their view of Russia, Soviet foreign policy at the beginning of the Cold War was unclear and in a state of flux.[49] Scholars have debated the origins of the Cold War for more than three decades. That debate seems likely to continue despite the newly available documents from the former Soviet Union—in part because there is still only scattered documentation of the plans and attitudes of top Soviet leaders.[50] Nevertheless, it seems safe to say that Stalin's policy toward the United States in 1945–46 was ambivalent. He appears to have been seeking great power cooperation with the United States along the lines that Franklin Roosevelt had outlined at Teheran and Yalta. Yet he was also suspicious that, with Roosevelt gone, the Americans and British would cheat him out of the gains he believed the Soviets had earned from the war. He thus was prepared to pursue Soviet security on a unilateral basis that entailed distance from but not necessarily hostility toward the United States and Britain.[51] The dictator appeared simultaneously proud of his nation's strength and achievements and worried that wartime experiences had undermined ideology and obedience, especially among returning soldiers, and that the Americans had trumped the Soviets with their atomic bomb. His election speech indicated the desire for time and space to reconstruct Soviet ideology and the economy.

In October, 1945, Stalin told Ambassador W. Averell Harriman that, rather than disputing American control over Japan, he was considering that "the Soviet Union should adopt . . . a policy of isolation."[52] Stalin meant an isolation that would keep Eastern Europe under Soviet dominance, a policy that violated American concerns with free elections and free markets. Two weeks before the February, 1946 speech, Harriman asked Stalin if he thought that "the political and social concepts" of the United States and the Soviet Union could be reconciled. Stalin replied that these concepts "related only to the internal policies of the two countries. With respect to foreign affairs it seemed to him that the two countries could find common ground. The United States would arrange their internal life according to their desires. The Soviet people would do the same."[53]

However, many Americans found Stalin's concept of self-isolation and separate spheres objectionable, especially when they made the logical leap that Soviet isolation would lead to Soviet expansion and that Soviet control would totally shut out American business.[54] By February, 1946, key State Department experts on the Soviet Union—including Francis "Doc" Matthews, Elbridge Durbrow, and George Kennan—were frustrated by the confusing mix in Stalin's words and actions, by Secretary of State James Byrnes's compromises with the Soviets at the December foreign ministers conference in Moscow, by the rapid pace of U.S. military demobilization, and by Truman's indecision and disengagement from foreign policy. These officials seized on Stalin's speech as clarifying, almost welcome proof that the Soviets were a political and/or military threat.

While Stalin used the fact of Soviet military victory as the basis for a myth about the efficacy of Communist ideology, some Americans used that Soviet fact and that Soviet myth as the basis for their own myth about the Communist military menace. Looking for definitive answers, Matthews found in Stalin's speech "the most important and authoritative guide to post-war Soviet policy." He predicted that the speech would become "the Communist and fellow-traveller Bible."[55] Knowing that in Moscow Kennan had been thinking through an analysis of the Soviet threat, Matthews informed him that the time was ripe for a harsher evaluation of Soviet foreign policy: "the importance of Stalin's statement has been realized by our press and public to a degree not hitherto felt."[56] That last word, "felt," pointed to the emotions sparked by alarmist interpretations of Stalin's speech—particularly by State Department officials influencing opinion makers.

One of the most effective opinion makers of the 1940s was Walter Lippmann. It was said that millions of Americans did not know what they thought about a foreign policy issue until they had read Lippmann's column in the morning newspaper. Until early February, 1946, Lippmann had been advocating that the United States remain a mediator between its rival allies, Britain and Russia. Then, in his columns of February 12 and 13, Lippmann shifted dramatically. The well-connected British embassy in Washington reported that Lippmann's change was "apparently in part the product of conversations with high State Department officials."[57]

In a column entitled "Stalin Chooses Military Power," Lippmann tried to convince readers that Stalin's speech meant that the ambivalence in Soviet foreign policy had ended, and that therefore the ambivalence in U.S. policy toward the Soviets should also end. Lippmann's rhetorical strategy was to replace doubt and nuance with simplified affirmation. The column's first two sentences read: "There is no mystery now about the central purpose of the Soviet Union. The main issue . . . has been decided." Similar declarations asserted that "there can be no misunderstanding" and that "we know what the Soviet Union intends to do in the next 15 or 20 years." Lippmann framed the "main issue" that "has been decided" as "whether, being invulnerable after the defeat of Germany and Japan, the Soviet Union would give priority to improving the standard of life of its own people or to the development of military power." By characterizing the Soviet Union as "invulnerable," Lippmann ignored the potential threat posed by America's atomic monopoly and air and naval superiority—a military disparity that Lippmann surely would have emphasized had the American and Soviet positions been reversed. Lippmann's framing of the issue also downplayed the introspective focus of Stalin's speech.[58]

Lippmann argued a reductive, hard-to-disprove, worst-case interpretation of Soviet intentions. He cast Stalin's statistical analysis of Soviet industrial power in World War II as a postwar challenge to the United States. Although Stalin had compared Soviet production to that of czarist Russia, Lippmann compared Soviet production to that of the United States. Lippmann's juxtaposition, and the readiness of others to interpret Soviet actions in terms of their potential impact on the United States, reflected a national self-focus and a tendency to relate to the Soviet Union not only as a concrete nation but also as an abstracted "other" and source of anxiety. While dismissing Stalin's pledge to improve civilian consumption and end rationing, Lippmann, like other influential analysts, equated heavy industry with military preparation—although reconstructing war damage would also require huge amounts of iron, steel, and coal. Heavy industry was certainly the basis for military power, but by declaring that economic reconstruction was unequivocally for military purposes, Lippmann exaggerated the concreteness of the threat. In arguing that "Stalin chooses military power," Lippmann at first acknowledged that the speech did not mention demography. However, he then cited "reliable" projections that the number of military-age men would rise faster in the Soviet Union than in Western Europe. Finally, he jumped to the conclusion: "So Stalin's calculation combines manpower and industrial power." But how could Lippmann definitively know "Stalin's calculation"?[59]

This phrase came at a key point in Lippmann's argument, and it is worth quoting the sentence in full: "So Stalin's calculation combines manpower and industrial power, and there is no ground for supposing that the Soviet Union lacks the means or the will to pursue the plan of military superiority."[60] Persuasive and resistant to refutation, Lippmann's language exemplified the emerging discourse on the Soviet menace. One could always make the argument that the Soviet Union, a populous, continent-sized nation, had "the means" for military superiority. Furthermore, how could anyone prove that the Soviets did *not* have "the will"? A "plan" could appear threatening even if distant or unrealizable. Finally, the phrase "military superiority" pushed emotional buttons about Hitler, Pearl Harbor, and more general fears of dominance by other nations. Similar leaps of logic, dubious analogies, scary extrapolations, and unwarranted certitude—in both the East and West—would power Cold War discourses and the Cold War paradigm for the ensuing forty-five years.

But what was Lippmann's purpose in portraying Stalin's speech as a dire challenge? The column's rhetorical structure suggests that Lippmann—like George Kennan in his famous Long Telegram written nine days later—first depicted the Soviet menace and then deployed that threat to justify bold action that focused not on the Soviet Union, but rather on the developing Western bloc.[61] The pivotal turn in Lippmann's argument came after he warned of Stalin's "calculation" for "military superiority." The columnist then asserted that "we, too, must make our calculations." Foreshadowing the postwar myth about America's global influence being an unsought burden, Lippmann argued that "now that Stalin has made the decision to make military power his first objective, we are forced to make a corresponding decision," namely to "reinforce, rebuild and modernize the industrial power of Western Europe, and to take a leading part in the development of . . . Asia."[62] From the exaggerated military threat came the impetus for the economic, political, and military construction of the "Free World."

In the final words of his column, Lippmann mentioned that Americans could build this community only "if we have the moral energy."[63] The need for "moral energy"—that is, a sense of righteousness, purpose, and drive—was a theme that Lippmann had developed in his previous day's column urging a more activist U.S. role in the Middle East. He argued that the Middle East needed the "new energy and . . . fresh hope" that could come only from massive U.S. economic investment. In terms that referred immediately to the Middle East but that applied also to what was becoming the "Free World," Lippmann called for "great work" that would "give men something else to do, something else to think about, something better to hope for" than their "dreary" past.[64] In the decades following Lippmann's remarks, the "great work" of containing an exaggerated Soviet threat, expanding the U.S. economy, and building the free world would generate "moral energy" and a happier future—at least for some—in the West. In the East, Soviet leaders would achieve their ideological control and their industrial goals, but in a dreary society where that ideological control would eventually stifle even industrial growth.

My purpose here has not been to offer yet another definitive interpretation of the origins of the Cold War, but rather to recall the prevalent ambiguity, ambivalence, and confusion of the immediate postwar era. Stalin and other Soviet leaders tried to make sense out of that turmoil and to create usable myths about the war and prewar periods. In almost every society, the past is constructed as a myth to serve particular purposes. In the pageant of the Soviet election campaign that construction was overt and heavy-handed, in keeping with an authoritarian political culture. We need to understand Soviet political culture on its own terms without, however, forgetting or justifying its repression. In the United States, the construction of usable myths was far less rigid and centralized and, perhaps for that reason, it was generally more successful.

Although no dictatorial regime directed Lippmann, the *New York Times*, and the State Department to exaggerate the threat adumbrated in Stalin's speech, these opinion-forming authorities encouraged each other in the task of mobilizing American power, emotions, and moral energy to contain the Soviet Union and construct the free world.

Notes

I wish to thank Walter LaFeber and Thomas Paterson for critiquing this essay, but they are in no way responsible for its contents.

1. James V. Forrestal diary, 17 Feb. 1946, Box 2, Seeley Mudd Library, Princeton University, Princeton, N.J.; also in James V. Forrestal, *The Forrestal Diaries*, ed. Walter Millis (New York: Viking, 1951), 134. Stalin's speech, "New Five-Year Plan for Russia," can be found in *Vital Speeches of the Day* 12 (Mar. 1, 1946): 300–304.

2. See Frank Costigliola, "'Unceasing Pressure for Penetration': Gender, Pathology, and Emotion in George Kennan's Formation of the Cold War," *Journal of American History* 83 (1997): 1331–37.

3. See, for example, Lynn Boyd Hinds and Theodore Otto Windt, Jr., *The Cold War as Rhetoric: The Beginnings, 1945–1950* (New York: Praeger, 1991), 74–78; Albert Resis, "Stalin, the Politburo, and the Onset of the Cold War, 1945–1946," Carl Beck Papers (Pittsburgh: University of Pittsburgh, 1988); Deborah Welch Larson, *Origins of Containment: A Psychological Explanation* (Princeton, N.J.: Princeton University Press, 1985), 252–55; Melvyn P. Leffler, *A Preponderance of Power* (Stanford, Calif.: Stanford University Press, 1992), 103–104; B. Thomas Trout, "Rhetoric Revisited: Political Legitimation and the Cold War," *International Studies Quarterly* 19 (1975): 251–81.

4. For an introduction to the study of collective memory see Iwona Irwin-Zarecka, *Frames of Remembrance* (New Brunswick, N.J.: Transaction, 1994); Alon Confino, "Collective Memory and Cultural History: Problems of Method," *American Historical Review* 102 (1997), 1386–1403. On Washington's consistent exaggeration of the Soviet threat see Thomas G. Paterson, "Harry S Truman, American Power, and the Soviet Threat," in *Meeting the Communist Threat* (New York: Oxford University Press, 1988), 35–53.

5. Dwight D. Eisenhower to John S. D. Eisenhower, Mar. 3, 1946, in *The Papers of Dwight D. Eisenhower*, ed. Louis Galambos, 13 vols. (Baltimore: Johns Hopkins University Press, 1970–89), 7:882.

6. Alexander Werth, *Russia: The Post-War Years* (New York: Taplinger, 1971), 81–83, 99–106.

7. *New York Times*, Feb. 10, 1946, 1.

8. *Foreign Relations of the United States, Diplomatic Papers* (hereafter *FRUS*), *1946*, vol. 6 (Washington, D.C.: GPO, 1969), 695; Stalin, "New Five-Year Plan," 300.

9. Minute by J. C. Donnelly on Weekly Political Situation in the United States, Feb. 21, 1946, F.O. 371/51606, Public Record Office, Kew (hereafter PRO).

10. Stalin, "New Five-Year Plan," 300–301.

11. Ibid.

12. Quoted in David Holloway, *Stalin and the Bomb* (New Haven, Conn.: Yale University Press, 1994), 73.

13. Dmitri Volkogonov, *Stalin: Triumph and Tragedy* (London: Weidenfeld and Nicolson, 1991), 409–13.

14. Alexander Werth, *Russia at War* (New York: Dutton, 1964), 691–99.

15. Kennan to Secretary of State, Mar. 9, 1946, Box 63, George M. Elsey Papers, Harry S. Truman Presidential Library, Independence, Mo. (Hereafter Truman Library.)

16. *FRUS, 1946,* 6:694.

17. R. C. Tucker, "Interpretative Report on Soviet Policy Based on the Press for Dec. 1945," 15 Jan. 1946, Box 186, W. Averell Harriman Papers, Library of Congress, Washington, D.C. (Hereafter Harriman Papers.)

18. Werth, *Russia,* 92.

19. V. M. Molotov, "Peace and Soviet Economic Development," Feb. 7, 1946, in *Soviet Monitor,* copy in F.O. 371/56725, PRO.

20. Stalin, "New Five-Year Plan," 303–304.

21. Ibid., 300–302.

22. Stalin also used the metaphors of "school" and "test" to frame his lessons on the supposed significance of the war. The war was "a hard school of trial and a testing . . . at the rear and at the front." The test of war had supposedly also provided "an opportunity to pass judgment on our party and our people." The opportunity to pass such "judgment" enabled Stalin to reshuffle leaders, ministries, and authority among the Communist Party, civilian government, and the military—all the while recentralizing power that had become diffused during the war. (Stalin, "New Five-Year Plan," 301). See also Werner H. Hahn, *Postwar Soviet Politics* (Ithaca, N.Y.: Cornell University Press, 1982), 19–66, esp. 22–23.

23. Stalin, "New Five-Year Plan," 301.

24. Ibid., 301.

25. Ibid.

26. Ibid.

27. Ibid.

28. Ibid.

29. Ibid.

30. Ibid.

31. Ibid.

32. Ibid., 301–302.

33. Ibid., 302.

34. Ibid.

35. Ibid., 302–303.

36. Ibid., 303.

37. Ibid.

38. Holloway, *Stalin and the Bomb,* 147–49.

39. President Harry Truman had announced in an October, 1945, speech that the United States would maintain its monopoly of the bomb as "a sacred trust" and that although the United States would in the future discuss "fundamental scientific information . . . these discussions will not be concerned with the processes of manufacturing the atomic bomb." (Truman, "Address on Foreign Policy at the Navy Day Celebration in New York City," Oct. 27, 1945, in *Public Papers of the Presidents of the United States, 1945* [Washington, D.C.: GPO, 1961], 437.) Even under the proposed Baruch plan, the Soviets would have the choice of either acceding to a long-term U.S. atomic monopoly or building their own bomb.

40. Stalin, "New Five-Year Plan," 303.

41. Ibid.

42. Frank Roberts to Ernest Bevin, Feb. 10, 1946, and Roberts to Bevin, Feb. 12, 1946, both in

F.O. 371/56725, PRO; Holloway, *Stalin and the Bomb,* 149; Resis, "Stalin, the Politburo, and the Onset of the Cold War," 16.

43. Molotov's election speech, not mentioned by the *New York Times,* did set the objective "to overtake and surpass economically the most developed capitalist countries of Europe and the United States of America. . . . Our country must produce no fewer industrial goods per head of the population than the most developed capitalist country." Although certainly ambitious, Molotov's speech did not threaten war. To the contrary, he stressed that to achieve this growth, "we need a lengthy period of peace and ensured security of our country. The peace-loving policy of the Soviet Union is not some transient phenomenon." (Molotov, "Peace and Soviet Economic Development.")

44. A secret intelligence analysis prepared for the White House tried to compare the speech passage for passage to "speeches made by Hitler." Although acknowledging that Stalin's "emphasis was on defense rather than aggression," the intelligence report labeled the speech "a cold and cynical analysis of the Soviet war potential" that "omitted almost all usual references to [the] civilian economy." Trying to end the debate about Soviet intentions, the analysis repeated that the industrial program "can have little other interpretation than a program for strengthening the Soviet war potential." ("Analysis of Stalin's Address to Moscow Constituency," Intelligence Review No. 2, Feb. 21, 1946, Box 63, George M. Elsey Papers, Truman Library.)

45. Geoffrey A. Hosking, "Memory in a Totalitarian Society: The Case of the Soviet Union," in *Memory: History, Culture and the Mind,* ed. Thomas Butler (New York: Blackwell, 1989), 115–29.

46. Joseph E. Davies Diary, Feb. 9, 1946, Box 23, Joseph E. Davies Papers, Library of Congress.

47. "Political Situation in the United States," Feb. 17, 1946, F.O. 371/51606, PRO.

48. "Minute by J. Donnelly," Feb. 21, 1946 on "Political Situation in the United States," Feb. 17, 1946, F.O. 371/51606, PRO.

49. In February, 1946, as the Truman administration sought to clarify rather than blur its differences with Moscow, Stalin's government continued to behave with a confusing mixture of caution and aggrandizement. The Soviets angered the United States with their continued occupation of northern Iran and Manchuria, with their pressure on Turkey for greater power in the Dardanelles, and with their defense of spies caught in Canada. Yet they evacuated northern Norway and Danish Bornholm, discouraged revolutionary activity in Western Europe, offered no leadership to Communist revolutionaries in Southeast Asia, and played to both sides in the Chinese civil war; further, they would allow free elections in Hungary, Czechoslovakia, and Finland. (See Leffler, *Preponderance of Power,* 133 and passim.)

50. See, for example, Odd Arne Westad, "Secrets of the Second World: The Russian Archives and the Reinterpretation of Cold War History," *Diplomatic History* 21 (1997): 259–71.

51. See Melvyn P. Leffler, "Inside Enemy Archives: The Cold War Reopened," *Foreign Affairs* 75 (1996): 120–35.

52. *FRUS, 1945,* vol. 6 (Washington, D.C.: GPO, 1969), 792.

53. Memorandum of conversation between Stalin and Harriman, Jan. 23, 1946, File 711.61/1-2346, General Records of the Department of State, Record Group (RG) 59, National Archives, Washington, D.C. (Hereafter NA.)

54. Thomas G. Paterson, *On Every Front: The Making and Unmaking of the Cold War* (New York: Norton, 1992), 41–69.

55. Matthews to James Byrnes and Dean Acheson, Feb. 11, 1946, Box 2, H. Freeman Matthews Papers, RG 59, NA.

56. Matthews to Kennan, Feb. 13, 1946, 861.00/2-1246, RG 59, NA.

57. Weekly Political Summary, Feb. 17, 1946, F.O. 371/51606, PRO.

58. Walter Lippmann, "Stalin Chooses Military Power," *Los Angeles Times,* Feb. 13, 1946. In 1945–47 Stalin demobilized two-thirds of the Red Army.

59. Ibid.

60. Ibid.

61. Costigliola, "'Unceasing Pressure for Penetration,'" 1334–35.

62. Lippmann, "Stalin Chooses Military Power."

63. Ibid.

64. Walter Lippmann, "The United States in the Middle East," *Los Angeles Times,* Feb. 12, 1946.

CHAPTER THREE

NSC (National Insecurity) 68

Nitze's Second Hallucination

ROBERT P. NEWMAN

The anti-Soviet diatribe known as NSC-68 was among the most closely held documents produced by the U.S. government. The reasons for the secrecy are important in any account of its construction. President Truman and Secretary of State Dean Acheson clearly were not anxious to aggravate Soviet-American relations by displaying fully the dark thoughts they held of their Cold War adversary, but there were also probably less obvious motives for such an extreme classification. Not all Americans in 1950 were prepared to believe that the Russians were nine feet tall. Not all experts on Soviet history thought Stalin had literally taken over Hitler's plans to subjugate the entire world, and many religious and academic leaders believed that Soviet prickliness was due to the massive destruction caused by invasions of Russian territory by Western powers. Had NSC-68 been released and its excesses subjected to public debate, the myth that it had overwhelming support could not have been sustained.

Of course the general thrust of the government's prime anti-Soviet tract did become known. Acheson himself cleaned up the harshest language for his many public statements about U.S. relations with the Soviet Union. But the raw charges of the document itself, the extremism of its "sky is falling" rhetoric, were never revealed until Henry Kissinger declassified it in February, 1975. At the time it was prepared, copies were numbered in Paul Nitze's office and a notation was made as to when each copy had been returned, shredded, or burned.[1] Even in 1975, although the text was released, the paper trail was not. Some of the maneuvering was included in volume one of *Foreign Relations of the United States (FRUS), 1950*, published in 1977, but much of the archive was not declassified until the 1990s. Even then, many documents were withheld from researchers. One archive box alone, containing records of the Department of State Policy Planning Staff (PPS) for 1950, included twenty-three cards identifying classified documents denied to the public as recently as 1999. Accounts of the gestation and birth of NSC-68, including this one, are thus based on less than full disclosure.

Early accounts, such as the influential attempt to contextualize NSC-68 by Paul Hammond, had to depend entirely upon testimony of the principals.[2] Even given an investigator of Hammond's formidable powers, this procedure had to be flawed. Many later accounts depended on interviews as well. And, given the controversial status of the Truman administration's Cold War moves, both hard-liners and revisionists were able to find actors in the NSC-68 drama to reinforce their prejudices. Until at least the Vietnam trauma of the late 1960s, hard-liners had the easiest time finding "memories" upon which to build pro-NSC-68 narratives. The most prominent hawks were more than willing to tell investigators how the document saved democracy. Revisionists, who suspected that there had been some flimflam on the part of pro-NSC-68 authors and thought that tripling the arms budget in one year was not absolutely necessary, could not directly attack the document. A *secret* formula for salvation is, after all, difficult to disprove.

For all these reasons, the corpus of NSC-68 criticism contains an overload of beliefs that cannot be sustained:

1. The document is alleged to be a blueprint for the conduct of the Cold War. (It *is* an impassioned statement of the *need* for such a blueprint.)
2. It did not recommend any innovations in American policy; it merely emphasized doing more of the things the United States started doing in 1947. (There *was* an innovation: The Soviet Union would have nuclear power sufficient to attack the United States in 1954.)
3. It was adopted with no great fuss by a unanimous government. (There was a *great* fuss, and enlightened opposition, which was ignored by Paul Nitze, the officer in charge.)
4. It was adopted only after furious arguments eventually settled by the Korean War. (The Korean War did precipitate its adoption, but the arguments continued.)
5. It governed U.S. national security policy until at least the time of détente and perhaps longer. (The most insidious part of NSC-68, the "rollback" doctrine, was rescinded by Dwight Eisenhower.)
6. It presented a rational, fully warranted approach to U.S.-Soviet relations. (It was a gross, catastrophic diatribe.)
7. It was constructed without input from George Kennan and Charles "Chip" Bohlen, the two foremost Soviet experts. (Both Kennan and Bohlen had much to say about it, all hostile.)

8. Its hard line was inevitable, given the Soviet threat to the American way of life, or to Western civilization. (The Soviet threat was political and psychological, not primarily military.)
9. It was produced in complete and final form on April 7, 1950, or on September 30, 1950, or sometime in December that year. (It was never in final form; versions of it were being produced up to 1953.)
10. It was largely responsible for the 1950 intensification of the Cold War and the massive increase in armaments that began then. (There is some truth in this, but the most incendiary event leading to the Cold War arms race was Korea.)

John Lewis Gaddis's 1982 *Strategies of Containment* is still the best account of the origin of NSC-68 and its relationship to the "Father of Containment," George F. Kennan. The macronarrative that follows draws much from Gaddis.[3]

From July, 1944, to April, 1946, Kennan served in the U.S. embassy in Moscow. It was clear to him that the Soviet Union was quite different from other European nations and from the United States. Kennan sent many dispatches to Washington analyzing the Soviet Union and recommending firm and vigilant dealing with the Soviets, but these fell on indifferent ears. Finally, in February, 1946, in response to a State Department telegram asking what could be expected from the Soviet Union in the future, Kennan composed his famous Long Telegram, which penetrated the Washington bureaucracy as nothing earlier had done. This message was "of primary importance in influencing official attitudes."[4]

The Long Telegram was different from Kennan's later "X" article in *Foreign Affairs,* which was composed under different circumstances. It was also a far cry from what the doctrine of containment became in NSC-68. Kennan spent much of the rest of his life distancing himself from the latter, insisting that he had not intended the universalism and fear mongering that went under the heading of "containment" in 1950. By 1947 Kennan realized that Truman's call for aid to Greece and Turkey was couched in language that committed the United States to an unending militaristic agenda with which he had no sympathy. The author of "containment" soon became the foremost opponent of the doctrines that he was alleged to have initiated.

It is therefore important to inspect the Long Telegram to see how it envisaged dealing with probable Soviet actions. There is room here for only the gravamen of Part 5 of that telegram, "Practical Deductions From Standpoint of U.S. Policy":[5]

In summary, we have here a political force committed fanatically to the belief that with US there can be no permanent *modus vivendi,* that it is desirable and necessary that the internal harmony of our society be disrupted, our traditional way of life be destroyed, the international authority of our state be broken, if Soviet power is to be secure. . . . This is admittedly not a pleasant picture. Problem of how to cope with this force is undoubtedly greatest task our diplomacy has ever faced and probably greatest it will ever have to face. . . . I cannot attempt to suggest all answers here. But I would like to record my conviction that problem is within our power to solve—and that without recourse to any general military conflict. And in support of this conviction there are certain observations of a more encouraging nature I should like to make:

1. Soviet power, unlike that of Hitlerite Germany, is neither schematic nor adventuristic. It does not work by fixed plans. It does not take unnecessary risks. . . . For this reason it can easily withdraw—and usually does—when strong resistance is encountered at any point. . . . If situations are properly handled there need be no prestige-engaging showdowns.
2. Gauged against Western World as a whole, Soviets are still by far the weaker force. Thus, their success will really depend on degree of cohesion, firmness and vigor which Western World can muster. . . .
3. Success of Soviet system, as form of internal power, is not yet finally proven. . . . Soviet internal system will now be subjected, by virtue of recent territorial expansions, to series of additional strains which once proved severe tax on Tsardom. . . .
4. All Soviet propaganda beyond Soviet security sphere is basically negative and destructive. It should therefore be relatively easy to combat it by any intelligent and really constructive program.

For these reasons I think we may approach calmly and with good heart problem of how to deal with Russia. . . . I wish only to advance, by way of conclusion, following comments:

1. Our first step must be to apprehend, and recognize for what it is, the nature of the movement with which we are dealing. We must study it with same courage, detachment, objectivity, and same determination not to be emotionally provoked or unseated by it, with which doctor studies unruly and unreasonable individual.
2. We must see that our public is educated to realities of Russian situation. I cannot over-emphasize importance of this. . . . I am convinced that there would be far less hysterical anti-Sovietism in our country today if realities of this situation were better understood by our people. . . . There is nothing as dangerous or as terrifying as the unknown. . . .

3. Much depends on health and vigor of our own society. World communism is like malignant parasite which feeds only on diseased tissue. . . .
4. We must formulate and put forward for other nations a much more positive and constructive picture of sort of world we would like to see than we have put forward in the past.
5. Finally we must have courage and self-confidence to cling to our own methods and conceptions of human society. After all, the greatest danger that can befall us in coping with this problem of Soviet communism, is that we shall allow ourselves to become like those with whom we are coping.

The story of how this telegram seized the imagination of official Washington has been often told. Kennan was brought back to the United States to lecture at the National War College, then, in May, 1947, Secretary of State George Marshall installed him as head of a new State Department operation, the PPS. For two and a half years Kennan was in charge of evaluating American diplomatic policies and suggesting future actions. Marshall's desire to have a planning staff that would be proactive rather than reactive was only partially successful, and Kennan soon found himself immersed in one crisis after another. He and his PPS were involved in the "crisis" in Greece and Turkey, the Marshall Plan, the Berlin affair, the creation of the North Atlantic Treaty Organization (NATO), the occupation of Japan, and lesser matters to the extent that it is hard to see how he accomplished *any* long-range planning.

But there was some, none more important than the production of the paper "U.S. Objectives with Respect to Russia," the forerunner of, and some say paradigm for, NSC-68. This paper was adopted by the National Security Council as NSC-20/1, and subsequent attempts to legitimate fire-breathing scenarios for dealing with the Soviets claimed its parentage.[6] This document responded to a request from Secretary of Defense James Forrestal, who wanted an assessment of "the proportion of our resources which should be devoted to military purposes. Because a large majority of the basic issues involved concern matters which are within the province of the Department of State, I have recommended that the State Department be asked to prepare a first draft of such a statement."[7] Kennan and his PPS drew the assignment.

The study was completed on August 18, 1948. Fifty-two pages long and composed in Kennan's elaborate style, NSC-20/1 considered U.S. objectives with respect to Russia under two headings: peacetime and war. Its most notable sections pointed toward the possibility of decreasing the Soviet threat by encouraging, or recognizing as they happened, the falling away from Soviet control and influence of peripheral countries (Tito's Yugoslavia was cited several times; the Sino-Soviet rift had not yet happened, but Kennan predicted it). It also emphasized that reducing the "power and influence of the Kremlin to limits in which they will no longer constitute a threat to the peace and stability of international society, . . . is an objective which can be logically pursued" in war *or* peace. And this was not an objective that imposed a time limit for achievement: "We are faced here with no rigid periodicity . . . that we must achieve our peacetime objectives by a given date 'or else'."[8] The Marshall Plan was a big factor in pursuing this objective and it probably contributed to the disaffection of Tito.

The completed NSC-20/1 was worked over by the PPS and NSC, and a variant (NSC-20/4) was approved by Truman on November 24, 1948. It was harsher than both NSC-20/1 and the Long Telegram: "Communist ideology and Soviet behavior clearly demonstrate that the ultimate objective of the leaders of the USSR is the domination of the world. . . . The resistance of the United States is recognized by the USSR as a major obstacle to the attainment of these goals."[9] Furthermore, the Soviet Union was increasing its bombing capabilities, so that no later than 1955 it would be able to launch air attacks on the United States with atomic, biological, and chemical weapons.

There was still an upside: the Soviets could not invade the United States, and the European Recovery Program, NATO, and internal dissension in the Soviet Union all might offset Soviet strength.[10]

There was no alarmism in these documents. The Soviets were not on their way to San Francisco. They had no timetable for world conquest. We could work to decrease their power even as we were working to increase ours. There was no statement that we were losing the Cold War, or that we would have to oppose every move the Soviets made even if it posed no threat to American interests. When Truman approved NSC-20/4 in November, 1948, it became the definitive statement of American policy toward the Soviet Union until December 14, 1950, when the president approved NSC-68/4.[11]

It can be fairly said that NSC-20/4 put Kennan's stamp on American Cold War policy. There were other specific decisions in which Kennan's judgment played a crucial role: the Marshall Plan owed much to Kennan, the "reverse course" in Japan that led to that country's economic dynamism was significantly influenced by Kennan's work, and he had much to do with the careful American response to Tito's break with Stalin. In addition to heading the PPS, Secretary of State Acheson made Kennan the State Department counselor.

However, Kennan's advice was not always followed. Treatment of Germany was constantly under review, and Kennan was firmly convinced that the postwar occupation should not be allowed to lead to a permanent division of Germany. He believed that Germany should be united, neutralized, and foreign troops withdrawn. Only then could the West and the Soviets "disengage" from central Europe and defuse the tinderbox Europe represented. Kennan lost this battle. Acheson and more hawkish advisers made the division of Germany firm and incorporated West Germany in the American-led bloc. This, according to Kennan, killed chances of getting the Russians out of central and Eastern Europe. As Wilson Miscamble says, "Kennan struggled to prevent this, and he failed. For a proud man the pain of this defeat struck deep."[12]

Kennan also backed a losing position with regard to China policy. He despised the Republican pro–Chiang Kai-shek fanatics, to whom Chiang was China's George Washington and Mao was subservient to Stalin. Kennan not only believed Chiang to be incompetent, he believed the only hope of crippling the Soviet drive for power in Asia was to stimulate Chinese independence from the Kremlin. He wanted to de-emphasize American relations with China, recognize the government in Beijing, and support the People's Republic of China's (PRC) membership in the United Nations. Toward the end of 1949 Kennan decided to resign as director of the PPS and accept a position at Princeton University's Institute for Advanced Study offered to him by J. Robert Oppenheimer. There, even if he could no longer influence policy, he could write about it. Acheson, however, persuaded him to delay his departure until June, 1950, make a tour of a much-neglected area (Latin America) and recommend policy initiatives there, and retain the title counselor. The year 1950 was the Point of No Return in the Cold War. Previous to that year, a modus vivendi with the Soviet Union was at least possible. By year's end no such outcome was conceivable.

During his last several months on duty in Washington, Kennan was drawn fully into the problem of the role the United States was to assign to nuclear weapons—both how they were to be used (if at all), and whether to expand the arsenal with a new fusion bomb (referred to during this period as the "Super"). Kennan's disagreements with PPS Deputy Director Paul Nitze assumed major proportions in late 1949. Acheson asked both Kennan and Nitze to study the question of building the H-bomb. Nitze, who had held various posts dealing with economics during the war, first met Kennan on a train in 1944. At the time, Nitze was en route to join the U.S. Strategic Bombing Survey (USSBS) team. His first stop was Germany, where he found most strategic bombing to be ineffectual, but the bombing of transportation and petroleum facilities to be significant. When Nitze went to Japan as acting head of the USSBS in the fall of 1945, he took the position that the conventional bombing of cities had been unnecessary but that destroying transportation and communication facilities had brought Japan to its knees.

Nitze believed that the Japanese, faced with the prospect of starvation in the summer of 1945, probably would have surrendered by October 1 without the atom bomb, without Soviet entry, and without an invasion. This startling conclusion, inserted by Nitze in the final USSBS reports, was, he claimed, based on "all the facts"—most of which came from the testimony of prominent Japanese officials. Unfortunately, when the papers of the USSBS investigation were released, it was immediately apparent that Nitze had no facts at all.[13] He was hallucinating.

In addition to his false conclusion about Japan's readiness to surrender in the late summer of 1945, Nitze was unimpressed by the power of the atom. The Hiroshima bomb damage could have been accomplished with the conventional explosives carried by a fleet of 210 B-29s. Furthermore, as he wrote in his memoirs:

> For instance, in Nagasaki, the railroads were back in operation forty-eight hours after the attack. Most of the rolling stock in the city had been destroyed, but the tracks suffered relatively minor damage. In Hiroshima, we learned that a train had been going through the city when the bomb went off. People sitting next to open windows suffered few cuts or other injuries from broken glass, but because they were directly exposed to radiation, many of them fell ill and later died. On the other hand, people sitting next to the closed windows, even though many were cut by flying glass, generally survived because the windows shielded them from the radiation. We also found that even in the immediate blast area, people who had taken to simple air raid tunnels emerged unscathed.[14]

For Nitze, a bomb was a bomb. Strobe Talbott, in his evenhanded biography, says "Nitze saw it as his task to demystify the bomb, to treat it as another weapon rather than the Absolute Weapon."[15] The contrast with Kennan, whose horrified reaction to the conventional bombing of Hamburg was total, did not prejudice their collaborative work on the PPS until after Truman announced on September 23, 1949, that the Soviets had detonated an atomic bomb. This unexpectedly early development stunned Washington into active consideration of the second generation of nuclear weapons: the Super, or H-bomb. Both Kennan and Nitze took Acheson's request to study the matter seriously.

Nitze's response was unqualified: We should build it.[16] As early as February, 1946, Nitze had interpreted Stalin's election eve speech to a Soviet party rally as "a delayed declaration of war against the United States."[17] If the Super could be built, Stalin would build it. For Nitze, the only question was its feasibility. Was it theoretically possible, or would we be pouring money down a rat hole? He called in Oppenheimer to advise him. Oppenheimer presented all the reasons why it should not be built, including moral reasons (H-bombs were clearly genocidal weapons) and technical doubts. We would, he said, be better off putting money and materials into improved fission bombs, which would be quite adequate to deter Soviet attack. Nitze was unpersuaded. He called in Edward Teller to give the other point of view. As David Callahan describes this encounter:

> For two hours he stood before the blackboard and tutored Nitze in his thick Hungarian accent on two possible methods of producing thermonuclear weapons. . . . "Ed Teller knew his subject so well that he was able to explain why this thing would work in just two hours time," Nitze said later. While Oppenheimer's technical doubts had seemed disjointed to Nitze, Teller had no question about feasibility and exuded total command of the scientific aspects of the problem. . . . As it later became clear, Edward Teller did not know what he was talking about. The methods that were used to build an H-bomb over the next three years bore little resemblance to the methods that Teller was promoting in 1949. . . . With little or no knowledge of physics, Nitze thought that he had followed Teller's calculations, and that those calculations proved the super's feasibility.[18]

Kennan, also responding to Acheson's request, launched a two-month investigation of the role of atomic weapons in American policy, including the question of the Super. He delivered a seventy-nine-page analysis of these problems to Acheson on January 15, 1950. In his *Memoirs,* Kennan says of this report: "I considered it to have been in its implications one of the most important, if not the most important, of all the documents I ever wrote in government."[19] At the end of the century, this report possesses a stature by comparison with which the tons of defense theoretical manuals produced in think tanks and military schools appear as obfuscation and madness. The seminal paragraph, as I see it, reads: "It is entirely possible that war will be waged against us again, as it has been waged against us and other nations within our time, under these concepts and by these weapons. If so, we shall doubtless have to reply in kind, for that may be the price of survival. I still think it vital to what it is we are about that we not fall into the error of initiating or planning to initiate, the employment of these weapons and concepts, thus hypnotizing ourselves into the belief that they may ultimately serve some positive national purpose."[20]

Acheson, who was not impressed, did not give Kennan's anguished analysis to Truman. As Peter Galison and Barton Bernstein show in their 1989 account of the H-bomb decision: "Secretary Acheson and military leaders wanted the weapon. They welcomed the strategic and political power they thought the bomb promised."[21] Truman decided on January 31, 1950, in favor of Acheson, Teller, and the hawks. However, he had sensed the reluctance of some of the doves and wanted serious study of the role nuclear weapons should play. His letter to Secretary Acheson announcing the decision on the Super thus included this charge: "I hereby direct the Secretary of State and the Secretary of Defense to undertake a reexamination of our objectives in peace and war and of the effect of these objectives on our strategic plans, in the light of the probable fission bomb capability and possible thermonuclear bomb capability of the Soviet Union."[22]

This sentence was the mandate for the NSC-68 series. There really was no precedent for drafting such a consequential document as the reexamination of the nation's national security objectives. Truman had commissioned the secretaries of state and defense to do it. Acheson, who was clearly to take the lead, appointed Nitze to take charge of what came to be known as the State-Defense Policy Review Group. Nitze chose four members of his PPS staff, the JCS chose four military members, and there were two representatives from the NSC. They started work on February 8, 1950.

Kennan was leaving on a lengthy mission to South America in his capacity as counselor just as Nitze's committee got underway. Knowing that fantasies of a Soviet steamroller crushing Western civilization were spreading in the government, Kennan composed an eight-page memorandum reviewing "our foreign policy in its entirety" and addressed it to Secretary Acheson. It was dated February 17, the day before Kennan left for Mexico. The memo was "circulated for the information of the staff" but never reached Acheson. This document shows more clearly than the Long Telegram, the "X" article, NSC-20, or any other Kennan statement *what NSC-68 would have looked like had Kennan rather than Nitze been in charge.*

The memo does not recapitulate the earlier Kennan products, it brings them up to date:

> There is little justification for the impression that the "cold war", by virtue of events outside of our control, has suddenly taken some drastic turn to our disadvantage. . . . Recent events in the Far East have been the culmination of processes which have long been apparent. The implications of these processes were correctly analyzed, and their results reasonably accurately predicted, long ago by our advisors in this field. . . . Mao's protracted stay

> in Moscow is good evidence that our own experts were right not only in their analysis of the weakness of the [Chinese] National Government but also in their conviction that the Russians would have difficulty establishing the same sort of relationship with a successful Chinese Communist movement that they have established with some of their eastern European satellites. [These Soviet difficulties are] not only *not* of our making but would actually be apt to be weakened by any attempts on our part to intervene directly. . . . The demonstration of an "atomic capability" on the part of the USSR likewise adds no new fundamental element to the picture. . . . The fact that this state of affairs became a reality a year or two before it was generally expected is of no fundamental significance. . . . The idea of their threatening people with the H-bomb and bidding them "sign on the dotted line or else" is thus far solely of our own manufacture.[23]

Other themes covered in Kennan's valedictory included de-emphasizing nuclear weapons, declaring a no-first-use policy, freeing trade from excessive tariffs, closely monitoring aid to underdeveloped areas so that it clearly benefits the people, and schooling American government officials so they can explain policies intelligently.

This agenda, no doubt because it was so calm and unexciting, appears nowhere in Cold War discourse. The Left, particularly, remembers only Kennan's attempt to convince Americans in the afterglow of World War II that Russia was not a democracy playing by our rules. Not one of Kennan's detractors can produce a policy agenda articulated in 1950 showing the foresight and realism of his February 17 memorandum.

Meanwhile, Nitze's committee was preparing for Armageddon. They did not necessarily envision it as an immediate, massive clash of arms. It might be a strangling envelopment of the Western world by the growth of Soviet hegemony everywhere, until the United States was isolated and compelled to give in. It might be a first strike by Soviet nuclear forces, which would be advanced enough by 1954 to cripple our retaliatory power. (The date was later moved forward to 1952.) Stuart Symington, chairman of the National Security Resources Board and a Nitze supporter, spoke at Baylor University on February 1, 1950, implying that the Soviet ready date could be as early as tomorrow.[24]

Six prominent citizens conversant with defense issues were brought before the Nitze committee; the first was Robert Oppenheimer on February 27.[25] Oppenheimer, who was lukewarm about the whole business, lectured the committee on the evils of H-bombs (too late, of course; that decision had been made). James B. Conant engaged the committee in a lengthy and profitable discussion on March 2. The most noteworthy item to emerge from this session was Conant's prediction that the Soviet Union would self-destruct by 1980.

Chester Barnard and Henry Smyth were brought in as consultants on March 10. Barnard liked the preliminary draft of the committee's opinions that he had seen and wanted a task force of prominent citizens to publicize them. Smyth's contribution was notable for his devotion to homiletics; the "one thing he missed in the paper was a gospel which lends itself to preaching."

Robert Lovett, soon to be deputy secretary of defense, introduced the most incendiary advice of any outsider on March 16. Lovett said the American posture vis-à-vis the Soviet Union should be vastly more combative, and suggested that the forthcoming document should state its conclusions in almost telegraphic style, or in what he referred to as "Hemingway sentences." Ernest O. Lawrence, who appeared before the group on March 20, *really* wanted a military buildup: "He labeled the cost of atomic developments as 'chicken-feed' and said that we should be spending ten times as much."

Nitze chose his consultants carefully: one dove, one chicken hawk, and four gung-ho belligerents.

Various apparently unsolicited letters appear in Nitze's files from this early period of the committee's work, two of them moderate and calming, but most wanting "go-for-broke" rhetoric. Of note is a memo from Nitze to Acheson dated March 29 reporting that General Eisenhower was not exactly on board. Nitze chided Eisenhower for giving a speech that showed alarming affinity for "the fallacy that Hans Morgenthau" touts: disarmament is a preventive for war. Furthermore, he said the general "does not indicate any awareness of the deep-seated nature of the drives behind totalitarianism, and of the critical importance of success in the cold war to prevent a shooting war."[26] Poor Eisenhower. By the time he entered the White House his affinity for Hans Morgenthau's fallacies was straightened out.

So we come to March 30, 1950, the date on which a first draft of what was to become NSC-68 was ready for circulation to and comment from fifteen second-level State Department officials and the full NSC.[27] The paper trail, as noted above, is not complete. However, what survives in the archives does not show a consensus.

The first response selected for inclusion in the *FRUS* volume on NSC-68 is from Llewellyn Thompson, Russian scholar and deputy assistant secretary of state for European affairs.[28] There was hardly a kind word from Thompson; he wanted the whole thing subjected to a "high level examination" by eight officials, whom he named. George W. Perkins, Thompson's boss, was less excoriating but still found nothing to his liking.[29] E. M. Martin, also of the Office of European Affairs, took two pages to offer his opinions:

> The objective is not clear . . . the mechanism by which increased political, economic, and military strength in the West will accomplish the objectives as I have interpreted it, is not clear. . . . The policy statement calls for [Soviet] withdrawal from the satellites. This is desirable on humanitarian grounds, but as the paper recognizes, they are an element of weakness. It might be at least worth examining whether the Kremlin . . . would not be strengthened by such a move . . . There are areas of the world to which our resources cannot possibly stretch with sufficient strength to revolutionize centuries old patterns of life, as for example in parts of the Middle and Far East. . . . We can hardly hope that over time we will avoid serious economic depressions . . . too much emphasis is put on more weapons and men, and not enough on improved technology. . . . There are references to cold war situations in which we cannot meet local forays without general war because our forces are too small.[30]

We know at least one thing about the government in 1950: Big Brother did not have all his minions brainwashed.

Willard Thorp, assistant secretary of state for economic affairs, offered perhaps the most damaging coherent attack: "One of the assumptions in this Report is the notion that the USSR is 'steadily reducing the discrepancy between its overall economic strength and that of the U.S.' So far as the evidence included in the Report is concerned, I do not feel that this proposition is demonstrated, but rather the reverse. . . . In fact, all the evidence in the report points the other way, that the actual gap is widening in our favor."[31]

Raymond A. Hare, acting assistant secretary for Near Eastern, South Asian, and African affairs, was polite and did not twist his knife. Instead he stuck it in deep: "For instance, are we yet certain that the Soviet venture in China will strengthen the USSR to the extent now feared? Have we, in fact, adequately explored the question of whether there may be a critical point in Soviet expansion beyond which the benefits to the USSR will turn to disadvantage?"[32] Hare apologized for his critical tone at the end.

James E. Webb, the undersecretary of state to whom Nitze reported, set a deadline of noon on April 5 for comments on the "State-Defense Staff Study" to reach his and Nitze's desks. The last memo to reach Webb and Nitze was surely the most probative, and by itself refutes the image of a single-minded administration heading into an unalloyed confrontation with the Soviet Union. Charles E. "Chip" Bohlen, the U.S. minister in Paris, was brought back to Washington in late March to assist in this study. His entire three-page memo deserves to be included here, but space permits only key parts. Bohlen agreed that the government needed to get its act together in dealing with Russia, of course, and he thought the "general conclusions" reached by Nitze and his team were unassailable. However, insofar as Bohlen was concerned:

> It is open to question whether or not, as stated, the fundamental design of the Kremlin is the domination of the world. . . . this carries the implication that all other considerations are subordinate and that great risks would be run for the sake of its achievement. It tends, therefore, to over simplify the problem, and, in my opinion, leads inevitably to the conclusion that war is inevitable. . . . I believe my chief suggestion concerning this report . . . is that the conclusions do not in every case stem directly from the argumentation. . . . Another point which might be made more precise would be an analysis of exactly what, in the present world, constitutes a deterrent to the launching of war by the Soviet Union. As you know, I believe that too much emphasis has been given to the atomic bomb as a deterrent in the past while we held the monopoly. I think it is difficult to deduce any evidence that this monopoly on our part influenced Soviet policy during this period or abated its aggressiveness.[33]

Bohlen was polite, but he concluded by rejecting a full-scale rearmament program and instead called for an emphasis on quality rather than quantity. He was clearly not on Nitze's wavelength.

When the deadline for comments on this first draft arrived, only one person consulted, Assistant Secretary of State for United Nations Affairs John D. Hickerson, could conceivably be classed as generally approving.[34] Nonetheless, on April 6, under the heading "Comments on State-Defense Staff Study," Nitze wrote a letter to Secretary Acheson that was almost as oblivious to the documents before him as he had been to the interrogations of Japan's leaders five years earlier when he wrote the USSBS reports:

> Mr. Secretary:
>
> I have received written comments from the following: Mr. Perkins, Mr. Hickerson, Mr. Thorp, Mr. Bohlen, Mr. Thompson, and Mr. Hare. In addition, I have discussed the paper with Mr. Jessup, Mr. Rusk, Mr. Byroade, and Mr. Kennan.
>
> 1. The conclusions and recommendations have found general support. The comments reveal no need to alter these in any major way, but it is suggested that you might wish to make the comment attached as Appendix 1 in forwarding them to the President. [This was to emphasize exploiting U.S. technology.]
> 2. Various comments of a helpful character have been received which relate to the Staff study. The nature of these is such that I believe they could best be reflected in the subsequent work of the Department in preparing programs to carry out the Conclusions and Recommendations.[35]

One can censure Nitze for seeing "no need to alter these in any major way." This report, like its USSBS predecessor, has ideology-induced bias written all over it.[36]

"United States Objectives and Programs for National Security," the sixty-eighth formal document accepted by the NSC, went to Harry Truman on April 7. Dean Acheson writes in his memoirs: "The purpose of NSC-68 was to so bludgeon the mass mind of 'top government' that not only could the President make a decision but that the decision could be carried out."[37] A little reflection suggests that if the president *and* the rest of the government's senior leaders had to be bludgeoned to do what Nitze and company wanted, what the report recommended was not exactly a consensus. Perhaps not even a majority opinion.

The table of contents of this scaremongering document gives an overview of how Nitze's review group intended to bludgeon the bureaucracy's mass mind:

I. Background of the Present World Crisis
II. The Fundamental Purpose of the United States
III. The Fundamental Design of the Kremlin
IV. The Underlying Conflict in the Realm of Ideas and Values Between the U.S. Purpose and the Kremlin Design
V. Soviet Intentions and Capabilities—Actual and Potential
VI. U.S. Intentions and Capabilities—Actual and Potential
VII. Present Risks
VIII. Atomic Armaments . . .
IX. Possible Courses of Action
  A The First Course—Continuation of Current Policies . . .
  B. The Second Course—Isolation
  C. The Third Course—War
  D. The Remainder Course of Action—A Rapid Buildup of Political, Economic, and Military Strength in the Free World
Conclusions
Recommendations[38]

Section I sounds the tocsin: "The issues that face us are momentous, involving the fulfillment or destruction not only of this Republic but of civilization itself. They are issues which will not await our deliberations."[39]

Section II piggybacks on the Constitution and Declaration of Independence; the "more perfect union" and so forth can actually be had with a "firm reliance on the protection of Divine Providence, we mutually pledge to each other our lives, our Fortunes, and our sacred Honor."[40]

Section III's second sentence declares that the Soviet design "calls for the complete subversion or forcible destruction of the machinery of government and structure of society in the countries of the non-Soviet world and their replacement by an apparatus and structure subservient to and controlled from the Kremlin." The United States, of course, is the principal obstacle to the Kremlin's fundamental design.[41]

Section IV gets into some theory of totalitarianism, contrasting it with Western individualism, the latter of which possesses "marvelous diversity . . . deep tolerance . . . and lawfulness." As such, the United States is a "permanent and continuous threat to the foundation of the slave society."[42] The glories of this "free society" are emphasized several times, as are the handicaps free societies face in competing with a tyranny, "which is able to select whatever means are expedient in seeking to carry out its fundamental design. . . . We have no such freedom of choice."[43]

Here we come to one of the unbelievable internal contradictions that make this polemic so reprehensible. Four paragraphs after the lament about our free society being handicapped in its choice of actions because of our value systems, we find this amazing disclaimer: "Our free society, confronted by a threat to its basic values, naturally will take such action, including the use of military force [including nuclear weapons], as may be required to protect those values. The integrity of our system will not be jeopardized by any measures, covert or overt, violent or non-violent, which serve the purposes of frustrating the Kremlin design, nor does the necessity for conducting ourselves so as to affirm our values in actions as well as words forbid such measures, provided only that they are appropriately calculated to that end and are not so excessive or misdirected as to make us enemies of the people instead of the evil men who have enslaved them."[44]

This is a jarring bit of sophistry: Our way of life abhors dirty tricks, but we can use them to preserve our way of life. Fortunately the archives reveal vigorous expressions of disdain from the mass mind of top government for the double standard issuing from Nitze's pen. Vigorous but impotent, for by the time this draft was finished, the Chinese Communists had seized U.S. consulate property, the Sino-Soviet mutual defense treaty had been signed, Alger Hiss had been convicted, Klaus Fuchs had confessed giving atomic secrets to the Russians, and Sen. Joseph McCarthy had begun his crusade to demonstrate that Communists really *did* dominate the State Department. The panic button had been pushed and cold warriors were on the move.

Section V, "Soviet Intentions and Capabilities," became the focus of sustained attack. The highlights expounded on in NSC-68 are these: "The Soviet

Union is developing the military capacity to support its design for world domination. The Soviet Union actually possesses armed forces far in excess of those necessary to defend its national territory."[45] Since the Soviet design is immutable, any negotiations we hold with Soviets will be mere window dressing for public relations purposes. The United States can survive only through a policy of military containment. We must strengthen our economy, arm our allies, and implement a civil defense program that includes fallout shelters.

But whatever we do, prospects are dim: "It is estimated that, within the next four years, the USSR will attain the capability of seriously damaging vital centers of the United States, provided it strikes a surprise blow and provided further that the blow is opposed by no more effective opposition than we now have programmed."[46] The point of maximum danger is 1954 because the Soviets will have a nuclear arsenal by then.

This section remained controversial to the end of the Truman administration, as did NSC-68's explicit rejection of Kennan's "no first use" (of nuclear weapons) doctrine. It stated Nitze's belief this way: "In our present situation of relative unpreparedness in conventional weapons, such a declaration would be interpreted by the USSR as an admission of great weakness and by our allies as a clear indication that we intended to abandon them."[47] Nowhere in the Nitze corpus is there any warrant for this assertion. How did Nitze know Russia and our allies would interpret a no-first-use pledge this way? It is certainly not obvious on the face of it.

As to the costs of the arms program called for in NSC-68, not to worry. "Budgetary considerations will need to be subordinated to the stark fact that our very independence as a nation may be at stake."[48] Not content to let this eschatological forecast stand alone, NSC-68 weaves it into a four-option finale. We have these choices: the present rearmament program, isolation, war, or the accelerated buildup recommended by NSC-68. It is never made clear how, if the Soviet Union is as belligerent and powerful as Nitze claims, even the tripling of defense expenditures would save us. Yet how could a president suffering from charges of being soft on communism and losing China choose any but the fourth option? Truman did not adopt NSC-68; he chose to bury it with studies. On April 12 he wrote James Lay, the NSC executive secretary: "I have decided to refer the report to the National Security Council for consideration, with the request that the National Security Council provide me with further information on the implications of the conclusions contained therein. I am particularly anxious that the Council give me a clearer indication of the programs which are envisaged in the Report, including estimates of the probable costs of such programs."[49]

Truman was, assuredly, a cold warrior at this time, but he was not a fanatic. He was aware of the inflationary pressures that had developed all over the world after major wars, he was conscious of the massive World War II American debt, and he was determined to balance the federal budget. The corporations that had grown fat on defense contracts were to be put on a lean diet. Defense expenditures in 1945 amounted to 38 percent of America's gross national product. By 1949 Truman had them down to 5.1 percent, and for 1950, 4.6 percent. He intended to hold steady at that figure—$13.1 billion—Cold War or no Cold War.[50] In 1949 he appointed Louis Johnson to serve as secretary of defense largely because Johnson saw a tight-fisted budget as an asset to his expected run for the presidency. On May 4, 1950, a month after receiving NSC-68, Truman told a press conference, "The defense budget next year will be smaller than it is this year."[51] Secretary Johnson stuck to his "no increase" line a month longer than Truman did. The gluttonous monster later christened the "military-industrial complex" by Dwight Eisenhower was nowhere in sight in the spring of 1950.

In April, 1950, the first version of NSC-68 lacked presidential approval, was without appropriation requests for its various programs, and was a sitting duck likely to be nibbled to death by both congressional committees and executive department budget balancers. For the hawks, it was time to retool. James Lay appointed a new ad hoc committee of eleven persons to begin gathering the "further information" requested by the president.[52] Once more in charge: Paul H. Nitze. He was joined by ten members from ten concerned branches of the government. His task? As I read bureaucratese, it was to "Plan the Cold War."

Nitze's coworkers this time were not from his own PPS shop. None was on the State Department payroll, and none was particularly deferential to a mere diplomat. The first indication of a rocky road to implementation of NSC-68 came from William F. Schaub, the committee's Bureau of the Budget representative. Dated May 8, Schaub's memo was directed not to Nitze, but to NSC Executive Secretary Lay:

> COMMENTS OF THE BUREAU OF THE BUDGET (ON NSC-68)
>
> **1. What, specifically, does the paper mean?**
>
> Military
>
> a. Do we anticipate that Russia will strike in 1954 and we should prepare to mobilize by that date? . . . This would require wartime controls in this country and be tantamount to notifying Russia that we intended to press war in the near future. . . . Is this the kind of national policy which we want to present to the world? . . .

General

1. What is the "sharp disparity between our actual military strength and our commitments"? what are our commitments?
2. Do we have a so-called "war plan" or "mobilization plan"? If not, what is being done to develop one? . . .
3. At what point do we intend to use military force to protect our "basic values"? . . .

2. Political and Psychological

b. Throughout NSC-68 appear such statements as "The idea of freedom is the most contagious idea in history, more contagious than the idea of submission to authority"; "The greatest vulnerability of the Kremlin lies in the basic nature of its relations with the Soviet people." . . . These statements reach toward the core of the problem dealt with by NSC-68, yet reference to policies and programs in the ideological war or war for men's minds are subordinated to programs of material strength; in fact, the only program dealt with in any detail is the military program. NSC-68 deals with this problem as being one involving "the free world" and "the slave world." While it is true that the USSR and its satellites constitute something properly called a slave world, it is not true that the U.S. and its friends constitute a free world. Are the Indo-Chinese free? Can the peoples of the Philippines be said to be free under the corrupt Quirino government?[53]

Schaub's tirade goes on to cover the vast superiority of the U.S. Air Force, U.S. Navy, fission bomb stockpile, economic health and military potential of our allies, and the location of U.S. allies near the borders of Russia. He finds it "hard to accept a conclusion that the USSR is approaching a straight-out military superiority."[54] There is an elaboration of the "unsound basis" of the document in "the neat dichotomy between freedom and slavery."[55] NSC-68 will "guarantee the eventual loss of the cold war through the proliferation and subsidization of unstable little tyrants."[56] It also "vastly underplays the role of economic and social change as a factor in 'the underlying conflict.'"[57] We have allowed the Communists to capture the banner of land reform and economic egalitarianism, and "we will never make use of our opportunities as long as the issue is submerged, as it is in NSC-68."[58] This is not the kind of pat budget-balancing one would have expected from these bureaucrats.

On any prudential judgment, Schaub's critique would demand powerful engagement by the Nitze group. In academia, such a devastating attack on a dissertation would send the candidate back to the drawing boards. In business, a board of directors, hearing so profound a list of deficiencies, would have taken a charge against profits and brought in a new manager. But this was government. Nitze was the boss's favorite, and the channel Schaub chose for voicing his challenge (NSC Executive Secretary Lay) was discrete. Secrecy was absolute. Nitze did not dominate this ad hoc committee as he had the earlier, smaller one, and he could not block the presentation of this challenge, but he seems to have been able to marginalize it. Schaub's memo appears in *FRUS* but there is neither discussion of it nor response to it. Nitze does not mention Schaub in his memoirs, yet Callahan's biography says Schaub's effort was "the most vehement attack on the paper yet made."[59] The minutes of committee meetings in the spring of 1950 read like the records of Lyndon Johnson's Vietnam strategy sessions after George Ball expressed his dissent a decade and half later: it was ignored and everyone moved on.

One maneuver, however, might indicate that there was at least some uneasiness on the part of the NSC-68 promoters. Newly appointed Assistant Secretary of State for Far Eastern Affairs Dean Rusk joined Nitze in obtaining from John Foster Dulles, the administration's channel to Republicans, a comforting memorandum dated May 18. Dulles put the imprimatur of Republicans on the belief that Armageddon was approaching: "The situation in Japan may become untenable and possibly that in the Philippines, Indonesia, with its vast natural resources may be lost and the oil of the Middle East will be in jeopardy. . . . This series of disasters can probably be prevented if at some doubtful point we quickly take a dramatic and strong stand that shows our confidence and resolution."[60] How can we do this? Defend Formosa (Taiwan), which "is gravely menaced by a joint Chinese-Russian expedition in formation. The eyes of the world are focused upon it." Dulles rang all the changes needed to "bludgeon the mass mind of top government;" his hallucination, the joint Chinese-Russian expedition, must have been sidetracked in the Shanghai red light district.

Argument over the assumptions, the rhetorical tone, and the specific programs to present to Truman in response to his January 30 directive continued up to the outbreak of the Korean War. The fifth meeting of the ad hoc committee, as reported by James Lay, revealed continuing confusion. The comparison that immediately comes to mind is with the Council of Nicaea in 325 A.D., where Athanasius battled Arius for the souls of the faithful. This 1950 ad hoc committee, lacking closure, decided (though not unanimously) to draft programs "under both sets of assumptions pending a decision by higher authority." The two sets of assumptions were those of Stuart Symington's NSRB and of State, Defense, and the Central Intelligence Agency (CIA).[61] The NSRB thought war might come immediately and that full mobilization was required. The other groups were more relaxed. They were convinced the Soviets would not be able to deal the United States a disabling blow until 1954. Having finessed the assumptions matter, the committee then turned to the inadequacy of the "general description of the [Cold War] program." It was "agreed that there should be added to the specific list of programs a statement on the program to build an adequate political and economic framework for the achievement of our long-term objectives."

Insight into the "NSRB versus everybody else" *casus belli* is found in a June 21 letter from Symington to Defense Secretary Johnson. Symington, who is having trouble getting information out of Johnson's office, simply *must* know what plans the Pentagon has for defending against a Soviet attack of 125–200 atomic bombs in 1954. What targets will these bombs reach? What is our retaliatory plan after such an attack? What resources will the United States need "for three years of war after said attack?"[62]

Government officials with time on their hands could argue about such future things on June 21, 1950. Four days later they could not. The whole world had changed. Kim Il-Sung had taken his Soviet-supported and supplied army across the 38th parallel into South Korea. Within a week the United States was at war. There are relatively few references to George Kennan in the documentary records of American foreign policy during the first six months of 1950. Paul Nitze, bureaucrat par excellence and in tune with Secretary Acheson, appears often. Now all that changed. The master plan for the Cold War (NSC-68) fell temporarily by the wayside. There was a real war on, and Kennan's departure from the government, scheduled at the end of June, was postponed. He once again had a voice. Kennan was quickly embroiled in a donnybrook whose outcome would temporarily legitimate the terror-ridden NSC-68 "proving" that Stalin had started on his world conquest. Again his voice did not prevail.

Kennan's first recorded participation in high-level councils on Korea was on June 29, in a meeting of NSC consultants that lasted all day.[63] Kennan dominated the discussion, which included Ambassador-at-Large Philip Jessup, assorted generals and admirals, and CIA Director Adm. Roscoe H. Hillenkoetter—all of whom listened to Kennan's judgment of Soviet intentions. Kennan did not absolve the Soviets of complicity, but he said "the USSR intended to avoid open involvement and did not intend to launch a general war." He was convinced that firm reaction to the invasion and United Nations support for the United States might modify Soviet calculations. The sensitive point for all was: What would the Russians do next? Several participants thought Stalin might attack Yugoslavia. Kennan disagreed. "Mr. Kennan said he did not believe that the USSR would attack Yugoslavia unless the Soviets became very jittery. Mr. Lay asked whether our actions in Korea would create jitters in Moscow. Mr. Kennan thought the Russians were not yet jittery; on the contrary, they were cool and calm, and somewhat surprised by our reaction in Korea." Kennan did think we needed to watch China closely. Dozens of other questions were discussed, the pattern being a remark or query either directed to Kennan or answered by him in such fashion that the note taker judged his response to be the only one that mattered. The *FRUS* indicates that Kennan prepared a draft of probable Soviet actions, which was then adopted as NSC-73.

There is one great, obvious void in the account of this discussion. No one had the gall to say: "What is all the excitement about? We wrote off Korea, put it outside our defense perimeter, and the secretary of state announced this publicly. We invited them to take over the south." Yet it is not clear that the discussion would have been more productive if this had come up.[64]

A similar meeting with different officials took place the next day, the Soviet specialist serving as prognosticator being Chip Bohlen, who "said that he saw no evidence that the Russians had changed their traditional tactic of probing for soft spots; that now they had found a hard spot they would probably not directly intervene; they would do their utmost to get the United States involved with Asiatic Communist troops, particularly Chinese. Mr. Bohlen stressed, however, that if we or any of our allies indicate an intention to strike Soviet territory in the neighborhood of Vladivostock or elsewhere the Soviets could be expected to react in a more primitive manner."[65] Five days into the Korean War, the government did not seem terror-stricken about the approaching end of Western civilization.

As the situation in Korea worsened, voices of doom began to appear. Chairman Symington of the NSRB warned on July 6 that the Soviets would attack the United States as soon as they believed they were ready.[66] John Foster Dulles, acting as a consultant to the Secretary of State, began the campaign to unite Korea after we repulsed the invaders, since the 38th parallel "was never intended to be a political line."[67] Secretary Acheson told a cabinet meeting on July 14 that "the feeling in Europe is changing from one of elation that the United States has come into the Korean crisis to petrified fright. . . . Our intentions are not doubted, but our capabilities are doubted."[68]

Dulles's concern about wiping out the 38th parallel as a political boundary and uniting Korea soon came to be the dominant issue in government circles. Hundreds of other documents discussing this matter fill the folders in State, Defense, White House, and other repositories. Both sides had cogent arguments.

In favor of unification, American opinion clearly demanded punishing the aggressors. Letting the Communists off without penalty would be appeasement. Allowing Kim Il-sung to stay in power would necessitate a permanent U.S. military presence in Korea. The UN resolution called for restoring peace and order on the whole peninsula, and so forth.

There was just one compelling argument for halting the UN advance at or near the 38th parallel, and Kennan, Bohlen, and other Kremlinologists made it. Neither the Soviet Union nor the PRC would tolerate hostile troops on their Yalu River border. The Chinese were particularly vocal about this, but official Washington paid no heed. The JCS warned General MacArthur to back off if Chinese or Soviet troops appeared in battle against him, but after his brilliant victory at Inchon, not even the Almighty Himself would have dared to tell MacArthur he was walking into a trap.

Well before MacArthur crossed the parallel it was clear that the worst-case scenario developed in NSC-68 was powerfully reinforced by the Communist aggression. Nitze saw to it that no one missed the significance of Korea. On August 1 Nitze wrote a three-page, top-secret document with only the heading "NSC-68," and distributed fifteen copies within the State Department. Each was tracked and eventually returned, and the master copy was marked "stencil burned." No clear reason for this degree of restriction appears. The three pages seem to be a preface or letter of transmittal to the report due in the president's office. Paragraph one reads: "This report is in response to the President's letter of April 12 requesting the National Security Council to provide him with further information on the implications of the Conclusions contained in NSC-68 . . ." along with costs, reappraisals due to the increased danger, and three important new corollaries.[69] The document brags about necessary defense measures that were in active preparation before the North Korean attack and about how Korea has "removed any doubt as to the willingness of the Communist leaders to employ force." It then says Korea is proof that the military buildup has to be continuous rather than designed to peak at a certain time, and that free world forces have to be able "to defeat aggression locally without the necessity of reacting globally."

Whether intended to accompany the full report to the president or designed solely for office circulation, to convince doubters that the long, contentious effort had been right, this document seems inoffensive. So why was it necessary to control it so closely and burn the stencil, when all it says is "I told you so!"? Perhaps Nitze was responding to a message from his antagonist Kennan, who was deprecating alarmism over Korea and calming the nervous hawks. Such a message was also in circulation, appearing in a formal statement from Kennan to Secretary Acheson dated August 8, 1950:

> I thought it might be useful if at this juncture I were to make a round-up of Communist intentions, as far as they seem to me discernible on evidence now available.
>
> 1. The Soviet Communists did not launch the Korean operation as a first step in a world war or as the first of a series of local operations designed to drain U.S. strength in peripheral theaters. They simply wanted control of South Korea; saw what looked to them like a favorable set of circumstances in which to achieve it; feared that if they did not achieve it now, time might run out on them. They did not think it likely that we would intervene militarily, and thought that if we did try to intervene we would get there too late. . . .
>
> 5. Furthermore, the Soviet leaders must be seriously worried over the proximity of the Korean fighting to their own borders and over the direct damage which can conceivably be done to their military interests. . . . Finally, it must be to them an intensely humiliating and irritating experience to be obliged either to keep their naval forces out of areas which seem to them almost part of their territorial waters or, alternatively, to risk their being molested and destroyed by U.S. and other naval units. . . .
>
> 8. As Bohlen emphasized when he was here, when the tide of battle begins to change, the Kremlin will not wait for us to reach the 38th parallel before taking action. When we begin to have military successes, that will be the time to watch out. Anything may then happen—entry of Soviet forces, entry of Chinese Communist forces, new strike for UN settlement, or all three together.[70]

We do not know if Acheson read this memorandum; however, we do know that he read Kennan's August 21 memo addressed to him. Also beautifully crafted, this memo was so prescient and so relevant to the witches' brew that was NSC-68 that it should have at least the readership Kennan got for the "X" article. It was the last memo Kennan wrote before leaving the State Department. In it he noted that Americans "are indulging themselves in emotional, moralistic attitudes toward Korea which . . . can easily [yield] real conflict with the Russians."[71] By allowing General MacArthur to determine "our policy in north Asian . . . areas we do not really have full control over . . . actions taken in our name . . ." our China policy is "almost sure to strengthen Peiping-Moscow solidarity rather than weaken it. . . . In Indo-China we are . . . guaranteeing the French in an undertaking which neither they nor we, nor both of us together, can win." In Korea, "it is not essential to us to see anti-Soviet Korean regime extended to *all* of Korea for all time." Similarly cogent, history-validated advice related to admitting China to the United Nations, creating a mobile combat force, enabling the Japanese to establish their own internal security force, and supporting a UN-conducted plebiscite on Formosa. The Republicans in Congress, Kennan admitted, would not go along willingly with this program.[72] Nevertheless, "there is a clear problem of responsibility here."

Acheson's comments on Kennan's parting advice were not kind. Although the secretary saw "flashes of prophetic insight," the suggestions were "of total impracticability."[73] However, one should not assume from this that Acheson was beyond listening to anyone who rejected the call to arms of NSC-68. On August 15, still smarting from a Republican attack in the Senate, he wired Chip Bohlen in Paris. The four senators involved had asserted, among other things, that Democratic administrations had failed "adequately to understand the Soviet mind and purposes," which had brought on present troubles. Acheson's plea: "Feel that you are best qualified to draw up answer to this charge. Would appreciate it if you could draft answer immediately and telegraph to Dept sometime August 16."[74] It is significant in the long, tangled history of the NSC-68 series that in the fall of 1950 Acheson was looking not to Nitze but to Bohlen for the best answer to his critics.

Truman had asked the ad hoc committee on NSC-68 in April to furnish specifics and clarifications by September 1. On August 22 Lay called the committee together and told the members that, war or no war, they had to produce, although he might be able to get the deadline extended to September 15. First, however, the NSC would draft a new version of NSC-73, which would address "Possible Further Soviet Moves in the Light of the Korean Situation."[75] That document was ready on August 25.

The new NSC-73/4 had something for everyone. There was still no consensus, and it included many contradictions. The Communists believed that war was inevitable, but Russia may retreat from adventures if strongly opposed. "In causing the attack to be launched in Korea, the Kremlin did not intend to bring about a global war. . . . on the other hand, the events of the past few weeks could be interpreted as the first phase of a general Soviet plan for global war." While the Soviets might launch widespread but coordinated attacks, "The Kremlin seems to have calculated its moves with a view to keeping the responsibility of the Soviet Government unengaged and its own military forces uncommitted."[76] There is as much of Kennan's opinion in this as there is of Nitze's. For Nitze, the Kremlin was always and everywhere ready to march.

September saw the spectacular Inchon landing, and morale in Washington shot up to the top of the chart. There was time again for the "blueprint." At the NSC's sixty-eighth meeting, held on September 30, 1950, the council, with Truman concurring, "Adopted the conclusion of NSC-68 as a statement of policy to be followed over the next four or five years, and agreed that the implementing programs will be put into effect as rapidly as feasible [pending further cost estimates.]"[77] Finally, after eight months of churning and feuding, was the blueprint for America's Cold War at last in place?

Not quite. Lay's minutes show that what was adopted was merely the sermon, the confession of faith, the Apostles's Creed as it were. The Ten Commandments were yet to be worked out. Bare and unadorned, "NSC-68" was approved. Meanwhile, NSC-68/1, which was to have the operational codes as annexes, was still under discussion. However, the council "Deferred action on NSC-68/1 pending a revision of the report to be prepared by the NSC staff for Council consideration not later than November 15, 1950."[78] Some writers describe this document as a done deal when it was first shown to Truman on April 7, whereas others say it was fully adopted on September 30. The documents, however, reveal that what was approved on September 30 was merely the purple prose. The wordsmiths had hardly begun to answer the question, "What does all this really mean?"

Policy Planning Staff member Charles Burton Marshall's October 3 letter to Nitze shows how things were shaping up. The long, homiletical center of NSC-68 was now to be supplemented by ten annexes, each one describing a separate program to be carried out by an operating agency, except for Annex 8, at first titled "The Strategy of Freedom."[79] This mysterious entity left little trace in the *FRUS* volumes, but the State Department files at the National Archives are full of it. Apparently it was as vigorously contested as the early NSC-68 drafts had been, and the paper trail is just as confusing. Annex 8 might have resulted from the squabbling over an "adequate political and economic framework for the achievement of our long-term objectives" that took place in the ad hoc committee on June 7. Whatever its genesis, Charles Marshall saw the matter this way on October 3: "Mr. Lay said as to Annex 8, the senior staff should meet on it very soon. He quoted Mr. Murphy of the White House as saying Annex 8 should be revised to show how the U.S. would use the progressively developing military shield; we should have to tell what our foreign policy aims are going to be. Mr. Lay said Annex 8 should be a kick-off on our long-term objectives. He said Mr. Acheson had indicated agreement. Mr. H. Cleveland, ECA, said Annex 8 should include a statement of political aims and methods and supervisory measures we need to take in order to make our dollar programs work."[80]

To an inquirer forty-nine years later this seems to indicate chronic confusion. Nothing in the archives modifies this judgment. Philip Jessup, ambassador-at-large and a powerful intellect in the State Department hierarchy until the "primitives" in Congress ran him out of the government, wrote to State's European agents requesting their evaluations of Annex 8, now retitled "Long-Term Political and Economic Framework."[81] This was perhaps the first chance for working-level diplomats to see what Nitze and his staff had constructed as the scenario under which they were supposed to be operating. Similar evaluations were requested of State Department employees in Washington. The result was a flood of criticism. Most of the responses did not rate inclusion in *FRUS,* but they are still in the files. Some of the objections were aired at a senior staff meeting on October 6.[82] To Williamson of the Western Europe desk, paragraphs 4, 5, and 6 "have no factual basis." Martin of Treasury said Annex 8 "does not leave the reader with any sense of a program." Admiral E. T. Wooldridge said Annex 8, unlike the preceding seven annexes, "gets away from the concrete into the abstract. We need concrete measures."

The senior person present at the October 6 meeting was Philip Jessup. After what must have been several hours of complaints and requests for guidance, or a least for an outline of what they should produce, the secretary recorded: "Mr. Jessup in response to a query from Mr. Lay said that he had no outline to suggest at that time. We have a tentative outline but only for our use in State. He felt that much of the discussion amounted to just a lot of words—thoughts were flying out as words and phrases came to mind."

Paul Nitze, project manager of this long effort to program Western defenses, reacting to the turbulence and discord of the October 6 senior staff meeting, felt it desirable to write his superior, putting a positive spin on things. His letter dated October 9 was standard boilerplate: all was on track, what we need now is to take the public into our confidence, there should be a "state paper" released rather than a "popular rewrite"—and NSC-68 will be "available for everyone to read. It is certain that there will be great numbers who will both read and understand."[83] Moreover, if Secretary Acheson had any doubts about the worthiness of the enterprise, Nitze told him: "The programs are not a quick response to an emergent situation. They mark a new course, not a tack. . . . They will result in a secular change in the national existence. Every person in the country will feel their impact."

Years later, when he wrote his memoirs, Nitze denied all this: "Equally erroneous is the contention that NSC-68 recommended a sharp departure in U.S. policy. On the contrary, the report concluded by calling for the reaffirmation of what was already approved policy in NSC-20/4."[84] Times had changed.

But Annex 8 remained short of any kind of group approval. Nitze sent copies of it as then constructed to twenty-four people on November 10. The copies noted that "Submission by the National Security Council to the President, not later than December 15, of revision of NSC-68/1 in its entirety" was to be made.[85] This distribution brought forth another round of criticism, most of it negative, some of it impolite. Among the polite memos was one from George Kennan at Princeton. Caustic responses came from Philip Jessup; Edward G. Miller, Jr., of Inter-American Affairs; Livingston Merchant of the Far East desk; and Park Armstrong in the Assistant to the Secretary's Office.[86]

The archives do not reveal precisely what happened with the Annex 8 draft after this last round of comment, but a complete copy of it incorporating some changes is in the files. However, *when NSC-68/3 was formally adopted and approved by the president on December 14, Annex 8—all seventy-eight pages of it—was not part of the document.*[87]

By December 14, 1950, NSC-68 and whatever annexes remained were hardly high priority. The December panic had struck. Douglas MacArthur, interpreting his orders liberally, had not only crossed the 38th parallel, he had driven to the Yalu—and the Chinese intervened in massive numbers, routing the Eighth Army and all but destroying Tenth Corps.[88] Defeat at the hands of the Chinese Communists dominated the agenda in Washington. NSC-68, and the "Strategy of Freedom" annex simply were not all that important anymore.

The two antagonists of the NSC-68 saga were at odds over basic decisions during the December panic also. By December 2, the dimensions of defeat in Korea became clear. In a high-level State Department meeting on that date, "Mr. Nitze raised the question as to whether it wouldn't be better to proceed secretly with negotiations [for a cease-fire] while at the same time maintaining a public attitude of firmness."[89] This may seem an unusual position for a certified hawk, but Nitze's rationale became clear in another meeting the next day: "Mr. NITZE said we would be better off if we had no hostilities with the Chinese . . . and then get ready for the Soviet Union."[90]

Kennan thought otherwise. On December 4 Kennan was discussing the same issues in a different group: "Mr. Kennan said that with regard to possible negotiations with the Russians, a request for a cease fire would look to the USSR as a suit for peace. The USSR would then want to extract every possible advantage and to damage wherever possible the prestige of the United States. . . . Mr. Kennan concluded by saying that now was the poorest time possible for any negotiations."[91] He was right, and this time his audience listened.

Those who emphasize Kennan's lack of influence on NSC-68 and his exclusion from the seats of power also overlook another instance when he, more than anyone, crafted a message that changed the course of events. MacArthur, having done a 180-degree turn from his braggadocio in October at Wake Island, wrote a dispatch on December 3 predicting disaster. Everything had turned against him: "This small command actually under present conditions is facing the entire Chinese nation in an undeclared war and unless some positive and immediate action is taken, hope for success cannot be justified and steady attrition leading to final destruction can reasonably be contemplated. . . . the situation here must be viewed on the basis of an entirely new war against an entirely new power of great military strength and under entirely new conditions."[92]

Kennan found similar defeatism throughout the State Department. He was especially concerned with the burden on Dean Acheson, toward whom he maintained friendly feelings despite Acheson's support of the Super and of the alarmism of NSC-68. Kennan therefore wrote a personal letter that Acheson received the next morning:

> Dear Mr. Secretary:
>
> On the official level I have been asked to give advice only on the particular problem of Soviet reaction to various possible approaches.
>
> But there is one thing I should like to say in continuation of our discussion of yesterday evening.
>
> In international, as in private, life, what counts most is not really what happens to some one but how he bears what happens to him. For this reason almost everything depends from here on out on the manner in which we Americans bear what is unquestionably a major failure and disaster to our national fortunes. If we accept it with candor, with dignity, with resolve to absorb its lessons and to make it good by re-doubled and determined effort—starting all over again, if necessary, along the pattern of Pearl Harbor—we need lose neither our self-confidence nor our allies nor our power for bargaining, eventually, with the Russians. But if we try to conceal from our own people or from our allies the full measure of our misfortune, or permit ourselves to seek relief in any reactions of bluster or petulance or hysteria, we can easily find this crisis resolving itself into an irreparable deterioration of our world position—and of our confidence in ourselves.[93]

Acheson read this letter at his staff meeting that morning. He and many who have written on the Korean War believe it to have been instrumental in stiffening American resolve. Perhaps the panic would have resolved itself without Kennan, but as Miscamble says: "Yet one must not dismiss the importance of key interventions by individuals at crucial moments and Kennan's may well have been one. He helped Washington keep together during one of the darkest moments of the postwar era."[94] His advice was fortunately validated by Gen. Matthew B. Ridgway's single-handed recreation of the U.S. Eighth Army into an effective fighting force. Conventional wisdom has it that the North Korean attack solidified the government behind NSC-68, if not in June, at least in November when the Chinese (who were Soviet puppets, of course) entered the fray. Truman asked for additional defense appropriations to carry out these "Programs for National Security" in the fall of 1950, and as a result, the defense budget tripled. But the defense budget increased mostly because of Korea, only secondarily because there was now known to be a hard-line national security policy.

But more than money was at issue. Melvyn Leffler is quite wrong in claiming that NSC-68 was nothing new, that "Nitze simply called for more, more, and more money to implement the programs and achieve the goals already set out."[95] It was a call to arms, a tocsin. It offered a theology, it divided the world into God-fearing people and satanic people, and, insofar as Nitze could prevail, it held that there could be no peace until the satanic types were converted or destroyed.[96] There was much opposition to the theological or ideological absolutes that crept into NSC-68, making the text so internally inconsistent and unpersuasive to many.

The alarmists (Nitzeans) were like religious fundamentalists and the moderates (Kennanites) like laid-back Unitarians. A confession of faith that had to encompass them both was bound to be confused, and the differences were never fully resolved. John Lewis Gaddis identifies the elements in the NSC-68 series that differed from Kennan's original position.[97] According to Nitze, the threat was primarily military, not political; it required perimeter defense, opposing the Soviet Union everywhere in the world, not just in those places where American interests were involved. The primary Soviet drive was to communize the world, not to preserve the power of the Moscow regime. Negotiations with such a regime could not be advantageous, and should be undertaken only as a public relations ploy.

Though his status in the government was not as strategic as Nitze's, Stuart Symington was even more of an alarmist. In early 1951, as chairman of the NSRB, Symington submitted to Truman a memo entitled "Current History of National Planning Policy—Diplomatic, Economic and Military" that showed no moderate influence whatever. It is hard to believe this script came from the same person who three years later stood up to Joe McCarthy. Truman's reaction to Symington's memo is important because it helps triangulate the administration's beliefs. According to Symington, the United States was losing the Cold War on nearly all fronts; the Soviet Union had put the United States on the defensive everywhere; we had no real organized program; the Communist-dominated peoples of the world had increased from 188 million to 800 million;

the United States resorted to a piecemeal policy called containment, and so on.[98] The editors of *FRUS* record a series of rebukes that Truman wrote in the margins of this document, found in the president's secretary's file: "Not true . . . Berlin, Greece, Turkey, Korea; . . . Not true: the formation of UN, Rio Treaty, Atlantic Treaty. . . . Bunk—all of it. . . . We have won this one. More bunk on the same false premise." On the last page, Truman wrote "My dear Stu, this is [as] big a lot of Top Secret Malarky as I've ever seen . . . H.S.T." The *FRUS* editors add, "No evidence has been found to indicate that it was ever returned to Symington." Truman, however anti-Communist, had not lost his senses.

Nitze's committee was still working on an old chestnut. On January 29, 1951, his assistant Charles Burton Marshall sent him "a revised draft of Annex VIII incorporating the revisions suggested from various sources during the review of the document in November and December."[99] Far from being out of the game, George Kennan was still a player. Of thirty-three revisions in this draft, seven came from Kennan. Five others came from theologian Reinhold Niebuhr. The Niebuhr contribution was not really anomalous; NSC-68 was as much theology as geopolitics.

Alarmists and moderates continued the battle to control the language in which national security policy should be expressed for the rest of the Truman administration. The alarmists never totally dominated, and they faced a new obstacle in March, 1951, when Chip Bohlen was made counselor and thus State Department representative on the NSC's senior staff. He picked up the cudgels for the moderate versions of Cold War doctrine immediately.

A four-page letter from Bohlen to Nitze on July 28 complains that the latest version of the NSC-68 series (identified in *FRUS* as NSC-114) perpetuated the old view of the Soviet Union as "a mechanical chess player, engaged in the execution of a design fully prepared in advance with the ultimate goal of world domination. The phrase 'world domination' is a misleading truth and tends to become related to the phenomenon of Hitler. . . . a false assumption of Soviet intention in this field may lead to a very radical conclusion which is found in paragraph seven. This paragraph states flatly that if this alleged aim of the Kremlin, i.e., to disrupt Western rearmament, cannot be done by the soft method, then there is a strong possibility that the Soviets will resort to preventive war."[100]

Also covered in Bohlen's letter: misrepresentations in the NSC-68 series of Soviet actions in Korea, in the Berlin blockade, and on the effect of Soviet nuclear capabilities on their actions. Bohlen wanted all of these questions reconsidered before the new version "becomes accepted as official U.S. Government doctrine."

Nitze, so far as the record shows, was unmoved. National Intelligence Estimates (NIE) continued to show "Soviet forces are in an advanced state of war-readiness and could initiate general war at any time with little or no warning."[101] The document went before the council on August 8, 1951, without addressing Bohlen's questions and was apparently approved as NSC-114/1.[102]

Tensions over strategic doctrine did not entirely eclipse the combatants' sense of humor. Everett Gleason of the NSC, not on Nitze's committee but privy to the various drafts of Annex 8, wrote Nitze on August 17: "I am aware that this is an exceptionally difficult task, but I can't help feeling that unless the October 1st report contains more than its predecessor in terms of positive political content, the total effect will be all the actors in a fine stage setting except Hamlet himself."[103]

Bohlen wrote his most thorough and compelling memos on August 22 and September 21. They are historical analyses of Soviet behavior since World War II of the highest order, as elegant as Kennan's prose but more effective because of the skill with which Bohlen demolishes Nitze's interpretations of the same events. On the basis of the available documents, no student of argument could say that at this time, in this arena, Bohlen failed to carry the burden of proof that the Soviet Union had *demonstrated* its unwillingness to precipitate war with the United States, and that U.S. national security policy should adapt to an opportunistic opponent rather than one programmed to seize control of the world.[104]

The argument went through many exchanges of heated memos. In my judgment, Nitze's responses are inadequate. He disavows the idea of a Soviet "timetable" and bemoans argument about Soviet intentions: "If every government official arrives at conclusions based on differing and personal images of the Soviet Union, the policy of the United States will soon be in a chaotic state."[105] Nitze's bottom line is that the Soviet Union is "implacably hostile" toward the United States, and nobody can prove that it will not attack if it thinks it can win, even if it sustains damage from every nuclear weapon in the U.S. arsenal.

During the fall of 1951, Nitze's dominance of his staff seems to have faded. Henry Koch and Robert Joyce of the PPS entered the debate with memos cautiously supporting Bohlen.[106] On October 8 Robert G. Hooker produced a scholarly effort that cited Nathan Leites, A. Rossi, and Hannah Arendt in the hope his argument "might illuminate the issues of the Bohlen-Nitze discussion."[107] Hooker was clearly on Bohlen's side.

Bohlen's equivalent of a summation for the jury was addressed to Acheson on October 9. In it he reviews his entire involvement in the NSC-68 series.[108]

No lawyer could have done better. He appears to have convinced the secretary. A memo dated October 26 indicates that, at senior staff request, Bohlen is to prepare "an analysis of Soviet intentions and internal vulnerabilities in connection with" reappraisal of NSC-114/2.[109]

Reappraisal and infighting continued to the very end. An "Editorial Note" in *FRUS* summarizes activity through August, 1952:

> The four papers which eventually comprised NSC-135/1 and NSC-135/1 Annex had been the subject of lengthy discussion, repeated drafts, and frequent refinements throughout the first eight months of the year. Although the assignment to reappraise national security objectives and programs had been formally assigned to the drafting group of Staff Assistants, documentation in Department of State files suggests that the drafting work on all papers save that dealing with "Relative Political, Economic and Military Capabilities" (Part II of the Annex) was undertaken by the Department's Policy Planning Staff under the general supervision and direction of Counselor Charles E. Bohlen who himself assumed responsibility for drafting what became Part I of the NSC-135/1 Annex.[110]

Nitze seems to have been eased out of his own shop at the crucial time.

Bohlen submitted his "NSC Staff Study on Reappraisal of United States Objectives and Strategy for National Security" to Acheson on August 22.[111] He clearly felt no need to be present to defend it before the NSC. In a cover letter to Acheson he announces that he is going on leave "for a couple of weeks," but the paper is in good shape and two of his assistants will be at the meeting to explain things.

The NSC met on September 3, 1952, and there was much discussion.[112] The NSRB wanted more emphasis on resources. The Defense Department representatives disagreed on how much emphasis to put on "perimeter actions" as compared with central reserves. Secretary of Defense Lovett, clearly a hawk, surprisingly said that the first paragraph "was too belligerent in tone and made no reference to our national aim to secure a lasting peace." Nitze was not present to complain about the absence of his favorite clause, "The Fundamental Design of the Kremlin is to control the whole world."

Bohlen and Nitze had worked out language that both could live with, although neither was completely happy with the draft. The final document was one that Kennan could easily have lived with, except perhaps for paragraph seven, which called for a massive civil defense program.[113]

Steven L. Rearden, in his admiring account of Nitze's early life published in 1983, writes "though he later held higher offices and had broader responsibilities, it is arguable that Nitze's most creative and enduring accomplishments came as director of the State Department's Policy Planning Staff in the early 1950s, when the drafting and implementation of NSC-68 took place. Never again would Nitze—or anyone else for that matter—be in such a key position to guide the development of a study that had as dramatic an impact on the nation's destiny."[114]

Nitze may have encouraged Rearden to believe this in 1983, but his attitude in 1952 had been quite different. Two years after the first version of NSC-68 was ready, constant tinkering and "reappraisal" had gotten nowhere near producing the clarion call Nitze had hoped to issue. Eventually NSC-68 merged into NSC-135, and drafts of the new version were sent out for comments in the summer of 1952. Nitze wrote his superior, Deputy Undersecretary Matthews, complaining about the new drafts:

1. I believe the papers [new drafts] tend to underestimate the risks which this country faces.
2. I believe they tend to underestimate U.S. capabilities.
3. I believe they hold forth inadequate goals for U.S. policy.
4. I believe they outline an inadequate strategy.
5. I believe they give inadequate, unclear or mistaken guidance to those who must prepare specific national security programs.[115]

In addition, Nitze wrote, "one of the difficulties is that they are internally inconsistent and that it is not entirely clear what they are trying to say." After two and a half years of battle, Nitze's efforts appear to him to have been in vain.

In one of his last memos to Acheson, Nitze complained bitterly that the latest reexamination was too soft. He pointed out that the United States was more vulnerable to Soviet nuclear attack than the report acknowledged, and that it was not developing nuclear weapons for tactical use as it should have. Worse still, actual armament programs had not fulfilled the requirements of any of the NSC papers: "The issue here is whether we are really satisfied with programs which in fact have the objective of making us a sort of hedge-hog, unattractive to attack, but basically not very worrisome over a period of time beyond our immediate position, or whether we take the objectives stated in NSC 20, 68, 114, and 135 sufficiently seriously as to warrant doing what is necessary to give us some chance of seeing these objectives attained."[116]

Could comparison with any animal so demean the United States as comparison with a hedgehog?

Those who hold that the intensity of the Cold War was inevitable and speak of "the scorpion and the tarantula in the bottle," as Louis Halle does, will not be interested in alternative scenarios.[117] Nevertheless it might have been different. The Cold War need not have been as dangerous as it was. The arms race was more costly and overkill capacity more insane than it had to be. The United States need not have been so traumatized in Korea. Truman was a cold warrior, but he was willing to listen to his advisers. Had Acheson not resonated with Nitze but instead retained Kennan as chief adviser, our Russophobia might have been lessened.

Kennan would have privileged his fellow Kremlinologists Bohlen and Thompson. Kennan knew that the Kremlin would never be able to control China as it did its European neighbors. Kennan would have moved heaven and earth to change MacArthur's orders and forbidden him to cross the 38th parallel at all. There would then have been no Chinese intervention, no defeat of the Eighth Army, no humiliating retreat below Seoul, no childish threat from MacArthur to evacuate the peninsula. Even had Kennan failed to change MacArthur's orders, he would have been able to soften the blow of Chinese intervention. After all, he had anticipated it, he did not believe it to be indicative of a Soviet desire to start a large-scale war, and he had taken the generally reasonable position that if a fire-breathing Communist general were approaching Texas and the Rio Grande from Mexico with hostile intent, we would have reacted just as the Chinese did in Korea.

Kennan was positioned to forcefully promote such policies. Who more than he had warned of Soviet recalcitrance? Consider the parallel case in 1972 when Richard Nixon went to Beijing and broke the spell of the Chiang lobby. No Democrat could have done that. Nixon was able to do it because he could not be outflanked on the right; he was a known anti-Communist. Kennan had the same stature in 1950 vis-à-vis the Soviet Union. Who could make a charge that Kennan was soft on Communism stick? Who could better mitigate the hysteria developing during the summer and fall of 1950? This is not to suggest that the Korean War would have had no impact on American Cold War policy, nor that there would have been no call for increased military expenditure when the North Koreans struck. The "macroforces" so beloved of political theorists would still have been working. What I do suggest is that had there been a steady, restrained voice governing State's Policy Planning Staff and chairing the State-Defense Policy Review Group, NSC-68 would have been a quite different document.

We cannot know what influence NSC-68 and its progeny exerted on U.S. policy. Had it not been for Korea, the answer should be "none." Since its precise wording was top secret, it could not influence the attentive public directly.

The aura and the ethos exuded by those in the know undoubtedly had influence; secret briefings given to Congress revealed much of the content. A less alarmist NSC-series would have produced less alarm all around.

The apocalyptic view of the Soviet challenge expressed in NSC-68 served anti-Soviet hard-liners, much as the *Protocols of the Elders of Zion* continues to serve anti-Semites. America's fever chart—so high in December, 1950, that the president declared a national emergency, big city mayors laid plans for evacuation, the vice president of Georgetown University wanted a preemptive strike against the Soviet Union, and Pacific Coast skiers organized as "defense guerrillas" to defend the Rocky Mountain passes against Communist invasion—slowly began to recede.

All of this was unnecessary. Soviet legions were not on the march, nor were North Korea and China Soviet satellites carrying out orders from the Kremlin. Had Nitze's hallucinations not dominated the government in 1950, had Kennan's advice not to cross the 38th parallel in Korea been heeded, had the United States not been so delusional and panicky, things could have been calmer. Kennan and Bohlen were voices of reason, out-shouted for a while by fanatics, but they saw the situation clearly and in its entirety.

Acheson and Nitze, peering through their Chicken Little lenses, saw only what they took to be the beginning of a Soviet plan to take over the world. They created not security but insecurity.

Notes

I am grateful to Francis A. Beer, Barton J. Bernstein, Kathleen Farrell, and Wilson D. Miscamble for helpful comments on early drafts of this essay.

1. See, for instance, Draft, SP:PHN, 8/1/50, Policy Planning Staff (hereafter PPS) Papers 1947–1953, Box 54, RG 59, National Archives (hereafter NA).

2. Paul Y. Hammond, "NSC-68: Prologue to Rearmament," in *Strategy, Politics and Defense Budgets,* ed. Warner R. Schilling et al. (New York: Columbia University, 1962), 95–134.

3. John Lewis Gaddis, *Strategies of Containment* (New York: Oxford University, 1982).

4. John Lewis Gaddis, "Containment: The Doctrine, 1946–48," in *Containment: Documents on American Policy and Strategy,* ed. Thomas H. Etzold and John Lewis Gaddis (New York: Columbia University Press, 1978), 49.

5. The "Long Telegram" is in *Containment,* ed. Etzold and Gaddis; quotations are from 61–63.

6. NSC-20/1, in *Containment,* ed. Etzold and Gaddis, 173–203.

7. Secretary of Defense (Forrestal) to the President, July 10, 1948, *FRUS, 1948,* vol. 1, pt. 2 (Washington, D.C.: GPO, 1976), 593.

8. Quotations from *Containment,* ed. Etzold and Gaddis, 178, 180.

9. NSC-20/4, Nov. 23, 1948, *FRUS, 1948,* vol. 1, pt. 663.

10. Ibid., 665.

11. NSC-68/4, Dec. 14, 1950, *FRUS, 1950,* vol. 1 (Washington, D.C.: GPO, 1977), 467.

12. Wilson Miscamble, "Rejected Architect and Master Builder: George Kennan, Dean Acheson, and Postwar Europe," *Review of Politics* 58 (1996): 446.

13. For Nitze and the USSBS, see Robert P. Newman, "Ending the War With Japan: Paul H. Nitze's 'Early Surrender' Counterfactual," *Pacific Historical Review* 64 (1995): 167–94; and Barton J. Bernstein, "Compelling Japan's Surrender Without the A-bomb, Soviet Entry, or Invasion: Reconsidering the US Bombing Survey's Early Surrender Conclusions," *Journal of Strategic Studies* 18 (1995): 101–48.

14. Paul H. Nitze, *From Hiroshima to Glasnost: At the Center of Decision* (New York: Grove, Weidenfeld, 1989), 42.

15. Strobe Talbott, *The Master of the Game* (New York: Knopf, 1988).

16. Nitze, 87–92.

17. Talbott, *Master of the Game,* 43. See also Frank Costigliola, "The Creation of Memory and Myth: Stalin's 1946 Election Speech and the Soviet Threat," in this volume.

18. David Callahan, *Dangerous Capabilities: Paul Nitze and the Cold War* (New York: HarperCollins, 1990), 76–77.

19. George F. Kennan, *Memoirs: 1925–1950* (Boston: Little, Brown, 1967), 472.

20. Memorandum by Counselor (Kennan), Jan. 20, 1950, *FRUS, 1950,* 1:39.

21. Peter Galison and Barton Bernstein, "In any light: Scientists and the decision to build the Superbomb, 1942–1954," *Historical Studies in the Physical and Biological Sciences* 19, no. 2 (1989): 328.

22. The President to the Secretary of State, Jan. 31, 1950, *FRUS, 1950,* 1:141–42.

23. Draft Memorandum by the Counselor (Kennan) to the Secretary of State, Feb. 17, 1950, *FRUS, 1950,* 1:160–67. Quotes are from 160–61.

24. Comments on remarks made by W. Stuart Symington, Feb. 17, 1950, Central Decimal Files (CDF) 1950–54, Box 2706, RG 59, NA.

25. Accounts of the appearance of the six experts before Nitze's committee are in *FRUS, 1950,* 1:169–75, 1:176–82, 1:190–95, 1:196–206.

26. Nitze to the Secretary, Mar. 29, 1950, PPS Papers 1947–1953, Box 54, RG 59, NA.

27. Memorandum by the Undersecretary of State (Webb), Mar. 30, 1950, *FRUS, 1950,* 1:210.

28. Memorandum by the Assistant Secretary of State for European Affairs (Thompson) to the Secretary of State, Apr. 3, 1950, *FRUS, 1950,* 1:213–14.

29. Memorandum by the Assistant Secretary of State for European Affairs (Perkins) to the Secretary of State, Apr. 3, 1950, *FRUS, 1950,* 1:214–16.

30. Perkins to Martin, Comments on State-Defense Staff Study, Apr. 4, 1950, PPS Papers 1947–1953, Box 54, RG 59, NA.

31. Memorandum by the Assistant Secretary of State for Economic Affairs (Thorp) to the Secretary of State, Apr. 5, 1950, *FRUS, 1950,* 1:218–20.

32. Memorandum by the Assistant Secretary of State for Economic Affairs (Hare) to the Undersecretary of State (Webb), Apr. 5, 1950, *FRUS, 1950,* 1:220–21.

33. Memorandum by Mr. Charles E. Bohlen to the Director of the Policy Planning Staff (Nitze), Apr. 5, 1950, *FRUS, 1950,* 1:221–25.

34. Memorandum by the Assistant Secretary of State for United Nations Affairs (Hickerson) to the Secretary of State, Apr. 5, 1950, *FRUS, 1950,* 1:216–17.

35. Nitze to the Secretary of State, Apr. 6, 1950, PPS Papers 1947–1953, Box 54, RG 59, NA.

36. Perhaps the clearest analysis of Nitze's ideological position is in Alan Tonelson, "Nitze's World," *Foreign Policy* 35 (1979), 74–90. Tonelson "places" Nitze; see Richard E. Neustadt and Ernest R. May, *Thinking in Time* (New York: Free Press, 1986), chap. 9.

37. Dean Acheson, *Present at the Creation* (New York: NAL/Signet, 1969).

38. NSC-68 is now available in several sources. I use the text in Ernest R. May, ed., *American Cold War Strategy: Interpreting NSC-68* (Boston: Bedford Books, 1993).

39. Ibid., 26.

40. Ibid.

41. Ibid., 26–27.

42. Ibid., 28.

43. Ibid., 31.

44. Ibid., 32.

45. Ibid., 37.

46. Ibid., 55.

47. Ibid., 57.

48. Ibid., 73

49. The President to the Executive Secretary of the NSC (Lay), Apr. 12, 1950, *FRUS, 1950,* 1:235.

50. See the table in Gaddis, *Strategies of Containment,* 359. A detailed study of Truman's budget aim is in Michael J. Hogan, *A Cross of Iron* (Cambridge: Cambridge University Press, 1998).

51. Harry S. Truman, Press conference of May 4, 1950, in *Public Papers of the Presidents of the United States, 1950* (Washington, D.C.: GPO, 1965), 286.

52. The President to the Secretary of the NSC (Lay), Apr. 12, 1950, *FRUS, 1950,* 1:234–35. See also Lay Memorandum, May 2, 1950, *FRUS, 1950,* 1:297–98.

53. Memorandum by the Deputy Chief of the Division of Estimates, Bureau of the Budget (Schaub) to the Executive Secretary of the NSC (Lay), May 8, 1950, *FRUS, 1950,* 1:298–306.

54. Ibid., 301.

55. Ibid., 302.

56. Ibid.

57. Ibid.

58. Ibid., 303.

59. Callahan, *Dangerous Capabilities,* 121.

60. Memorandum by Mr. John Foster Dulles, Consultant to the Secretary of State, May 18, 1950, *FRUS, 1950,* 1:314–16.

61. Memorandum for Jessup et al. from the Executive Secretary of the NSC (Lay), June 8, 1950, PPS Papers 1947–1953, Box 54, RG 59, NA.

62. Memorandum for the Secretary of Defense (from W. Stuart Symington), June 21, 1950, PPS Papers 1947–1953, Box 54, RG 59, NA.

63. Memorandum of NSC Consultants' Meeting, Thursday, June 29, 1950, *FRUS, 1950,* 1: 324–30.

64. Acheson insists in *Present at the Creation* that his speech about the defense perimeter could not have led the Communists astray (see 467).

65. Memorandum of Conversation by Mr. Frederick E. Nolting, June 30, 1950, *FRUS, 1950,* vol. 7 (Washington, D.C.: GPO, 1976), 258–59.

66. Statement by the Chairman of the National Security Resources Board (NSRB) (Symington) to the National Security Council, July 6, 1950, *FRUS, 1950,* 1:338–41.

67. Memorandum by Mr. John Foster Dulles, Consultant to the Secretary of State, to the Director of the Policy Planning Staff (Nitze), July 14, 1950, *FRUS, 1950,* 7:386–87. There are many good studies of the problem of crossing the parallel; see Walter LaFeber, "Crossing the 38th: The Cold War in Microcosm," in *Reflections on the Cold War,* ed. Lynn Miller and Ronald Preussen (Philadelphia: Temple University, 1974), 71–90; and James I. Matray, "Truman's Plan for Victory: National Self-Determination and the Thirty-Eighth Parallel Decision in Korea," *Journal of American History* 66 (1979): 314–33.

68. Memorandum of Conversation by the Secretary of State, July 14, 1950, *FRUS, 1950,* 1: 344–46.

69. "NSC-68," (Nitze to fifteen officials identified only by initials), Aug. 1, 1950, PPS Papers 1947–1953, Box 54, RG 59, NA.

70. Memorandum by the Counselor (Kennan) to the Secretary of State, Aug. 8, 1950, *FRUS, 1950,* 1:361–67.

71. Memorandum by the Counselor (Kennan) to the Secretary of State, Aug. 14, 1950, *FRUS, 1950,* 7:574–76.

72. Transcripts of the Executive (Secret) session of the Senate Foreign Relations Committee for fall 1949 through 1950 show 206 pages devoted to excoriating the State Department for the loss of China and other Asian problems, and only 119 pages devoted to the rest of the world. See U.S. Senate, Foreign Relations Committee, 81st Cong., 1st and 2d sess., Executive Sessions (Historical Series) (Washington, D.C.: GPO, 1976).

73. Acheson, *Present at the Creation,* 578.

74. PRIORITY EMBASSY PARIS—FOR BOHLEN (from Acheson) Aug. 15, 1950, CDF 611.00/7-350–611.00/9-3050, Box 2706, RG 59, NA.

75. Memorandum of Conversation by the Executive Secretary of the National Security Council (Lay), Aug. 23, 1950, *FRUS, 1950,* 1:373–74.

76. Report by the NSC, Aug. 25, 1950, *FRUS, 1950,* 1:375–89.

77. Report to the NSC by the Executive Secretary (Lay), Sept. 30, 1950, *FRUS, 1950,* 1:400.

78. Ibid.

79. Nitze to Marshall, Oct. 3, 1950, PPS Papers 1947–1953, Box RG 59, NA.

80. Ibid.

81. To Perkins and Matthews from Jessup, Oct. 4, 1950, PPS Papers 1947–1953, Box 58, RG 59, NA.

82. Williamson's comment is in Byington to Perkins, Oct. 6, 1950, PPS Papers 1947–1953, Box 58, RG 59, NA; Martin, Woolridge, and Jessup are in Notes on Senior Staff Meeting, NSC, Oct. 6, 1950, PPS Papers 1947–1953, Box 58, RG 59, NA.

83. To Secretary of State from Nitze, Oct. 9, 1950, PPS Papers 1947–1953, Box 54, RG 59, NA.

84. Nitze, *From Hiroshima to Glasnost,* 97.

85. Memorandum by the Secretary of the NSC (Lay), Nov. 14, 1950, *FRUS, 1950,* 1:403.

86. These memos are in PPS Papers 1947–1953, Box 58, RG 59, NA.

87. See editorial footnote, *FRUS, 1950,* 1:404.

88. See William Stueck, *The Korean War: An International History* (Princeton, N.J.: Princeton University Press, 1995). Short but useful accounts are Roger Dingman, "1950: The Fate of a Grand Design," *Pacific Historical Review* 47 (1978): 465–71; and Robert Jervis, "The Impact of the Korean War on the Cold War," *Journal of Conflict Resolution* 24 (1980): 563–91.

89. Memorandum of Conversation by Mr. Lucius D. Battle, Dec. 2, 1950, *FRUS, 1950,* 7:1301–1305.

90. Memorandum of Conversation by the Ambassador at Large (Jessup), Dec. 3, 1950, *FRUS, 1950,* 7:1323–24.

91. Memorandum by Mr. Lucius D. Battle, Dec. 4, 1950, *FRUS, 1950,* 7:1345–47.

92. Commander in Chief, United Nations Command (MacArthur) to the Joint Chiefs of Staff, Dec. 3, 1950, *FRUS, 1950,* 7:1321.

93. This letter is in Acheson, *Present at the Creation,* 615–16; and Kennan, *Memoirs,* 31.

94. Wilson D. Miscamble, *George F. Kennan and the Making of American Foreign Policy, 1947–1950* (Princeton, N.J.: Princeton University Press, 1992), 331. See also Stueck, *Korean War,* 34–35.

95. Leffler, *Preponderance of Power,* 356.

96. See Samuel F. Wells, "Sounding the Tocsin: NSC-68 and the Soviet Threat," *International Security* 4 (1979): 116–58.

97. Gaddis, *Strategies of Containment,* chap. 4.

98. Memorandum by the Chairman of the National Security Resources Board (Symington) to the President, undated, *FRUS, 1951,* vol. 1 (Washington, D.C.: GPO, 1979), 21–33. Truman's comments are on 21, 22, 33.

99. Marshall to Nitze, Jan. 29, 1951, PPS Papers 1947–1953, Box 58, RG 59, NA.

100. The Counselor (Bohlen) to the Director of the Policy Planning Staff (Nitze), July 28, 1951, *FRUS, 1951,* 1:106–109.

101. Memorandum by the CIA, Aug. 2, 1951, *FRUS, 1951,* 1:120–27.

102. Report to the President by the NSC, Aug. 8, 1951, *FRUS, 1951,* 1:127–29.

103. Gleason to Nitze, Aug. 17, 1951, PPS Papers 1947–1953, Box 58, RG 59, NA.

104. Memorandum by the Counselor (Bohlen), Aug. 22, 1951, *FRUS, 1951,* 1:163–66; Memorandum by the Counselor (Bohlen), Sept. 21, 1951, *FRUS, 1951,* 1:170–72. These memos are fundamental to any evaluation of the construction of the NSC-68 series. One must read them against the alarmism of CIA estimates from 1951, for instance, which show the Soviets as able to undertake military campaigns against Britain, submarine and air offensives against Western sea lines of communications, and "aerial attack (conventional and atomic) against Canada and most of the United States." The Soviet Union would launch all of these campaigns simultaneously, with 180–200 divisions, more than eleven thousand tactical aircraft, and 850 light and medium bombers, and still retain an adequate reserve. (Cited in Matthew Evangelista, "Commentary: The 'Soviet Threat': Intentions, Capabilities, and Context," *Diplomatic History* 22 [1998]: 445.) A favorable view of Bohlen's argument on the Soviet threat is in Robert B. Bowie and Richard H. Immerman, *Waging Peace* (New York: Oxford University Press, 1998), chap. 1; Admiral Fechteler's powerful Jan., 1950, derogation of Soviet power is on page 99. See also Robert H. Johnson, *Improbable Dangers* (New York: St. Martin's, 1994).

105. Policy Planning Staff Memorandum, Sept. 29, 1951, *FRUS, 1951,* 1:172–75.

106. Koch's memo is in *FRUS, 1951,* 1:166–69; Joyce is in *FRUS, 1951,* 1:169–70.

107. "Soviet Objectives and the Danger of War," Oct. 8, 1951, PPS Papers 1947–1953, Box 59, RG 59, NA.

108. The Counselor (Bohlen) to the Secretary of State, Oct. 9, 1951, *FRUS, 1951,* 1:180–81.

109. Memorandum by the Counselor (Bohlen) to the Executive Secretary of the Policy Planning Staff, Oct. 26, 1951, *FRUS, 1951,* 1:244.

110. Editorial note, *FRUS, 1952–1954,* vol. 2 (Washington, D.C.: GPO, 1984), 56–57.

111. Annex to a Report to the NSC by the Executive Secretary (Lay), Aug. 22, 1952, *FRUS, 1952–1954,* 2:89. Bohlen's cover letter is on 2:87–88.

112. Memorandum for the President of Discussion at the 122d Meeting of the NSC on Wednesday, Sept. 3, 1952, *FRUS, 1952–1954,* 2:117–26.

113. Statement of Policy by the NSC, undated, *FRUS, 1952–1954,* 2:144–56.

114. Steven L. Rearden, *The Evolution of American Strategic Doctrine* (Boulder, Colo.: Westview, 1984), 33–34.

115. Memorandum by the Director of the Policy Planning Staff (Nitze) to the Deputy Undersecretary of State, July 14, 1952, *FRUS, 1952–1954,* 2:58–59.

116. Memorandum by the Director, Policy Planning Staff (Nitze) to the Secretary of State, June 12, 1953, *FRUS, 1952–1954,* 2:202–205.

117. Louis J. Halle, *The Cold War as History* (New York: Harper Colophon, 1967), xiii.

CHAPTER FOUR

Militarizing America's Propaganda Program, 1945–55

SHAWN J. PARRY-GILES

As Louis J. Halle contends, "most persons regard the Cold War as essentially an ideological war"[1]—a "war of words" in which propaganda replaced bombs and tanks. In the early postwar years, though, propaganda was an ill-understood practice, or at least one known only in terms of the negative connotations attached to its uses in World Wars I and II.[2] As America progressed from two world wars into a cold war, Washington and the country's first two Cold War presidents became more interested in the strategic potential of propaganda.[3]

From 1945 to 1955, Presidents Harry S. Truman and Dwight D. Eisenhower experimented with and refined the practice of propaganda as a presidential tool for fighting the Cold War. In doing so, their administrations replaced a journalistic conception of propaganda with a militarized paradigm.[4] The militarization of America's propaganda program allowed for enhanced presidential direction over propaganda planning. In order to understand the militarization of the Cold War propaganda program, I first examine the private and once classified strategic documents that exhibit presidential motives. Second, I analyze the public documents (congressional debates, administrative speeches, and propaganda texts) that actualized these motives.

Decentralization of Propaganda Planning

Six months after the United States entered World War II, the Office of War Information (OWI) began operations. Dogged by the criticisms aimed at its World War I predecessor, the Committee for Public Information (CPI), OWI hurriedly organized an international and domestic propaganda program as it addressed concerns about a government-sponsored news bureau.[5] Some of the strongest objections to the program concerned OWI's domestic branch, which used radio to boost morale at home and to convince Americans to serve the country's war effort.[6] By the end of the war, members of the public, the Congress, and the media continued to harbor negative attitudes toward a government-sponsored propaganda program, clinging to the view that the "private media were the appropriate instruments for public information."[7] As Truman settled into the White House, his administration initiated a campaign to gain support for the controversial practice of propaganda.

The Truman Administration's Campaign to Influence the Media

Given the reservations about the government's dissemination of propaganda, the eventual passage of the Smith-Mundt Act on January 27, 1948, which legalized America's first *official* peacetime propaganda program, demonstrates the Truman administration's commitment to propaganda activities. Through the leadership of William Benton, assistant secretary of state for public affairs, the Truman administration relied on a journalistic propaganda paradigm in the early years of the Cold War to help achieve the passage of the Smith-Mundt Act. Such a paradigm equated propaganda with news and required the testimony of leading editors and journalists to evidence propaganda's utility. This model placed propaganda operations in the hands of multiple news outlets, resulting in a diffuse and ineffective propaganda operation. While successful domestically, the journalistic paradigm produced propaganda problems abroad that culminated in the militarization of propaganda operations.

A cordial relationship between America's propaganda program and the private news media was essential to the media's eventual support of the Smith-Mundt Act. In September of 1945, Truman appointed Benton, a former advertiser,[8] to direct the State Department's interim propaganda program and to lead the campaign to gain its legalized status. As Benton acknowledged years later, one of the major obstacles that he faced in legalizing America's first propaganda program regarded the resistance emanating from "commercial broadcast interests and the wire services."[9]

Attempting to garner support for the Smith-Mundt bill, Benton lobbied media moguls and formed special committees composed of media personnel, who were asked to recommend changes in propaganda operations. A State Department press release in May, 1946, publicized the statements of five radio executives who broadcast under contract with that department and who fulfilled Benton's request to critique congressional budget cuts. Those providing very positive appraisals of the government's propaganda efforts included: RCA chairman David Sarnoff, Westinghouse vice president Walter Evans, GE chairman Philip D. Reed, CBS president Frank Stanton, and Crosley Corporation vice president J. D. Shouse. Stanton, for example, asserted, "the dangers incident to even a temporary interruption of international short-wave broadcasting are so great that we feel it both proper and necessary for us to make this recommendation to you."[10]

Beyond forming the shortwave radio force, Benton also grouped publishers, educators, and radio officials together into a Radio Advisory Committee, which commented on "the effectiveness of the State Department's [propaganda] efforts."[11] The committee assembled such notable individuals as scholar Harold Lasswell and broadcaster Edward R. Murrow, in addition to Gardner Cowles, Jr., publisher of the *Des Moines (Iowa) Register and Tribune.*[12] The eight-member committee determined that the available funds "for international broadcasting [were] inadequate to do the job required and . . . [had to] be expanded . . . to avoid a serious set-back in the development of its proper relations with the rest of the world."[13]

In addition to these two committees, Benton lobbied the American Society of Newspaper Editors (ASNE) to study the interim propaganda program and to offer public support for its continuation. While members of the ASNE were initially hostile toward the program,[14] the board eventually appointed a committee to examine the "problem of world dissemination of news" during its 1946 convention. This group consisted in part of seven editors from major newspapers such as the *New York Times, St. Louis Post-Dispatch,* and *Baltimore Sun.* The group concluded that the "present uncertainties in international relations justify an effort by the United States Government to make its activities and its policies clear to the people of the world through the agency set up in the State Department."[15] Not surprisingly, Benton highlighted this committee's startling conclusions privately and publicly in order to bolster his lobbying efforts.[16]

While the activities and recommendations of these three committees were generally publicized, the actions and even the existence of a separate committee remained hidden. In order to achieve the passage of the Smith-Mundt Act, Benton formed a secret advisory committee, the membership of which is still not fully known. Benton personally covered the committee's operating costs, although he received additional funding from two major Republican Party contributors, Henry Luce of *Time* and Gardner "Mike" Cowles of Cowles Publications. The committee reportedly used the OWI alumni network to solicit favorable coverage from former staffers.[17] Benton referred to such OWI alum's as his "under-cover workers . . . [who were] of great help" in advertising the necessity of a peacetime propaganda program. Benton felt such recognition would help produce more favorable coverage of the Smith-Mundt bill by those "back at their jobs on the newspapers and magazines."[18]

Beyond Benton's activities, members of the State Department strategized ways to involve the press in advising roles so as to generate more favorable coverage. Two major State Department assumptions led to such a plan. The first was that poor relations existed between State and the press,[19] and the second was that State needed to take a more active role in "initiat[ing] the news."[20] M. J. McDermott, special assistant to the secretary of state, urged, for example, that only through more "intimate" contact could press relations be improved.[21] Edward G. Miller, Jr., a member of the assistant secretary of state's staff, concluded that "an informal advisory committee of members of the press . . . be loosely constituted to advise on matters of press policy." Miller, while urging "strict confidential[ity]," argued that improving press relations was essential to "maintain[ing] a consistent foreign policy." As Miller predicted, "the more information we [give] out the more sympathetic the press [becomes] to our total aims."[22]

These connections between the propaganda program and the private news media served as evidence for both the constitutionality and the necessity of a peacetime propaganda program in the debates over the Smith-Mundt bill. Benton predictably relied on testimony from his special media committees to silence opposition over the government's involvement in international broadcasting. Cited most extensively was the ASNE study, the results of which were placed in the February, 1947, *Congressional Record,* and the May, 1947, subcommittee hearings of the House Committee on Foreign Affairs.[23] Employing the testimonials of ASNE members, Benton thus equated propaganda with news, furthering the journalistic paradigm. As Benton proclaimed, "If we did not play the news straight, as the ASNE agreed in their study, in my opinion we would not have such press support for this program."[24]

Benton evinced the media's support further by excerpting the Radio Advisory Committee's report and featuring testimonies from "friends" of propaganda. At the same May, 1947, House subcommittee hearings, Benton placed into the record more than seven pages of editorial passages from newspapers and magazines across the country, including *Life* and the *New York Times,* and from business leaders like RCA's Sarnoff and GE's Reed.[25] Reed also testified on behalf of the Smith-Mundt bill before the subcommittee of the Senate Foreign Relations Committee in July, 1947, claiming that "the simple truth about the United States . . . widely told throughout the world, will do more to reduce the risk of war, and thus to reduce the need for a multibillion dollar military force, than any other single factor."[26] Such a view fashioned propaganda as a substitute for military involvement, elevating the importance of a government-sponsored *news* agency. The successes of Benton's rhetorical efforts can best be seen in the coverage of the nation's most noted newspaper.[27]

The "Voice" of the *New York Times*

The *New York Times*'s coverage of the debate surrounding the Smith-Mundt Act demonstrates how the *Times* engaged in a public relations campaign for the propaganda program. This coverage illustrates how the news media seemingly functioned as the domestic arm of America's international propaganda program, illustrating the existence of a more "camouflaged" propaganda, where the actual source and the propagandistic nature of the material is invisible to its intended readers.[28]

Some *Times* reporters served as active advocates for the propaganda program. *Times* journalist, Edwin L. James, for example, linked the propaganda program to the Marshall Plan, arguing that "there is a job to be done in getting to a greater number of people our story of what we are attempting to do with the Marshall Plan."[29] Anne O'Hare McCormick, a well-known *Times* editorial writer,[30] championed an increase in propaganda funding during a speech before a group of teachers in which she equated a lack of news in Europe with a greater peril to peace than "hunger, cold or the atom bomb."[31] McCormick argued that the dissemination of news and information was of greater importance than diplomatic and military measures and thus was the "first answer to the atomic bomb."[32]

When covering the debates over the Smith-Mundt bill, the *Times* often featured "friends" of Benton's propaganda program in their stories. As Russell Porter covered the semiannual meeting of the Academy of Political Science, he de-emphasized other featured speakers in favor of GE's Reed, an outspoken supporter of the Smith-Mundt bill. In discussing the relationship between free enterprise and the government, Porter reported Reed's concern that "foreigners [were] especially lacking in news about the standard of living of American workers and about the aid the United States has given other countries." The central theme that Reed promulgated, Porter reported, was "the need for education in defense of the American way of life."[33]

The *New York Times* demonstrated its support for America's propaganda program even after the passage of the Smith-Mundt Act, when it featured a four-part series on the Voice of America (VOA).[34] In defining VOA's mission, Austin Stevens perpetuated the State Department's rehabilitated views of propaganda in his front-page story. According to Stevens, the "'Voice' and other media, is telling facts abroad about international developments and setting forth the United States's position in areas where it may not be known."[35] Commenting on Stevens's feature, an unidentified *Times*'s editorial writer championed the Voice while highlighting the positive slant that the feature writer gave to the government's short-wave radio broadcast: "We believe that a reading of the series of articles in this newspaper by Austin Stevens that has just been concluded will convince most thoughtful persons and members of Congress that the program is at present soundly visualized and that an effort is being made to give it the best direction possible." In the end, the *Times*'s editors concluded that the United States Government *reluctantly* entered the "war of words"—a contest in which the United States had to prevail: "This war was not of our making but is one we must win. In it lies a better hope for world peace than the winning of a hot war of arms could bring."[36]

Benton was quite pleased by the news media's support of America's propaganda program. He boasted that his own "propaganda" helped spawn "editorials favoring" the Smith-Mundt Act in the *New York Times*.[37] Such coverage thus reveals the effectiveness of Benton's rhetoric on the news media—the kind of rhetorical feat that typifies administrative discourse.[38] Just as Benton intended, the news media helped rally support for peacetime propaganda—a propaganda grounded in a journalistic paradigm. However, although successful at home, the Truman administration's earliest peacetime propaganda efforts were failing miserably abroad.

America's International Voice

Intended audiences and congressional watchdogs objected vehemently to certain "news" shows that were beamed abroad in 1947 and 1948. In implementing the journalistic paradigm, the State Department contracted with NBC to write a VOA radio broadcast for Latin American audiences, known as *Know North America (KNA)*, which aired in that region between November 27, 1947, and March 8, 1948. Ultimately, this controversy helped prompt the centralization of propaganda strategy in the State Department, and the eventual centralization of propaganda activities in the White House. For some members of Congress, the Truman administration's earliest propaganda efforts were simply too diffuse.

All of the *KNA* broadcasts followed a similar format, with each covering the travels of one individual from Venezuela and another from Cuba as they explored the United States. The show's producers intended for one of the travelers to raise prejudices that Latin Americans might have about the United States, and the other to counter such stereotypes. Such a show presumably served America's propaganda mission of "promot[ing] a better understanding between people of the United States and the people of other countries," as outlined by the Smith-Mundt Act.[39] Each broadcast was beamed to Latin America in Spanish and was designed to be an entertaining travelogue complete with music, sound effects, and humor. Although NBC created the idea, the State Department approved the series and the format.[40]

As part of each broadcast, a narrator began with a statement similar to the following: "The National Broadcasting Company presents: *Know North America,* a weekly program in which we narrate the spiritual adventures of two travelers as they discover the numerous miracles of the historical and present-day life of the United States."[41] Each broadcast focused on a particular state, providing listeners with background on that state, its cities, and important landmarks. The broadcasts all featured descriptions of the state's natural resources, which highlighted American wealth and riches.[42]

Know North America was more than just a travelogue, though. All of the scripts drew ideological conclusions primarily from the historical background of each state, and those conclusions attracted the attention of congressional overseers. One broadcast, for example, featured humorous stories about polygamy in Utah and divorce rates in Nevada,[43] which attracted negative attention from members of Congress. Another broadcast that drew congressional scrutiny involved the state of Alabama, which represented a place *KNA* producers believed could be used to "educate" Latin American listeners on the history of America's racial divisions. Of a street that was named "Jefferson Davis Avenue," the first traveler asked, "Wasn't that the President of the Southern Confederation?" The narrator answered affirmatively and added: "On this avenue . . . only Negroes live." The first traveler interrupted and elaborated: "And he defended slavery and was the most bitter enemy of Lincoln's ideals." Concluding, the second traveler stated: "That will show you that the dead do not return, because if they did the spirit of Davis would have removed the signs of this street." The narrator then declared: "In no other part of the United States has the colored race struggled and suffered so much as here."[44] For Sen. Homer E. Capehart (R-Indiana) at least, such a statement had no place in a program designed to promote America's image in foreign countries. As Capehart sarcastically declared during the hearings on the program: "I am certain that the people of Alabama who pay State . . . and Federal taxes will appreciate the fact their money is being used to advertise them to the world in such light."[45]

Congressional leaders were also outraged by the overall content of the *KNA* series. Senator Carl A. Hatch (D-New Mexico), for example, stated that while he had been "one of the strong supporters" of a peacetime propaganda program, he demanded an end to the "drivel, nonsense and downright falsehoods . . . set forth" in the *KNA* broadcasts. Senator Lister Hill (D-Alabama) referred to the broadcasts as "base slander," while Sen. Millard E. Tydings (D-Maryland) went so far as to claim that the broadcasts looked like "a calculated attempt to portray the United States in the most degrading way that radio technique would allow." Senator Thomas Connally (D-Texas) demanded that the program be abolished if it continued to "plaster all over the world . . . slanderous, [and] outrageous stories regarding the different States of the Union."[46]

All of these complaints ultimately led to questions about who was responsible for the content of *KNA* broadcasts. Questions were raised about Alberto Gandero, who supervised the writing of the project. According to the testimony of Charles V. Denny, vice president and general counsel of NBC, Gandero headed the Spanish language section and directed Dr. Renè Borgia to script the *KNA* series.[47] Congressional objections centered more on the lack of oversight of these Spanish texts by NBC and State Department officials who were unfamiliar with the Spanish language. Congressional leaders were quite alarmed that *KNA* scripts were not translated into English and checked over before being aired. Evidencing such shock, Senator Homer Ferguson (R-Michigan) concluded: "Congress [did] not intend that there should be divided responsibility."[48] The message seemed clear in that members of Congress wanted the State Department rather than independent journalists to assume control over the program's content.

The Truman administration also learned other lessons from America's propaganda during the first few years of the program's peacetime existence. Just as members of Congress found the *KNA* broadcasts troubling, many within the international community also reacted negatively to America's propaganda. Rather than creating greater understanding of the United States around the globe, the propaganda instead created hostility and instilled jealousy in the very people it was designed to persuade. As propaganda specialist Fitzhugh Green explains: "Foreigners were treated to copious descriptions of America's prosperity in terms of millions of automobiles, washing machines, and bathtubs for every citizen." Intending to contrast the material benefits of democracy with the substandard living conditions under Communism, the program instead created "envy" and "resentment" in many parts of the world.[49]

While State Department officials were bragging about America's wealth and prosperity in propaganda programs like *KNA*, the Soviets were allegedly engaged in a campaign to discredit American credibility abroad, simultaneously promoting their own foreign policy aims. Mose Harvey of the State

Department's Division of Research on the Soviet Union indicated that the "hate America" campaign was launched on January 21, 1950, during which time the Soviets also stressed a desire for "peaceful coexistence" with all countries.[50]

The alleged failure of America's international propaganda and the new Soviet "attacks" against the United States led U.S. officials to reconsider propaganda aims and techniques. Thus, while the Truman administration, through the leadership of William Benton, experienced success at home with attempts to influence the domestic news media, the administration quickly learned that its international strategies were naive and fell short of congressional expectations. In order to meet this changing propaganda environment and the new exigencies of the Cold War, the administration responded with a more determined propaganda effort in April, 1950, with Truman personally launching the new "Campaign of Truth."[51] In the process, the administration abandoned the journalistic approach to propaganda and moved toward an intensified and militaristic model of propaganda.

Militarizing America's Propaganda Program

The Cold War began to intensify even before the Truman administration's propaganda program achieved its legalized status.[52] In response to increased Communist activity, the ineffectiveness of the journalistic approach to propaganda, and the new Soviet-sponsored hate America campaign, the administration sought to implement new overt as well as covert propaganda strategies. The covert channels were invested primarily in the newly established Central Intelligence Agency (CIA),[53] and by 1950 in the Psychological Strategy Board (PSB). The overt activities, however, were under the propaganda arm of Truman's Campaign of Truth. When faced with the need for an enhanced governmental propaganda program during what seemed more like an impending warlike crisis, the administration began to metaphorically equate propaganda with weapons. Such a rhetorical move, whether intentional or not, served as a more familiar linguistic paradigm for government officials than did the language of news.

The Truman Administration's Psychological Warfare Activities

Concerns over Soviet propaganda gains were articulated soon after the propaganda program achieved legalized status in 1948. Fearful that the overt propaganda apparatus would be ineffective on its own, the administration expanded its secret psychological warfare activities, hiding such actions from Congress and the American people. The progression to a psychological warfare apparatus shifted the practice of propaganda away from the journalistic paradigm and toward a militaristic vision. The archival documents concerning covert activities and the establishment of the PSB reveal a progression toward centralizing propaganda strategy in the White House, reducing congressional input, and militarizing communication strategies. Combined with a language that equated propaganda and weaponry, this structure initiated the process whereby psychological warfare and eventually propaganda would become instruments under the direct control of the president.

The Truman administration institutionalized a covert structure by creating the CIA through the National Security Act of 1947. Only five months after the CIA's establishment, the Truman administration expanded anti-Soviet propaganda activities, which were placed under the direction of the CIA and supervised by the National Security Council (NSC). While responsive to the NSC, the NSC-4/A document of December 9, 1947, clearly granted the CIA unrestricted actions in its operations, indicating that "nothing contained herein shall be construed to require the Central Intelligence Agency to disclose operational details concerning its secret techniques, sources or contacts."[54]

Six months later, Truman expanded the CIA's activities to include psychological warfare and paramilitary maneuvers. Still under the authorization of the National Security Act of 1947, NSC-10/2 empowered the CIA to conduct "espionage and counter-espionage operations abroad." NSC-10/2 also established the parameters of covert actions, which referenced activities "conducted or sponsored by this Government against hostile foreign states . . . or in support of friendly foreign states . . . but which [were] so planned and executed that . . . if uncovered the US Government [could] plausibly disclaim any responsibility for them."[55] As John Prados explains, NSC-10/2 established for the first time "a mechanism designated by the President to approve and manage secret operations . . . [that were] responsible to him."[56]

One clear outgrowth of this covert structure involved the development of two CIA-sponsored radio stations, commonly known as Radio Free Europe (RFE) and Radio Liberty (RL). Developed under the guise of private sponsorship, which placed them outside of congressional control, the CIA's involvement with both stations was not confirmed publicly until 1971.[57] Radio Free Europe began broadcasting in 1950 under the "government's intelligence apparatus" of the National Committee for a Free Europe, which technically represented a "private" organization. Radio Liberty went on the air in 1953 under the sponsorship of the American Committee for Freedom for the Peoples of the USSR, Incorporated. As the title of RL's "dummy" foundation implies, it existed to beam messages to the Soviet Union, using former Soviet citizens as broadcasters.[58] However, RFE targeted Eastern Europe, including Poland, Czechoslovakia, Hungary, Romania, and Bulgaria.[59] As Martin J. Medhurst explains, one of the goals of these new radio services was "to keep the Soviets so preoccupied with their own captive people that they would not have the inclination to take on any more trouble spots."[60]

Beyond the covert apparatus that allowed for CIA sponsorship of RFE and RL, the Truman administration ordered the development of further psychological warfare research via NSC-59 and NSC-74. Truman sanctioned a comprehensive program for psychological warfare by establishing a staff devoted to researching and planning through the institutionalization of NSC-59 in 1949. In 1950, Truman approved "A Plan for National Psychological Warfare."[61] Throughout this period, political officials devoted considerable attention to defining the framework and meaning of psychological warfare,[62] with NSC-74 offering a sense of its parameters: "Psychological warfare is an instrument of national policy and an integral part of the national war effort."[63] A more explicit definition of "psychological warfare" was reported in a PSB file that featured the Joint Chiefs of Staff (JCS) conception of its practice. According to the JCS, psychological warfare involved "the planned use by a nation of propaganda . . . to influence the opinion, emotions, attitudes and behavior of enemy, neutral or friendly foreign groups in such a way as to support the accomplishment of its national policy and aims."[64] Thus while psychological warfare related to wartime activities only, propaganda possessed utility for wartime *and* peacetime.

As political officials sought to conceptualize psychological warfare activities, battles erupted over the appropriate oversight of such a program among the officials of the CIA and the Departments of Defense and State. In the end, a compromise structure was reached with the formation of the PSB.[65] For many involved, the final solution required the "same kind of unified leadership as in a military struggle."[66] In his April, 1951, implementing directive Truman appointed some of the government's highest officers to the PSB. Those involved in such psychological planning included the undersecretary of state, the deputy secretary of defense, and the CIA director. In addition, a JCS representative was required to "sit with the Board as its principal military advisor." The NSC supervised the PSB's activities, which made all psychological warfare activity subject to the guidance and control of the president as commander in chief.[67] Any activity connected to the PSB was deemed "very highly classified" by its members because of the "sensitive subjects affecting . . . national security."[68] Recently declassified minutes of the PSB reveal its "broad" scope, which included any activity "except overt shooting and overt economic warfare."[69] As Prados maintains, the PSB became a "stimulant" for intensifying the Cold War.[70]

Not only did the PSB's structure move psychological warfare and propaganda strategy closer to a military paradigm, so too did the language employed in the conversations over such strategies. Documents pertaining to psychological strategy reveal how political officials relied heavily on artillery metaphors in conceptualizing psychological warfare, propaganda, and their appropriate structures. C. D. Jackson, for example, identified RFE as a "mighty weapon in the struggle for freedom,"[71] while the unknown authors of a PSB draft statement not only used the term *weapon* on three separate occasions in referring to psychological strategy, but also called such strategies "indispensable *arms* of United States policy for peace."[72] Other internal documents intensified the metaphorical use of weaponry images, with one PSB document equating psychological warfare with such weapons as "the airplane, the 155 millimeter gun, the Patton Tank, and the bazooka."[73] Such a militaristic construction of propaganda's role within the Cold War influenced not only the private debates surrounding its operations, but also penetrated the public debates as well, particularly during Truman's Campaign of Truth.

The Campaign of Truth

As an outgrowth of the intensifying Cold War and the increased militarization of secret psychological warfare activities, Truman initiated the Campaign of Truth in 1950. As Truman became more visibly involved in promoting propaganda, he centered the public debate on increasing propaganda expenditures. Just as in the private discourse concerning covert psychological warfare operations, a militaristic paradigm began to replace the journalistic one in deliberations over Truman's Campaign of Truth.

In March, 1950, William Benton, by then a U.S. senator, and twelve of his colleagues, called for an enlarged information program, a "Marshall Plan in the field of ideas."[74] Plans for such a program were already being made within the administration. When Truman informed newly appointed Assistant Secretary of State for Public Affairs Edward W. Barrett of his desire to launch a major propaganda offensive against the Soviet Union, Barrett convinced him to label the effort a "Campaign of Truth," so as to avoid the stigma of propaganda. This new propaganda campaign was designed to target twenty-eight critical areas of the world, including Iran, South Korea, Indochina, Thailand, Greece, Afghanistan, Finland, and the Soviet satellite regions.[75]

President Truman used the bully pulpit to launch the Campaign of Truth in front of the ASNE on April 20, 1950.[76] A subcommittee of the Senate Foreign

Relations Committee investigated the need for such a program in July of that same year. In order to support the campaign publicly, the administration engaged in a massive effort to marshal support for the program inside and outside of Congress. From April 20, 1950, through January 16, 1951, for example, State Department officials made some fifty-four speeches about the campaign to private groups.[77]

Interestingly, in justifying increased funds for the State Department's propaganda program, wartime imagery pervaded the congressional debates over the Campaign of Truth. Even though incensed that the Soviets would portray the United States as a warmongering nation,[78] the new language in the Campaign of Truth likewise articulated war images rather than the peaceful ones more common in the Smith-Mundt debates. The American-Soviet struggle had become, according to supporters of the program, a "war of words," a "war of ideologies," a "propaganda war," or a "battle for the minds of men."[79] Propaganda and the Campaign of Truth were frequently referred to as instrumental weapons in the Cold War.[80] Edward Barrett, for instance, argued that the Campaign of Truth represented the "weapon which [possessed] the firepower to pierce the iron curtain . . . [and] the explosive force to rip the camouflage from the Soviet position."[81] Officials even talked of win/loss ratios, counting the number of "victories" by each side. In a speech entitled "Mobilization of American Strength for World Security," Barrett argued that the Kremlin had "nine nations lined up on their side," to "53 nations lined up on the side of the free world."[82] Unless the United States continued to deploy the "T-Bomb" aggressively,[83] as supporters referred to the Campaign of Truth, the "Big Lie"[84] of Soviet propaganda would undoubtedly lead to more Soviet victories.

By using the language of all-out warfare, proponents of the Campaign of Truth lobbied Congress with a rhetoric of crisis. America needed to take Soviet propaganda seriously, they argued, studying the content of the Communist message and designing better weapons to counter its effects.[85] This rhetoric produced a significant change in American propaganda strategy during the Campaign of Truth and resulted in the expansion of propaganda expenditures. Truman's campaign, for example, received approximately $111.7 million dollars for fiscal year 1951, inspired largely by the North Korean invasion of South Korea on June 25, 1950. This budget outlay increased propaganda expenditures some threefold. For the next two fiscal years, appropriations continued to rise by similar amounts.[86] The language of war translated into a call for a more aggressive and bellicose propaganda, which was buttressed by the secret deliberations concerning America's covert propaganda activities. Such rhetorical successes illustrate the effectiveness of the Truman administration's discourse on congressional elites.

By the end of the Truman presidency, the military paradigm appeared to replace the journalistic one used to legalize the Smith-Mundt Act. Part of the transformation is reflected in the language used in the private discussions among policy planners as well as throughout the debates over the Campaign of Truth. Such language usage reveals the naturalized equation of weaponry images with propaganda/psychological warfare. By equating weapons and propaganda, this language paradigm contextualized communication principles within a confrontational model, evidencing the belief systems of the political participants. The actual propaganda that was produced as part of the Campaign of Truth likewise evidenced this paradigmatic shift.

Militarizing the VOA

Not surprisingly, many of those involved in the VOA's operations during the Campaign of Truth came from the ranks of practicing journalists.[87] Such journalists-turned-propagandists quickly learned that news in the service of propaganda during the Campaign of Truth operated under a wholly different set of constraints—constraints now more closely regulated by the PSB and State Department officials. While trained to be "objective," to present both sides of an issue, or to attribute their material to reliable sources,[88] the VOA "journalists" had to answer to different standards in the aftermath of the *KNA* hearings. During the Campaign of Truth, State Department officials tightened their control of the "news" aired by the VOA, and the individual "journalists" became little more than readers of carefully prepared scripts.

After the *KNA* hearings, Congress held hearings focused on America's propaganda program so as to examine its material more closely. In 1951, the Senate Committee on Foreign Relations and the House Committee on Foreign Affairs jointly investigated VOA's news operation. Reacting to the congressional call for stricter control over the program's output, Edward Barrett reported that the program initiated more intense training for employees. According to Barrett, "two months of *indoctrination* by some courses in the Foreign Service Institute" were required of all field employees. These individuals also studied the principles of American democracy and various aspects of American foreign policy. Barrett stressed that lectures and writings were offered to reinforce "the *indoctrination*" that was required for their position with VOA.[89]

In order to monitor the effectiveness of VOA's message, Barrett explained that the program used "local panels of cross sections of the audience in each country" to provide feedback on their broadcasts. These groups listened to certain broadcasts, filled out questionnaires, and offered advice on the programming. Except for daily newscasts, Barrett reported, "no publication" was sent into the field "until the manuscript [had] been gone over by the Embassy Staff, tried out on a local audience, [or] edited in accordance with the Embassy's best judgment."[90] The directives for most story lines were sent to VOA offices around the world from officials within the State Department or from VOA administrators. The VOA reporters were directed to highlight remarks made by the president, the secretary of state, and other high-ranking U.S. government officials.[91]

In the VOA's actual news broadcasts, the Soviet Union of course served as the evil instigator of the Cold War. In a March 6, 1951, feature, this view was reinforced by an emphasis on the "existence of huge military forces behind the Iron Curtain." The broadcaster explained that in 1945 the "U. S., Britain, and the rest of the free world disarmed drastically." At this time, the United States spent only "6 percent of its national income on armaments," whereas the Soviet Union reportedly devoted some "eighteen percent of [its] national income . . . on military spending."[92]

A March 23, 1951, broadcast in a VOA series entitled *The Iron Curtain,* placed the resolution of the Cold War in the hands of the Soviet leaders. This particular newscast described the views of three American officials: Secretary of State Dean Acheson; Sen. Brien McMahon, chairman of the Congressional Atomic Energy Commission; and George Kennan, former ambassador to the Soviet Union. The broadcast closed with the following statement: "The conclusion reached by all three experts is [that] . . . the Iron Curtain is a matter of deepest concern to everyone [because] it constitutes a danger to world peace. Until it is lifted, there can be no abiding security anywhere."[93]

Other VOA broadcasts accented the dismal living conditions in the Communist regions with living standards in the West serving as the logical alternative. In a VOA series entitled *Life Behind the Iron Curtain,* individual stories were selected that exemplified life in those areas. All of the narratives opened with a description of the program's intent, which involved presenting "the happenings in the daily lives of men and women in the Soviet Union and the oppressed areas under communistic control." In Bulgaria, for instance, the VOA reported that "due to excessive Soviet demands," shortages of "fuel and firewood" existed, along with shortages of "vegetables and dairy foods particularly potatoes, cabbages, onions, butter, eggs and milk." All shortages were attributed to the "communists' distribution plans."[94] During a February 15, 1951, news feature entitled *Spotlight on Dictatorship,* VOA compared how much time a person would have to work to buy products in Romania, France, and the United States. The VOA reported that to buy a loaf of bread a Romanian would have to work three hours and thirty minutes, compared to only twenty-five minutes in France and fifteen minutes in the United States. The purpose of the report, the broadcaster declared, was to dispel the myth that dictators had "lifted living standards higher than . . . [in] capitalistic lands."[95]

Thus, because of the *Know North America* debacle and increased interagency coordination, VOA exacted tighter controls over its journalists by indoctrinating them into their propaganda system and by providing them with propaganda scripts. Such practices allowed little room for journalistic freedom. This lack of journalistic freedom evidences the increased militarization and centralization of propaganda policy by the end of the Campaign of Truth. The enhanced control under which VOA employees labored was reminiscent of military training and maneuvers. Propaganda practitioners by then had become the Truman administration's newest "soldiers," who merely followed PSB orders.

In spite of these significant changes in tone, and in spite of the increased coordination between the PSB and the State Department, a new kind of unexpected backlash appeared that questioned the propaganda program's mission once again. As Wilson P. Dizard alleges, the Soviets noticed America's more defensive propaganda posture, which they used for their own propaganda ends. For the Kremlin, America's "hysteria" over Communism actually proved Communism's political virility and democracy's fragility, further empowering the Soviets.[96] Even though the government enhanced the coordination of its propaganda strategy, political officials continued to agree that even tighter coordination was needed in order to elevate the effectiveness of its propaganda and psychological warfare planning.[97] As Walter L. Hixson claimed, "the PSB failed to achieve its 'manifest destiny' of uniting the national security bureaucracy behind a coordinated psychological warfare effort that would force the retrenchment of Soviet power."[98] By the time Dwight Eisenhower entered office, the propaganda program, while more militarized, still experienced discord over its structure and its message.

The Centralization of Propaganda Policy

Shortly after his election Eisenhower formed the President's Committee on International Information Activities (Jackson Committee) and directed that it investigate America's peacetime propaganda program. At the time of the investigation, the Eisenhower administration determined that "no publicity" should be given "to the [Jackson] Committee or its work,"[99] with the bulk of its recommendations remaining classified until the 1980s. However, it has become quite clear that the Jackson Committee played a very important role in the Eisenhower administration's entire approach to the Cold War.

Recently declassified materials on the Jackson Committee's activities help to illuminate the Eisenhower administration's deep devotion to propaganda, revealing how this presidential administration developed new strategies for undertaking the propaganda offensive against the Soviet Union. The Jackson Committee redefined America's propaganda mission, recommending a more centralized operation with the president at the helm, and calling for a more positive and empathic message as a means to improve the effectiveness of American propaganda. At the same time, the Jackson Committee and the PSB helped increase covert operations even beyond the clandestine actions of the Truman administration.

Internationally, the official channels, such as the VOA, assumed a much more positive tone and disseminated news rather than the more combative propaganda of Truman's Campaign of Truth. "Private" (covert) agencies were assigned the task of distributing the more polemical propaganda, which was driven by a stepped-up psychological planning apparatus. At bottom, the propaganda approach of the Eisenhower administration blended the journalistic and militaristic paradigms. The U.S. Information Agency (USIA), which was established by Eisenhower, essentially became a "news" organization that masked the intricate and massive covert propaganda activities that were publicly disassociated from the U.S. government. Despite the journalistic appearance of the overt channels of propaganda, the entire program assumed a militarized structure. This pyramid of propaganda operations allowed Eisenhower to serve as commander in chief of the propaganda program, with the White House functioning as the central command post. In the end, this structure served to lessen outside congressional interference and to expand presidential powers.

The Jackson Committee

As defined by Eisenhower's directive, the members of the Jackson Committee were empowered to evaluate "international information policies and activities" as they related to "international relations and the national security" of the United States.[100] Named for its chair, New York businessman and former CIA Deputy Director William Jackson, the committee began its inquiry on January 26, 1953, and issued its final report on June 1 of that same year.[101] During the six-month study, committee members interviewed 250 witnesses and advocated the abolition of Truman's PSB in favor of an Operations Coordinating Board (OCB) designed to coordinate national security policy and psychological operations.[102]

The Jackson Committee determined that the Truman administration's propaganda program still lacked centralization. Members of the committee argued, for example, that "opportunities had been missed to take the offensive in global propaganda campaigns." Many of the current and past programs, committee members believed, had been "merely defensive." Beyond that, committee members complained that "the United States [had spoken] with a multitude of voices," resulting in a "haphazard projection of too many and too diffuse propaganda themes."[103]

In order to combat these centralization problems, the Jackson Committee resolved that American propaganda needed to be refashioned. First, the committee called for more direction "from the President." The committee wanted the NSC to direct America's propaganda operations, which were to become more centralized in the White House. Beyond that, the Jackson Committee called for a decrease in the use of official propaganda channels. The committee also recommended that shortwave broadcasts be halted in some areas, and that fewer pamphlets, magazines, and films bear the government seal.[104]

The Jackson Committee members believed that tactically sound foreign policies supported by an effective propaganda machine could prove the winning combination in America's "war of words" with the Soviet Union. But in order for the program to achieve heightened effectiveness, such propaganda strategy needed greater synchronization and centralization from the White House. Eisenhower clearly agreed with the committee's assumptions and recommendations, and, in fact, began implementing them even before the USIA was officially formed.

The USIA is Formed

Like the Jackson Committee members, President Eisenhower regarded "communism as humanity's primary enemy," and thus led his administration on a "thorough and ambitious" crusade against it.[105] Following the committee's recommendations, Eisenhower's new propaganda program, the USIA, was established on August 1, 1953, as an independent agency, separate from the State Department's propaganda operations. Directed from the White House, with the commander in chief assuming more responsibility in the agency's day-to-day and long-range plans, the USIA centralized America's propaganda operations and cultivated the ethos of a "news" agency. The intent was for the USIA to disseminate "positive" material while relegating the more strident propaganda to "private" channels. Even though the aggressive psychological warfare materials would not bear the government's seal, the administration would strictly control and coordinate the entire propaganda program, demonstrating the institutionalization of a militarized propaganda structure, and thus, the expansion of presidential power.

When the USIA was established, agency officials were directed to "report to the President through the National Security Council."[106] The PSB's successor, the OCB, was set up as an arm of the NSC and functioned to insure that the plans developed by the NSC and the president were enacted rather than filed away.[107] The functions of the OCB and the NSC were established more clearly in a July 8, 1953, press release in which the administration explained that the OCB would "coordinate . . . national security policies," and would also help further what Eisenhower called the "reconstitution and revitalization of the National Security Council." The OCB's membership consisted of the "Under-Secretary of State (chair), the Deputy Secretary of Defense, the Deputy Director for Mutual Security, the Director of Central Intelligence, and a Special Assistant to the President"—an integrated constituency that reflected, in part, the design of the PSB. The president, of course, was empowered to appoint a chief executive officer of the OCB, and, in order to insure complete coordination, required the secretary of state to provide "full guidance" to the USIA director on issues of foreign policy.[108]

Eisenhower clearly supported this militarized apparatus. In a preliminary document on the reorganization of government, Eisenhower advocated that "a clear line of responsibility" be established with "adequate authority . . . for all operations, so the people will always know who is responsible for carrying out any particular job." Eisenhower also threatened to replace any administrator who "fail[ed] to perform" his grand plans.[109] With reference to foreign policy planning and particularly to wartime, Eisenhower especially wanted to insure secrecy among his executive departments like the OCB and the NSC.[110]

The structure that Eisenhower established under NSC-5412/1 2 gave his administration full license to conduct foreign policy with little congressional oversight. With NSC-5412, Eisenhower called for "the overt foreign activities of the U. S. Government" to be "supplemented by covert operations," which NSC-5412 defined as "propaganda, political action; economic warfare; preventive direct action, including sabotage, anti-sabotage, demolition; escape and evasion and evacuation measures . . . deception plans and operations." Grounded in the legislative authority of the National Security Act of 1947, NSC-5412 empowered the CIA to conduct these covert operations on instructions received from the NSC. Eisenhower also involved the OCB by making this group the "normal channel for securing coordination of support among the Departments of State and Defense and the Central Intelligence Agency."[111]

While Truman relinquished more control of such covert operations to subordinates, Eisenhower increased presidential involvement in directing such activities via the NSC. In NSC-5412 he designated a planning group to oversee such CIA-initiated operations. This secret group included presidential appointees from the Departments of State and Defense and other presidential representatives.[112] As Prados asserts, NSC-5412 awarded these "secret warriors with the broadest possible charter." While Eisenhower maintained close contact with the "5412 group," he also wanted to preserve his "'deniability' by not actually participating" in the group's activities.[113] The term *deniability* epitomized this 5412 group. Eisenhower wanted the government to "plausibly disclaim any responsibility" for such covert actions.[114]

As the Jackson Committee called for streamlining overt activities, it simultaneously elevated USIA's role in the overall stature of American foreign policy and refashioned its tone. According to an OCB "Progress Report" dated September 30, 1953, USIA's broadcasts were to "present a full exposition of the United States actions and policies." The OCB determined that while "the tone and content should be forceful and direct," a "propagandist note should be avoided." In order to cultivate the ethos of a news agency, the OCB concluded that VOA broadcasts should "consist of factual news reporting supplemented by commentaries designed to provide sober and responsible interpretations of events . . . policies . . . and actions of the United States."[115] In a letter to William Benton dated May 1, 1953, Eisenhower explained that this more "careful regard for the truth" would result in the USIA becoming more "respected and trusted throughout the world."[116]

To further its reorganization efforts, the Eisenhower administration expanded the polemical, psychological warfare materials dispersed over covert mediums just as the Jackson Committee urged. These secret operations were also highly coordinated with overt actions. Eisenhower directed that "clandestine arrangements" be made with "magazines, newspapers . . . and book publishers in some countries" to supplement official propaganda operations.[117] According to the PSB, the USIA was to attribute propaganda to the United States only when such attribution functioned as an "asset," while at the same time, utilizing more "private American organizations" for the advancement of U.S. objectives. In the end, America's propaganda program was to become the center for a "psychological warfare offensive" against the Soviet Union, involving the exploitation of available propaganda channels so as to explicate the "meaning and purposes" of presidential initiatives and objectives.[118] Such directives would be developed and orchestrated by the PSB-turned-OCB.

Overall, when the Eisenhower administration created the USIA, it centralized all propaganda and psychological warfare operations in a manner reminiscent of military operations. While granting the agency its independence from the State Department, Eisenhower assumed more control over its activities—implementing a military structure for propaganda operations. To that end, to call the USIA an independent agency is a misnomer, given the control Eisenhower exerted through groups like the OCB. This centralization process resulted in the White House's increased command over America's message, making the USIA an extended voice of the president. The administration turned the more strident propaganda, some of which permeated the airways of VOA under the Campaign of Truth, over to the covert agencies. Following the Jackson Committee's recommendation, the VOA spoke with the "authority of the United States Government," while stations like Radio Free Europe and Radio Liberty could purport "to be the voice of the freedom forces of the respective target countries."[119] All of these strategies were designed to increase the USIA's credibility abroad.

Such overt actions helped to mask covert psychological warfare activities. Most noticeably, the administration coordinated the government's overt and covert propaganda activities. Such processes involved the construction and synchronization of broad-based propaganda offensives focused around major presidential addresses that served as centerpieces of grand and ubiquitous propaganda campaigns.

Eisenhower's Peace Message

Even before Eisenhower moved into the White House, the theme of peace became central to the construction of his political ideology. As Martin J. Medhurst maintains, Eisenhower "associated [Truman] . . . with war and himself with peace" during his 1952 presidential bid. Eisenhower's conception of peace grew out of what Medhurst calls a "direct outcome of strength— military strength, economic strength, and spiritual strength."[120] Robert L. Ivie references Eisenhower's attempt to construct himself "as a benign warrior for peace who dedicated his presidency to a failed quest for détente with the Soviet Union." Ivie critiques Eisenhower's peaceful image, arguing that this misperception "severely underestimates [Eisenhower's] . . . impact as an agent of Cold War acculturation."[121]

The synchronization of Eisenhower's rhetorical strategies around a campaign of peace can also be seen in the messages that Eisenhower delivered during the first years of his presidency—messages that were promulgated by a newly restructured propaganda program. As the commander in chief of a militarized propaganda program, Eisenhower took his 1952 campaign theme and transformed it into a global propaganda campaign with both international and domestic implications. The first of these campaigns surrounded the death of Joseph Stalin and was publicly referred to as the "Chance for Peace" campaign. As recently declassified materials reveal, the Eisenhower administration actually transformed the Truman administration's strategy of containing Communism to a goal of total extinction, with Eisenhower preparing for a full-scale war against Communism if necessary. The public peace rhetoric served to mask these preparations, evidencing how propaganda texts can camouflage rhetorical motives.

Much of the scholarship surrounding Stalin's death centers on Eisenhower's April 16, 1953, Chance for Peace speech. However, the administration's attempt to gain the propaganda advantage during the Soviet exchange of power extended far beyond the few months surrounding Stalin's death. In fact, Eisenhower's political operatives used Stalin's death as the beginning point in their long-term goal of eradicating Communism. The PSB and later the USIA and the OCB developed propaganda and psychological warfare strategies toward that end, beginning as early as October, 1952, and continuing well into 1954. The Chance for Peace campaign themes were perpetuated in propaganda mediums ranging from Radio Free Europe to the USIA's domestic and international academic journal, *Problems of Communism (POC)*. Once launched, campaign organizers feared the potential success of their own campaign and thus sought to insure that any peace overtures offered by the Soviet Union would be viewed skeptically by America's Cold War allies. The activities surrounding the Chance for Peace campaign provide insight into the offensive and defensive strategizing of the newly militarized propaganda program, which crafted synchronized, long-term propaganda and psychological warfare efforts.

Even though Stalin did not die until March 5, 1953, the PSB curiously began preparing for his imminent death some five months earlier.[122] In part, the PSB sought to seize "the psychological initiative" with Stalin's death.[123] Additional hidden aims existed as well, with propagandists wanting to exacerbate the turmoil resulting from a Soviet transfer of power. As PSB staff member William J. Morgan articulated on March 4, 1953, "*Our strategic guiding principle, as well as our secret goal, should be to do everything to encourage and promote chaos within the USSR.*"[124] Moreover, George A. Morgan, the acting PSB director, claimed that such a rhetorical exigence offered an opportunity "for world leadership by the President."[125] In order to achieve the psychological advantage, to promote chaos in the Soviet Union, and to elevate Eisenhower to a supreme leadership position, the PSB called for "all information media under United States Government control, both overt and covert, [to] . . . be given standing instructions in the event of Stalin's death."[126]

As the PSB planned the Chance for Peace campaign, they simultaneously anticipated a Soviet response. Edward P. Lilly, a PSB historian and operative, feared that "Russian leaders might attribute all the difficulties to Stalin's control and as a propaganda gesture indicate even with specific action that they were willing to terminate the Korean war." In countering such a Soviet action, Lilly recommended that rather than have a senior government official denounce any "peaceful" gestures, contacts be made with "the more responsible American columnists and even editorial writers," to warn them of the "dangerous implications to American long-range policy of falling into a Soviet trap." Such contacts were to be made even before the Soviet Union implemented such a plan so as to thwart its "psychological impact."[127] To that end, Lilly viewed any Soviet response as a mere propaganda ploy—even one that eventually brought about the end of the Korean War.

The PSB planners clearly felt that Stalin's death provided a grand opportunity for the Eisenhower administration to gain a psychological advantage in democracy's battle against Communism. Charles R. Norberg, acting deputy assistant director of the PSB, asserted that the Soviet transfer of power and Eisenhower's Chance for Peace address offered "a gold mine of psychological warfare opportunities and obligations."[128] The Chance for Peace address was the president's first public pronouncement of his administration's campaign to "exploit" the changing events in the Soviet Union. Delivered before the ASNE, the Chance for Peace address dichotomized the peaceful intent of the "free world" versus the warlike behavior of the Soviet Union after World War II. Eisenhower charged that the United States sought "true peace" in the postwar years whereas the Soviet government exhibited "force: huge armies, subversion, rule of neighbor nations." In looking toward the future in light of the current Cold War tensions, Eisenhower feared either the realization of an "atomic war," or the "perpetual fear" of its occurrence.[129]

Despite the dim outlook, Eisenhower outlined his vision for achieving a worldwide "peace that [was] neither partial nor punitive." Emphasizing that the United States was "ready to assume its part," and prepared to dedicate its "strength to serve the needs, rather than the fears, of the world," the president urged the Soviet Union to take action: to sign the "Austrian treaty"; to offer an "honorable armistice in Korea"; and, most importantly, to reduce "the burden of armaments now weighing upon the world." Such measures, he stressed, provided world governments with a "precious chance to turn the black tide of events" and conform to a "firm faith that God created men to enjoy, not destroy, the fruits of the earth and their own toil."[130] Such themes set into motion a multitude of post-address propaganda activities.

Promulgating Eisenhower's Peace Message

Part of the PSB's synchronized plan involved RFE, an organization over which the Eisenhower administration exacted tight control. Prados alleges that in 1953 RFE also "introduced a technique of 'saturation broadcasting' to counter Soviet jamming."[131] This saturation can clearly be seen by the manner in which RFE perpetuated the Chance for Peace themes, portraying the United States as the seeker of genuine peace and the Soviet Union as merely providing highly questionable peace overtures. For example, RFE portrayed American peace as "total," "sincere," "complete," "true," "just," "honest," "lasting," "global," "real," and the peace of the "future," in broadcasts to Poland, Hungary, Albania, and Czechoslovakia the day of, and the day following, Eisenhower's speech.[132] By contrast, RFE attempted to arouse suspicion concerning Soviet peace claims, labeling their peace as "so-called," "false," "maneuvers," "overtures," "ambiguous," and "empty" in broadcasts to Poland, Bulgaria, Hungary and Romania.[133]

As the Eisenhower administration worked to co-opt peace for the United States, RFE helped portray America's peace as beneficial to all through a form of defector propaganda. During a broadcast to Albania on April 17, 1953, for example, the anchor identified himself as an Albanian,[134] and stressed that Eisenhower "is talking to us. . . . He has laid down . . . the terms of a peace that would . . . benefit all people."[135] In the Czechoslovakian broadcast that same day, the commentator stressed: "We Czechoslovaks, and the enslaved peoples behind the Iron Curtain can be deeply gratified by Eisenhower's statements. It puts an end to the period of containment."[136] As the PSB intended, the U.S. government's peaceful intentions were being stressed while simultaneously portraying Eisenhower as a newly emerging world leader and champion of world peace. The use of RFE also met the Jackson Committee's goals by using propaganda channels not publicly connected to the government.

The Chance for Peace campaign not only manifested international propaganda objectives but domestic ones as well. Even though the USIA was forbidden from propagandizing American citizens,[137] Congress allowed the USIA to produce and market one academic journal domestically (and internationally), entitled, *Problems of Communism (POC)*. Attempting to develop an "academic propaganda,"[138] *POC*'s editors maintained that the journal functioned "to make readily available significant background information and documentary material on the theoretical and political aspects of world communism today, with particular emphasis on the policies and aims of the Soviet Union."[139]

For a year following Eisenhower's Chance for Peace address, *POC* published various stories that perpetuated the PSB's propaganda aims. In the second 1953 issue, the editor commemorated Stalin's death and rearticulated Eisenhower's dichotomous construction of the future: "The successor regime stands at a crossroads. It can pursue the course set by the Stalin regime since World War II, continuing policies of open aggression and overt hostility toward the non-communist world. Or it can, if it chooses, embark on a new course, repudiating the attitudes and policies linked to Stalin's name and seeking a peaceful *modus vivendi* with the outside world."[140]

The four articles that followed this "editor's note" all related to "A New Chapter in Soviet History," and were connected to the Chance for Peace campaign. The first article of this series centered on "The First Steps of the New Regime," and summarized the events in the Soviet Union during the aftermath of Stalin's death. Just as the PSB proposed and RFE likewise complied, *POC* writers questioned the sincerity of Soviet peace activities after Stalin's death, asserting that "a number of contradictory elements should be noted" in the Communist's more recent "peace offensive." Along with highlighting and excerpting Eisenhower's April 16 speech, the article also questioned the Soviet Union's most recent peaceful gestures, by placing quotation marks around the word *peace* when referring to the Soviet Union's past conciliatory actions. Following Lilly's dictates closely, *POC* writers also construed the Soviet's new efforts toward peace as "completely erroneous" and urged their academic readers to "temper hope with utmost caution, keeping in mind the lessons of the past, maintaining a defensive strength, and waiting for concrete demonstration that the communist leadership is ready for a settlement of outstanding issues."[141] Such a move prevented any Soviet action in the wake of Stalin's death from being viewed as a positive step toward peace. Eisenhower's public rhetoric of détente thus covered up his administration's more hardened Cold War stance.

So concerned were America's propagandists that the Soviet's new actions might be embraced by the world community, the PSB revamped the Chance for Peace campaign beginning in May, 1953. The new tactics targeted the United Nations and its member countries. Since this part of the Chance for Peace campaign has only recently been declassified, not all of its details are fully clear. Yet from the archival documents now available, the "Lodge Project" represented the point at which PSB planners became so paranoid of Communism's wrath that its extinction became the Cold War goal of the Eisenhower administration.

The Lodge Project

In May, 1953, U.S. ambassador to the United Nations and Eisenhower adviser Henry Cabot Lodge, Jr., initiated "a strong anti-Soviet-bloc" psychological warfare campaign, supported by the PSB and designed to use the UN General Assembly for the second stage of the Chance for Peace campaign.[142] Working closely together, Lodge and C. D. Jackson sought to insure that any Soviet peace overture would be viewed as a propaganda ploy. As defined by Lodge and interpreted by the PSB, the goals of the Lodge Project would be to: "attack, minimize and ridicule the doctrinal basis of Soviet positions"[143]; to remind "the free world officially of the enduring truth concerning the world communist menace";[144] "to deflate considerably the Soviet peace offensive; to exert . . . adverse effects within the enemy camp; and to unify . . . the free world."[145] Attempting to encourage more nations to join the United States in its fight against Communism beginning in April, 1953, the UN served as a propaganda venue for the United States. The PSB declared that the UN represented the "greatest single sounding board in the world . . . a kind of global amplifier of information."[146] In the end, the Lodge Project revealed how the Eisenhower administration's public rhetoric of détente masked the PSB's more militarized language of war, which made the administration less open to peaceful resolutions to the Cold War in 1953–54.

The Lodge Project clearly became an extension of the Chance for Peace campaign, and once again, targeted Soviet vulnerabilities. Not only did PSB planners call for the perpetuation of Eisenhower's Chance for Peace address, they asked that "relevant citations" from the speech be included in the public presentations and position papers linked to what they called Project Cosmos.[147] As with the initial phases of the Chance for Peace campaign, the PSB wanted to undermine Soviet vulnerabilities through documents related to the Lodge Project. In particular, the PSB looked to gather information on Soviet vulnerabilities that would hold "'bullet proof' authenticity" for audiences so as to increase the material's "dramatic attention-getting quality."[148]

The depth of the PSB's secrecy is most noticeable in its private proclamation that peace policies were weak and ineffective. By the summer of 1953 the Eisenhower administration's shift from a policy of containing Communism to one of extinguishing it was complete, which seemingly necessitated heightened psychological warfare efforts and an enhanced nuclear buildup in preparation for what some PSB/OCB staffers believed would be a war with Communism. As the PSB articulated in July, 1953, "no good policy was ever made with either peace or compromise as its main ingredient."[149] A month later the PSB was calling for a strengthened foreign policy plan, which resulted in the "unequivocal [pronouncement] for the eventual *extinction* of world communism." When referencing this "policy of extinction," the PSB acknowledged that such a policy shift would "increase rather than diminish the likelihood of an early global shooting war." Members of the PSB justified this more strident policy-through-power shift on the grounds that "to balk at action because of an uncertain fear of precipitating war is to increase the risk of defeat in the world struggle." Realizing that such a policy transformation could create an international backlash, the PSB's plans remained hidden from the public until very recently, with the PSB determined to work toward the policy of extinction gradually through propaganda and "appropriate non-attributable actions." Determined to proceed with the Lodge Project in some form, the PSB sought to "alert the free world to the communist peril" in a more vigorous manner,[150] while keeping its ultimate motives hidden.

Given the recently declassified nature of the Lodge Project, the number of public pronouncements that were influenced by the PSB's planning is uncertain. The one public presentation that clearly reflected the strategizing of the Lodge Project though was delivered by Secretary of State John Foster Dulles during the eighth meeting of the UN General Assembly. In an address titled, "Easing International Tensions: The Role of the UN," delivered on September 17, 1953, Dulles constructed the Cold War in a manner that mirrored the prescriptions of the Lodge Project. Reflecting the enhanced threat that emanated from the PSB planners, Dulles discussed the current "disharmony" between the free world and Communist nations as "menacing" and "dangerous." Dulles alluded to the potential for nuclear holocaust, asserting that "physical scientists have now found means which . . . can wipe life off the surface of this planet." Given that potentiality, Dulles urged that the United Nations face the "universal problem of saving the human race from extinction."[151]

In portraying a historical context of fear, which pitted Communism against democracy, Dulles reminded his UN peers that the Soviets could not be trusted. In an attempt to reduce what he termed a "summarizing fact," Dulles historicized that "since 1939 some 600,000,000 people of some 15 nations have been brought into the Soviet camp of dictatorships" involuntarily. Just as the

PSB planned, Dulles inoculated his audience against Soviet peace claims, arguing that "mere words do not instantly or totally reassure us [because] we have heard them before."[152]

In order to counter this menacing Communist force, Dulles expanded on the peaceful efforts articulated by Eisenhower in the Chance for Peace address to include the entire international community. Speaking in terms of "a community defense system," "international groupings," and a "world community," Dulles attempted to harmonize neutral and satellite countries in the fight. Portraying American peace efforts as the UN's peace efforts, Dulles returned to Eisenhower's April 16 address, speaking of the necessary faith that Eisenhower stressed throughout his speech and the need for close surveillance and reduction of armaments. At bottom, Dulles called upon the UN members to "seize [the] moment" and help secure "international agreements limiting armaments."[153]

The Eisenhower administration thus worried that any Soviet actions, which might be viewed as a step toward a peaceful resolution of the Cold War, would thwart America's Cold War aims. The intricate and anticipatory strategizing that took place behind closed doors revealed that the propaganda of peace masked America's hard-line anti-Communist policies. The PSB's goals, while perceived to be militarily sound, lacked effective popular appeal. Much of these policies remained hidden from public purview while the PSB deemed that someone other than Eisenhower had to deliver the more strident speeches in order to preserve the president's peace posture. For many at least, the administration's propaganda policies achieved new levels of propaganda effectiveness.[154]

Ending in 1954 with C. D. Jackson's return to the private sector, the Lodge Project had clearly helped implement a more militarized propaganda structure. The language of war that pervaded these private discussions led to a more militarized mind-set that lessened the likelihood for peaceful solutions to the Cold War during the project's duration. As Caroline Pruden argues, "the emphasis on psychological warfare therefore may have discouraged more pacific tendencies in the Soviet Union. It [the Lodge Project] thus bears at least some responsibility for contributing to the 'lost opportunity' to improve relations between the superpowers." Beyond that, Pruden claims, the Lodge Project "undermined the UN's ability to serve as a forum for negotiation" as American "propaganda victories" alienated "the Communist bloc . . . and put off many neutral nations as well."[155] A propaganda program thus initially designed to reduce the likelihood of war now aided in heightening global tensions. The interdepartmental constituency of the PSB/OCB[156] undoubtedly influenced the move toward a stepped-up foreign policy that privately critiqued a rhetoric of peace and promoted a mentality of aggression.

Conclusion

From 1945 to 1955, the Truman and Eisenhower administrations militarized America's propaganda program. During this time, propaganda progressed from an activity directed by journalists to one commanded more by military officials. The military mind-set heavily influenced the language used to talk about the propaganda and eventually influenced the overall organization of the propaganda program. As Paul A. Chilton maintains, language "constitutes our main evidence as to the underlying belief systems that underwrite international political discourse."[157] Grounded in belief systems, metaphors become literalized over time. As Robert L. Ivie writes, "we are in the presence of literalized metaphors when we act upon the figurative as if it were real, not recognizing that two domains of meaning have been merged into one despite their differences." In examining Cold War metaphors in particular, Ivie posits that they often "illustrate the rhetorical essentials of the logic of confrontation."[158] By militarizing propaganda, this language usage clearly contextualized this communication form within a confrontation model, which influenced PSB planners to the extent that peace was no longer viewed as a viable option in the Cold War. Such cold warriors privately anticipated the extinction of Communism through psychological *and* perhaps military means.

Militarizing propaganda led to a second consequence, which involved the increased presidential control over its activities. By the end of 1953, propaganda policy was controlled from the White House through the leadership of the NSC and the OCB, which operated without congressional oversight. Such an organizational strategy offered the president increased outlets to disseminate his Cold War message. Even though Eisenhower did not voice the words articulated by the RFE, RL, VOA, *POC,* or Dulles, for example, these organizations and individuals reinforced Eisenhower's public message and served as his rhetorical surrogates. Their messages in fact were as presidentially orchestrated as the Chance for Peace address. Throughout their terms of office both Truman and Eisenhower achieved rhetorical success with Congress, the media, and international audiences through both overt and covert messages.

The study of Cold War propaganda evinces finally how orators' motives may not be discernible from public texts. To fully understand the practice of propaganda and the power of the presidency, we must broaden our study of presidential communication to include the means of production as well as the accompanying public discourse that enacts, and at times camouflages, rhetorical motives. A study that only examines public discourse can be incomplete because, as in the case of propaganda, its hallmark can be the masking of such rhetorical motives. Likewise, a study that only analyzes private strategies fails to demonstrate how such motives are publicly articulated. By combining an examination of production modes with the actual public texts, we gain a more complete understanding of how propaganda evolved in the earliest years of the Cold War.

Notes

1. Louis J. Halle, *Cold War as History* (New York: Harper Colophon, 1967), 3.

2. See Erika G. King, "Exposing the 'Age of Lies': The Propaganda Menace as Portrayed in American Magazines in the Aftermath of World War I," *Journal of American Culture* 12 (1989): 37; and Stephen Vaughn, *Holding Fast the Inner Lines: Democracy, Nationalism, and the Committee on Public Information* (Chapel Hill: University of North Carolina Press, 1980), xi–18.

3. Oren Stephens, *Facts to a Candid World: America's Overseas Information Program* (Stanford, Calif.: Stanford University Press, 1955), 18. For the purposes of this essay, propaganda is conceived of as strategically devised messages that are disseminated to masses of people by an institution for the purpose of generating action benefiting its source. The sole source of interest in this essay is the U.S. government's official and nonofficial propaganda (information) channels.

4. I am equating the term *paradigm* with perspective. Like Klaus Krippendorff, I view dialogue or discourse as foundational to any paradigm, particularly one involving the study of communication. Language thus demarks paradigmatic distinctions that work to construct reality. See Klaus Krippendorff, "On the Ethics of Constructing Communication," in *Rethinking Communication: Paradigm Issues,* ed. Brenda Dervin, Lawrence Grossberg, Barbara J. O'Keefe, and Ellen Wartella (Newbury Park, Calif.: Sage, 1989), 67–68.

5. For background information on the CPI and the criticism brought against that World War I agency, see George Creel, *How We Advertised America* (New York: Arno, 1972); Thomas A. Hollihan, "Propagandizing the Interest of War: A Rhetorical Study of the Committee on Public Information," *Southern Speech Communication Journal* 49 (1984): 241–57; J. Michael Sproule, "Propaganda Studies in American Social Science: The Rise and Fall of the Critical Paradigm," *Quarterly Journal of Speech* 73 (1987): 60–78; J. Michael Sproule, "Social Responses to Twentieth-Century Propaganda," in *Propaganda: A Pluralist Perspective,* ed. Ted J. Smith III (New York: Praeger, 1989), 5–22; J. Michael Sproule, *Propaganda and Democracy: The American Experience of Media and Mass Persuasion* (Cambridge: Cambridge University Press, 1997), 1–52; and Charles A. H. Thomson, *Overseas Information Service of the United States Government* (Washington, D.C.: Brookings Institute, 1948), 309. For background information on the Office of War Information, see J. Fred MacDonald, *Don't Touch that Dial: Radio Programming in American Life, 1920–1960* (Chicago: Nelson-Hall, 1979), 61–81; Sproule, *Propaganda and Democracy,* 178–223; and Holly Cowan Shulman, *The Voice of America: Propaganda and Democracy, 1941–1945* (Madison: University of Wisconsin Press, 1990), 13–52.

6. J. Fred MacDonald, *Television and the Red Menace: The Video Road to Vietnam* (New York: Praeger, 1985), 6–7.

7. David M. Abshire, *International Broadcasting: A New Dimension of Western Democracy* (Beverly Hills, Calif.: Sage, 1976), 26.

8. "William Benton: A Biographical Sketch," n.d., Guide to the William Benton Papers, Department of Special Collections, University of Chicago Library, 1–3.

9. William Benton, "My Overview of the Nineteen Forties," *The Times in Review: 1940–1949* (New York: Arno, 1973), n.p.

10. "Status of American International Broadcasting," *Department of State Bulletin* 15 (May 26, 1946): 900–904.

11. "Radio Advisory Committee Urges Strengthening of Voice of America," *Department of State Bulletin* 16 (May 25, 1947): 1038.

12. For more information on Harold Lasswell's work with government propaganda, see J. Michael Hogan, "George Gallup and the Rhetoric of Scientific Democracy," *Communication Monographs* 64 (1997): 161–79; Christopher Simpson, *Science of Coercion: Communication Research and Psychological Warfare, 1945–1960* (New York: Oxford University Press, 1994), 26–27, 82; and "Radio Advisory Committee Urges Strengthening of Voice of America," *Department of State Bulletin* 16 (May 25, 1947): 1038.

13. "Report of Radio Advisory Committee to the Assistant Secretary of State for Public Affairs," *Department of State Bulletin* 16 (May 25, 1947): 1041.

14. Sidney Hyman, *The Lives of William Benton* (Chicago: University of Chicago Press, 1969), 354.

15. American Society of Newspaper Editors, "Proceedings: Twenty-Fifth Anniversary Convention—ASNE," Apr., 1947, American Society of Newspaper Editors' Archives, Reston, Va., 24.

16. "Radio Advisory Committee Urges Strengthening of Voice of America," *Deparment of State Bulletin* 16 (May 25, 1947): 1038. See also William Benton to President Truman, May, 1947, Papers of Harry S. Truman, Official File, Harry S. Truman Presidential Library, Independence, Mo. (hereafter Truman Library), 1.

17. Hyman, *Lives of William Benton,* 383.

18. Transcript, William Benton Oral History Interview, 1968, by the Columbia University Oral History Collection, pages 182, 176, Columbia University.

19. Edward G. Miller, Jr., to William Benton, Sept., 1945, William Benton Papers, Box 375, Department of Special Collections, University of Chicago, 1–5.

20. M. J. McDermott, "Mechanics of and Possible Improvement in the Department's Relations with the Press," Sept., 1945, William Benton Papers, Box 375, Department of Special Collections, University of Chicago, 8.

21. Ibid., 11.

22. Miller, Jr., to Benton, 1, 4–5.

23. See *Congressional Record,* 80th Cong., 1st sess., 1947, 936–39; and Subcommittee of the House Committee on Foreign Affairs, *United States Information and Educational Exchange Act of 1947,* 80th Cong., 1st sess., 1947, 96–102.

24. Subcommittee of the House Committee on Foreign Affairs, 104.

25. Ibid., 105–25.

26. Subcommittee of the Senate Committee on Foreign Relations (hereafter SFRC), *United States Information and Educational Exchange Act of 1947,* 80th Cong., 1st sess., 1947, 48.

27. See James Aronson, *The Press and the Cold War* (New York: Monthly Review, 1970), 17; Bernard Cohen, *The Press and Foreign Policy* (Princeton, N.J.: Princeton University Press, 1963), 136; Donald O. Dewey, "America and Russia, 1939–1941: The Views of the *New York Times,*" *Journalism Quarterly* 44 (1967): 62.

28. Shawn J. Parry-Giles, "'Camouflaged' Propaganda: The Truman and Eisenhower Administrations' Covert Manipulation of the News," *Western Journal of Communication* 60 (1996): 146–67.

29. Edwin L. James, "Better Prospects Now for 'Voice of America,'" *New York Times,* Jan. 18, 1948, sec. 4, 3.

30. Marion Turner Sheehan, ed., *The World at Home: Selections from the Writings of Anne O'Hare McCormick* (New York: Knopf, 1956), x–xii.

31. "Lack of News Held Danger to Europe: Anne O'Hare McCormick Tells Teachers that Information for Decisions is Absent," *New York Times,* Mar. 12, 1947, 6.

32. "Seminar Speakers Deplore Slash in Funds for Voice of America," *New York Times,* Apr. 25, 1947, 4.

33. Russell Porter, "U. S. Called to Aid of Free Economy," *New York Times,* Apr. 18, 1947, 24.

34. In February, 1942, the U.S. government launched a shortwave radio station called the Voice of America (VOA). Launched just seventy-nine days after the Japanese attack on Pearl Harbor, VOA became the largest section of the State Department's propaganda program. Cold War propagandist Hans N. Tuch claims that the VOA "has often been called the tail that wags the USIA dog." See Laurien Alexandre, *The Voice of America: From Détente to the Reagan Doctrine* (Norwood, N.J.: Ablex, 1988), 1–13; Thomas C. Sorensen, *The Word War: The Story of American Propaganda* (New York: Harper and Row, 1968), 10; Cedric Larson, "Religious Freedom as a Theme of the Voice of America," *Journalism Quarterly* 29 (1952): 188; Julian Hale, *Radio Power: Propaganda and International Broadcasting* (Philadelphia: Temple University Press, 1975), 32.; and Hans N. Tuch, *Communicating with the World: U.S. Public Diplomacy Overseas* (New York: St. Martin's, 1990), 87.

35. Austin Stevens, "'Voice of America' Girds for Battle," *New York Times,* Aug. 11, 1948, 3.

36. "Propaganda for Freedom," *New York Times,* Aug. 16, 1948, 18.

37. Transcript, William Benton Oral History Interview, 182.

38. George Edwards argues that the "real influence of rhetoric may be on . . . journalistic coverage." See George C. Edwards III, "Presidential Rhetoric: What Difference Does it Make?," in *Beyond the Rhetorical Presidency,* ed. Martin J. Medhurst (College Station: Texas A&M University Press, 1996), 215.

39. Committee on Foreign Relations, *United States Information and Educational Exchange Act of 1948,* 80th Cong., 2d sess., 1948, 1011.

40. Subcommittee of the SFRC *Investigation of "Voice of America" and "Know North America" Series of Broadcasts,* 80th Cong., 2d sess., June 2, 1948, 89–90.

41. *Know North America—Colorado,* Feb. 5, 1948, Charles Hulten Papers, Box 15, Truman Library.

42. See ibid., and *Know North America—Texas,* Dec. 11, 1947, Charles Hulten Papers, Box 15, Truman Library.

43. *Know North America—Utah,* Feb. 2, 1948, Charles Hulten Papers, Box 15, Truman Library.

44. *Know North America—Alabama,* Dec. 18, 1947, Charles Hulten Papers, Box 15, Truman Library.

45. *Congressional Record,* 80th Cong., 2d sess., 1948, 6465.

46. Ibid., 6462–73.

47. See Subcommittee of the SFRC, *Investigation of the "Voice of America" and "Know North America" Series of Broadcasts,* 80th Cong., 2d sess., June 3, 1948, 220; and Subcommittee of the SFRC, June 2, 1948, 97–101.

48. Subcommittee of the SFRC, June 2, 1948, 117–25, 161.

49. Fitzhugh Green, *American Propaganda Abroad* (New York: Hippocrene, 1988), 24–25.

50. Subcommittee of the House Committee on Appropriations, *Departments of State, Justice, Commerce, and the Judiciary Appropriations for 1953*, 82d Cong., 2d. sess., 1952, 408.

51. Robert William Pirsein, *The Voice of America: An History of the International Broadcasting Activities of the United States Government, 1950–1962* (New York: Arno, 1979), 199.

52. On March 12, 1947, President Truman enunciated the Truman Doctrine to Congress, which offered economic aid, weapons, and military advice to Greece and Turkey as a way to combat the Communist pressure in that region. At the same time, France and Italy were experiencing significant economic problems that threatened the entire economic stability of Europe, opening the door to possible Communist infiltration. In an effort to aid Europe, Secretary of State George C. Marshall unveiled his plan during a Harvard University commencement address on June 5, 1947, at which he invited all European countries to participate in the recovery efforts. The Communists's seizure of the former Czechoslovakia in 1948 and increased Communist activity in Berlin were further cause for concern. Beyond the European exigencies, the Far East was also experiencing political and economic problems. By June, 1950, China had fallen to the Communists, the UN had committed ground troops in Korea, and the Soviet Union had successfully detonated its first atomic bomb. See Michael J. Hogan, *The Marshall Plan: America, Britain, and the Reconstruction of Western Europe, 1947–1952* (Cambridge: Cambridge University Press, 1987), 43–45; Edward Lilly, Dec., 1951, "PSB: A Short History. White House Office, National Security Council Staff Papers, 1948–1961," Psychological Strategy Board (hereafter PSB) Central Files Series, Box 6, Dwight D. Eisenhower Presidential Library, Abilene, Kans., 31–33, 45, 85–86; Martin J. Medhurst, "Truman's Rhetorical Reticence, 1945–1947: An Interpretive Essay," *Quarterly Journal of Speech* 74 (1988): 52–70; and Harry S. Truman, *Years of Trial and Hope: Memoirs by Harry S. Truman*, vol. 2 (New York: New American Library, 1956), 263–68, 339–41, 351–52, 377–80.

53. Stephen F. Knott asserts that the OSS "served as a hatchery for a score of future CIA figures." See Stephen F. Knott, *Secret and Sanctioned: Covert Operations and the American Presidency* (New York: Oxford University Press, 1996), 157. See also Lawrence C. Soley, *Radio Warfare: OSS and CIA Subversive Propaganda* (New York: Praeger, 1989), 68–69, 220–22. It is important to note that secret activities seemingly increased with the inauguration of the CIA.

54. For further analysis of NSC-4/A, see John Prados, *Presidents' Secret Wars: CIA and Pentagon Covert Operations Since World War II* (New York: Morrow, 1986), 28–29; and "A Report to the National Security Council by the Executive Secretary on Psychological Operations," NSC-4/A, Dec., 1947, Records of Organizations in the Executive Office of the President, RG 429, Truman Library, 4.

55. "A Report to the National Security Council by the Executive Secretary on Office of Special Projects," NSC-10/2, June, 1948, Records of Organizations in the Executive Office of the President, RG 429, Truman Library, 1–3.

56. Prados, *Presidents' Secret Wars*, 29.

57. See Hale, *Radio Power*, 39–40; Cord Meyer, *Facing Reality: From World Federalism to the CIA* (New York: Harper and Row, 1980), 110; and David D. Newsom, *Diplomacy and the American Democracy* (Bloomington: Indiana University Press, 1988), 184. See also Tuch, *Communicating with the World*, 16. Tuch explains that RFE and RL were blended into one radio station in 1973, received congressional funding, and were directed by the Board of International Broadcasting.

58. Joseph G. Whelan, *Radio Liberty: A Study of Its Origins, Structure, Policy, Programming, and Effectiveness* (Washington, D.C.: Congressional Research Service, Library of Congress, 1972), ii. See also Sig Mickelson, *America's Other Voice: The Story of Radio Free Europe and Radio Liberty* (New York: Praeger, 1983), 1–2; and George R. Urban, *Radio Free Europe and the Pursuit of*

Democracy: My War Within the Cold War (New Haven, Conn.: Yale University Press, 1997), 1–73.

59. See Abshire, *International Broadcasting,* 30; and Paul S. Smith, *On Political Warfare* (Washington, D.C.: National Defense, 1989), 198.

60. Martin J. Medhurst, "Eisenhower and the Crusade for Freedom: The Rhetorical Origins of a Cold War Campaign," *Presidential Studies Quarterly* 27 (1997): 652.

61. See Prados, *Presidents' Secret Wars,* 83–84. The NSC believed such actions were warranted because a "war will be forced upon the United States by the USSR or its Satellites." See "A Report to the National Security Council by the Undersecretary of State on A Plan for National Psychological Warfare," NSC-74, July, 1950, 1; and "A Report to the National Security Council by the Undersecretary of State on the Foreign Information Program and Psychological Warfare Planning," Dec., 1949, 1–4; both in Records of Organizations in the Executive Office of the President, RG 429, Truman Library.

62. Lilly, "PSB: A Short History," 4.

63. "Report to the National Security Council . . . on A Plan for National Psychological Warfare," 2.

64. PSB File, Jan., 1953, White House Central Files, 1953–1961, Confidential File, Box 61, Eisenhower Library, 6.

65. For secondary accounts concerning the activities of the PSB and psychological warfare strategies, see Stephen E. Pease, *Psywar: Psychological Warfare in Korea, 1950–1953* (Harrisburg, Pa.: Stackpole, 1992), 16–18; Prados, *Presidents' Secret Wars,* 84–86; Simpson, *Science of Coercion,* 75. See also, Psychological Strategy Board Minutes (Aug., 1951), White House Office, NSC Staff: Papers, 1948–1961, NSC Registry Series, 1947–1962, Box 17, Dwight D. Eisenhower Presidential Library, 5. The PSB was also directed to coordinate "psychological strategy" with "all activity in the Government" related to its practice.

66. Lilly, "PSB: A Short History," 4.

67. Gordon Gray, Report to the President, Feb., 1952, Gordon Gray Papers, 1946–1976, Box 3, Eisenhower Library, 6–7. For the organization and personnel structure of the NSC, the PSB, the Department of Defense, the Department of State, and the CIA, see William E. Daugherty, "Post–World War II Developments," in *A Psychological Warfare Casebook,* ed. William E. Daugherty and Morris Janowitz (Baltimore: Johns Hopkins University Press, 1958), 143; and Michael McClintock, *Instruments of Statecraft: U.S. Guerrilla Warfare, Counter-insurgency, and Counter-terrorism, 1945–1990* (New York: Pantheon, 1992), 35–39.

68. "Handbook on Psychological Strategy Board Functions and Procedures," Feb., 1953, White House Office, NSC Staff: Papers, 1948–1961, PSB Central Files Series, Box 23, Eisenhower Library, 6.

69. PSB Minutes, July, 1951, White House Office, NSC Staff: Papers, 1948–1962, Box 17, Eisenhower Library, 2.

70. Prados, *Presidents' Secret Wars,* 86.

71. C. D. Jackson to Crusaders, May, 1951, William Benton Papers, Box 7, Department of Special Collections, University of Chicago, 2.

72. Draft of Statement for PSB Meeting, n.d., Gordon Gray Papers, 1946–1976, Box 3, Eisenhower Library, 1. Emphasis added.

73. PSB File, Jan., 1953, White House Central Files, 1953–1961, Confidential File, Box 61, Eisenhower Library, 8.

74. Charles A. Thomson and Walter H. C. Laves, *Cultural Relations and U.S. Foreign Policy* (Bloomington: Indiana University Press, 1963), 80.

75. See Edward W. Barrett, *Truth Is Our Weapon* (New York: Funk and Wagnalls, 1953), 73; Sorensen, *Word War,* 26; and Senate Committee on Appropriations, *Supplemental Appropriations for 1951,* 81st Cong., 2d sess., 1950, 308.

76. Harry S. Truman, "Going Forward with a Campaign of Truth," *Department of State Bulletin* 22 (May 1, 1950): 669–72.

77. Subcommittee for the House Committee on Appropriations, *Department of State Appropriations for 1952,* 82d Cong., 1st sess., 1951, 747–57, 761–62.

78. See Subcommittee of the Senate Committee on Appropriations, *Departments of State, Justice, Commerce and the Judiciary Appropriations for 1953,* 82d Cong., 2d sess., 1952, 1084; Subcommittee of the SFRC, *Expanded International Information and Education Program,* 81st Cong., 2d sess., 1950, S. Rept., 243, 39; Subcommittee of the House Committee on Appropriations, *The Supplemental Appropriation Bill for 1951,* 3; and Senate Committee on Appropriations, *Supplemental Appropriations for 1951,* 316.

79. See *Congressional Record,* 81st Cong., 2d sess., 1950, 8624, A6730; *Congressional Record,* 82d Cong., 1st sess., 1951, 8774, 8954, 10619, 10631, 10639–40, 10646, 10649; *Congressional Record,* 82d Cong., 2d sess., 1952, 3527; Edward W. Barrett, "USIE Capitalizes on Soviet Propaganda Blunders," *Department of State Bulletin* 23 (Sept. 11, 1950): 414; Edward W. Barrett, "The Turn of the Tide," *Department of State Bulletin* 24 (Feb. 26, 1951): 354; John M. Begg, "The American Idea: Package It for Export," *Department of State Bulletin* 24 (Mar. 21, 1951): 409; Thurman L. Barnard, "Truth Propaganda and the U.S. Information Program, *Department of State Bulletin* 25 (Nov. 26, 1951): 853; Wilson Compton, "An Organization for International Information," *Department of State Bulletin* 26 (Mar. 26, 1952): 444; Wilson Compton, "Mutual Security Requires Mutual Understanding," *Department of State Bulletin* 26 (Apr. 28, 1952): 670; Wilson Compton, "The Voice of America at the Water's Edge," *Department of State Bulletin* 26 (June 2, 1952): 865; Wilson Compton, "Crusade of Ideas," *Department of State Bulletin* 27 (Sept. 8, 1952): 345; and Wilson Compton, "Paving a Road to Peace," *Department of State Bulletin* 27 (Oct. 20, 1952): 604.

80. See Subcommittee of the SFRC, 1950, 141; Edward W. Barrett, "U. S. Informational Aims in the Cold War," *Department of State Bulletin* 22 (June 19, 1950): 992, 995; Begg, "American Idea," 410; and Wilson Compton, "An Organization for International Information," *Department of State Bulletin* 26 (Mar. 24, 1952): 444.

81. Edward W. Barrett, "Expanding Techniques for a Truth Strategy," *Department of State Bulletin* 23 (Dec. 11, 1950): 946.

82. Edward W. Barrett, "Mobilization of American Strength for World Security," *Department of State Bulletin* 23 (Nov. 6, 1950): 736.

83. See Subcommittee of the SFRC, 1950, 28; *Congressional Record,* 1950, 9914, A6730.

84. See *Congressional Record,* 1950, 9908; and *Congressional Record,* 1951, 7294, 8954.

85. Subcommittee of the House Committee on Appropriations, *The Supplemental Appropriation Bill for 1951,* 26.

86. See Barrett, *Truth Is Our Weapon,* 82–85; Pirsein, *Voice of America,* 209, 224, 227; and Ronald I. Rubin, *The Objectives of the U.S. Information Agency: Controversies and Analysis* (New York: Praeger, 1966), 113.

87. Stephens, *Facts to a Candid World,* 132–35.

88. See Peter B. Clark, "The Opinion Machine: Intellectuals, the Mass Media, and American Government," in *The Mass Media and Modern Democracy,* ed. Harry M. Clor (Chicago: Rand McNally, 1974), 38, 57–58; John Corry, *TV News and the Dominant Culture* (Washington, D.C.: Media Institute, 1986), 1; Herbert J. Gans, *Deciding What's News* (New York: Vintage, 1979), 41–42; Roderick P. Hart, *The Sound of Leadership: Presidential Communication in the Modern Age* (Chi-

cago: University of Chicago Press, 1987), 121; William A. Henry III, "News as Entertainment: The Search for Dramatic Unity," in *What's News: The Media in American Society,* ed. Elie Abel (San Francisco: Institute for Contemporary Studies, 1981), 153; and Gaye Tuchman, "Objectivity as Strategic Ritual: An Examination of Newsmen's Notions of Objectivity," *American Journal of Sociology* 77 (1972): 676.

89. SFRC and the House Committee on Foreign Affairs, *The Voice of America,* 82d Cong., 1st sess., 1951, 13–15. Emphasis added.

90. Ibid., 9–10.

91. "General Policy Considerations for Initial Russian Broadcasts," n.d., Charles Thayer Papers, Box 5, Truman Library.

92. "Causes of International Tension: Armaments of the Paris Meeting," Mar. 6, 1951, Charles Hulten Papers, Box 18, Truman Library.

93. *The Iron Curtain,* Mar. 23, 1951, Charles Hulton Papers, Box 18, Truman Library.

94. *Life Behind the Curtain*—no. 44, Dec. 28, 1950, Charles Hulton Papers, Box 18, Truman Library.

95. *Spotlight on Dictatorship,* Feb. 15, 1951, Charles Hulton Papers, Box 18, Truman Library.

96. Wilson P. Dizard, *The Strategy of Truth: The Story of the U.S. Information Service* (Washington, D.C.: Public Affairs, 1961), 43.

97. Robert E. Elder, *The Information Machine: The United States Information Agency and American Foreign Policy* (Syracuse, N.Y.: Syracuse University Press, 1968), 37. Elder argues that the PSB "apparatus had little influence upon actions."

98. Walter L. Hixson, *Parting the Curtain: Propaganda, Culture, and the Cold War, 1945–1961* (New York: St. Martin's Griffin, 1998), 18–19.

99. "Appraisal Survey of Our Cold War Effort," Nov. 26, 1952, U.S. President's Committee on International Information Activities (Jackson Committee): Records, 1950–1953, Box 1, Eisenhower Library.

100. Dwight D. Eisenhower to James S. Lay, Jr., Jan. 24, 1953, U.S. President's Committee on International Information Activities (Jackson Committee): Records, 1950–1953, Box 1, Eisenhower Library.

101. The other members of the Jackson Committee were C. D. Jackson, Eisenhower's special assistant; Gordon Gray, former army secretary; John C. Hughes, National Committee for a Free Europe; Sigurd Larmon, president of Young and Rubican; Robert Cutler, special assistant to the President for National Security Affairs; Berklie McKee Henry, director of corporations and institutions; Roger M. Keyes, undersecretary of defense; and Abbott Washburn, the committee's executive secretary. See Pirsein, *Voice of America,* 318–19; and Prados, *Presidents' Secret Wars,* 84.

102. See "List of Jackson Committee Witnesses," n.d., U.S. President's Committee on International Information Activities (Jackson Committee): Records, 1950–1953, Box 11, Eisenhower Library; See also "Tentative List of Witnesses and/or Interviews," n.d., U.S. President's Committee on International Information Activities (Jackson Committee): Records, 1950–1953, Box 11, Eisenhower Library, 1–10; and John W. Henderson, *The United States Information Agency* (New York: Praeger, 1969), 51.

103. The President's Committee on International Information Activities, "Report to the President," June 30, 1953 (hereafter Jackson Committee Report), U.S. President's Committee on International Information Activities (Jackson Committee): Records, 1950–1953, Box 14, Eisenhower Library, 56–60.

104. Ibid., 58, 68, 71, 73, 99, 106.

105. Blanche Wiesen Cook, *The Declassified Eisenhower: A Divided Legacy* (Garden City, N.Y.: Doubleday, 1981), vi, xxi.

106. James C. Hagerty, Press Release, June, 1953, White House Central Files, 1953–1961, Official File, Box 461, Eisenhower Library, 3.

107. Fred I. Greenstein, *The Hidden-Hand Presidency* (New York: Basic Books, 1982), 133.

108. James C. Hagerty, Press Release, July, 1953, U.S. President's Committee on International Information Activities (Jackson Committee): Records, 1950–1953, Box 52, Eisenhower Library, 2–3; and Hagerty, June, 1953, 3.

109. Dwight D. Eisenhower, Draft of Reorganization Plans, Mar., 1953, White House Central Files, 1953–1961, Official File, Box 460, Eisenhower Library, 1–2. See also NSC Meeting, July, 1953, Papers as President of the United States, 1953–1961, Ann Whitman File, NSC Series, Box 4, Eisenhower Library, 17.

110. NSC Meeting, July, 1953, Papers as President of the United States, 1953–1961, Ann Whitman File, NSC Series, Box 4, Eisenhower Library, 17.

111. NSC-5412, Mar., 1954, NSC Directive on Covert Operations, White House Office, Office of Special Assistant for National Security Affairs: Records, 1952–1961, NSC Series, Policy Papers Subseries, Box 10, Eisenhower Library, 1–3. See also NSC-5412/1, Mar., 1955, 1–3; and NSC-5412/2, Dec., 1955, 1–3; both in White House Office of Special Subseries for National Security Affairs: Presidential Subseries, Box 2, Eisenhower Library.

112. See Christopher Andrew, *For the President's Eyes Only: Secret Intelligence and the American Presidency from Washington to Bush* (New York: HarperCollins, 1994), 3–4; McClintock, *Instruments of Statecraft,* 137, 161; and NSC-5412/2, 3.

113. Prados, *Presidents' Secret Wars,* 112.

114. NSC-5412/2, 2.

115. "Progress Report to the National Security Council on Implementation of the Recommendations of the Jackson Committee Report," Sept. 30, 1953, White House Central Files, 1953–1961, PSB File, Box 22, Eisenhower Library, 8, Annex A, 1.

116. Dwight Eisenhower to William Benton, May, 1953, D. D. E. Diary Series, Box 3, Eisenhower Library, 1–2.

117. Ibid.

118. "Proposed Plan for a Psychological Warfare Offensive," n.d., PSB, White House Office: NSC Staff: Papers, 1948–1961, NSC Series, Box 9, Eisenhower Library, 1–3, 5.

119. Jackson Committee Report, 36.

120. Martin J. Medhurst, *Dwight D. Eisenhower: Strategic Communicator* (Westport, Conn.: Greenwood, 1993), 30, 86.

121. Robert L. Ivie, "Eisenhower as Cold Warrior," in *Eisenhower's War of Words: Rhetoric and Leadership,* ed. Martin J. Medhurst (East Lansing: Michigan State University Press, 1994), 7.

122. PSB Minutes, Oct., 1952, White House Office, NSC Staff: Papers, 1948–1961, NSC Registry Series, 1947–1962, Box 17, Eisenhower Library, 2.

123. "Working Draft," Jan., 1953, White House Office, NSC Staff: Papers, 1953–1961, PSB Central Files Series, Box 8, Eisenhower Library, 1–2.

124. William J. Morgan to Dr. H. S. Craig, Mar., 1953, White House Office, NSC Staff: Papers, 1953–1961, PSB Central Files Series, Box 8, Eisenhower Library, 1. Emphasis in original.

125. George A. Morgan, Memorandum for the PSB, Mar., 1953, White House Office, NSC Staff: Papers, 1953–1961, PSB Central Files Series, Box 8, Eisenhower Library, 1.

126. "Working Draft," 1.

127. Edward P. Lilly, Memo to George A. Morgan, Mar., 1953, White House Office, NSC Staff: Papers, 1953–1961, PSB Central Files Series, Box 8, Eisenhower Library, 1–2.

128. Charles R. Norberg to Paul B. Comstock, Apr., 1953, White House Office, NSC Staff: Papers, 1953–1961, PSB Central Files Series, Box 8, Eisenhower Library, 1.

129. Dwight D. Eisenhower, "Address 'The Chance for Peace' Delivered Before the American Society of Newspaper Editors," in *Public Papers of the Presidents of the United States, 1953* (Washington, D.C.: GPO, 1960), 179–82. For further analysis of the "Chance for Peace" address, see Robert L. Ivie, "Dwight D. Eisenhower's 'Chance for Peace': Quest or Crusade?" *Rhetoric and Public Affairs* 1 (1998): 227–43.

130. Eisenhower, "Chance for Peace," 183–88.

131. Prados, *Presidents' Secret Wars,* 123, 126.

132. See "Sunday Talk," no. 51, Radio Free Europe—Poland, Apr., 1953; Radio Free Hungary, n.d.; "Eisenhower's Speech," Radio Free Europe—Albania Desk, Apr., 1953; "Our New York Correspondent Reports," Radio Free Europe—Czechoslovak Desk, Apr., 1953, 1–4; and "International Commentary," Radio Free Europe—Poland, Apr., 1953, 1–8; all in White House Office, NSC Staff: Papers, 1953–1961, PSB Central Files Series, Box 8, Eisenhower Library.

133. See "International Commentary," Radio Free Europe—Poland; "Special Commentary on the Occasion of President Eisenhower's Speech," Radio Free Europe—Bulgaria, Apr., 1953; Radio Free Europe—Hungary; and "Daily Commentary," Radio Free Europe—Romania, Apr., 1953; all in White House Office, NSC Staff: Papers, 1953–1961, PSB Central Files Series, Box 8, Eisenhower Library.

134. See Meyer, *Facing Reality,* 120; and Paul A. Smith, Jr., *On Political War* (Washington, D.C.: National Defense University Press, 1989), 199. Meyer and Smith discuss RFE's practice of recruiting exiled indigenous news personnel.

135. "Eisenhower's Speech," Radio Free Europe—Albania, 6–8.

136. "International Commentary," Radio Free Europe—Czechoslovakia, 4.

137. Gil Cranberg, "Propaganda and the United States," *Etc.* 41 (1984): 184–86.

138. Tuch, *Communicating with the World,* 24, 61. Tuch also explains that the U.S. Congress allowed one other periodical to be published by the USIA and marketed in the United States. This second periodical is entitled *English Teaching Forum* and is targeted to English teachers.

139. Editorial Statement, *Problems of Communism* 3 (1954): i.

140. "A New Chapter in Soviet History," *Problems of Communism* 2 (1953): 1.

141. "The First Steps of the New Regime," *Problems of Communism* 2 (1953): 1–5.

142. Wallace Irwin, Jr., Memorandum to George A. Morgan, May, 1953, White House Office, NSC Staff: Papers, 1953–1961, PSB Central Files Series, Box 23, Eisenhower Library, 1–2. For information on the relationship between Eisenhower and Lodge, see Caroline Pruden, *Conditional Partners: Eisenhower, the United Nations, and the Search for a Permanent Peace* (Baton Rouge: Louisiana State University Press, 1998), 5–9.

143. "Lodge Project Within the United Nations," n.d., White House Office, NSC Staff: Papers, 1953–1961, PSB Central Files Series, Box 23, Eisenhower Library, 1.

144. "The Lodge Project and the World Conflict: Notes for a General Policy Approach," Aug., 1953, White House Office, NSC Staff: Papers, 1953–1961, PSB Central Files Series, Box 24, Eisenhower Library, 1.

145. "Notes for a General Policy Approach to the Lodge Project," July, 1953, White House Office, NSC Staff: Papers, 1953–1961, PSB Central Files Series, Box 23, Eisenhower Library, 2–3.

146. "Notes on Ambassador Lodge's Meeting with Contributors to GA Project," Aug., 1953,

White House Office, NSC Staff: Papers, 1953–1961, PSB Central Files Series, Box 23, Eisenhower Library, 2–3.

147. See Cosmos, July, 1953, Annex A, 1; and Wallace Irwin, Jr., Memorandum to George A. Morgan, Sept. 1, 1953, 1; both in White House Office, NSC Staff: Papers, 1953–1961, PSB Central Files Series, Box 24, Eisenhower Library.

148. Irwin to Morgan, Sept. 1, 1953, 5.

149. "Notes for a General Policy Approach to the Lodge Project," 14–15.

150. "The Lodge Project and the World Conflict," 1, 23, Annex A. Emphasis in original.

151. John Foster Dulles, "Easing International Tensions: The Role of the U.N.," *Department of State Bulletin* 29 (Sept., 1953): 403–404. The same speech was titled "Harmonizing the Actions of Nations: Major Causes of Present Tension," in *Vital Speeches of the Day.* This version of the speech also contains content variations from the one included in the *Department of State Bulletin.* See John Foster Dulles, "Harmonizing the Actions of Nations: Major Causes of Present Tension," *Vital Speeches of the Day* 19 (1953): 748–51. I examine and cite the *Department of State Bulletin* text.

152. Dulles, "Easing International Tensions," 403–406.

153. Ibid., 403, 407–408.

154. Several scholars point to the effectiveness of the Eisenhower administration's propaganda program, including Robert E. Elder, who argued that the interagency coordinating bodies of the NSC and the OCB improved under Eisenhower, allowing for greater coordination between propaganda strategy and foreign policy. Blanche Wiesen Cook argues that the "Chance For Peace" campaign represented the "top side of political warfare," labeling his speech "stunning." The Eisenhower administration likewise appeared pleased with its own propaganda accomplishments, as the report by the President's Committee on Information Activities, commonly referred to as the Sprague Committee, asserted in 1960 that Eisenhower's peace campaigns "contributed greatly to the positive image of the United States as a peace-seeking nation." See Elder, *Information Machine,* 40; Cook, *Declassified Eisenhower,* 180–81; and President's Committee on Information Activities Abroad, "Conclusions and Recommendations," Dec., 1960, Ann Whitman File—Administrative Series, Box 33, Eisenhower Library, 21–22.

155. Pruden, *Conditional Partners,* 85.

156. "Operations Coordinating Board Established by the President," *Department of State Bulletin* 29 (1953): 420–21. The PSB became the OCB in September, 1953.

157. Paul A. Chilton, "The Meaning of Security," in *Post-Realism: The Rhetorical Turn in International Relations,* ed. Francis A. Beer and Robert Hariman (East Lansing: Michigan State Unversity Press, 1996), 195.

158. Robert L. Ivie, "Cold War Motives and the Rhetorical Metaphor: A Framework of Criticism," in *Cold War Rhetoric: Strategy, Metaphor, and Ideology,* by Martin J. Medhurst, Robert L. Ivie, Philip Wander, and Robert L. Scott (East Lansing: Michigan State University Press, 1997), 72.

CHAPTER FIVE

The Science of Cold War Strategy

Propaganda and Public Opinion in the Eisenhower Administration's "War of Words"

J. MICHAEL HOGAN

We have sent our forces into this new type of warfare armed only with pea shooters and B.B. guns.

—George Gallup

In 1952 the Senate Foreign Relations Committee established a special subcommittee, chaired by Sen. Bourke Hickenlooper of Iowa, to investigate and recommend improvements in America's overseas information programs. Conducting two days of preliminary hearings in November, 1952, and more extensive hearings the following year, the Hickenlooper Committee drew its authority from Senate Resolution 74 of the Eighty-second Congress, which called for "a full and complete study" of existing "foreign information programs" and for "the prompt development of techniques, methods, and programs for greatly expanded and far more effective operations in this vital area of foreign policy." The Senate's urgency was palpable. "Whereas the first weapon of aggression by the Kremlin is propaganda designed to subvert, to confuse and to divide the free world, and to inflame the Russian and satellite peoples with hatred for our free institutions," the resolution proclaimed that the "security of the free world" now rested on "not only military and economic strength but a psychological offensive in behalf of our democratic principles and aspirations." During the 1952 campaign Eisenhower had called "for a great expansion in our campaign of truth," the resolution noted, and the Senate resolved to support the president-elect in making "the international propagation of the democratic creed" an "instrument of supreme national policy."[1]

In fulfilling its mandate, the Hickenlooper Committee solicited statements and testimony from seventy witnesses, including administrators of the existing information programs, public relations and advertising specialists, executives from the broadcasting and entertainment industries, educators, and journalists. Of all the witnesses, however, George Horace Gallup, popularly known as the "father" of modern polling, perhaps best reflected the spirit of S.R. 74 itself. Testifying before the Hickenlooper Committee on April 1, 1953, Gallup warned that the United States was badly "losing" the "most important struggle in the world today"—the "struggle to win the minds of men"—and he called for enormous increases in expenditures on propaganda. The Soviet Union, Gallup declared, was "15 to 20 years ahead of us in knowledge of propaganda and in skill in using it," and it would take something on the order of *five billion dollars*—about *fifty times* the amount then being spent on overseas information—to catch up.[2]

For nearly three years prior to his appearance before the Hickenlooper Committee, Gallup had been sounding similar warnings in speeches before influential groups of lobbyists and corporate leaders, as well as in articles in popular periodicals. Yet in both those statements and in his testimony before Congress, Gallup also spoke optimistically of ultimate victory. Even as he claimed that the Soviets were "15 to 20 years ahead" in their ability to use propaganda, he observed that the United States was "10 to 20 years ahead of the Russians" in "the development of research techniques." The United States, he argued, now had "the methods or tools" to "build a program of ideological warfare" that could "equal or excel, in effectiveness, that of Russia."[3] How could the United States both be "losing" the Cold War and be ten to twenty years ahead in "new" methods and procedures? What new methods and procedures did Gallup have in mind? What, in short, were the "weapons" needed to win the Cold War? The answer did not require more tanks nor even more atomic bombs, but rather the new communication sciences: advertising, public relations, and, of course, public opinion polling.

Gallup spoke with the credibility of perhaps the best-known social scientist in America, and the incoming Eisenhower administration listened to Gallup and like-minded social scientists. Radically changing the mission and the character of American propaganda, Eisenhower and his propaganda advisers brought a whole new attitude toward propaganda to the White House. Moreover, they changed the information program in ways that shaped the character and direction of the Cold War for years to come.

I begin my analysis with a brief history of propaganda in the twentieth century. In the process, I suggest how domestic political factors, as well as scholarly and popular understandings of the term "propaganda" itself, constrained both the scope and the character of American propaganda programs prior to the Cold War by relegating them to the status of a "necessary evil" in wartime. Next, I review George Gallup's critique of the prevailing conceptions of propaganda and his campaign for taking the offensive in the Cold War. As we shall see, Gallup was indeed pessimistic about the course of the early Cold War. Yet he was equally confident of ultimate victory, assuming that Americans could be "educated" about the nature of the Cold War and the methods and techniques available for fighting it. Finally, I illustrate how many of the basic ideas Gallup articulated in his campaign were reflected in the Eisenhower administration's transformation of the American propaganda program in 1953. Focusing on the recommendations of the so-called Jackson Committee, a committee appointed by Eisenhower to reassess the propaganda program, I show how the committee aspired to a more "scientific" approach to propaganda. In the end, however, Eisenhower personally called off the first major campaign based on the Jackson Committee report, dubbed Operation Candor, as overly pessimistic and frightening. Sensing that scaring the public would not work, Eisenhower ordered work to begin on his more hopeful alternative: "Atoms for Peace."

Politics, Propaganda, and the New Communication Sciences

The popular connotations of the word *propaganda* historically have been shaped by its practical applications: the causes it has served, the backgrounds and areas of expertise of its practitioners, and its perceived results. So too have scholarly conceptions of propaganda been shaped by political and pragmatic concerns. J. Michael Sproule contends that a "paradigm shift" took place in the academic study of propaganda between the late 1930s and early 1950s during which critical, humanistic studies of propaganda (under the rubric of "propaganda analysis") gave way to a new paradigm of "communication research" committed to studying "social influence in truly scientific terms." Sproule says that this new paradigm did not emerge out of an epistemological debate among scholars. Rather, it was shaped by a combination of political factors, some within the academy, others on a larger political stage.[4]

In the twentieth century, the defining moments in the history of propaganda—the moments that most significantly shaped both popular and scholarly understandings of the term itself—were, of course, the two world wars. With the term *propaganda* entering the "general public lexicon" in sensational exposés of German plots to influence American public opinion prior to World War I, the term came to be understood popularly as "dishonest communication orchestrated in underhanded campaigns by a foreign enemy."[5] Not surprisingly, Woodrow Wilson shunned the label as he established the government's first official propaganda agency: the Committee on Public Information

(CPI). Yet the CPI only further delegitimized propaganda by overzealously selling World War I both at home and abroad.

Headed by progressive journalist George Creel, the CPI had three major functions: to weaken the enemy, to influence positively the perceptions of allies and neutrals, and to motivate the American people themselves to support the war. Overseas, the Creel Committee deployed field agents, wireless cable, news and photographic releases, posters and broadsides, and displays at overseas American retail outlets to influence allies and neutrals. To reach German citizens and soldiers, the CPI dropped propaganda leaflets by airplane and balloon and even blasted them out of cannon.[6] At home, meanwhile, the Creel Committee's "all-pervasive system of communication" included press handouts, editorial cartoons, posters, school curricula, exhibits and war expositions, "Americanization Committees," and seventy-five-thousand traveling speakers known as the "Four-Minute Men." The CPI "eschewed the heavy-handed press censorship characteristic of the European belligerents," as Sproule has noted.[7] Yet "under Creel's ministrations," the war "pervasively enveloped American citizens at every venue in their personal lives."[8]

Criticism of the Creel Committee first emerged in Congress, where Republicans accused Creel of promoting Wilson more than the national interest. In 1919 the critics prevailed and Congress cut off the CPI's funding. The agency "disappeared without a trace."[9] Subsequently, revisionist thinking about the origins of the war (including exposés of British and French propaganda), along with disappointment over the Versailles treaty, led to further disillusionment with the CPI. In a sense, as Scott Cutlip has suggested, the CPI had been victimized by its own success. It had so raised expectations of "a world made safe for democracy" that postwar disillusionment with the Versailles treaty not only discredited the CPI, it led to the further "corrosion of the word *propaganda*" itself, reinforcing its connotations as a "derogatory, pejorative term."[10]

With the Creel Committee as their chief example, it comes as little surprise that the first generation of propaganda scholars reinforced the term's negative connotations. Under the rubric of "propaganda analysis," scholars inspired by the writings of John Dewey and Walter Lippmann painted a portrait of an agency that had "hoodwinked" the American people "by confidently transforming wishful thinking, ignorance, and half-truths into a self-serving dogma designed to fuel the Wilson Administration's war policies."[11] Institutionalized in the Institute for Propaganda Analysis (IPA) in the 1930s and 1940s,[12] this attitude arose out of a fundamental ideological question that would constrain American propaganda efforts during World War II and into the Cold War: How could the democratic commitment to a free "marketplace of ideas" be reconciled with state-sponsored propaganda, especially propaganda directed at the American public itself? For the reform-minded progressives at the IPA, the answer was clear: propaganda was antidemocratic and citizens needed to be "educated" to recognize and resist it.[13]

The approach of World War II brought an ideological backlash against "propaganda analysis." Suspicious of progressive, reform-minded exposés of propaganda, critics began attacking such studies in the late 1930s as "socially damaging, even unpatriotic."[14] In 1941 the House Committee on Un-American Activities investigated the IPA itself, and upon America's entry into World War II the notion that Americans ought to be "educated" to be critical consumers of *all* propaganda—including, of course, their own government's—ran counter to efforts to mobilize for war. Nevertheless, propaganda continued to be seen as, at best, a necessary wartime evil. Roosevelt, like Wilson, thus settled on a more benign label for his wartime propaganda agency: the Office of War Information (OWI). Still, the OWI, like the CPI, was dismantled when the war ended.[15]

The Cold War posed a serious dilemma for American policy makers. By definition a "war of words," the Cold War seemed to demand a propaganda response, yet policy makers remained constrained by the fact that the United States remained technically at peace. For advocates of anti-Communist propaganda, the solution to this dilemma was to "literalize" the Cold War metaphor—to convince Americans that a "war of words" was no less a *real* war than one fought with bullets and bombs. This they managed to do, as Shawn Parry-Giles has suggested, by "constructing a new portrait of the Soviet Union in the wake of World War II," a portrait emphasizing its human rights abuses, its atheism, and its imperialistic aims.[16] This portrait helped win congressional approval of a bill establishing the first permanent, peacetime propaganda program in U.S. history: the Smith-Mundt Act.

Reflecting continuing uneasiness over a democratic society engaging in peacetime propaganda operations, the Smith-Mundt Act authorized an information program designed only to "promote a better understanding of the United States in other countries"—openly and with "truthful information." Furthermore, it explicitly prohibited propaganda agencies from targeting the American people themselves. The result was a program reflecting what Parry-Giles has called a "naive" approach to propaganda—a program that merely showcased the American way of life in foreign countries. If foreign peoples only knew the truth about life in a democracy, the bill's supporters assumed, they would "naturally" embrace it.[17]

The seemingly inexplicable string of Communist advances between the end of World War II and Dwight Eisenhower's election in 1952 undermined this "naive" conception of propaganda. In short order, America's wartime ally enslaved Eastern Europe, rejected the Marshall Plan, blockaded Berlin, and developed, by 1949, its own atomic bomb. Then came the Alger Hiss case, the "loss" of China, and Joseph McCarthy railing against the "known Communists" in the State Department. Then, as if to confirm McCarthy's charge that Communists were "working and shaping the policy of the State Department," North Korean troops equipped with Soviet-made weapons poured south across the 38th parallel in June, 1950. With the Cold War turning hot on the Korean peninsula, it finally became clear to American propaganda strategists that celebrating the American way of life was not enough. Indeed, as John Henderson has written, such rhetoric appeared only "to fuel envy, jealousy, and resentment in underdeveloped countries."[18]

Already under pressure for being weak on Communism, Truman had little choice but to respond forcefully, not only militarily in Korea but on the propaganda front as well. Hence, the Truman administration launched a new, more hard-hitting propaganda campaign, "the Campaign of Truth." Focused less on democracy and more on the evils of Communism, American propaganda now assumed a much more combative, even "hysterical" tone, as Parry-Giles has argued, portraying Communism as a "living creature" spreading out of control and feeding on the flesh and blood of the people.[19] However, this approach also failed—indeed, it backfired—as it "scandalized a good many foreigners" accustomed to the more positive themes of earlier American propaganda. Communist propagandists even offered such messages as evidence of American "hysteria" and "immaturity."[20] In a sense, the Campaign of Truth was no less "naive" about how propaganda works than earlier efforts to showcase America. It too reflected American perceptions and values—the increasingly perfervid fears of America in the McCarthy era—rather than those of the target audiences.

The failure of both the "naive" and "hysterical" approaches to American propaganda might have been predicted—even quantified—by postwar communication researchers. Since the 1930s, humanistic propaganda scholarship gradually had given way to a quantitative field of communication research that focused on attitudes and public opinion more than on the ethics of propaganda messages. Some of this research was purely academic, but much of it came out of the "booming" public relations industry of the 1920s.[21] In addition, the field of advertising, newly reinvented as a "science" of persuasion, contributed to the change,[22] as did government-sponsored propaganda research during World War II.[23] After the war, all of these various strains of academic, commercial, and government-sponsored "applied" research consolidated into what came to be known as the "communication sciences."[24] Focused on mass communication, empirical and quantitative in methodology, and ultimately concerned with audience effects, the new communication scientists brought about a shift from the "conception of direct, undifferentiated, and powerful effects" implicit in earlier propaganda studies "to an understanding of effects as highly limited because of processes of psychological and social mediation" within audiences.[25]

Returning to universities and research institutes after the war, most of these new communication scientists rejected the "politically suffused work" of earlier communication researchers and set out to develop a genuine "social science of communication aimed at theory development."[26] Although George Gallup did not join his colleagues in this pursuit, he did become a visible popularizer of the new communication sciences. More an ideologue and entrepreneur than a scholar, he advocated putting the new theory to work in a vastly expanded "war of words" against the Communists. Like most cold warriors, Gallup "naively" believed in the "natural" superiority of democracy and at times was barely less "hysterical" about Communism than Joseph McCarthy himself. As a scientist, however, he insisted that he could explain *why* the earlier programs had failed and *how* the United States might do better in this new kind of war—this "war of words."

George Gallup and the "War We Are Losing"

Since predicting the *Literary Digest*'s miscall of the 1936 presidential election, George Gallup had become America's best-known pollster, a man celebrated in a 1948 *Time* magazine cover story as a "big, friendly, teddy bear of a man with a passion for facts and figures."[27] Later that same year, Gallup's credibility, and the credibility of polling in general, would suffer from the most embarrassing miscall in the history of the industry: the prediction that Thomas E. Dewey would defeat Harry Truman in the presidential election. However, the polling industry recovered quickly from that embarrassment largely because of Gallup's own success at portraying the debacle as a useful learning experience—a "blessing in disguise." Out of a pair of investigations into the 1948 miscall came theoretical and methodological breakthroughs that Gallup promised would improve not only polling but all of the human and communication sciences.[28] As empirical communication research in particular "crystallized into a distinct discipline" in the early 1950s,[29] Gallup became not only the "informal historian and popular interpreter of the polls,"[30] but also the best-known advocate of the new communication sciences.

Gallup, however, was more than a champion of science. He was also a cheerleader for democracy. Waxing political in his many speeches, books, and articles, Gallup routinely polarized the world into two antagonistic camps: those who believed that a "small ruling clique" ought to govern the masses, and those who believed that the "common people" should "be free to express their basic needs and purposes."[31] In no uncertain terms, Gallup sided with the democrats, identifying the former camp with Hitler and Mussolini, the latter with Jefferson and Theodore Roosevelt. He also answered at great length the argument of those who were "fearful of the people" or who felt that the "common people" were insufficiently interested, informed, or wise to govern themselves. Countering with the results of his own polls, Gallup repeated two simple themes over and over throughout his fifty-year career: that the polls showed that the public typically was not only right about most political issues, but also "far, far ahead of the parties and politicians."[32]

Unlike the progressives at the IPA, Gallup did not fret over whether propaganda conflicted with democratic principles. For Gallup, no method of "selling" democracy to the rest of the world raised ethical dilemmas. At the same time, he recognized that democracy's superiority was rarely so "obvious" to the rest of the world. "The worst folly in the world," he argued in a speech to the American Petroleum Institute in 1950, "is to assume that everywhere in the world the superiority of our system of government and our way of life are recognized." Even nations "friendly to us in Western Europe" saw "no great advantage in democracy as opposed to Communism," and "certainly not enough to warrant fighting to save their countries from Communist domination."[33]

That was the "reality" that Gallup set out to change between 1950 and 1953. Delivering dozens of speeches around the country and publishing articles in *Look*, *Reader's Digest*, the *New York Times Magazine*, and other popular periodicals, Gallup stressed three major themes as he elaborated how science could better promote democracy: (1) that the American propaganda program needed to be reorganized, given higher priority, and integrated into the long-range planning of American foreign policy; (2) that it needed to exploit new media and better understand and target its audiences; and (3) that it needed a whole new kind of message—simple, repetitious, and designed not to showcase America nor to vilify the Communists but to demonstrate the audiences' own self-interest in fighting for democracy. More importantly, Gallup changed his tune about the wisdom of the American people, at least as it pertained to the threat posed by Communism. According to Gallup, the public simply did not understand the nature of the Cold War and what would be necessary to win it. In Gallup's view, the "war of ideas" needed to be won at home before it could be won overseas.

In one of the early speeches of his campaign, an address before the Red Banks, New Jersey, Lions Club in December of 1950,[34] Gallup reflected on how radically the world had changed in the preceding twenty years. Proclaiming it "childlike and disastrous to think of the problems that face us today in the classic historical manner," Gallup argued that a "new kind" of war had begun—a war "for the minds of men"—and that this war would be fought not just against Russia but against "a world-wide revolutionary movement." Even if the war in Korea developed into World War III, and even if we won that war and liberated not only Korea but all of the Soviet satellites, it would count for nothing if we lost "this war of ideas." Suppose that we won World War III, Gallup imagined. Could you envision "the problem we would face . . . if we had to police hundreds of millions of hostile people—unless we had first won over to our point of view a large segment of the population of these lands?" And suppose we even "insisted upon their setting up democratic election machinery." What would we then do if the people of these nations took "full advantage of our democratic processes" and "promptly vote[d] in a communist regime?"[35]

In Gallup's view, American political leaders remained "surprisingly unaware of this battle for the minds of men." They foolishly committed "all our energies and resources" to conventional armed defenses. As a result the United States was taking a "hell of a beating" in the war of words.[36] In Italy, France, and China, impoverished peasants were being won over to Communism with offers of land and a better way of life. In Iran, the Russians had "mobile motion picture trucks" touring the country "showing the peasants how Russia would improve their standards of living."[37] In a major address at Georgetown University in April, 1952, Gallup claimed that "some 100 Communist newspapers with a total circulation running into the millions" were already publishing daily in Western Europe, and that "some five or six million card-carrying Communists" were engaged in "missionary work" there as well. Meanwhile, the free world countered with little more than shortwave radio broadcasts and a few balloons set adrift "bearing our message in pamphlet form." That effort, Gallup argued, was like putting "a spindly 2-year-old child into the ring with the world's champion."[38] In a series of rhetorical questions, Gallup summarized the result in his speech to the Petroleum Institute: "How many nations of the world are willing to send their troops into a war against Russia at our bidding? How many millions of men and women outside this country are willing to devote their time and money to furthering the cause of America? How many millions of fanatics do we have on our side—ready and willing to die for our cause?" In Gallup's opinion, merely asking such questions sufficed to "prove how pitifully inadequate have been our own attempts in this new type of warfare."[39]

Gallup thus proposed to mobilize for this "new kind of warfare"—"ideological warfare"—just as vigorously as we had mobilized for the two world wars. That meant, among other things, spending much more money. Gallup routinely threw out the figure of $5 billion, but he insisted in his Georgetown address that even that amount represented only the "minimal expenditure" necessary "if we want to make headway in this battle for the minds of men." For Gallup, it would still be a bargain if we spent many times that amount, for in his view, "every dollar spent in winning the war of ideas will accomplish as much as $10 spent for the conventional weapons of war." In other words, ideological warfare was not only a bargain but could *substitute* for spending on the hardware of conventional warfare. Gallup thus proposed that the $5 billion come straight out of the defense budget, assuring Americans that $5 billion spent on "today's tanks, guns, and battleships" would "make far less difference in achieving ultimate victory over communism" than $5 billion spent on ideological warfare.[40]

In addition to adequate funding, Gallup suggested that the "colossal task of winning over the world to our way of thinking" would require a "whole new department" of propaganda, a department "separate and independent" of the State Department and called, perhaps, the "Department of Ideological Warfare."[41] Such a department could engage in the "long-range thinking" necessary to win the war of ideas, and it could be staffed with the "best brains of the country drawn from the fields of publishing, broadcasting, public relations, and advertising."[42] The war of ideas likely would last fifty, perhaps even a hundred years or more, according to Gallup, and his proposed Department of Ideological Warfare would need "specially trained personnel" with "many different talents." According to Gallup, the United States had not yet even "begun to appreciate the strength of the forces we are fighting," much less to "map out a campaign of the dimensions necessary to bring success to our side." What was most needed, he concluded, was a modern-day Clausewitz to "set out the principles and philosophy of this new kind of warfare," a strategist with "a keen understanding of people and of human behavior."[43]

Gallup did not himself claim to be that "Clausewitz," yet he was certain that such an authority on psychological warfare would recognize certain "basic facts" about human nature and persuasion.[44] In his Georgetown University address, a speech published in essentially the same form in *Look* magazine in December, 1952,[45] Gallup enumerated those "facts," in the process sketching out both his critique of existing American propaganda programs and his blueprint for change. Gallup's "basic facts" reflected the new communication scientists' rejection of the direct, undifferentiated-effects model of propaganda and their faith in the ability of new experimental and survey methods to point the way toward more effective approaches. In effect, Gallup offered the American people a layman's primer on the new communication sciences and how they could be used to win the Cold War.

Some of Gallup's "facts" clearly reflected the new communication science's focus on audiences and the "social contexts" of persuasion. These included Gallup's observations that "the people of all nations" aspired to "a better way of life," and that all shared certain "universal goals" such as "the desire for peace" and the desire "to run one's own country without interference from other nations." According to Gallup, the free world had shown little more than "a passing interest" in the poor and downtrodden, whereas Communists had "brought millions into their fold" with the "mere promise" of "a better life"—however "false and insincere" that promise. Articulating the principle involved, Gallup observed: "People who are leading a miserable existence are ready to follow anyone who holds the slightest hope for a better life."[46]

Similarly, Gallup argued that the Communists had been more successful than the United States in associating themselves with the "universal goals" of peace and self-determination. According to Gallup, the Soviets were winning the Cold War because they had a "two-pronged" propaganda strategy: a long-term, worldwide campaign associating the Soviet Union with peace and the United States with imperialism and colonialism, combined with "a special brand of propaganda for each nation."[47] The United States needed to adopt a similarly "long-time point of view," Gallup concluded, dwelling for many years upon those ideals that "transcend national boundaries," while not losing sight of "short-term objectives" dictated by differences among nations.

In elaborating on the need for better understanding of foreign audiences, Gallup observed that Americans "unconsciously" had the habit of "peopling the world with persons like ourselves." That is, Americans assumed that everybody in the world shared their values and life experiences. As a result, they talked to "all the inhabitants of the globe" as they talked to their friends. Americans had trouble relating to people who never got enough to eat, and it was "almost impossible" for Americans even to believe that "large segments of the world" remained illiterate. The advanced education of the so-called experts crafting America's propaganda only exacerbated the problem. "If you are a college graduate and most of your friends are college graduates," Gallup observed, "you want to talk with all the inhabitants of the globe in the same manner that you communicate with your friends." Gallup concluded sarcastically: "The impulse of doctors of philosophy is to broadcast messages that only doctors of philosophy can understand."[48]

As Gallup elaborated on the content of propaganda messages, his "facts" reflected two more "lessons" recognized in "every field" dealing with persuasion, especially advertising: simplicity and repetition. One of Gallup's "facts" was a simple principle of advertising: "If you would sell ideas, concentrate on selling them one at a time." If he were asked to cite his chief criticism of American propaganda efforts, Gallup claimed that it would be that "we have never followed this simple rule. We say one thing today, another tomorrow." As a result, "we sell nothing. We leave only a blur in the minds of our auditors." Gallup insisted that "the advertiser who tries to get over one major sales point about his product, at a time, does far better than the advertiser who brings up 10 reasons for buying his product." Nazi and Communist propagandists, he concluded, "never made this mistake of scattering their fire. Their whole strategy has been aimed at doing a rifle, and not a shotgun job," and their "success" testified to "the importance of this principle of ideological warfare."[49]

Another basic "fact" was that "an idea will register on the minds of the millions and be accepted by them only if it is repeated *ad nauseam.*" According to Gallup, repetition was "at the very heart of the problem of selling ideas," and "scores of vehicles" had to be found "to carry the idea." This meant that "speakers must harp upon it; it must be dramatized by international conferences, painted on the walls of factories, plastered on sidewalks and billboards, carried on the front pages of newspapers, screamed over the radio, made the subject of international petitions." There must be, he concluded, "no escape from it." Again, the Soviets seemed intuitively to grasp this point, as they had so often repeated the idea that "Communists are for peace, we are warmongers" that the very word *peace* had become their most potent weapon. Scrawled on walls "everywhere" across Europe, peace now evoked images of a "war crazy" America bent on starting another world war.[50]

Gallup actually downplayed the power of mass propaganda in another of his "facts": that in dealing with the "illiterate people" in much of the world, "word-of-mouth" had to be "the chief way of selling people." This meant, of course, that the United States had to recruit "agents, advocates, friends native to the country and working for our cause in every land where . . . we need to sell our ideas." Once again, the Communists understood this and had developed a "great advantage" over us in "recruiting agents" through promises of "power" and "a high place in the Communist hierarchy." The United States could not employ the same methods, of course, but "some kind of pay or reward" for foreign agents would not be "too heavy a burden." Such incentives needed to be viewed as "part of the job of selling our point of view in those areas of the world where our ideas and ideals have been grossly distorted by the Communists."[51]

One last "fact," in Gallup's view, was "all important": American propaganda needed to be "based upon the truth." Yes, Gallup argued, a lie *could* be "sold by endless repetition," but the truth could be sold "more easily than lies" if repeated "just as endlessly." This "fact" had "escaped many in the propaganda field," Gallup contended, no doubt because of the success of "Herr Goebbels" in World War II. Sounding more like a preacher than an objective scientist, Gallup offered a value-laden counterexample: Christ and his disciples also stood "among the best propagandists" in the history of the world, and they (he let it go without saying) told the truth.[52]

Gallup's "basic facts" thus involved both media and messages, both technique and substance, and they articulated principles that, while perhaps obvious and simplistic by today's standards, were revelations to a generation schooled in the "direct effects" model of propaganda. With regard to media, Gallup's program envisioned going beyond reliance on shortwave radio and exploiting all available media, including motion pictures, "picture books," textbooks "for the children of the world," and as many newspapers around the world as the United States could afford to buy and publish.[53] With regard to the character of the message, all of Gallup's suggestions implied criticisms of both the "naive" and "hysterical" approaches to propaganda, for neither rested on sound understandings of foreign audiences and social contexts. Indeed, Gallup criticized the "naive" approach directly, insisting that showcasing the "good fortune of this country and of its people probably inspires more hatred than good will on the part of those who live in poverty-stricken lands." For years, he argued, the United States had been guilty of "telling people of the world how wonderful we are without realizing how few friends this type of boasting brings us."[54]

As Gallup spoke of a more scientific approach to propaganda and the "new research techniques" that made it possible, his pessimism about "losing" the Cold War gave way to a confident optimism. For the first time in history, Gallup declared, it was now possible "to supplant much of the guesswork about the way propaganda works with definitive knowledge." Not only could scientists now answer the concern that propaganda in general might be a "waste of money," but they could empirically test the effectiveness of both Communist and American messages. As Gallup explained: "Specifically it is possible today to find out just what propaganda ideas of the enemy are being accepted in any country. Likewise it is possible to find out which of our ideas have made an impact on the minds of people in those nations. . . . We can learn with a high degree of accuracy just what the people of any country think of us, and what they think of the Communists, what arguments carry weight with these people, which they reject. In short, it is possible to discover just who is winning the propaganda battle, and why." In addition, "research techniques . . . developed in recent times" now made it possible "to find out the best way of answering or nullifying the enemies' propaganda program" in advance of launching a propaganda campaign, and "to measure the effects of these ideas in winning converts after they have been made a part of an action program."[55]

Gallup did not specifically identify the new "techniques" and "methods" that could provide such evidence. Clearly, however, he had two sorts of research in mind: (1) experimental or laboratory studies in persuasion and attitude change, and (2) survey research based on newly developed sampling techniques. The former might be used to "pre-test" propaganda themes, while the latter could be used both to analyze audiences and to follow up on the success of "action programs."

For years, as Parry-Giles has shown, American propaganda officials responded to congressional demands for "proof" of the program's effectiveness with little more than anecdotal evidence that Russians hungered for American news or had been "converted" by American propaganda. After 1950, congressional skeptics began to demand more conclusive proof—quantitative proof—of the program's effectiveness. But propaganda officials could respond with little more than statistical estimates of the number of radio receivers in foreign countries, counts of letters received by the Voice of America, or numbers indicating declines in Communist Party membership in nonaligned nations.[56] For years Gallup had been busy behind the scenes building his own organization's ability to survey foreign audiences. By 1953 he had established fifteen so-called Public Opinion Institutes in foreign countries,[57] and these Gallup "affiliates" now stood poised to answer the growing demands from congressional critics for quantitative evidence that America's propaganda dollars were dollars well spent.

Gallup stood even better prepared to aid the government in overcoming what he insisted was the greatest obstacle to winning the Cold War: the ignorance and apathy of the American people. At first glance, Gallup's refrain that the American public needed to wake up to the Communist threat seemed to contradict his faith in the people's collective wisdom. Even during the Cold

War he sounded his usual refrain that the public was "years ahead" of their leaders. He insisted that "the people" recognized the need to "go all-out to sell our point of view to the world," even if it cost a "billion dollars and more to do the job."[58] Yet now Gallup worried that, due to a "lack of information," the public lacked the political will to fight a protracted "war of words" against the Communists. As he wrote in the *New York Times Magazine* in 1951, the American people did not understand the threat posed by Communism and they could not "envisage the awesome effect" of another world war. They had deluded themselves into thinking that, should World War III come, the United States could win it "quickly" by dropping "the bomb" and "live happily ever after."[59] In addition, Gallup worried that "the people of this country . . . had deluded themselves" into believing that we already were "actually undertaking all-out ideological warfare." In reality, America's propaganda effort was comparable to an army of a "couple of hundred men equipped with squirrel rifles" or an air force with "a half dozen Piper Cubs fitted out with shot guns."[60]

Nevertheless, Gallup remained confident that the American people, were they to know the truth, would *demand* that their leaders "face up to the job that has to be done—the hardest, toughest selling job that any nation of the world has ever faced—against the greatest odds and for the greatest stakes."[61] Although the Smith-Mundt bill prohibited propaganda turned inward to shape domestic public opinion, Gallup envisioned an assault not just against ignorance about the Cold War but against the whole cultural ethos of postwar America. According to Gallup, the politicians had not leveled with the American people, but the problem ran deeper than that. Both the educational system and the mass media had cultivated a culture "so bent on entertainment" that few Americans now kept "abreast of the times." Teachers and journalists needed to recapture their "sense of mission," Gallup insisted, by keeping the public "interested in, and informed about, the important problems of the day." Not surprisingly, Gallup promised that the pollsters would help by "uncovering and reporting the more serious 'areas of ignorance.'"[62]

Gallup's plan for winning the Cold War thus rejected not only the style and substance of the existing propaganda program but the whole notion that a democratic nation should not propagandize its own people. And he was not alone in his thinking. As President Eisenhower settled into office, his chief advisers on propaganda also developed a comprehensive and long-range plan for revamping the American propaganda program, and those advisers, like Gallup, viewed the apathy and ignorance of the American people as perhaps the greatest obstacle to winning the Cold War. As a result, the Eisenhower administration blurred the line between foreign and domestic propaganda. Indeed, that line was obliterated in planning for the administration's first major propaganda offensive in 1953: a campaign targeted at domestic public opinion and dubbed Operation Candor. In the end, however, Eisenhower's rhetorical intuition, not "science," dictated the tone of American propaganda during his presidency.

The New "Science" and the Jackson Committee Report

On January 24, 1953, President Eisenhower appointed a special committee whose recommendations would dramatically change the role of propaganda in American foreign policy: the so-called Jackson Committee.[63] Charged with investigating and recommending changes in American propaganda programs, the Jackson Committee developed "a considered policy of the entire Government to win World War III without having to fight it."[64] Gallup did not serve as a member of the committee, but he did testify before it and he corresponded regularly with top presidential aides working closely with the committee. Whatever his direct role, the Jackson Committee's report to the president, dated June 30, 1953,[65] reads like it could have been written by George Gallup himself.

Declassified in 1986, the top-secret Jackson Committee report echoed Gallup on everything from the need to reorganize American propaganda efforts, to the appropriate types of propaganda themes, to the principles of persuasion that must guide effective propaganda. Calling for radical changes in the American propaganda program, the report urged what Gallup had been advocating for years: that propaganda be made a top priority and, in the words of a White House press release on the report, be considered an aspect of "every diplomatic, economic, or military policy and action."[66] Most notably, it echoed Gallup in calling for a concerted effort to "educate" the American people about Soviet Communism, the threat of nuclear war, and the challenge posed by a protracted Cold War. Calling public "misunderstanding" a significant "disability under which the information program has labored,"[67] the Jackson Committee devoted the entire last chapter of its report to "Informing the American Public."

Beginning with reflections on "The Nature of the Conflict," the committee declared that U.S. policies must be "based upon the assumption that the purpose of the Soviet rulers is world domination."[68] Like Gallup, however, the committee argued that the Soviets would pursue this goal, not by military means, but through a new kind of warfare: "political warfare," including propaganda and subversion. In fact, the committee downplayed the Soviet military threat, emphasizing instead the psychological dimensions of the Cold War: "It is our belief that the Soviet rulers will strive to avoid general war, primarily because of fear that their regime could not be maintained in power after a devastating atomic attack and because the opportunities for expansion by political warfare still seem good."[69] The real threat, the committee argued, would come from propaganda, and like Gallup the committee insisted that the Soviets were years ahead of the free world in their skills and knowledge of this new kind of warfare: "For the last 30 years the Soviet propaganda program has been large and centrally directed. From the time they seized power, the bolsheviks have given high priority to propaganda, both internal and external. As a result of this long experience, the Soviet Union possesses a large group of propagandists which is continually replenished by new and well-trained recruits."[70]

Criticizing the "confusion" surrounding America's own propaganda "mission,"[71] the Jackson Committee recommended that propaganda be given higher priority in the long-term planning of American foreign policy. In addition, the committee urged that propaganda operations be reorganized and more centralized, if not in a new government department, then at least by means of a new special assistant to the president "with particular responsibility in regard to 'cold war' activities" and an "Operations Coordinating Board" affiliated with the National Security Council (NSC).[72] The existing organizational structure was based upon "a basic misconception" that "psychological strategy" could be separated from actual foreign policy making, when in fact there was a "psychological" aspect "inherent in every diplomatic, economic, or military action."[73] According to the Jackson Committee, "the previously clear dividing line between peace and war" had been "blurred."[74] That "compelling reality" dictated not only "a more unified effort" but also better leadership, continuity, and training of personnel—personnel with not only "technical competence" but also "a broader understanding of the significance of their own assignments."[75]

Like Gallup, the Jackson Committee stressed the need for a whole new approach to propaganda messages, urging singular, more focused propaganda themes as the key to successful, long-term, global campaigns. In the past, the committee argued, "lack of coordination has resulted in the haphazard projection of too many and too diffuse propaganda themes." Like Gallup, the committee complained that "no single set of ideas" had been "registered abroad through effective repetition" and credited much of the Soviet Union's propaganda success to a better understanding of these principles of focus and repetition: "This is in sharp contrast to the technique of the Soviets, who have consistently hammered home a few carefully selected central themes: land reform, peace, anti-imperialism, youth."[76]

Also echoing Gallup, the committee criticized what Parry-Giles has called the "naive" conception of propaganda. "The note of self-praise and the emphasis on material achievements," the committee declared, "frequently creates envy and antagonism" in foreign countries.[77] Instead of praising ourselves, the committee argued, the "primary and overriding purpose" of American propaganda needed to be to "persuade foreign peoples that it lies in their own interests to take action consistent with the national objectives of the United States."[78] By the same token, the Jackson Committee critiqued the "hysterical" tone of the Truman administration's Campaign of Truth, declaring that it was "not enough just to be anti-Communist" and repeating that the United States needed to appeal to foreign nations "in terms of their own self-interest."[79] For the Jackson Committee, as for Gallup, long-term, global campaigns needed to revolve around basic or transcendent themes grounded in universal aspirations, which could then be adapted to short-term objectives in particular "local situations."[80]

The Jackson Committee did not share Gallup's emphasis on economic concerns, but it did agree that foreign propaganda, to be effective, had to emphasize transcendent themes grounded, not in uniquely American values, but in universal aspirations. In sketching its own ideas about possible themes for a long-term, global campaign, the Jackson Committee sounded a more "spiritual" note than Gallup, calling for a new emphasis on "the deeper spiritual values uniting this nation with the rest of the world."[81] Above all, the committee concluded, American propaganda needed to project a vision of a better world—a vision that would "arouse . . . an understanding and a sympathy for the kind of world order which the United States and other free nations seek to achieve."[82]

Like Gallup, the Jackson Committee envisioned spreading this "vision" over a much wider array of media, including not only shortwave radio but commercially published books, local newspapers, motion pictures, and even the newly emerging medium of television. According to the committee, the Soviet Union's production of published materials "considerably" exceeded that of the United States, and there was a need to use newspapers and books "to much better advantage than in the past in advancing national objectives."[83] Citing one specific problem, the committee noted that "cheap communist books" had been "dominating local markets" in some foreign nations, and hence that the United States should make available more "equally inexpensive non-communist books."[84] Likewise, motion pictures had not been used to full advantage, and the committee urged that "every effort . . . be made . . . to increase the positive contribution of commercial films to the United States propaganda and information programs."[85] Even television, the committee argued, was "expanding rapidly outside the United States" and offered "a new propaganda medium of potential effectiveness which Government information agencies have thus far hardly attempted to utilize."[86]

The Jackson Committee also echoed Gallup's call for propagating America's message by word of mouth by establishing more "agents" friendly to the United States in other nations. Focusing on "exchange programs" that brought foreigners to America and sent Americans abroad, the committee observed that such programs could effectively promote U.S. interests as long as "great care" was exercised in "placing and looking after exchanges." Exchange programs involving tens of thousands of individuals already had been successfully employed by the Soviet Union, the committee observed, "to provide skilled local communist leaders in foreign countries and to win friends and sympathizers for the Soviet Union."[87]

The Jackson Committee agreed with Gallup that American propaganda ought to be based on "the truth," but they clearly were more concerned that it have the *tone* of objective news, at least on such overt or "attributed" media as the Voice of America (VOA). With specific reference to VOA broadcasts to the Soviet Union, for example, the committee found it "difficult to envisage any positive results" from "provocative propaganda," and insisted that the "basis for VOA output" should instead be "objective, factual news reporting." Only as "a source of truth and information about world events," the committee argued, did VOA have "value for the Soviet listener."[88] Similarly, the committee argued that, "to be effective," American propaganda in the free world also had to be "dependable, convincing, and truthful."[89] This did not preclude editorializing or news analysis, but it did mean that "a tone of exhortation and abuse" had to be avoided and that refutations of Soviet accusations and claims, while "forceful," also needed to be "dignified" and "factual."[90]

The Jackson Committee thus echoed Gallup on virtually every major topic relating to the purposes, character, and media of American overseas propaganda. The Eisenhower administration, in turn, implemented virtually all of the committee's recommendations, most notably by establishing a new, independent agency in charge of overseas information—the U.S. Information Agency (USIA)—and by directing it to propagate the positive themes of Eisenhower's "Chance for Peace" speech. "It is the purpose of this instruction," read a blueprint for the USIA's first year of operations known simply as "The Plan" among insiders, "to translate the broad principles of our foreign policy, as laid down by the President in his speech of 16 April, into terms meaningful for the information program and to establish a world-wide plan of action." Directly invoking the Jackson Committee report, The Plan called for stressing those "goals and desires" we held "in common" with other nations, and it identified two aspects of the president's speech that made for "good propaganda": "the Faith" and "the Vision." "We must now employ proven techniques of mass communication to carry our message of the Faith and the Vision to the farthest corners of the globe," The Plan concluded. "This message must be expressed in a few simple concepts appropriately presented in every medium and repeated, repeated, repeated."[91]

The architects of the USIA's first-year plan considered it but a "modest plan" containing "the seeds of a much larger and more dynamic program in which all the agencies of the Government, as well as the American people, could actively participate."[92] That theme—that government and the people must work together to win the Cold War—echoed throughout the Jackson Committee report as the committee argued that the "drive and resources" the government devoted to overseas propaganda efforts depended on "the national will," or the "composite thought of the American people." Like Gallup, the Jackson Committee worried that the American people did not yet "fully understand the dangers that confront them, the power of the enemy, the difficulty of reducing that power, and the probable duration of the conflict." Like Gallup, the committee suspected that the public felt protected by the atom bomb.[93] As a result, the committee called for repeal of the Smith-Mundt Act's prohibition against "informing the American people" about "information" activities, urging that propaganda officials be "authorized to release domestically, without request, information concerning the program."[94] More than that, though, the committee urged "a greater degree of candor toward the American people" about nuclear weapons and the Soviet threat. The public did not yet understand that "the rapid growth of the Soviet atomic capability" had brought "the communities of the United States into the front lines" and placed "in doubt the claim that quantitative atomic superiority is a conclusive deterrent to attack." Nor did the public "yet grasp the import of the President's recent words that we live in an age, not an instant, of peril."[95] For these reasons, the committee dismissed concerns about a democratic nation propagandizing its own people and rendered it something of a moral imperative to do just that. "Only a clear and consistent exposition of the United States program can produce that measure of public understanding and support which will constitute the great moral foundation required for the effective conduct of external relations."[96]

The Jackson Committee did not specify themes or even the tone of a campaign of "candor." In planning for the Eisenhower administration's first propaganda campaign, the president's advisers thus turned to the atomic scientists and pollsters for guidance in framing their message. They finally settled on a rhetoric of fear, emphasizing the destructiveness of atomic weapons. Eisenhower himself, however, saw a better way. Instead of scaring people, he spun hopeful visions of peaceful uses of the atom.

Operation Candor: Fear, Faith, and American Public Opinion

The Jackson Committee's call for "candor" reflected the influence of the so-called Oppenheimer Panel, which had been appointed during the Truman administration as an advisory committee on nuclear weapons and disarmament. Chaired by Los Alamos director J. Robert Oppenheimer, the five-member committee's report to Secretary of State Dean Acheson caught the attention of the incoming administration, and members of the panel met twice with the NSC in the first half of 1953.[97] As McGeorge Bundy has written, the Oppenheimer Panel's report presented a very "stern picture of the nuclear world,"[98] and Oppenheimer carried that message not only to the NSC but to a broader public in an article in *Foreign Affairs* in July, 1953. Warning that the "terrifyingly rapid accumulation" of bombs on both sides had left the United States and the Soviet Union like "two scorpions in a bottle, each capable of killing the other, but only at the risk of his own life," Oppenheimer declared that "our twenty-thousandth bomb" would not "in any deep strategic sense offset their two-thousandth." In other words, he dismissed the basic assumption behind America's entire defense policy: that we were protected by our quantitative and qualitative atomic superiority. Even if we did manage to maintain our superiority, Oppenheimer concluded, we were still "probably faced with a long period of cold war" during which the "atomic clock" would only tick "faster and faster."[99]

Perhaps constrained by such "somber conclusions," the Oppenheimer Panel made what Bundy has called only "modest recommendations."[100] Yet the Oppenheimer Panel's call for a "policy of Candor" toward the American people had far-reaching implications for the *rhetoric* of the Cold War and for democratic governance in the nuclear age. In summarizing the panel's recommendation in *Foreign Affairs*, Oppenheimer seemed more the political philosopher than the atomic scientist, arguing that the "political vitality" of the country depended upon "the conflict of opinion and debate" and "a public opinion which is based on confidence that it knows the truth." The immediate, practical reason for confronting the "truth" about atomic weapons was to avoid stumbling blindly into war: "I believe that until we have looked this tiger in the eye, we shall be in the worst of all possible dangers, which is that we may back into him." But for Oppenheimer, not telling the people the truth about the arms race had larger implications: "More generally, I do not think a country like ours can in any real sense survive if we are afraid of our people."[101]

Eisenhower generally agreed with the idea of a "policy of candor," and he put C. D. Jackson to work on an "opening gun" speech to launch such a policy.[102] Jackson, a robust cold warrior and "an enthusiastic supporter of Oppenheimer's basic idea," pursued the task vigorously. He described the atomic threat so candidly that his speech drafts came to be known among insiders as the "Bang! Bang! papers."[103] Meanwhile, James Lambie, special assistant and assistant staff secretary to the president, oversaw planning for a larger, "follow-up" campaign. Dubbed Operation Candor, the campaign was to emphasize the central theme of Eisenhower's radio address of May 19: that the Cold War represented not merely an "instant" of danger but an "Age of Peril."[104]

In planning Operation Candor, Lambie envisioned a program of "considerable magnitude" to be "executed over a period of several months." It was to involve four nationwide radio and TV "talks" by top administration officials, summarized in a final speech by the president himself and supported by a "major campaign" by the Advertising Council employing "newspapers, magazines, radio, TV, house organs, and car cards."[105] As the plan evolved, it grew to six "talks," each hosted by a White House spokesman in an "Ed Murrow" role "to insure full Presidential authority for the series." Among the talks planned were one featuring both the president and Secretary of State Dulles on the "Nature of Communism" (addressing the "implacability" of the "unprecedented Soviet Communist menace"), another on the "Capabilities of the Enemy" (with Allen Dulles and Gen. Walter Bedell Smith discussing the "probable effects of a surprise attack on the U.S."), and a third with Adm. Arthur W. Radford on the "retaliatory" deterrent and "defensive preparedness."[106] All of the talks were to emphasize the "realities" of the "Age of Peril."

Gallup enthusiastically endorsed Operation Candor in correspondence with Lambie in June and July, 1953. On June 16, Gallup wrote that he was "keenly interested" in the project and offered to share "a small mountain" of relevant data. He also offered to add new questions to his ballot that might help "guide" the effort.[107] Lambie accepted this offer in a letter dated June 26. It would be "useful," Lambie wrote, to pose such questions as: "From developments since Stalin's death, would you say the Soviet menace had diminished or increased or stayed about the same?" And "how long do you think the 'cold war' . . . is likely to go on—another year or so, 5 years, 10 years, 20 years,

50 years?" Lambie also wanted to know, among other things, whether the American people thought that the Russians already had the capability of "knocking out" the United States with a "swift all-out attack," and whether they thought that the "eventual goal of Russian communism" was "world domination." Lambie also wanted to know "the degree of 'awareness' with which we have to deal" as he contemplated how to "educate" the public about the Soviet menace.[108]

Gallup obliged, promising in a letter dated June 30 to "cover many of the issues on our next ballot." In addition, Gallup enclosed some "unpublished results" that already had addressed Lambie's question about perceptions of Stalin's death. According to the poll taken in "about the middle of May," nearly a quarter of the American people (23 percent) thought there had been a "real change" in Soviet policy since Stalin's death, while a majority (60 percent) thought "no change" had become evident. Gallup also offered to send Lambie additional "unpublished results" on public attitudes toward the Soviet Union, as well as "any material which we think shows 'a dissatisfaction or misunderstanding of basic attitudes or approaches to national problems on the part of the President or his administration.'" Finally, Gallup reflected on the mutual benefits of the developing relationship between the administration and America's best-known pollster: "It occurs to me that we can be of real help to you and that you can be of real help to us."[109]

Gallup followed up on his promise to pursue additional questions of interest to the administration in his public polls in the summer and fall of 1953. One poll that appeared in the newspapers in August used Lambie's exact wording and imagery in asking about public attitudes toward the Soviet Union's atomic capabilities: "Do you think Russia would be able, now, to knock out the United States with a surprise all-out atom bomb attack?"[110] Another Gallup poll that appeared in August pursued Lambie's question about the "eventual goal" of the Communists: "As you hear and read about Russia these days, do you believe Russia is trying to build herself up to be the ruling power of the world—or do you think Russia is just building up protection against being attacked in another war?" These polls seemed to confirm what had led administration strategists to propose Operation Candor in the first place. They suggested that while the public recognized Soviet ambitions,[111] they downplayed Soviet power and the threat of an atomic attack. Only about a fifth of the public believed that the Soviet Union could "knock out" the United States with a "surprise all-out" attack,[112] while another Gallup poll revealed that only 32 percent thought there was a "good chance" their own community would be attacked with an atom bomb in "another World War."[113] Yet another Gallup poll revealed that 14 percent of the public did not even believe that the Soviets had a "workable atomic bomb."[114] In short, the public did not recognize the seriousness of the threat.

Although the problem seemed clear, Lambie continued to press for additional research to help determine the best way to frame Operation Candor's *message*. In thanking Gallup for his unpublished data on perceptions of the Soviet menace, for example, Lambie wrote on July 11 asking Gallup about his "newly-developed technique of trying to measure the intensity of opinion."[115] Lambie observed that it would be "immensely more valuable to know how strongly 60 percent of the people, say, feel that there has been no change in Russia's policy than that, at any given time, they do feel that way." He felt that by getting "an inkling of the depth of the conviction as to the 'total menace,'" it would be "easier to guess" how those opinions might change.[116]

On the same day, Lambie also sent a memo to C. D. Jackson calling for additional "attitude and motivation research" to aid in deciding "what to say" and "how to say it." Research of the "proper kind" could be of "immeasurable help" in "sharpening lines of attack" and in answering such questions as: "How do [people] go about making up their minds—what kind of events or pronouncements influence their opinions? How strongly do they feel as they feel?" "Two jobs" required additional research, according to Lambie: "One is to find out what the story has to be. The other is to find out what will make people believe it and act on it." Lambie noted that "any of the good university outfits (such as Harvard's Laboratory of Social Relations, Samuel A. Stouffer) could do the job" and concluded: "This is no more than a business corporation would do before launching a campaign. It would discover who comprised its market, what their prejudices and predilections, what they knew and didn't know, what they would accept and wouldn't accept, etc, etc."[117]

In the end, the administration scuttled Operation Candor—not because additional scientific studies suggested a different approach, but because Eisenhower personally rejected draft after draft of Jackson's speech.[118] Repeatedly directing Jackson to tone the speech down and "find some hope,"[119] the president insisted that the emphasis be on "vigilance and sobriety, not on panic."[120] The whole project then stalemated until Eisenhower himself suddenly "hit upon" a whole new approach to the issue in September, 1953: the idea of proposing "a common fund" of isotopes to be developed for "peaceful purposes."[121] Eisenhower again put Jackson to work, this time along with Atomic Energy Commission (AEC) chairman Lewis Strauss, and the idea evolved into Eisenhower's "Atoms for Peace" speech of December 8, 1953. Like Operation Candor, Atoms for Peace involved elaborate follow-up plans, and eventually it evolved into a "persuasive campaign" so ambitious and far-reaching, as Martin Medhurst has observed, as to "stagger the imagination."[122] Yet the rhetorical thrust of Atoms for Peace was quite the opposite of Operation Candor. Instead of scaring the public, Atoms for Peace aimed to "help take the curse off the atom" and thus, in Medhurst's view, "create the time and psychological space needed to effect completion of the New Look."[123]

Yet Atoms for Peace was more than a diversionary tactic. It also was more consistent with Eisenhower's personality and rhetorical persona than a rhetoric of fear. From his first day in office, as Rachel Holloway has noted, Eisenhower made "faith" the key term of his rhetoric about nuclear weapons, creating a "sense of urgency" with his descriptions of the Soviet threat but also a "sense of hope."[124] In his inaugural address, the president's rhetoric of "faith"—a term he used twelve times in the speech—rendered nuclear weapons no different than any other weapons: evil when in the hands of "Communist aggressors," but good, even reassuring, when wielded by the "protectors of freedom."[125] Even after a test of the hydrogen bomb in 1954 completely vaporized the test island and irradiated a Japanese fishing crew, Eisenhower refused to concede the frightful power of the bomb. At a news conference after the blast, AEC chairman Strauss remarked that the H-Bomb now could be built large enough to "take out a city. . . . Any city."[126] The country, as Holloway has noted, was "shocked."[127] Yet just four days later, Eisenhower appeared on national television urging the public not to "get panicky." The H-bomb was not in itself "a great threat to us," the president counseled, but "merely a dramatic symbol" of "how far the advances of science have outraced our social consciousness." America would face the challenges of the atomic age with "courage and faith" and become "ever stronger," not just in weapons, Eisenhower assured his viewers, "but particularly in this spiritual sense, in the belief—the faith that we can do certain things," the "faith that comes from a study of our own history."[128]

In Holloway's view, Eisenhower's "rhetoric of faith"—his refusal "to scare the public"—demonstrated his "own lack of candor."[129] It also seemed to defy public opinion, for according to Gallup, a large majority of Americans favored the government providing "more information about the destructiveness of the atom and hydrogen bombs, and about the danger to this country in case of an atom attack by Russia."[130] Yet Eisenhower worried about the security risks involved in the release of atomic information.[131] He also worried that scary rhetoric might set off a congressional frenzy of defense spending.[132] Above all, however, he seemed to sense that scaring the public simply would not work.

In coming to this conclusion, Eisenhower had recent history on his side.

Shortly after the bombing of Hiroshima, a group of atomic scientists had campaigned for international control over atomic energy and a ban on all atomic weapons. When polls showed public indifference to their efforts, they launched their own campaign of candor about atomic weapons—a five-year campaign of "shameless propaganda" based "almost wholly on fear." Their aim, explained one of the scientists, was to "scare the pants off the public," while another opined: "Only one tactic is dependable—the preaching of doom." Scientists speaking before citizens' groups were advised to "make this a blood and thunder speech" or, more simply, to "scare the living hell" out of people. The campaign won widespread support from political leaders, civic groups, and editorial writers, but as an effort to change public opinion it proved worse than a failure; it actually seemed to backfire, only encouraging more hawkish public attitudes. By 1951, even Eugene Rabinowitch, a key figure in the effort, conceded that the movement had failed. In "trying to frighten men into rationality," Rabinowitch lamented, the scientists had succeeded only in promoting "abject fear or blind hatred."[133]

The lesson of the scientists' movement is, in fact, the lesson of apocalyptic movements throughout history: the rhetoric of doom, if it is to persuade and motivate, must not only frighten but also hold out *some* hope of ultimate "salvation," some "assurance of deliverance."[134] Moreover, that historical lesson seemed confirmed by the first generation of empirical communication research on "fear-arousing appeals"—research being published at the very time the administration was debating whether to scare the public with candor about the nuclear threat. In a now-classic book published in 1953, for example, Carl Hovland, Irving Janis, and Harold Kelley reported that "threat" appeals were likely to produce "opinion change" only when accompanied by "reassuring recommendations" that immediately "elicit anticipations of escaping from or averting the threat." Indeed, the research showed how intense fear appeals could backfire altogether, producing such "defensive reactions" as inattentiveness, avoidance, or even hostility toward the communicator. The research even showed how a "strong threat appeal" might not only fail to produce support for the communicator's recommendations but have the "unintended effect" of motivating the audience to adopt "magical," "wishful," or "other types of reassuring beliefs" that were directly "antithetical to the communicator's purposes."[135] That, of course, appears to be precisely what happened in the case of the "scientists' movement": an effort to "scare up" support for disarmament instead produced support for building *more* bombs.

Ironically, then, Dwight Eisenhower seemed more in tune with the new communication research than the scientists who advised him. He sensed that "scaring the pants off the public" would not—by itself—produce support for administration policies, and throughout his first year in office he personally insisted on counterbalancing the candor advocated by both the atomic and communication scientists with the "reassurances" of his own faith and vision. Holloway may be right that by pacifying and reassuring the public, Eisenhower's "rhetoric of faith" discouraged "public participation and democratic debate."[136] Yet a rhetoric of candor and fear, especially in the absence of the president's soothing reassurances, likely would have been equally debilitating—or worse. In the final analysis, Eisenhower seemed to sense intuitively what both history and the communication scientists of his day already had shown. In the absence of hope and faith in the future, the rhetoric of atomic fear leads, at best, to the sort of psychology that Robert Jay Lifton would later dub "psychic numbing"—a psychology of denial and apathy.[137] At worst, it scares the public into demanding that still more bombs be built for "protection."

Conclusion

It has become fashionable of late to condemn the first generation of communication scientists for their cozy relationship with government propagandists. In *Science of Coercion*, for example, Christopher Simpson laments that between 1945 and 1960 communication researchers "helped elaborate rationales for coercing groups targeted by the U.S. government and Western Industrial culture generally."[138] In rhetoric scarcely less "hysterical" in its own way than the Campaign of Truth, Simpson condemns the researchers. Without reflecting on "where contemporary Western ideology comes from, whose interests it serves," and their own role "in its propagation," according to Simpson, the communication researchers served as accomplices to policy makers who were "rapacious, destructive, tolerant of genocide, and willing to sacrifice countless people in the pursuit of a chimera of security that has grown ever more remote."[139]

Yet even Simpson concedes that, at the time, communication scientists viewed their service to the government as "proper, even noble." They believed that propaganda and even covert violence could be "cheaper, more flexible, and sometimes less brutal than conventional war, or that it could actually mitigate or avoid conflicts."[140] Even with the nation technically at peace, most communication researchers remained convinced of the necessity and nobility of propagandizing not just foreign audiences but the American people themselves. Literalizing the Cold War metaphor and conceptualizing domestic propaganda as "education" for survival, few doubted the morality of their efforts to help win the Cold War.

George Gallup's campaign to expand the propaganda program does raise questions about the ethics of research and the role of the social scientist in public affairs. Clearly, Gallup was not what he publicly cast himself to be: the disinterested social scientist whose "responsibility ends with the objective reporting of survey results."[141] Nor did he always evidence, behind the scenes, his public expressions of faith in the "good common sense" of the American people.[142] Instead, Gallup deployed his science as a weapon, not only helping to design campaigns to reshape American public opinion, but later in measuring the effects both of those campaigns and of American propaganda around the world. Establishing a network of affiliates in more than fifty foreign nations over the next two decades,[143] Gallup eventually realized his early Cold War dream: the ability to assess "with a high degree of accuracy just what the people of any country think of us, and what they think of the Communists, what arguments carry weight with these people, which they reject."[144] In effect Gallup became not just a social scientist but something akin to a government intelligence agent.

That, in turn, raises questions about the purposes and integrity of the polls Gallup syndicated to hundreds of American newspapers. Asking survey questions framed by administration officials, and clearly interested not just in *measuring* but in *shaping* public opinion, Gallup did not merely report the anti-Communist public sentiment that protected Joseph McCarthy and sustained hard-line policies. He actively promoted that sentiment not only in his speeches and essays, but also with the polls themselves. The very act of polling so frequently on the Communist threat helped to elevate the issue to the top of the public agenda. Moreover, some of Gallup's polls seemed *designed* to demonstrate public support for stronger anti-Communist policies. In short, Gallup was no mere "weatherman" of public opinion, as he insisted when critics accused him of political bias.[145] On the contrary, he contributed significantly to the chilly political climate of the postwar years, both with his anti-Communist rhetoric and with the results of his own polls.

Finally, this study adds a few brush strokes to the revisionist portrait of Dwight Eisenhower. Unlike the "Ike" of conventional wisdom, Eisenhower did not stand aloof from the planning of his administration's Cold War propaganda strategy. He instigated a debate over propaganda by appointing the Jackson Committee in the first place, and he closely monitored the committee's work. When the committee finished its report, Eisenhower worked hard to implement its recommendations. When both the atomic scientists and some of his closest propaganda advisers pushed for candor about the horrors of an atomic attack, Eisenhower personally rejected the idea, insisting on his more "positive" alternative: Atoms for Peace. In the area of Cold War planning, at least, Eisenhower hardly seemed the "passive-negative" president criticized by James David Barber.[146] Instead, he was the "intelligent, decisive, and perceptive" Ike of the revisionist portrait,[147] the Ike for whom rhetoric was an important "weapon in the arsenal of the Cold War."[148]

Eisenhower was no doubt a hard-line cold warrior, no less convinced of the Soviet threat than John Foster Dulles and the administration's other hawks. Yet Eisenhower frequently disagreed with Dulles and the hard-liners about the best way to counter that threat.[149] Rejecting the rhetoric of terror and ultimatums, Eisenhower sought to de-escalate the "war of words" with a rhetoric of "faith" and "vision." Refusing to "scare the hell" out of the public, he instead mesmerized the world with his vision of Atoms for Peace—a vision of the world made better, not more fragile, by the secrets of the atom. Although no less propagandistic than a rhetoric of fear, Eisenhower's rhetoric of peaceful cooperation did bring at least a temporary pause in the escalating war of words between the United States and the Soviet Union. For a war-weary world, Atoms for Peace held out at least a measure of hope that the atomic age might be not only survivable but also an age of great human progress.

Notes

1. Senate Committee on Foreign Relations (SFRC), *Overseas Information Programs of the United States: Hearings Before a Subcommittee of the Committee on Foreign Relations,* 82d Cong., 2d sess., Nov. 20–21, 1952, pt. 1, 1–2.

2. SFRC, *Overseas Information Programs of the United States: Hearings Before a Subcommittee of the Committee on Foreign Relations,* 83d Cong., 1st sess., Mar. 6, 1953, pt. 2, 773–93.

3. SFRC, *Overseas Information Programs,* pt. 2, 779.

4. J. Michael Sproule, "Propaganda Studies in American Social Science: The Rise and Fall of the Critical Paradigm," *Quarterly Journal of Speech* 73 (1987): 60–78.

5. J. Michael Sproule, "Social Responses to Twentieth-Century Propaganda," in *Propaganda: A Pluralist Perspective,* ed. Ted J. Smith III (New York: Praeger, 1989), 7–8.

6. Fitzhugh Green, *American Propaganda Abroad* (New York: Hippocrene, 1988), 12–14.

7. Sproule, "Social Responses," 6–7

8. J. Michael Spoule, *Propaganda and Democracy: The American Experience of Media and Mass. Persuasion* (Cambridge: Cambridge University Press, 1997), 10.

9. Green, *American Propaganda Abroad,* 15.

10. Scott M Cutlip, *The Unseen Power: Public Relations. A History* (Hillsdale, N.J.: Lawrence Erlbaum, 1994), 106.

11. Sproule, "Social Responses," 9.

12. See Sproule, *Propaganda and Democracy*, 129–77.

13. Sproule, "Propaganda Studies," 67–68.

14. Ibid., 72.

15. Green, *American Propaganda Abroad*, 18.

16. Shawn Parry-Giles, "Rhetorical Experimentation and the Cold War, 1947–1953: The Development of an Internationalist Approach to Propaganda," *Quarterly Journal of Speech* 80 (1994): 450.

17. Ibid., 450–53.

18. John W. Henderson, *The United States Information Agency* (New York: Praeger, 1969), 46–47.

19. Parry-Giles, "Rhetorical Experimentation," 453–56.

20. Ibid., 456.

21. See Cutlip, *The Unseen Power*, 105–523.

22. See Jesse G. Delia, "Communication Research: A History," in *Handbook of Communication Science*, ed. Charles R. Berger and Steven H. Chaffee (Newbury Park, Calif.: Sage, 1987), 46–50.

23. As Simpson has documented, the earliest of the "modern communication research" grew directly out of the work of the Creel Committee in World War I, and virtually all of the prominent communication scientists of the 1950s were involved in government-sponsored "applied" research during World War II. See Christopher Simpson, *Science of Coercion: Communication Research and Psychological Warfare, 1945–1960* (New York: Oxford University Press, 1994), 15–30.

24. Delia, "Communication Research," 54–63.

25. Ibid., 21.

26. Ibid., 59.

27. "The Black and White Beans," *Time*, May 3, 1948, p 21.

28. See J. Michael Hogan, "George Gallup and the Rhetoric of Scientific Democracy," *Communication Monographs* 64 (1997): 163–65.

29. Simpson, *Science of Coercion*, 3.

30. Jean M Converse, *Survey Research in the United States: Roots and Emergence, 1890–1960* (Berkeley: University of California Press, 1987), 116.

31. George Gallup and Saul Forbes Rae, *The Pulse of Democracy: The Public-Opinion Poll and How It Works* (New York: Simon and Schuster, 1940), 6.

32. "Interview with Dr. George Gallup: '68 Election Size-Up," *U.S. News and World Report*, July 29, 1968, 34.

33. George Gallup, "We Have Been Outsold," *Vital Speeches of the Day* 17 (Dec. 15, 1950): 141–43. Gallup illustrated his point with the story of one Korean asked by another about the importance of a UN victory in their country. If you are a "blade of grass," the first Korean replied, it makes "little difference whether you were eaten by a cow or by a horse" (141).

34. George S [sic] Gallup, "The Struggle for the Minds of Men," speech before the Red Banks Lion Club, Dec. 19, 1950, William Benton Papers, Box 347, University of Chicago Library. This speech so impressed one member of the club, one J. D. Tuller, that he personally distributed more than a thousand copies to "friends and acquaintances," as well as to all the members of Congress. See J. D. Tuller to Sen. William Benton, Feb. 5, 1951, William Benton Papers, Box 347, University of Chicago Library.

35. Gallup, "Struggle for the Minds of Men," 1–2.

36. Ibid., 1.

37. Gallup, "We Have Been Outsold," 142.

38. George Gallup, "Why We Are Doing So Badly in the Ideological War," *Vital Speeches of the Day* 18 (June 1, 1952): 502–503.

39. Gallup, "We Have Been Outsold," 141.

40. Gallup, "Why We Are Doing So Badly," 502.

41. Ibid. Earlier in his campaign, Gallup had suggested a less warlike title: the Department of World Relations. See "Struggle for the Minds of Men," 4.

42. Gallup, "Struggle for the Minds of Men," 1, 4.

43. Gallup, "Why We Are Doing So Badly," 502.

44. Ibid.

45. George Gallup, "The Battle We Are Losing," *Look,* Dec. 2, 1952, 101.

46. Gallup, "Why We Are Doing So Badly," 502–503.

47. Ibid., 503.

48. Ibid.

49. Ibid.

50. Ibid.

51. Ibid., 503–504.

52. Ibid., 503.

53. Gallup, "We Have Been Outsold," 142; and Gallup, "Struggle for the Minds of Men," 5.

54. In elaborating this principle, Gallup also cited perhaps the only popularizer of persuasion techniques better known in his day than Gallup himself: "Certainly Dale Carnegie wouldn't recommend this as a way to win friends and influence people" (Gallup, "Why We Are Doing So Badly," 504).

55. Ibid.

56. Shawn Parry-Giles, "Propaganda, Effect, and the Cold War: Gauging the Status of America's 'War of Words,'" *Political Communication* 11 (1994): 203–13.

57. See George Gallup, *The Sophisticated Poll Watcher's Guide* (Princeton, N.J.: Princeton Opinion, 1972), 231.

58. Gallup, "Why We Are Doing So Badly," 502.

59. George H Gallup, "What We Don't Know Can Hurt Us," *New York Times Magazine,* Nov. 4, 1951, 12.

60. Gallup, "Why We Are Doing So Badly," 502.

61. Gallup, "We Have Been Outsold," 143.

62. Gallup, "What We Don't Know Can Hurt Us," 50–51.

63. The President's Committee on International Information Activities, the so-called Jackson Committee, was named for its chair, William Jackson, but the driving force behind the committee was C. D. Jackson. The latter served as Eisenhower's psychological warfare chief during World War II and came to the White House to fill the peculiarly Cold War post of Special Assistant to the President for Psychological Warfare. In that capacity, C. D. Jackson served as one of Eisenhower's closest advisers and chief speechwriters. Over the objections of Secretary Dulles and the State Department, Jackson played a major role in drafting the two major presidential addresses that anchored the administration's "peace offensive" against the Soviets in 1953: the "Chance for Peace" speech in April and the "Atoms for Peace" speech in December. See Thomas F. Soapes, "A Cold Warrior Seeks Peace: Eisenhower's Strategy for Disarmament," *Diplomatic History* 4 (1980): 70; Green, *American Propaganda Abroad,* 28–29; and J. Michael Hogan, "Eisenhower and Open Skies: A Case Study in 'Psychological Warfare,'" in *Eisenhower's War of Words: Rhetoric and Leadership,* ed. Martin J. Medhurst (East Lansing: Michigan State University Press, 1994), 139–40.

64. C. D. Jackson, Memorandum to General Eisenhower, Dec. 17, 1952, Psychological Warfare, Box 29, Administration Series, Whitman File, Eisenhower Library.

65. The President's Committee on International Information Activities, "Report to the President," June 30, 1953 (hereafter Jackson Committee Report), U.S. President's Committee on International Activities (Jackson Committee): Records, 1950–1953, Box 14, Eisenhower Library.

66. James C Hagerty, White House press release, July 8, 1953, Time Inc./Jackson Committee, Box 52, C. D. Jackson Papers: 1934–1967, Eisenhower Library, 3.

67. Jackson Committee Report, 64.

68. Ibid., 1.

69. Ibid., 4.

70. Ibid., 59.

71. Ibid., 56.

72. Ibid., 91.

73. Ibid., 90.

74. Ibid., 95.

75. Ibid., 102.

76. Ibid., 60.

77. Ibid., 61.

78. Ibid., 75.

79. Ibid., 105.

80. Ibid., 60.

81. Ibid.

82. Ibid., 55.

83. Ibid., 72.

84. Ibid., 74.

85. Ibid., 73.

86. Ibid., 74–75.

87. Ibid., 70.

88. Ibid., 34.

89. Ibid., 55.

90. Ibid., 68.

91. "The USIA Program for 1954," July 15, 1953, Official File 247, Box 909, White House Central Files, Eisenhower Library.

92. John Read Burr to Abbott Washburn, July 15, 1953, Official File 247, Box 909, White House Central Files, Eisenhower Library.

93. Jackson Committee Report, 104.

94. Ibid., 64.

95. Ibid., 104. The committee's reference is to Eisenhower's radio address to the American people on May 19, 1953, in which the president concluded: "The truth is that our danger cannot be fixed or confined to one specific instant. We live in an age of peril." See Dwight D. Eisenhower, "Radio Address to the American People on the National Security and Its Costs, May 19, 1953," in *Public Papers of the Presidents of the United States* (hereafter *Public Papers*), *1953* (Washington, D.C.: GPO, 1960), 307.

96. Jackson Committee Report, 106.

97. See the memorandum to Robert Cutler, May 25, 1953, and the editors' note 1 in the secret memorandum to C. D. Jackson, Aug. 24, 1953, in *The Papers of Dwight David Eisenhower*, vols. 14–

17, *The Presidency: The Middle Years,* ed. Louis Galambos and Daun Van Ee (Baltimore: Johns Hopkins University Press, 1996), 14:251–52, 487.

98. McGeorge Bundy, *Danger and Survival: Choices About the Bomb in the First Fifty Years* (New York: Random House, 1988), 289.

99. J. Robert Oppenheimer, "Atomic Weapons and American Policy," *Foreign Affairs* 31 (1953): 528–29.

100. Bundy, *Danger and Survival,* 289.

101. Oppenheimer, "Atomic Weapons," 531–32.

102. See the editors' note 1 to the secret memorandum to C. D. Jackson, Aug. 24, 1953, in *Papers of Dwight David Eisenhower,* 14:487.

103. Stephen E Ambrose, *Eisenhower: Soldier and President* (New York: Touchstone, 1990), 339.

104. Eisenhower, "Radio Address to the American People," 307.

105. James Lambie, "Proposal for Operation Edify: A Public Information Program to Acquaint the American People with the Realities of this 'Age of Peril,'" July 15, 1953, Candor and United Nations Speech—Dec. 8, 1953, Box 12, White House Central Files, Eisenhower Library.

106. "Project 'Candor'—To Inform the Public of the Realities of the 'Age of Peril,'" July 22, 1953, PSB 091-4 U.S. (2), Box 17, White House Central Files, Eisenhower Library.

107. George Gallup to James M Lambie, Jr., June 16, 1953, Chronological File: May–June 1953 (1), Box 3, James M. Lambie, Jr.: Papers, 1953–1961, Eisenhower Library.

108. James M Lambie, Jr. to George Gallup, June 26, 1953, Candor and United Nations Speech—Dec. 8, 1953, Box 12, White House Central Files, Eisenhower Library.

109. George Gallup to James M Lambie, Jr., June 30, 1953, Candor and United Nations Speech—Dec. 8, 1953, Box 12, White House Central Files, Eisenhower Library.

110. George H Gallup, *The Gallup Poll: Public Opinion, 1935–1971,* 3 vols. (New York: Random House, 1972), 2:1161–62.

111. According to the poll, 79 percent agreed that Russia was "trying to build herself up to be the ruling power of the world," whereas only 10 percent thought Russia was just "building up protection against being attacked in another war," and 11 percent had no opinion. See Gallup, *Gallup Poll,* 2:1163.

112. Gallup asked this question twice, both before and after news that Russia had tested a hydrogen bomb. In the poll reported in August, only 17 percent thought Russia could, at that time, "knock out" the United States with a "surprise all-out atom bomb attack." When Gallup repeated the poll the following month, the question read: "Do you think Russia would be able, now, to knock out the United States with a surprise all-out atom and hydrogen bomb attack?" The addition of "and hydrogen" produced only a sight change in the results, increasing the "yes" responses from 17 to 21 percent. See Gallup, *Gallup Poll,* 2:1161–62, 1174.

113. Ibid., 2:1162.

114. Ibid., 2:1120.

115. Lambie apparently had in mind what Gallup had been touting in the technical literature as the "quintamensional approach" to question design. See George H. Gallup, "The Quintamensional Plan of Question Design," *Public Opinion Quarterly* 11 (1947): 385–93.

116. James M Lambie, Jr., to George Gallup, July 11, 1953, Candor and United Nations Speech—Dec. 8, 1953, Box 12, White House Central Files, Eisenhower Library.

117. James M Lambie, Jr., "Memorandum for C. D. Jackson: Research as an Aid to Operation Candor," July 11, 1953, Candor and United National Speech—Dec. 8, 1953, Box 12, White House Central Files, Eisenhower Library. Lambie estimated the cost of this research at $15,000 to $20,000 and suggested that the Ford Foundation might be persuaded to pick up the tab.

118. In his memoirs, Eisenhower charitably credited Jackson with agreeing that "the exposition left the listener with only a new terror, not a new hope." However, Eisenhower's rejection of multiple drafts of the speech suggest that the two men did not see eye-to-eye on the basic approach to the speech. See Dwight D. Eisenhower, *Mandate for Change, 1953–1956: The White House Years* (Garden City, N.Y.: Doubleday, 1963), 252.

119. Ambrose, *Eisenhower: Soldier and President,* 340.

120. See the editors' note 1 to the secret memorandum to C. D. Jackson, Aug. 24, 1953, in *Papers of Dwight David Eisenhower,* 14:487.

121. Eisenhower, *Mandate for Change,* 252.

122. Martin J. Medhurst, "Eisenhower's 'Atoms for Peace' Speech: A Case Study in the Strategic Use of Language," *Communication Monographs* 54 (1987): 204.

123. Martin J. Medhurst, "Atoms for Peace and Nuclear Hegemony: The Rhetorical Structure of a Cold War Campaign," *Armed Forces & Society* 23 (1997): 590.

124. Rachel L Holloway, "'Keeping the Faith': Eisenhower Introduces the Hydrogen Bomb," in *Eisenhower's War of Words,* ed. Medhurst, 54.

125. Dwight D Eisenhower, "Inaugural Address, Jan. 20, 1953," in *Public Papers, 1953,* 1.

126. "Text of Statement and Comments by Strauss on Hydrogen Bomb Tests in the Pacific," *New York Times,* Apr. 1, 1953, A20.

127. Holloway, "Keeping the Faith," 64

128. Dwight D Eisenhower, "Radio and Television Address to the American People on the State of the Nation," in *Public Papers, 1954* (Washington, D.C.: GPO, 1960), 372–89.

129. Holloway, "Keeping the Faith," 61.

130. According to the poll, 65 percent favored such disclosure, whereas 26 percent were opposed. See Gallup, *Gallup Poll,* 2:1174.

131. See the editors' note 1 to Eisenhower's memo to C. D. Jackson, Aug. 24, 1953, in *Papers of Dwight D. Eisenhower,* 14:487.

132. Ambrose, *Eisenhower: Soldier and President,* 339.

133. Paul Boyer, *By the Bomb's Early Light: American Thought and Culture at the Dawn of the Atomic Age* (New York: Pantheon, 1985), 68, 70–71, 93.

134. As Barry Brummett writes, predictions of disaster or the end of the world have been, in most apocalyptic rhetoric throughout history, "secondary to, and derivative from," the ways in which such discourse "comforts and empowers" audiences in contexts of "anomie and chaos." See Barry Brummett, *Contemporary Apocalyptic Rhetoric* (New York: Praeger, 1991), 31, 38.

135. Carl I. Hovland, Irving L. Janis, and Harold H. Kelley, *Communication and Persuasion: Psychological Studies of Opinion Change* (New Haven, Conn.: Yale University Press, 1953), 56–98.

136. Holloway, "Keeping the Faith," 69.

137. Robert Jay Lifton, *Death in Life: Survivors of Hiroshima* (New York: Random House, 1968).

138. Simpson, *Science of Coercion,* 115.

139. Ibid., 117.

140. Ibid., 94, 116.

141. George Gallup, "Foreword," in John M Fenton, *In Your Opinion: The Managing Editor of the Gallup Poll Looks at Polls, Politics, and the People from 1945 to 1960* (Boston: Little, Brown, 1960), ix.

142. George Gallup, "Main Street Rates the Issues," *Vital Speeches of the Day* (Jan. 1, 1948): 177

143. See Gallup, *Sophisticated Poll Watcher's Guide,* 230–32.

144. Gallup, "Why We Are Doing So Badly," 504.

145. Gallup, "Foreword," in Fenton, *In Your Opinion,* ix–x.

146. James David Barber, *The Presidential Character: Predicting Performance in the White House,* 3d ed. (Englewood Cliffs: Prentice-Hall, 1972), 134–48.

147. Mary S McAuliffe, "Commentary: Eisenhower, the President," *Journal of American History* 68 (1981): 625.

148. Martin J. Medhurst, "Introduction," in *Eisenhower's War of Words,* ed. Medhurst, 2.

149. As Richard Immerman has observed, the conventional portrait of Eisenhower suggested that Eisenhower's foreign policies were largely designed by Dulles. Yet Eisenhower clearly disagreed with Dulles about rhetorical strategy. While Dulles "methodically prosecuted the Soviets for their actions," Eisenhower believed that his secretary of state "neglected to emphasize sufficiently the constructive aspects of U.S. policy." See Richard H. Immerman, "Eisenhower and Dulles: Who Made the Decisions?" *Political Psychology* 1 (1979): 36.

CHAPTER SIX

Liberals All!

Politics and Rhetoric in Cold War America

H. W. BRANDS

Ten years past the end of the Cold War and twenty years after the collapse of liberalism as the defining motif in domestic American politics, it is sometimes difficult to remember how closely intertwined those two phenomena were. Certainly the rhetoric of the Cold War suffused the liberal initiatives of the post–World War II period. Determining strict causality in history is a fool's game; however, working on the premise that what elected officials *say* bears some resemblance to what they *mean,* a strong case can be made that the Cold War in fact provided significant impetus for some of the most important liberal reforms of the postwar era.

A full examination of this topic would require nothing less than a history of postwar America. Such is not attempted here. Rather, three presidencies are investigated: those of Dwight Eisenhower, John Kennedy, and Lyndon Johnson. The topic is Cold War liberalism during the sixteen years from 1953 to 1969, which encompassed both the institutionalization of the Cold War and the efflorescence of liberalism. A look at this stretch, although hardly definitive, may nonetheless be instructive.

First, however, a remark about the nature of liberalism is in order. The term has had a dozen definitions since coming into popular use in the nineteenth century. Self-styled liberals have attached all manner of positive attributes to it, and conscious conservatives have denied those and substituted a host of negative traits. In the late twentieth century about the only thing both sides agree on is that liberals have greater confidence in the efficacy of government than conservatives do. Put another way, if you think government is or can be part of the solution to important social problems, you are a liberal; if you don't, or you at least have grave doubts, you are a conservative.

Waging Peace

Eisenhower was a conservative by instinct. As president he constantly fretted that big government would disrupt the working of the American market economy, and he endlessly lectured his cabinet and anyone else who would listen on the need to balance the federal budget. At times even members of his own administration thought he was carrying his cost cutting to extremes. "If we ever go to the American people and tell them that we are putting a balanced budget ahead of national defense," warned Defense Secretary Charles Wilson, at a moment when Eisenhower's defense policy seemed to many to be doing just that, "it would be a terrible day." [1]

On the other hand, having spent almost his entire adult life working for the federal government, Eisenhower was not as completely convinced that Washington would screw up anything it set its hand to as some of his conservative friends were. He was also realistic enough to recognize that once certain government responsibilities had been incorporated into people's expectations, shedding those responsibilities would be painful—to the people themselves and to whatever party was behind the shedding. "Should any political party attempt to abolish social security and eliminate labor laws and farm programs, you would not hear of that party again in our political history," he told his brother Edgar. The president recognized that some Republicans—including Edgar—advocated just such abolition. But he did not take them seriously. "Their number is negligible and they are stupid." [2]

Eisenhower had more respect for the captain-of-industry types with which he filled his cabinet. Yet these were no swashbuckling Harrimans and Carnegies and Rockefellers. Defense Secretary Wilson, formerly president of General Motors, best exemplified the new model of corporate executives who had made their peace with the welfare state and were making their profits with the Cold War—in some cases directly, in some cases from the overall prosperity the Cold War rearmament helped spur. (This prosperity came as no surprise to those who ordered the rearmament program. The authors of NSC-68 had predicted: "The economic effects of the program might be to increase the gross national product by more than the amount being absorbed for additional military and foreign assistance purposes. One of the most significant lessons of our World War II experience was that the American economy, when it operates at a level approaching full efficiency, can provide enormous resources for purposes other than civilian consumption while simultaneously providing a high standard of living." [3]) As executives like Wilson recognized, social security, unemployment insurance and other federal guarantees to workers helped stabilize the labor force and broadened the base for programs corporations might otherwise have had to pay for themselves. In any event, during a period of economic growth such costs as these programs created for businesses could be passed along to consumers.

Eisenhower did not disagree with the liberalism as social-stabilizer argument. Indeed, not content with defending social security against conservative attack, he insisted that the program be enlarged. At his prodding Congress raised benefits to recipients and extended coverage to some ten million people previously excluded.

But Eisenhower was equally concerned with what the federal government could do to fortify American society in its contest with Communism. This concern led him to support projects that would not have passed his muster on their domestic merits alone. A modest example was the Saint Lawrence Seaway. Many Republicans—and more than a few Democrats—wondered why the president placed such a priority on completing the series of locks and canals that would facilitate ship traffic between the Great Lakes and the Atlantic. Conservatives who still daydreamed of dynamiting dams of the Tennessee Valley Authority looked on the Saint Lawrence project as another federal boondoggle. But Eisenhower closely heeded studies indicating that the mother lode of American iron ore, the Mesabi range in Minnesota, would fail before long, leaving the steelmakers of the Great Lakes—and the American arms makers who needed the steel to fabricate their weapons—dependent on ore from abroad. The Saint Lawrence Seaway would ensure that this ore found its way to the blast furnaces and rolling mills and thence to the ship hulls and artillery barrels. For Eisenhower the national security argument provided just the hammer to beat down the budget hawks, and he pounded the appropriation through Congress.

Eisenhower's support of the interstate highway system revealed similar considerations. In the decade since Detroit had reconverted from tanks and planes to cars, Americans had taken to the highways with a vengeance—almost literally, in consequence of the inadequacy of roads that had not been updated since before the Great Depression and that now exacted an alarming toll of fatal mishaps. As a country boy, Eisenhower appreciated what good roads could mean to those who had to travel long distances to markets and towns. But as a Republican he appreciated how much the roads cost—and how roads and highways had been chiefly the responsibility of the states.

What tipped the balance for Eisenhower was the argument that good roads would enhance national defense. At a time when the threat of Soviet air attack was growing, and when antiaircraft defenses were unreliable and antimissile defenses nonexistent, the only hope of materially reducing civilian casualties in the event of general war was to evacuate targeted cities. The proposed new highways—four-lane, limited-access roads without stoplights or other obstructions—would move people out of cities many times faster than the current tangle of roads left over from the horse-and-buggy era. Moreover, the federal responsibility for this aspect of the program was irrefutable. Since the eighteenth century, national defense had been a federal responsibility; it remained so now more than ever.

So was the Cold War therefore responsible for what turned out to be the largest public-works project in world history? Not by itself. Concrete makers, truckers, property owners along likely rights-of-way, congressmen from congested suburbs—these and dozens of other interest groups had reasons for supporting the interstate system that had nothing to do with the danger of a Soviet air raid. But major legislation always subsumes a congeries of motives—and almost always generates substantial opposition. In this case, the defenders of the status quo— including not simply taxpayers' advocates and philosophical antifederalists but also railroad executives and unions and barge and pipeline owners and other groups that expected to be damaged by competition from the new highways—had been holding off the road gangs for years. The Cold War was the new element in the situation, and it provided just the additional argument needed to bulldoze the opposition and get the graders moving.

The connection between the Cold War and another manifestation of Eisenhower era liberalism was more straightforward. From the start of his administration the president had resisted conservative demands to cut federal aid to education. At one early cabinet meeting the secretary of health, education, and welfare, Oveta Culp Hobby, unveiled plans to trim school spending. Eisenhower objected at once. "I am amazed at the thought of an education cut!" he told the assembled group. "This is the most important thing in our society." Looking straight at Hobby he declared, "Every liberal—including me—will disapprove."[4] Yet, liberal or not, Eisenhower at first was not prepared to expand federal aid to education, citing budgetary restrictions and the longstanding tradition of local and state responsibility for education.

Early in his second term the Cold War erased his qualms—along with those of millions of other Americans. In October, 1957, the Soviet Union launched the first successful artificial earth satellite. Sputnik astonished the world and stunned Americans, who until then had complacently assumed that their country enjoyed a secure scientific lead over the Communists. The implications of Sputnik were sobering: a political system that could launch a satellite clear around the earth could soon—if not already—launch a warhead halfway around the earth from Russia to America. Not only was American prestige on the line; so also was American security.

Besides predictably sparking demands for increased spending on defense and space exploration, the Sputnik scare made liberals out of nearly everyone on the education issue. Congress immediately began searching for ways to produce scientists and engineers who would equal Russia's. Hearings had not even started before it became obvious that the legislature would order a major package of aid to science and technical education; the only question was the size and shape of the package. Eisenhower found himself in the congenial—for a Republican president—position of acting as a brake on the more liberal designs of Democrats on Capitol Hill. But when all the maneuvering and negotiating ended in August, 1958, the National Defense Education Act authorized the spending of nearly $1 billion over four years—$1 billion that almost certainly would not have been spent absent the spur of the Cold War.

If Eisenhower had to be nudged into greater federal activism on education, he had to be dragged kicking and screaming into a larger role on race. His reluctance here may have reflected what he had learned in school of the history of his home state: how race had made "bleeding Kansas" the first battlefield of the Civil War. Perhaps the Kansas origins of the seminal 1954 Supreme Court case *Brown v. Board of Education of Topeka* somehow contributed to his determination to keep hands off. For whatever reasons, he essentially left race matters alone for three years after *Brown.*

But the cost of avoiding the issue increased with passing time. The 1955 Montgomery, Alabama, bus boycott brought Jim Crow—and Martin Luther King, Jr.—to national attention. More to the point for Eisenhower, it brought the American race problem to international attention. Foreign visitors had long remarked on the discrepancy between the rhetoric of American equality and the practice of American discrimination. But as the European colonial empires crumbled after 1945 and the new states of Asia and Africa gained independence and sent representatives to Washington and the United Nations in New York, America's racial situation grew more embarrassing than ever. It also grew potentially dangerous to American national interests. Henry Cabot Lodge, Eisenhower's UN ambassador, made this point repeatedly in messages to the president. "At the United Nations General Assembly," Lodge declared, "you see the world as a place in which a large majority of the human race is non-white. The non-white majority is growing every year, as more African states gain their independence." Lodge asserted that America would have great difficulty winning the allegiance of the new nations unless it could demonstrate its bona fides on the issue of racial equality.

The problem of world opinion grew critical during the autumn of 1957 when Gov. Orval Faubus of Arkansas abetted the violent obstruction of federal integration orders at Little Rock's Central High School. Lodge was dismayed. "Here at the United Nations I can see clearly the harm that the riots in Little Rock are doing to our foreign relations," he wrote. Once again he urged the president to demonstrate the nation's commitment to racial equality.[5]

Eisenhower was as reluctant as before to involve the federal government in what he considered social engineering, but the Little Rock resistance left him no choice. How could the U.S. government lead the Free World if it could not enforce its authority within America? In announcing his decision to send federal troops to Little Rock, Eisenhower made it plain that he personally did not agree with court-ordered integration, yet he went on to say that "our personal opinions about the decision have no bearing on the matter of enforcement." The responsibility and authority of the Supreme Court to interpret the Constitution were "very clear," as was the duty of the executive branch to uphold the Court's ruling. The Little Rock matter had the most serious implications not only for public order in America but for the fate of freedom around the world:

> At a time when we face grave situations abroad because of the hatred that Communism bears toward a system of government based on human rights, it would be difficult to exaggerate the harm that is being done to the prestige and influence, and indeed to the safety, of our nation and the world.
>
> Our enemies are gloating over this incident and using it everywhere to misrepresent our whole nation. We are portrayed as a violator of those standards of conduct which the peoples of the world united to proclaim in the Charter of the United Nations. There they affirmed "faith in fundamental human rights" and "in the dignity and worth of the human person" and they did so "without distinction as to race, sex, language or religion."
>
> And so, with deep confidence, I call upon the citizens of the State of Arkansas to assist in bringing to an immediate end all interference with the law and its processes. If resistance to the Federal Court orders ceases at once, the further presence of Federal troops will be unnecessary and the City of Little Rock will return to its normal habits of peace and order and a blot upon the fair name and high honor of our nation in the world will be removed.[6]

Diehard segregationists scoffed at Eisenhower's appeal to patriotism and national security. Some even turned the argument around, calling the president a Hitler and a Stalin for employing military force against American citizens. But for those many in the middle on the race question—those who would ultimately determine the outcome of the struggle against the segregationist system—the linking of civil rights to America's Cold War fortunes provided a powerful new argument for racial equality.

The New Frontier Thesis

John Kennedy made the link between liberalism and the Cold War explicit from the beginning of his administration. "Let every nation know," he announced at his inauguration, "whether it wishes us well or ill, that we shall pay any price, bear any burden, meet any hardship, support any friend, oppose any foe to assure the survival and success of liberty." This was the cold warrior speaking, but the liberal quickly chimed in. "If a free society cannot help the many who are poor," the new president explained, "it cannot save the few who are rich." Kennedy made a particular pledge to the nations of the Western Hemisphere, lately beguiled by the Castro revolution in Cuba: The United States would "assist free men and free governments in casting off the chains of poverty." To the world at large he extended a promise of cooperation in the "struggle against the common enemies of man: tyranny, poverty, disease and war."

Like Eisenhower, Kennedy perceived an intimate connection between what Americans did abroad and what they did at home. On behalf of his "new generation of Americans" he asserted a national refusal "to witness or permit the slow undoing of those human rights to which this nation has always been committed, and to which we are committed today at home and around the world." The same spirit of endeavor that must motivate Americans domestically would energize the advocates of freedom overseas. "My fellow Americans: ask not what your country can do for you—ask what you can do for your country. My fellow citizens of the world: ask not what America will do for you, but what together we can do for the freedom of man."[7]

Kennedy marched boldly forward in both foreign and domestic affairs. In April, 1961, he ordered the invasion of Cuba by a small contingent of CIA-trained and -supported anti-Castro exiles. The operation immediately exploded in his face, failing spectacularly and convincing him to be more circumspect in the future, although not necessarily more cautious. He set aside further invasion plans in favor of attempts to assassinate Castro.

The Bay of Pigs fiasco prompted Nikita Khrushchev to try to slip some Soviet nuclear missiles into Cuba. When discovered by American spy satellites in the autumn of 1962 the Cuban missiles provoked the most terrifying hundred hours in the entire history of the Cold War. Americans clustered around their television sets—those who were not out digging bomb shelters in their backyards—to determine whether Kennedy's demand for the missiles' withdrawal and his imposition of an anti-Soviet blockade of Cuba would trigger the holocaust many had feared since the beginning of the Cold War. To the world's relief, Khrushchev accepted Kennedy's public promise not to invade Cuba and his private pledge to withdraw U.S. missiles from Turkey, and pulled the Russian rockets out.

Kennedy emerged from the crisis as the model cold warrior: a cool but implacable foe of Communism. Although some Americans, and doubtless a larger percentage of foreigners, wondered whether it had been strictly necessary to push to the brink of nuclear war to restore the strategic status quo in the Caribbean, Kennedy's performance won him the plaudits of his compatriots. His approval rating jumped sharply—from 62 percent in the last Gallup poll before the crisis to 74 percent in the first one afterward.[8] Americans were reminded, in terms that could scarcely have been more arresting, that the world was a dangerous place, and most were willing to accept that their safety required decisive action by their government.

It was Kennedy's belief, and again one that a majority of Americans seemed willing to accept, that similar decisiveness was required in domestic affairs. In April, 1962, the United States Steel Corporation announced a price increase of 3.5 percent in its basic product line, and within days the other major steel firms followed suit. Kennedy had spent the previous months jawboning steelworkers to keep their wage demands within the 3 percent guideline established by his Council of Economic Advisers to restrain inflation. The steel unions, complaining that their members had already lost ground but unwilling to defy a popular Democratic president, grumblingly agreed. The president hardly had time to savor his victory before the steel corporations unveiled their price hike, which implicitly made Kennedy appear a shill for U.S. Steel and its fellow oligopolists. Privately he muttered, "My father always told me that all businessmen were sons of bitches, but I never believed it till now."[9] To the nation he decried the price hike as "a wholly unjustifiable and irresponsible defiance of the public interest."

In particular, the actions of the steel companies jeopardized American security. "In this serious hour in our Nation's history," Kennedy declared, "when we are confronted with grave crises in Berlin and Southeast Asia . . . when we are asking reservists to leave their homes and families for months on end and servicemen to risk their lives—and four were killed in the last two days in Vietnam— . . . at a time when restraint and sacrifice are being asked of every citizen, the American people will find it hard, as I do, to accept a situation in which a tiny handful of steel executives whose pursuit of private power and profit exceeds their sense of public responsibility can show such utter contempt for the interests of 185 million Americans." Kennedy explained that the Defense Department had calculated what the steel hike would cost the country's military. "It would add, Secretary McNamara informed me this morning, an estimated $1 billion to the cost of our defenses, at a time when every dollar is needed for national security and other purposes." Besides the direct cost to weapons purchases, the hike would make it more difficult for the government to improve the American balance of trade and to stem the outflow of American gold. The gold drain was especially troublesome. "It is necessary to stem it for our national security, if we're going to pay for our security commitments abroad."[10]

With the nation's security at risk, the president felt justified in bringing the full weight of the federal government to bear to force repeal of the price hike. He announced investigations by the Justice Department and the Federal Trade Commission into the possibility of criminal price-fixing in the steel industry. He ordered the Pentagon to review its procurement practices and steer the public's business away from the offending firms. Administration allies in Congress launched their own probes, making it clear that special legislation targeting the big steel companies was a strong possibility.

The steel executives, unaccustomed to public pillory for lack of patriotism and reckless disregard of national security, folded in the face of Kennedy's counterattack. Within days they capitulated and rolled back their prices.

It had been an astonishing display of executive power. The price controls of the world wars had lapsed long before, but Kennedy insisted on reimposing them, in effect, against one of the most basic and powerful industries in the country. Needless to say, conservatives cried that the sky was falling. The *Wall Street Journal* blistered the president's cavalier use of "naked power"; the Republican congressional leadership warned darkly of "police state methods." The president of the American Chamber of Commerce declared, "We should remember that dictators in other lands usually come to power under accepted constitutional procedures."[11]

Kennedy shrugged off the criticism, expecting no better from those boardroom SOBs. He had a harder time ignoring another response from Wall Street: the collapse of the stock market a month later. Not since 1929 had stocks tumbled so alarmingly. Naturally, conservatives and other Kennedy critics laid the swoon on the White House's doorstep.

Kennedy was not willing to accept the blame, but neither could he ignore the ominous portents of the stock dive for the economy. In 1962 the country was not so far from the Great Depression that Americans could not recall how the last such stock plunge had ushered in a decade of economic and social distress and led, at least indirectly, to World War II. Kennedy's economic advisers, led by Walter Heller, had been urging him to employ the tools of Keynesian theory to stimulate the economy. Although the president sympathized, until now he had judged that the political costs of a stimulus package of budget deficits outweighed the economic benefits. But the stock crash demonstrated the downside of doing nothing, and he threw his support to the deficit squad.

Not completely, though. While Heller and the others advocated unbalancing the budget by raising spending, Kennedy chose to cut taxes. By itself the tax cut might have been taken as indicating a conservative shift—a curtailment of government activity. And, indeed, Kennedy soothed the jitters of the financial classes by presenting it in just such terms. In a speech to the Economic Club of New York he asserted, "The best means of strengthening demand among consumers and business is to reduce the burden on private income and the deterrents to private initiative which are imposed by our present tax system."[12]

But the proposed tax cut, far from signifying a retreat from government activism, really represented a signal advance. By embracing Keynesianism, Kennedy assumed on behalf of the federal government the responsibility for managing the national economy. For decades the connection between federal fiscal policy and the condition of the economy had been recognized, if not entirely agreed upon, but not until now had any administration openly claimed a mandate for manipulating tax and spending policies to spur the economy to faster growth. As before, Kennedy downplayed the liberal implications of his decision, portraying it as an essentially technical matter. "What is at stake in our economic decisions today," he told a commencement crowd at Yale University in June, 1962, "is not some grand warfare of rival ideologies which will sweep the country with passion but the practical management of a modern economy. What we need is not labels and cliches but more basic discussion of the sophisticated and technical questions involved in keeping a great economic machinery moving ahead."[13]

Significantly, Kennedy justified both his proposed tax cut and what he saw as the overall federal responsibility for economic management in terms of national security. In his New York Economic Club address—delivered while the world was still getting over its nervousness from the Cuban missile crisis—he declared: "Less than a month ago this Nation reminded the world that it possessed both the will and the weapons to meet any threat to the security of free men. The gains we have made will not be given up, and the course that we have pursued will not be abandoned. But in the long run, that security will not be determined by military or diplomatic moves alone. It will be affected by the decisions of finance ministers as well as by the decisions of Secretaries of State and Secretaries of Defense; by the deployment of fiscal and monetary weapons as well as by military weapons; and above all by the strength of this Nation's economy as well as by the strength of our defenses." Kennedy reminded the assembled bankers, brokers, and manufacturers that Khrushchev had predicted that history would turn decisively in socialism's direction when the Soviet economy out-produced the American economy, which it surely would. Khrushchev's prediction—warning, rather—made the health of the American economy an issue of highest national security, a matter "not merely our own well-being, but also very vitally the defense of the free world." Under such circumstances the federal government could not shirk responsibility for managing the economy.[14]

Kennedy's deliberate deficit had the anticipated effect of stimulating the economy, although he did not live to see this vindication of the Keynesian gospel. Neither did he live to see the attainment of the most ambitious pledge of his administration, one that, perhaps better than any other, summarized both the intimate connection between foreign and domestic policy during the Cold War and the can-do spirit of 1960s liberalism. In May, 1961, the president declared, "I believe that this nation should commit itself to achieving the goal, before this decade is out, of landing a man on the moon and returning him safely to earth." The context of Kennedy's challenge made clear that this was no disinterested call for expanding human knowledge of the cosmos. The space pledge was part of a special supplementary State of the Union message. The president acknowledged that State of the Union messages were traditionally annual affairs but added that the tradition had been broken in extraordinary times. He went on: "These are extraordinary times. And we face an extraordinary challenge. Our strength as well as our convictions have imposed upon this nation the role of leader in freedom's cause."

Most of Kennedy's address dealt with the nuts and bolts—literally, in the case of the new weaponry he requested of national defense. Beyond the new helicopters, armored personnel carriers, and howitzers the army wanted, he asked for increased funding for American "special forces" (notably the Green

Berets), for American economic and military aid to friends and allies abroad, for counter-Communist informational activities, for civil defense (fallout shelters and the like), and for other activities traditionally within the realm of national defense. He also emphasized his theme of the centrality of a healthy economy to national defense, and in this vein he proposed a manpower development and training program.

But as important as anything material was what America could do to win the moral support of those peoples beyond the superpower alliance systems. "The great battleground for the defense and expansion of freedom today is the whole southern half of the globe—Asia, Latin America, Africa and the Middle East—the lands of the rising peoples. Their revolution is the greatest in human history." American arms and American money could help these peoples defend themselves, but arms and money would not suffice. What was required additionally was a demonstration of the dynamism of the free world. Unfortunately, recent events—especially the Soviet Union's successful orbiting of cosmonaut Yuri Gagarin—suggested that the Soviet system was the one destined to dominate the future. "If we are to win the battle that is now going on around the world between freedom and tyranny, the dramatic achievements in space which occurred in recent weeks should have made clear to us all, as did the Sputnik in 1957, the impact of this adventure on the minds of men everywhere, who are attempting to make a determination of which road they should take." Kennedy did not deny that the Soviets had a lead in space technology, but he refused to surrender the heavens to the Communists. "While we cannot guarantee that we shall one day be first, we can guarantee that any failure to make this effort will make us last. . . . We go into space because whatever mankind must undertake, free men must fully share."

Kennedy acknowledged the huge costs of the adventure he was proposing: up to $10 billion during the next six years alone. The effort would mirror, in many ways, the mobilization of wartime. "This decision demands a major national commitment of scientific and technical manpower, materiel and facilities, and the possibility of their diversion from other important activities where they are already thinly spread. It means a degree of dedication, organization and discipline which have not always characterized our research and development efforts." Neither scientists alone nor the government would be the ones putting that first American on the moon. "It will be an entire nation. For all of us must work to put him there." Only a united, national effort would enable the country to "move forward, with the full speed of freedom, in the exciting adventure of space."[15]

All the Way with LBJ

Along with much other unfinished business, Kennedy bequeathed the moon to Lyndon Johnson. The thirty-sixth president was as much a Cold War liberal as the thirty-fifth, but where Kennedy came to Cold War liberalism from the Cold War side, Johnson arrived from the liberal side. Where Kennedy had reveled in the grand politics of war and peace and merely tolerated the pedestrian politics of bill drafting and vote counting, Johnson did just the opposite. Johnson's first love was legislating, his passion the flesh-and-blood business of cloakroom cajoling, the imploring, intimidating, berating, promising process of improving the lives of ordinary Americans by building a new school here, underwriting job training there, subsidizing rent across the street, and paying for medical care around the corner. Johnson accepted the Cold War the way many people accept their parents' religion: it explained prominent features of the world he inhabited, most of the people he knew believed in it, and he saw no reason to question it. But while his foreign affairs theology was strictly high church, his domestic faith was tent meeting revivalist. Brother Lyndon was born again in the gospel of government activism, and he devoted his career to spreading the good news.

The Great Society marked the apogee of twentieth-century American liberalism. From the Civil Rights Act of 1964 to the Voting Rights Act of 1965, from the War on Poverty to Medicare, from the Elementary and Secondary Education Act to Model Cities, from the National Wilderness Preservation System to the Water Quality Act of 1965 and the Air Quality Act of 1967, Johnson's reform program enormously expanded the federal government's scope and responsibilities.

Some of these measures were purely domestic, having nothing to do with foreign affairs or national defense. Not even the most ingenious cold warriors could figure out what a national recreation area had to do with American security, except perhaps provide a place for city dwellers to flee to in the event of nuclear attack.

Yet many of the liberal programs *were* drawn into the Cold War nexus. Federal aid to elementary and secondary education had, among other purposes, a goal similar to that of the National Defense Education Act of the Eisenhower administration: to fashion the informed intelligences that would guarantee America's scientific and technological edge over the Communists into the next generation. The War on Poverty would strengthen the economy—and hence the country—overall.

Beyond this, the success of the Great Society would reinforce American security by demonstrating to the world that the American way of life was the one worth emulating. After the Cuban missile crisis, Americans more than ever understood that the struggle between ideological systems must not be by military means alone or even primarily. Rather it must be a contest to determine which system delivered the better life to its people. American prosperity had long been unchallenged, but until now America's commitment to equality was questionable. The Great Society would remedy that, and in the process win the hearts and minds of those billions abroad who would ultimately render the verdict between democracy and Communism.

In his January, 1965, State of the Union address Johnson explicated what he saw as the intimate link between liberalism at home and American success abroad. The United States, he declared, was "at the beginning of the road to the Great Society." The road was long, so the nation needed to get started at once. "I propose that we begin a program in education to ensure every American child the fullest development of his mind and skills. I propose that we begin a massive attack on crippling and killing diseases. I propose that we launch a national effort to make the American city a better and a more stimulating place to live. I propose that we increase the beauty of America and end the poisoning of our rivers and the air that we breathe. I propose that we carry out a new program to develop regions of our country that are now suffering from distress and depression." And so on, through guaranteeing the right to vote, honoring and underwriting the arts, preventing crime and juvenile delinquency, and ending government waste and inefficiency.

Why must the nation tackle this agenda? Partly for the good of Americans, to be sure, but also because the quality of life in America was indissolubly linked to the quality of life in the world, and the quality of life in the world had a direct bearing on American security. "Our concern and interest, compassion and vigilance, extend to every corner of a dwindling planet. . . . We were never meant to be an oasis of liberty and abundance in a worldwide desert of disappointed dreams. Our Nation was created to help strike away the chains of ignorance and misery and tyranny wherever they keep man less than God means him to be." At one time Americans had believed they could seek their salvation apart from the world, but no longer. Speaking a hundred years after the end of the war to save the Union, Johnson proclaimed that America must strive for a new, more perfect form of national unity, and asserted: "The unity we seek cannot realize its full promise in isolation. For today the state of the Union depends, in large measure, upon the state of the world."[16]

Left to his own devices, Johnson might have wished that things were otherwise—that the state of the American union did *not* depend on the state of the world. Where Eisenhower had wanted domestic problems like race to go away so that he could concentrate on the Cold War, Johnson wanted the Cold War to go away so that he could concentrate on domestic problems like race. But neither got what he wanted, and both found the two sets of issues—the foreign and the domestic—irretrievably conflated.

In Johnson's case, the Democratic president understood that tending to the Cold War, in particular its current incarnation in Vietnam, was the cost of maintaining his ability to accomplish domestic reform. "I knew that if we let Communist aggression succeed in taking over South Vietnam," he later explained, "there would follow in this country an endless national debate—a mean and destructive debate—that would shatter my Presidency, kill my administration, and damage our democracy. I knew that Harry Truman and Dean Acheson had lost their effectiveness from the day the Communists took over in China. I believed that the loss of China had played a large role in the rise of Joe McCarthy. And I knew that all these problems, taken together, were chickenshit compared with what might happen if we lost Vietnam."[17]

Of course Vietnam would not have been Johnson's to lose if his Cold War predecessors had not staked American credibility on the survival of a non-Communist regime in Saigon. First Truman, then Eisenhower, and then Kennedy had made Vietnam an American project. Aid to France had transmuted into money and arms for Ngo Dinh Diem; American advisers had followed American arms; the advisers were followed in turn by American combat troops. Nothing had worked for long, and Johnson found himself facing a choice between further escalating the American commitment and watching a decade and a half of American effort, along with the attached prestige, collapse in ignominy. Johnson's orthodox view of the world included the antiappeasement belief that aggression had to be halted at the outset wherever it occurred. Yet even if he had not bought in to the philosophy of global containment, the commitment he inherited from Kennedy would have bound him politically, and he could hardly have done other than he did.

As it was, he sought desperately to keep Vietnam from derailing the Great Society. Despite growing chaos in Saigon after Diem's assassination, Johnson refused for more than a year to take strong action in Vietnam. He cast himself as the peace candidate, against the frightening—to judge by voters' response—Barry Goldwater, and he carefully cultivated congressional support for escalation, most portentously via the Gulf of Tonkin resolution. Even after safely winning election in his own right, and after deciding that escalation was unavoidable, he revealed his decision in careful stages. He delayed large-scale bombing of North Vietnam until after he unveiled the four score antipoverty programs that would form the heart of the Great Society and after he announced his intention to seek what became the Voting Rights Act. He procrastinated on major increases in ground troops until after winning approval of the voting bill, Medicare, and the Elementary and Secondary Education Act. Throughout his presidency he refused to declare a national emergency, call up the reserves, or take any action not absolutely necessary that might jeopardize his domestic reforms.

Johnson appreciated the difficulty of his task. "I knew from the start," he said later, "that I was bound to be crucified either way I moved. If I left the woman I really loved—the Great Society—in order to get involved with that bitch of a war on the other side of the world, then I would lose everything at home. All my programs. All my hopes to feed the hungry and shelter the homeless. All my dreams to provide education and medical care to the browns and the blacks and the lame and the poor. But if I left that war and let the Communists take over South Vietnam, then I would be seen as a coward and my nation would be seen as an appeaser and we would both find it impossible to accomplish anything for anybody anywhere on the entire globe."[18]

The Dilemma of Cold War Liberalism

Johnson's dilemma was the crux of the problem of Cold War liberalism. By linking liberalism so closely to the Cold War, liberals inadvertently made themselves hostage to the success of American Cold War policy. When that policy failed in Vietnam, the blowback battered domestic liberalism. To trace the demise of liberalism would be impossible in the present space; let three observations suffice.

First, by discrediting the most liberal of postwar presidents (indeed, the most liberal president in American history), the debacle in Vietnam made it easy for conservatives to discredit liberalism. Perhaps the Great Society overreached; almost certainly it could never fulfill the ambitious goals set for it by Johnson. But after Vietnam, critics of the Great Society did not have to debate Johnson's reforms on their merits. It was enough that Johnson was in disgrace. Simply by association—one of the oldest rules in politics—so were his policies.

Second, Vietnam shattered the coalition at the heart of Cold War liberalism. Perhaps the strains of the civil rights movement, the War on Poverty, emerging feminism, the counterculture and the various other manifestations of the turbulence of the 1960s eventually would have shattered the Democratic

Party, but Vietnam was the issue that actually did it. It was the detonator of the explosion at the 1968 Democratic convention and the key to the nomination of George McGovern in 1972—one of the most politically disastrous selections in modern American history, and one that made a liberal comeback essentially impossible.

Third, the debacle in Vietnam largely destroyed the popular faith in government on which liberalism ultimately rested. From the beginning of World War II until the mid-1960s, Americans had given government the benefit of the doubt in its efforts to defend them against the Nazis and Japanese militarists and then the Communists. By the evidence of the world war and the early Cold War, this trust was well placed. Moreover, human psychology being what it is, Americans tended to extrapolate their trust from foreign to domestic affairs. If the president said civil rights reform was necessary to American security, Americans were inclined to believe him, just as they had believed the president who declared that the development of the hydrogen bomb was necessary to American security. But then Vietnam gave the lie to a generation of presidents—and in the process showed, through the Pentagon Papers, Watergate, and other evidence, that presidents and their top advisers had quite literally been lying. Americans naturally asked, If elected officials had lied about Vietnam, why should they be trusted on anything else? When trust went out the window with Vietnam, liberalism could not be far behind. And it was not.

Notes

1. H. W. Brands, "The Age of Vulnerability: Eisenhower and the National Insecurity State," *American Historical Review* 94 (1989): 970.

2. Alonzo L. Hamby, *Liberalism and Its Challengers: From F.D.R. to Bush,* 2d ed. (New York: Oxford University Press, 1992), 121.

3. "NSC-68," in *Foreign Relations of the United States, Diplomatic Papers, 1950,* vol. 1 (Washington, D.C.: GPO, 1976), 235–92.

4. Stephen E. Ambrose, *Eisenhower: Soldier and President* (New York: Touchstone, 1990), 115.

5. H. W. Brands, *Cold Warriors: Eisenhower's Generation and American Foreign Policy* (New York: Columbia University Press, 1988), 171.

6. Dwight D. Eisenhower, "Radio and Television Address to the American People on the Situation in Little Rock, Sept. 24, 1957," in *Public Papers of the Presidents of the United States* (hereafter *Public Papers*), *1957* (Washington, D.C.: GPO, 1958), 694.

7. Eisenhower, Jan. 20, 1961, in *Public Papers, 1961* (Washington, D.C.: GPO).

8. George H. Gallup, "Gallup Polls for Oct. 10 and Dec. 5, 1962," in *The Gallup Poll: Public Opinion, 1935–1971,* 3 vols. (New York: Random House, 1972), 3:1786, 1793.

9. James N. Giglio, *The Presidency of John F. Kennedy* (Lawrence: University Press of Kansas, 1991), 131.

10. John F. Kennedy, "The President's News Conference of April 11, 1962," in *Public Papers, 1962*, (Washington, D.C.: GPO, 1963), 315–22.

11. Thomas C. Reeves, *A Question of Character: A Life of John F. Kennedy* (New York: Free Press, 1991), 332; Allen J. Matusow, *The Unraveling of America: A History of Liberalism in the 1960s* (New York: Harper and Row, 1984), 41.

12. Kennedy, Dec. 14, 1962, in *Public Papers, 1962.*

13. Kennedy, June 11, 1962, in *Public Papers, 1962.*

14. Kennedy, Dec. 14, 1962, in *Public Papers, 1962.*

15. Kennedy, May 25, 1961, in *Public Papers, 1961.*

16. Lyndon B. Johnson, Jan. 4, 1965, in *Public Papers, 1965* (Washington, D.C.: GPO, 1966).

17. Doris Kearns, *Lyndon Johnson and the American Dream* (New York: St. Martin's, 1991), 252–53.

18. Ibid., 251–52.

CHAPTER SEVEN

The Rhetoric of Dissent

J. William Fulbright, Vietnam, and the Crisis of International Liberalism

RANDALL BENNETT WOODS

Of fundamental importance to the Vietnam majority that Lyndon Johnson inherited from John F. Kennedy were Cold War liberals. The activist foreign policies of the post–World War II era that produced the war in Southeast Asia were a product of the melding of conservative anti-Communists who defined national security in terms of bases and alliances and who were basically xenophobic, and liberal reformers who were determined to safeguard the national interest by exporting democracy and facilitating overseas economic development. Products of World War II, these internationalists saw America's interests as being tied up with those of the other members of the global community. They opposed Communism because it constituted a totalitarian threat to the principles of cultural diversity, individual liberty, and self-determination that they hoped would prevail at home and abroad. Moreover, as a number of historians have pointed out, in the overheated atmosphere of the early Cold War period, anti-Communism was a political necessity for liberals whose views on domestic issues made them ideologically suspect.[1] For them, the war in Vietnam was nothing less than a crusade to extend the blessings of democracy and individual liberty, and to guarantee stability and prosperity to a people threatened by Communist imperialism. The discrediting of liberal internationalism and the disillusionment of its adherents helped destroy the Vietnam consensus that Lyndon Johnson had inherited. No American played a more significant role in that process than did J. William Fulbright.[2]

A number of factors underlay Fulbright's opposition to the war. Some have argued that the Arkansan acted out of personal pique, miffed at President Johnson's decision not to make him secretary of state.[3] But there was more to his dissent than resentment over thwarted ambition. At various times he blamed the war on the radical right and its hysterical fear of Communism, on the burgeoning military-industrial complex, and on Lyndon Johnson's Texas heritage and Alamo mentality. In the end, however, Fulbright came to believe the liberal internationalist philosophy that he had espoused from 1944 to 1964 was the real culprit. In his view, the union of New Deal liberalism and militant anti-Communism had spawned a foreign policy that was at the same time both idealist and imperialist. Because he came to see in Lyndon Johnson the embodiment of misguided liberalism, Fulbright's opposition to the war focused not only on the issues but on the man he had nominated for the presidency in 1964 and in whom he had placed such high hopes.

On August 2, 1964, the commander of U.S. forces in the Pacific notified the White House that North Vietnamese torpedo boats had staged an unprovoked attack on two American destroyers in international waters in the Gulf of Tonkin. Two days later President Johnson went on television to tell the nation that a second attack had occurred and that he had ordered U.S. planes to retaliate against North Vietnamese patrol boat installations and oil storage facilities. Before his public announcement, the president called members of the congressional leadership to the White House, told them what he intended to do, and asked for a congressional resolution of approval. "Some of our boys are floating around in the water," he added with typical hyperbole.[4]

The Senate debated the Gulf of Tonkin resolution for less than ten hours. During much of that time the chamber was less than one-third full. Fulbright carefully shepherded the resolution through, choking off debate and amendments. The vote in the Senate was an overwhelming 88 to 2, with only Wayne Morse and Ernest Gruening dissenting. Consideration in the House was even more perfunctory. Passage required a mere forty minutes; the vote was unanimous. Uppermost in Fulbright's and the rest of the Democratic leadership's minds were that 1964 was an election year and that Barry Goldwater and the radical right were working frantically to persuade the electorate that Lyndon Johnson specifically and Democrats in general were soft on Communism.[5]

Indeed, by the time of the Tonkin Gulf incident J. William Fulbright was obsessed with the Goldwater candidacy, seeing in it a potential Trojan horse that the radical right intended to use to seize control of American political life. Fulbright had been the first and only U.S. senator to vote against funding for Joe McCarthy's Internal Security Subcommittee, and his experience in the early 1950s made him extremely sensitive to the threat of a third red scare. In fact, by 1961 the "Ultras"—as *Time* termed the religious fundamentalists, Russophobes, militarists, and political opportunists who made up the new right—were a force to be reckoned with. Robert Welch, Billy James Hargis, Dan Smoot, and George Benson had created a world in the minds of their adherents that was fraught with shrewd, unscrupulous, and blood-thirsty Communist agents just waiting for the appropriate moment to seize power and launch a new reign of terror. Members of the radical right saw their enemies as godless murderers, sociopaths enslaved by Marxist ideology who would stop at nothing to obtain their objectives. The enemy had penetrated federal and state government, co-opting various politicians and converting them into fellow travelers.[6]

In 1962 Fulbright had discovered that active-duty military officers in conjunction with John Birchers and members of other radical organizations were holding "Strategy for Survival" seminars in Arkansas and other parts of the country. Not only did speakers at these meetings warn against the dangers of Communist military aggression, they implied that any politician who supported Medicare, Medicaid, or the War on Poverty was a fellow traveler. When Fulbright persuaded the Kennedy administration to issue an order banning such activities by military personnel, he immediately went to the head of the radical right's hate list.[7]

When Lyndon Johnson won a landslide victory over Goldwater in 1964, the Arkansan rejoiced, certain in the knowledge that the election had been a mandate for moderation. He noted with satisfaction that when the issue of Vietnam had come up during the campaign, Johnson had repeatedly insisted that "we are not about to send American boys nine or ten thousand miles away from home to do what Asian boys ought to be doing for themselves."[8] The consensus in the Fulbright camp was that the president would not escalate the war in Vietnam. Admitting that a Communist triumph would insure that "the birch society will get a new lease on life," Fulbright and his chief of staff, Carl Marcy, nevertheless reasoned that Johnson had been elected in 1964 because he had promised to keep the United States out of a land war in Asia, and if the president wanted to win reelection in 1968 he would have to live up to his promises.[9]

In February, 1965, in an effort to bomb North Vietnam into submission, Lyndon Johnson and his advisers launched Operation Rolling Thunder and, when that failed, sent several divisions of American combat troops to South Vietnam. The war had begun in earnest.

Following several conversations with McGeorge Bundy and the president, Walter Lippmann advised his long-time friend Fulbright that he believed the assumptions underlaying American policy in Vietnam were erroneous. More ominously, perhaps, Lippmann and Fulbright began to suspect that the president was capitulating to the very forces he had defeated in the 1964 election,[10] a suspicion that crystallized into certainty following the 1965 intervention in the Dominican Republic. Following a Senate Foreign Relations Committee

(SFRC) investigation that disproved Johnson's claims that fifteen hundred people had been shot by Castroite guerrillas in that unfortunate nation, and that the goal of American intervention had been to prevent a return to power by Juan Bosch, a non-Communist liberal, Fulbright broke with his old friend. The Arkansan took to the Senate floor to blast Johnson for poor judgment and for succumbing to the advice of Cold War ideologues within the administration.[11]

Although the Dominican speech shattered Fulbright's relationship with Johnson, the Arkansan did not openly break with the administration over Vietnam until early the following year. On January 25, 1966, with the Christmas bombing halt in its thirty-second day, Fulbright called for an indefinite extension of the pause and the inclusion of the National Liberation Front in any negotiations. He and his advisers were convinced that "the present bombing pause and negotiation initiative offer the last clear chance to stop short of unlimited escalation," as Marcy put it.[12] However, Robert McNamara and McGeorge Bundy convinced the president that the situation was so desperate in Vietnam that the United States must end the bombing halt and assume direct control of the war.[13] When the U.S. planes resumed their bombing campaign shortly thereafter, Fulbright concluded that the much-publicized halt and accompanying search for negotiations had been a public relations stunt. The Sunday following Johnson's decision to resume the air war, Fulbright appeared on a CBS national television broadcast to declare the conflict in Southeast Asia morally wrong and contrary to the nation's interests.[14]

Fulbright's decision to have the SFRC hold televised public hearings on the war in 1966 constituted a new chapter in the history of the antiwar movement. A host of distinguished Americans, including Lt. Gen. James Gavin and George Kennan urged the administration to proceed with extreme caution in Vietnam. The committee grilled Maxwell Taylor and Robert McNamara for hours, and Fulbright read a letter from an anonymous soldier who declared that the United States was losing the war. America, argued the disillusioned GI, had simply replaced France in the role of the hated Western foreigner in the eyes of both the North and South Vietnamese. Fulbright's disgust with the administration, and especially Secretary of State Dean Rusk, was palpable.[15]

Not surprisingly, the SFRC hearings alarmed the White House and infuriated the president. On February 19 Richard Goodwin called Joseph Califano to tell him that at every speaking engagement, he, Goodwin, was running into deep concern about Vietnam. The Fulbright hearings, he said, were doing a great deal to "confuse" the American people.[16] Johnson, not surprisingly, was fuming. During his February meeting in Honolulu with Nguyen Cao Ky he denounced "special pleaders who counsel retreat in Vietnam." Relations between Fulbright and Johnson, the White House, and the SFRC deteriorated steadily during the next year and a half. "I had lunch with Senator Fulbright yesterday and found him rather 'hurt' about his relations with you," presidential counselor Douglas Cater informed Johnson. Cater suggested a dinner with wives to patch things up. "He is a cry baby," Johnson retorted, "and I can't continue to kiss him every morning before breakfast."[17] Fulbright's attitude toward the president quickly hardened. "Tell the son-of-a-bitch I'm playing golf," he instructed a relative when Johnson attempted to call him in Fayetteville in 1966.[18] As the war intensified, Fulbright worked furiously to alienate the administration's moderate and conservative supporters.

Over the next two years Fulbright came to the conclusion that the war in Vietnam was essentially a civil war and that the United States was simply supporting one side against the other. Indeed, by the time Lyndon Johnson left the White House, Fulbright was insisting that the insurgency in the South was chiefly a response to the repressive policies of the Saigon government and its American ally. In doing so he was anticipating an argument made by historian George Kahin some twenty-five years later.[19]

Fulbright initially believed that Lyndon Johnson had decided to stick America's fist into the Vietnam tar baby for the same reason he had sent marines to the Dominican Republic. The president had been captured by the very forces he and Fulbright had struggled against in the 1964 campaign—the true believers in total victory over Communism, the radicals, and the know-nothings. By late 1966, however, he was beginning to see American involvement in Vietnam as something more than a sellout to the Ultras; the war represented nothing less than the perversion of the very liberal internationalism he and Lyndon Johnson had been espousing.

Throughout the spring and summer of 1961 it was Fulbright, more than any other figure associated with the Kennedy administration, who had articulated the liberal activist philosophy that underlay Camelot's foreign policy. Effective resistance against the forces of international Communism involved not only military strength, he told the Senate in June, but willingness to help developing nations "toward the fulfillment of their own highest purposes." Noting that the principal Cold War antagonists were then focusing on the underdeveloped and newly emerging nations, Fulbright insisted that America's greatest contribution to the struggle was not its "affluence, or our plumbing, or our clogged freeways," but its values, "liberty and individual freedom . . . international peace, law and order, and constructive social purpose."[20] Like ancient Athens, Fulbright told the Senate, the United States stood at a crossroads in its history. Shortly after the beginning of their brief ascendancy, the Athenians had made a distinction between themselves and those who were dependent upon them for security and leadership. In denying those peoples access to the ideas and institutions that had made their city-state great, the Athenians lost the respect and hence support of their erstwhile allies in the struggle against Sparta. America could be truly secure, he seemed to be saying, only in a community of nations whose institutions and values closely resembled its own.[21]

Fulbright's subsequent support of a comprehensive foreign aid program coupled with "flexible response" in defense policy seemed a logical extension of the position he had adopted during the early days of the Cold War. During his first term in the Senate, which began in 1944, Fulbright had been the quintessential Cold War activist. He railed against isolationism during World War II, cosponsored the Fulbright-Connally resolution, founded the international exchange program that bore his name, and ardently supported both the Truman Doctrine and Marshall Plan. During the Eisenhower years he simultaneously blasted Dulles for being a narrow-minded ideologue and the president for being too passive in combating Communism, particularly in the developing world.[22]

And yet, during the 1950s, deeply influenced by the arguments of George Kennan, Fulbright rejected the globalism inherent in NSC-68. He advocated military preparedness but not indiscriminate intervention. The Arkansan supported the war in Korea, but he did so unenthusiastically. "If we are confronted by alternatives which you mentioned," he wrote a constituent, "that is, an all-out effort in Korea or an evacuation, I would prefer the latter."[23] America's resources were limited and its interests specific. In a subsequent speech in early 1951 Fulbright attempted to carve out a middle ground between the globalist philosophy of Paul Nitze and Averell Harriman, and the neoisolationism then being advocated by Robert Taft and Herbert Hoover. "Broadly speaking," he told the Senate, "there may be said to be three policies that have been advanced in recent weeks. . . . First, the limitation of our commitments to the defense of the Western Hemisphere with emphasis upon air and sea power. Second, the so-called Truman Doctrine of opposing aggression in every area where it appears. Third, participation in the creation of a land army in Western Europe, in addition to the defense of the Western Hemisphere."[24] It was this last course, "the Truman Doctrine with limitations," that he urged on Congress and his countrymen.

During this period, Fulbright's stance on domestic issues was that of a classic progressive. He had won in Arkansas without the help of the national Democratic organization, and he welcomed the freedom his independence allowed him. As a progressive and an independent Democrat, as a practitioner of republican virtue, as guardian of the liberties of the people, and as representative of the interests of his fellow Arkansans, Fulbright believed that it was not only his privilege but his duty to pick and choose among New Deal programs.[25] He challenged conservatives in Arkansas and Congress by championing the cause of public power and supporting the Farm Security Administration. He favored a progressive corporate income tax and fought courageously against corruption and cronyism in the Truman administration. He was, moreover, a prominent opponent of Joe McCarthy. At the same time, he voted against the minimum wage bill, opposed the Fair Employment Practices Commission, supported the Taft-Hartley Act, and signed the Southern Manifesto.[26]

During the early 1960s, when he expanded his vision of containment to include more than the Western Hemisphere and Western Europe, Fulbright showed signs of becoming a full-fledged liberal in domestic matters as well. He was attracted to the liberal intellectuals with whom Jack Kennedy had surrounded himself. He had known John Kenneth Galbraith for years and had joined with him in attacking the "materialism" of the Eisenhower years. Arthur Schlesinger, Jr., was a frequent correspondent, and the development theories of Walt Rostow began to appear in Fulbright's speeches even before the Massachusetts Institute of Technology economist came to Washington in 1961. Two events, Kennedy's assassination and the killing of four African American children in an Alabama church bombing, caused Fulbright to cast caution to the winds. After the bombing, he called Bobby Kennedy and promised him he would do what he could to help get future civil rights legislation through Congress.[27] The Birmingham murders and the assassination were part of the same cloth of bigotry and hatred, he subsequently told the Senate. The nation should seek "redemption" from these murders through "a national revulsion against extremism and violence, and from a calling forth of the basic decency and humanity of America to heal the wounds of divisiveness and hate."[28] During the early days of the Johnson administration Fulbright became an ardent advocate of various Great Society programs. His particular passions were the Office of Economic Opportunity and the Food Stamp Program. These programs, he told the Senate, were designed "to help those people—and particularly those children who did not have the wisdom and foresight to be born of the right parents or in the right place."[29] There was, then, a certain parallel between Fulbright's activist foreign policy views during the Kennedy administration and his increasingly liberal views on domestic socioeconomic issues.

Although he came to include portions of the developing world not yet overrun by Communism as crucial to American interests, and though he believed the United States should learn from Athens's mistakes and make its foreign policies an extension of its liberal domestic programs, Fulbright continued to reject the globalism of NSC-68. In the spring of 1964 Fulbright delivered his famous "old myths and new realities" speech on the floor of the Senate. He declared that coexistence with Russians and even Fidel Castro was possible. He called for a realistic assessment of U.S. policy toward Latin America and the Far East based on the recognition that there were limits to American power and pressing domestic needs that demanded attention. In anticipation of the inevitable overthrow of "feudal oligarchies" in Latin America, the United States should consider opening communications with the revolutionary movements that would replace them. America should be ready to adopt a more "flexible" attitude toward Communist China and, indeed, the entire Communist world. Treating different Communist countries differently would encourage diversity and independence that would inevitably work to America's advantage. Finally, he called for a reevaluation of America's Vietnam policy, not with an eye to withdrawal or neutralization, but with the objective of Vietnamization.[30] Fulbright was not arguing that the United States should stop competing with Communist China and the Soviet Union for the hearts and minds of the Third World, only that it employ sophisticated means and that it avoid identification with European colonialism. Given time and the freedom to choose, the peoples of the world would opt for a system characterized by democracy, individual liberty, and free enterprise.

Like Fulbright, Lyndon Johnson had become converted to the principles of liberal internationalism during and immediately after World War II. A disciple of Franklin D. Roosevelt and a staunch support of the New Deal, he became convinced that generous programs of technical and economic aid to war-torn and developing nations were in the economic and strategic interests of the United States.[31] But for Lyndon Johnson, as numerous historians have noted, an activist foreign policy was more than just a matter of national self-interest. There was a strong messianic strain in the Texan's personality that his accession to the presidency only served to accentuate. The thought of defending the weak against totalitarian injustice, of bringing the blessings of liberty, free enterprise, and indoor plumbing to the less fortunate of the world, was a continuing and intoxicating source of inspiration to him. Among Johnson's most influential advisers were Dean Acheson, Averell Harriman, and Dean Rusk.[32] All of these men were "present at the creation" and, like Johnson, were strongly committed to civil rights. Historian Eric Goldman touched a responsive chord in Johnson following Kennedy's assassination by invoking a presidency based on unity and ministration to the needs of all the people.[33] Following the 1964 election, Averell Harriman appealed to Johnson to extend that vision to the international arena. Because of his overwhelming mandate, the president had the opportunity to unify the peoples of the free world, Harriman argued, through the proclamation of an updated version of Roosevelt's Four Freedoms. He called upon Johnson to do nothing less than extend the War on Poverty to foreign lands; the Texan responded enthusiastically.[34] For Harriman, Acheson, Lyndon Johnson, and other liberal activists, the effort to save the developing nations from the scourge of Communism was part and parcel of the crusade to end discrimination and ensure that African Americans enjoyed equality under the law.[35]

Though he was proud, frequently oversensitive, and given to fits of machismo, Lyndon Johnson was not an anti-Communist ideologue, and when he entered office, the United States was working toward détente with the Soviet Union. Military preparedness and realistic diplomacy would contain Communism within its present bounds, it seemed. The United States must continue its "flexible response" of military aid, economic assistance, and technical/political advice to those in the developing world threatened by Communism, but there was nothing wrong with negotiating with the Soviets in an effort to reduce tensions. Above all, he projected the image of a flexible, pragmatic cold warrior, an image very congenial to J. William Fulbright.[36]

Kennedy and Johnson's pragmatic diplomacy toward the Soviet Union following the Cuban missile crisis and the administration's rhetorical commitment to peaceful change around the world were reassuring, but Fulbright realized that the pressure to deal with the world in simplistic, Cold War terms remained intense. He sensed, he told the Senate in the same speech in which he declared that the United States must align itself with the forces of social progress, that there were powerful voices abroad in the land declaring that any change in the status quo around the world was the result of a Communist conspiracy and must be met by force.[37] His fears, of course, turned out to be well-founded.

A number of factors combined to ensure that Lyndon Johnson would not unilaterally withdraw from South Vietnam or seek a negotiated settlement that would lead to neutralization of the area south of the seventeenth parallel. In the first place, he was, as McGeorge Bundy has noted, "a hawk."[38] The memory of the Munich pact made him a staunch cold warrior and it shaped his attitude toward the challenge in Vietnam. He would not reward "aggression" with "appeasement."[39] In addition, as vice president in 1961, Johnson had made a personal commitment to the survival of an independent non-Communist government in South Vietnam. He seemed smitten with Diem and with the determination of the "brave people of Vietnam" to resist a Communist takeover.[40]

Johnson was just as fearful of the radical right as Fulbright. His concern, however, was not that the Ultras would dictate his foreign policies but that they would join with conservative southern hawks such as Richard Russell (D-Georgia) and James Eastland (D-Mississippi) to hamstring his domestic programs should South Vietnam fall to Communism. He would never forget the McCarthyites's hounding of Harry Truman following Mao's conquest of China. Even though, as he indicated in his conversations with Fulbright, he may have wanted to question the assumptions that underlay the original containment policy, including the monolithic Communist threat and the domino theory, he dare not, lest the debate fracture the domestic consensus he so desperately desired. In a word, Lyndon Johnson had no intention of allowing the charge that he was soft on Communism to be used against him to destroy the Great Society.[41]

In trying to decide what methods to use to prevent a Communist takeover in South Vietnam, Johnson was caught in a bind. Shortly after he became president he observed to his advisers that there had been too much emphasis on social reconstruction in the aid program to Vietnam. All too often when the United States became involved in the affairs of another country, it tried to make it over in its own image.[42] Yet as he became aware of the political vacuum in South Vietnam and as he became caught up in the effort to build a society able to stand on its own, Johnson threw caution to the winds. Confronted with the exigencies of the Cold War, he gave free rein to his liberal impulses and became a crusading nation builder. Following the Buddhist crisis of 1966 the United States made pacification a top priority in South Vietnam. "Dammit," Johnson exploded on one occasion, "We've got to see that the South Vietnamese government wins the battle . . . of crops and hearts and caring."[43]

Fulbright was unable to decide whether Johnson's determination to raise living standards, establish a viable political system, and defeat Communist totalitarianism in Vietnam stemmed from an authentic commitment to human rights or whether his humanitarian arguments were merely a justification for policies he pursued to placate conservatives, the military-industrial complex, and the radical right. In the end, he decided that it did not matter. The president was using liberal internationalist arguments to mobilize and sustain support for the war and thus it was those arguments that would have to be discredited. It was Carl Marcy who pointed out the relevance of the missionary impulse to the war in Vietnam and the consensus that sustained it. In August,

1965, the SFRC's chief of staff wrote an impassioned assessment of American foreign policy for Fulbright. Where do we stand, he asked? Détente with the Soviet Union had been swallowed up in the administration's quest for consensus. The United States had chosen to challenge an enemy of dubious importance ten thousand miles from home. America's credibility in the United Nations and within the world at large was rapidly evaporating. What had happened, he asked, to bring his beloved country so low? What had happened to "turn the liberal supporters of President Kennedy into opponents of the policies of President Johnson?" The answer was fairly obvious, Marcy argued. "We have tried to force upon the rest of the world a righteous American point of view which we maintain is the consensus that others must accept. Most of the tragedies of the world have come from such righteousness."[44] Marcy's critique struck a responsive chord within Fulbright. Given his support of liberal internationalism generally and the Gulf of Tonkin resolution specifically, its resonance in time would cause bitter self-reproach. Recognition of his own culpability gave a special edge to his criticism of Lyndon Johnson and his foreign policies.

Appalled by the carnage in Vietnam, the conversion of hundreds of thousands of sedentary villagers into homeless refugees, and the inability of the United States to raise up and work through any sort of broad-based political system in the South, Fulbright launched a devastating critique of American foreign policy. Addressing the Cold War interventionists—former isolationists who believed that if America could not hide from the world, it would have to dominate it—he declared the war to be a monstrous strategic error. The domino theory had never been proven in history. Whenever a great power threatened to dominate a particular region, a coalition had always emerged to challenge that power, regardless of ideological considerations.[45] It just might be necessary, he suggested, for the United States to accept the legitimacy of an independent, nationalist, and united Vietnam, even with a Marxist-Leninist government. This Yugoslav style entity would serve not as a puppet but as a counterweight to an expansionist China.[46]

Implicit in Fulbright's philosophy of containment, developed in the late 1940s and early 1950s, was the notion that revolutions inevitably pass through stages, moving from an initial totalitarian, radical stage toward Thermidorean moderation. During his spring, 1966, speaking tour he reread Crane Brinton's *Anatomy of Revolution.* Using Brinton's study of the French revolution as a model, Fulbright argued that the Chinese revolution, and by extension, Communism in Vietnam, would inevitably moderate. Like other revolutionary societies, it would become a "more or less normal society with a more or less normal relation with the outside world."[47] The United States must be patient and do all in its power to encourage a trend toward moderation. As visualized by its architects, containment was designed to prevent the spread of Soviet aggression, he told Martin Agronsky and Eric Severeid on a CBS television news program. As it had evolved under Johnson it was an attempt to contain a worldwide movement toward self-government and self-expression by peoples formerly yoked to European empires.[48]

Analogies from Thucydides' history of the Peloponnesian Wars, absorbed during his years at Oxford as a Rhodes Scholar, continued to haunt the chairman of the SFRC. Decrying the Johnson administration's huge military budget and the militarization of American foreign policy, Fulbright told a joint congressional committee in 1967: "Contrary to the traditions which have guided our nation since the days of the Founding Fathers, we are in grave danger of becoming a Sparta bent on policing the world." But modern American imperialism, "welfare imperialism," Fulbright called it, was particularly pervasive and virulent because it combined militarism and idealism. America had decided to export its Athenian ideals using Spartan means. The United States, he told a college audience at Storrs, Connecticut, would have to decide which of the two sides of its character would prevail—"the humanism of Lincoln or the aggressive moralism of Theodore Roosevelt."[49] The "arrogance of power," "the tragedy of American foreign policy," "myth and reality in Soviet-American relations,"—those and other phrases in Fulbright's rhetoric underscored his disillusionment with liberal internationalism. In the heat of war, frustrated by the nation's inability to win a clear-cut victory, Congress and the American people were deferring to an avaricious executive captivated by a burgeoning military-industrial complex whose existence was justified on the grounds that it was bringing social justice, a higher standard of living, and the possibility of democracy to those peoples of the world threatened by international Communism.

Idealism and imperialism could not continue to exist side by side, Fulbright proclaimed to Congress, the American people, and Lyndon Johnson. The great question before America, he told a 1967 meeting of the American Bar Association, was whether the United States could simultaneously pursue imperialism abroad and republicanism at home. They were, to him, "morally incompatible roles." In a terrible irony, given its lofty goals, the Vietnam War was not only polarizing the country but eroding the political liberties of its citizens.[50] Fulbright said he was fearful that, in its efforts to preserve its hegemony in Southeast Asia, America was turning its back on the Jeffersonian heritage of limited government, restraint in foreign policy, and representative democracy.

What was emerging in the United States was an imperial presidency—"an elective dictatorship," Fulbright termed it.

It was this perception that caused the Arkansan in the wake of the 1966 hearings to abandon his long-time advocacy of executive predominance in foreign policy. Fulbright's ultimate commitment was not to a particular interpretation of the Constitution but to rational pursuit of enlightened self-interest. In the aftermath of World War II, in his view, with the tide of isolationism still running strong and deep in the United States, a vigorous, assertive executive was needed to advance the cause of internationalism and keep the peace. But over the years the stresses and strains of fighting the Cold War under the shadow of a nuclear holocaust had taken their toll. The executive branch, its actions at times circumscribed and at times dictated by a fanatical anti-Communism at home, had adopted a missionary posture that assumed that America had the duty and the power to make the world over in its own image.[51] So certain was the Johnson administration of the righteousness of its cause that it had concealed its policies in Southeast Asia from the American people and then persecuted those who dissented. If the liberties of the people were to be safeguarded and future Vietnam's avoided, Congress would have to reassert its prerogatives in foreign affairs.

Johnson, needless to say, was not impressed. Early in 1966 George McGovern, then a young first-term senator from South Dakota, paid a visit to the Oval Office to express his doubts about the war. McGovern dared to point out that the Chinese and Vietnamese had been fighting each other for a thousand years. "It's hard for me to believe that Ho Chi Minh is a stooge of the Chinese," he told the president. Johnson exploded: "Goddamn it, George, you and Fulbright and all you history teachers down there. I haven't got time to fuck around with history. I've got boys on the line out there. I can't be worried about history when there are boys out there who might die before morning."[52]

For Fulbright the embodiment of liberal internationalism was the foreign aid program. It was at once the symbol of the nation's idealism and the vehicle of its imperialism. From being one of foreign aid's staunchest defenders, the SFRC chairman moved to being its most ardent and destructive critic. At the dawning of the Cold War Fulbright had supported the British Loan, the Marshall Plan, and the Mutual Security Act. During the Eisenhower administration he had led the fight for the Development Loan Fund, and under Kennedy had championed the Alliance for Progress. While it is true that he became increasingly alarmed at the emphasis on military over nonmilitary aid and Washington's tendency to support repressive client governments in the name of anti-Communism, he continued to support foreign aid throughout the

Kennedy administration—support that was crucial given that Fulbright was the SFRC chairman.[53] In the wake of Johnson's escalation of the war, however, he turned on the program with a vengeance. The foreign aid network, with its dual emphasis on armaments and infrastructure, symbolized the imperial marriage between liberals and conservatives. Conservatives were willing to accept nonmilitary aid because they were convinced that it was essential to halting the rise of Communism, whereas liberals could reconcile themselves to massive military assistance on the grounds that America was simply protecting the recipients of its global social experiment.[54]

In July, 1966, the administration submitted its $3.2 billion request for fiscal year 1968. As usual, military and nonmilitary aid was lumped together, and the administration asked for a five-year rather than a one-year authorization. Insisting that approval of the measure would be portrayed by President Johnson and his advisers as approval of the war in Vietnam, Fulbright persuaded the SFRC and the Senate to separate military and nonmilitary aid for the first time in history. Reversing the position he had taken on previous aid bills, Fulbright, the measure's floor manager, led the fight to cut the authorization from five years to one. "I would be much more inclined to support multi-year authorizations if there were not this tendency to escalate our commitments," he told the administration.[55] Fulbright subsequently introduced an amendment to cut the administration's Food for Peace program from $5 billion for two years to $1 billion for one year.[56] When Johnson's supporters angrily pointed out that the Arkansan was doing an about-face on foreign aid, Fulbright replied, "it seems to me that anyone at all perceptive should change his opinion about the interference of our country in the internal affairs of other countries, and what it leads to."[57]

The pacification program in Vietnam had convinced Fulbright that much of the foreign aid program was futile if not counterproductive. No matter how well-intentioned, American aid was ripping the fabric of Vietnamese life, distorting the nation's economy, undermining its religious beliefs, disparaging its material culture, and threatening its very identity. He was not surprised, he declared, at the anti-American tone of the demonstrations that took place in Danang and Hue in 1966. The Vietnamese were suffering from the "'fatal impact' of the rich and strong on the poor and weak." Dependent on it though the Vietnamese were, "our very strength is a reproach to their weakness, our wealth a mockery of their poverty, our success a reminder of their failures."[58]

Lyndon Johnson regarded Fulbright's dissent as an attack on his motives as well as his methods. Egged on by Dean Rusk and Walt Rostow, the president came to blame the Arkansan's opposition to the war on his racism. Johnson convinced himself that Fulbright was willing to abandon the Vietnamese to forces of international Communism because they were poor and yellow.[59] Significantly, Fulbright's opposition seemed to stimulate the Texan's missionary impulse. At the same White House meeting at which he learned that the 1966 SFRC hearings had knocked his public approval rating down thirteen points, the president blurted out: "Why don't we do a real study on brown men—and Asia—Task Force on Asia—heavy thinking on Asia—potentialities and solutions—liven it up—Asian Task Forces."[60] That summer, at White Sulphur Springs, West Virginia, Johnson declared that the United States was a Pacific power and would seek to use its resources to promote prosperity and cooperation throughout the entire region. The future was secure for the people of the Pacific Rim as long as "we stand firm in Vietnam against military conquest."[61] For Fulbright, the "Asian Doctrine," as the press subsequently dubbed Johnson's pledge, confirmed his worst fears concerning the perversion of liberal internationalism. Without consulting Congress or the American people, the president had made a sweeping commitment to build Western-style democracies throughout the Far East and to defend them with force.

Fulbright's opposition to the war and his feud with Lyndon Johnson came to a head during a meeting between the president and congressional leaders the last week in July, 1967. When Johnson thanked the group for its "experience, friendship and judgment," and invited comments, Fulbright exclaimed: "Mr. President, what you really need to do is to stop the war. That will solve all your problems." The Texan's faced reddened. "Vietnam is ruining our domestic and our foreign policy. I will not support it any longer." By now Johnson's steely gaze was fixed on the Arkansan. The group was absolutely still. "I expect that for the first time in 20 years I may vote against foreign assistance and may try to bottle the whole bill up in committee," Fulbright warned.[62]

Johnson exploded. If Congress wanted to tell the rest of the world to go to hell, that was its prerogative. "Maybe you don't want to help the children of India, but I can't hold back," he said. If Fulbright and his colleagues did not like the war, they could repeal the Gulf of Tonkin resolution and cut off funds for troops in the field: "you can tell General Westmoreland that he doesn't know what he is doing."[63]

Six days later Fulbright introduced his national commitments resolution. That measure sought a nonbinding Senate endorsement for the proposition that a "commitment" made by the executive to a foreign power would not be viewed as a commitment unless it had received congressional approval.[64] Using the same constitutional arguments he had employed in attacking various civil rights bills, Fulbright had been working for more than a year to convince southern hawks like Richard Russell (D-Georgia), Sam Ervin (D-North Carolina), and John Sparkman (D-Alabama) not only that the war was strategically counterproductive but that it was unlawful. No sooner had Fulbright introduced his bill than Russell leapt to his feet. "I know of nothing that is more in need of clarification than the present state of the alleged commitment of the United States all over the world," he told the Senate. "The Senator from Arkansas has rendered a real, a lasting, and a most significant service to the country," Ervin chimed in.[65] A host of others followed—doves, hawks, northerners, southerners, liberals, and conservatives. Although the Senate did not pass the national commitments resolution until 1969, it marked the beginning of the process that culminated in the 1970 Cooper-Church and 1971 Hatfield-McGovern resolutions, as well as various other end-the-war resolutions passed by Congress in the late summer of 1973.

Fulbright's participation in the crusade against civil rights during the postwar period enabled him to communicate with disgruntled hawks when other members of the antiwar movement could not. In fact, the White House was not entirely wrong in believing that Fulbright's critique of liberal internationalism stemmed from his conservative, southern roots. As a southerner and a segregationist, not to mention the founder of the international exchange program that bore his name, Fulbright was especially jealous of the sanctity of indigenous cultures. Like so many other leaders of the New South, he never forgot that Arkansas and the entire region were one-time economic colonies of the North.[66] Both his views on the South as an economic appendage of the North and his resentment at what he believed to be that region's efforts to impose its racial views on Dixie instilled in him an intense commitment to the principle of cultural and political self-determination. As an individual with a strong sense of class, kinship, and place, he believed it no less abhorrent that the United States should force its culture, political institutions, and economic theories on Vietnam than that the North should impose its mores on the South. "American interests are better served by supporting nationalism than by opposing communism," he told the Senate, "and . . . when the two are encountered in the same country, it is in our interest to accept a Communist government rather than undertake the cruel and all but impossible task of suppressing a genuinely national movement."[67] Fulbright's insights into the causes of the war as well as his effectiveness as an opponent of it stemmed in no small part from his experiences as a crusader on behalf of two apparently contradictory causes—internationalism and segregation.

In many ways Fulbright's critique of American foreign policy paralleled that of the New Left which was, in the main, a revolt among American intellectuals and college students against liberal politics.[68] By the mid-1960s the great Satan of the New Left had become "corporate liberalism." The men who engineered the war in Vietnam "are not moral monsters," Carl Oglesby declared. "They are all honorable men. They are all liberals." The American corporate machine they oversaw was the "Colossus of history," taking the riches of other nations and consuming half of the world's goods. Being decent men, corporate liberals rationalized their rapacity and their policy of counterrevolution with the ideology of anti-Communism, defining all revolutions as Communist and Communism as evil.[69]

Like Tom Hayden, I. F. Stone, and Staughton Lynd, Fulbright railed against the military-industrial complex. His argument—that in its obsessive anti-Communism the United States had everywhere arrayed itself against indigenous revolution thus identifying itself with a dying colonialism—paralleled the soft revisionism of such young historians as Thomas Paterson. His frank portrayal of the United States as an avaricious empire certainly conformed to the writings of William Appleman Williams and Gabriel Kolko. Indeed, Ronald Steel, whose *Pax Americana: The Cold War Empire and the Politics of Counter-Revolution* appeared in 1967, was a former SFRC staff member and was heavily influenced by Fulbright. But the SFRC chairman was not of the New Left.

Fulbright did not believe in "participatory democracy"; he remained committed to the vision of America as a meritocracy based on education and equality of opportunity. During the 1960s he had been converted to the notion that inequality was the product of socioeconomic disadvantages and that the government had a responsibility to create conditions in which learning and achievement could take place. Thus, while he came to support the War on Poverty, he never endorsed the notion of equality of condition, and he remained wedded to the free enterprise system. Fulbright did indeed share the New Left's distrust and fear of the military-industrial complex, but he did not buy the idea of a pervasive corporate elite that was inherently immoral and exploitative. There were vast differences in interest, intent, and public-spiritedness in the American corporate structure. Fulbright's indictment was of the defense industry and the degree to which it was dominating the country's foreign policy and politics.

Fulbright's disillusionment both paralleled and accelerated disillusionment within the nation's preeminent liberal organization, the Americans for Democratic Action (ADA). As Steven Gillon has pointed out, Vietnam destroyed the delicate balance of power within American liberalism between "politics and vision," between an idealism that called for a commitment to social justice and a realism that required a militant anti-Communism.[70] Although his civil rights record and his advocacy of a "balanced" approach toward the Middle East ensured that Fulbright would never be a member of the ADA, his opposition to McCarthyism, militarism, and Barry Goldwater had forever endeared him to the likes of Chester Bowles, Arthur Schlesinger, and John Kenneth Galbraith. Like them, Fulbright had accepted the need after World War II to embrace anti-Communism and link it with a higher ideal. That heritage made his critique of contemporary American foreign policy all the more devastating. He was among the first Cold War activists to see that in harnessing their obsession with social justice to anti-Communism, liberals had turned the Cold War into a missionary crusade that blinded the nation to the political and cultural realities of Southeast Asia. It also made possible an unholy alliance between realpolitikers preoccupied with markets and bases, and emotionally committed to the domino theory, and idealists who wanted to spread the blessings of freedom, democracy, and a mixed economy to the less fortunate of the world. In Fulbright's view, Jack Kennedy's and Lyndon Johnson's agenda had not triumphed over that of Barry Goldwater—the two had become joined.

Notes

1. Steven Gillon, *Politics and Vision: The ADA and American Liberalism, 1947–1985* (New York: Oxford University Press, 1987), 16–32.

2. Several books have been written on Fulbright's life and his opposition to the war. The two best are Haynes Johnson and Bernard M. Gwertzman, *Fulbright: The Dissenter* (Garden City, N.Y.: Doubleday, 1968) and William C. Berman, *William Fulbright and the Vietnam War* (Kent, Ohio: Kent State University Press, 1988). It should be noted that two of the most comprehensive and careful histories of the antiwar movement, Melvin Small's *Johnson, Nixon, and the Doves* and Charles DeBenedetti's and Charles Chatfield's *An American Ordeal* discuss Fulbright only in terms of his actions in opposition to the war. They make no attempt to portray him as representative of a particular culture or philosophy. See Melvin Small, *Johnson, Nixon, and the Doves* (New Brunswick, N.J.: Rutgers University Press, 1988), 49, 72, 78–81, and 107–108, and Charles DeBenedetti and Charles Chatfield, *An American Ordeal: The Antiwar Movement of the Vietnam Era* (Syracuse, N.Y.: Syracuse University Press, 1990), 110, 113, 124, 152–54, and 358–59.

3. Marcy to Valenti, Oct. 14. 1965, Box 5, Folder Oct. '65, Papers of Carl Marcy (hereafter Marcy Papers), Papers of the Senate Foreign Relations Committee, RG 46, National Archives (hereafter NA). This snub, if it was indeed perceived as such, was followed by the White House's refusal to provide an air force jet to fly Fulbright and other members of the SFRC to attend a meeting of the British Commonwealth Parliamentarians Association in Wellington, New Zealand, in November, 1965. Carl Marcy, the committee's influential chief of staff, regarded the refusal as a slap in the face of Fulbright and the committee, and, more importantly, a reflection upon his personal power. Fulbright's relegation to a lumbering prop plane converted Marcy to an unrelenting dove. (Marcy to Hubert H. Humphrey, May 7, 1965, Folder May '65, Marcy Papers.)

4. "Notes Taken At Leadership Meeting, Aug. 4, 1964," Meeting Notes File, Box 1, Papers of Lyndon B. Johnson, Johnson Library, Austin, Tex. (hereafter Johnson Papers). Perhaps hyperbole is the wrong term in light of the fact that the second attack never occurred. (Robert McNamara, interview with author, Washington, D.C., 1990.)

5. J. William Fulbright, interview with author, Washington, D.C., 1988; and George McGovern, interview with author, Washington, D.C., 1991.

6. "The Ultras," *Time,* Dec. 8, 1961; George Barrett, "Close-Up of the Birchers' 'Founder'," *New York Times Magazine,* May 14, 1961; and Phillip Horton, "Revivalism on the Far Right," *The Reporter,* July 20, 1961.

7. Fulbright to Kennedy, June 28, 1961, White House Office Files (WHOF), Box 639, Papers of John F. Kennedy, JFK Library, Boston; and John Birch Society, *Bulletin for Oct.,* Oct. 2, 1961.

8. Quoted in Kathleen J. Turner, *Lyndon Johnson's Dual War: Vietnam and the Press* (Chicago: University of Chicago Press, 1985), 95.

9. Marcy to Fulbright, Jan. 10, 1966, Box 6, Folder Jan. '66, Marcy Papers. At the outset of the first Indochinese war Fulbright fully accepted the need to help the French and the anti-Communist forces in Vietnam. He shared Roosevelt's views on the bankruptcy of Western colonialism, but he believed that the European powers, led by Britain's example in India, were committed to a responsible program of decolonization. "The primary objective of this effort [American aid to France]," he wrote a constituent in 1953, "is not to perpetuate the colonial domination of Indo-China by France but to prevent the Communists from taking complete control of that unfortunate country." The French, he insisted, would move rapidly toward giving the Vietnamese full independence once the battle was won. See Fulbright to Fred Hutt, June 8, 1953, BCN 87, Box F3, Papers of J. William Fulbright, Mullins Library, University of Arkansas, Fayetteville, Ark. (hereafter Fulbright Papers).

10. Bundy to Johnson, Mar. 15, 1965, NSC File, Memos to President, Box 3, Johnson Papers; Marcy to Fulbright, Mar. 30, 1965, Folder Mar. '65, Marcy Papers; and Walter Lippmann, "On the Way to the Brink," *Washington Post,* Mar. 30, 1965.

11. Pat Holt, interview with author, Washington, D.C., 1988; Memo of Conversation between Peter H. Freeman, and Holt, July 26, 1965, Series 48:14, Box 38:5, Fulbright Papers; and "The Situation in the Dominican Republic," July 14, 15, 16, 19, 23, and 29 and Aug. 3, 1965, Executive Sessions, SFRC Papers, RG 46, NA.

12. Marcy to Fulbright, Jan. 10, 1966, Box 6, Folder Jan. '66, Marcy Papers.

13. Bundy to Johnson, Jan. 27, 1965, NSC File, Memos to President, Bundy, Box 2, Johnson Papers. As Johnson subsequently put it to the NSC, "We face the choice of going for war or running. . . ." and "we have chosen the first alternative." Partial Record of Meeting with President of Group prior to NSC Meeting, Feb. 8, 1965, NSC Meeting Notes, Box 1, Johnson Papers.

14. Berman, *Fulbright and Vietnam,* 33.

15. As early as July 1965 Carl Marcy confided to Douglas Cater that there was feeling among Hill liberals that Rusk was not vigorous in presenting foreign policy points of view to the president—that he had been a good secretary for Kennedy, who had his own policy, but that Johnson needed a stronger secretary. (Marcy, Memo of Conversation, July 24, 1965, Box 5, Folder July '65, Marcy Papers.)

16. Joe Califano to Johnson, Feb. 19, 1966, Box 219, White House Central Files (WHCF), National Security-Defense, ND19/CO 312, Johnson Papers.

17. Douglas Cater to Johnson, Feb. 8, 1965, Memos to the President, Box 13, Office Files of Douglas Cater, LBJ Library.

18. Jacqueline Douglas, interview with author, Fayetteville, Ark., 1989.

19. See George McT. Kahin, *Intervention* (New York: Knopf, 1986). After the Paris peace talks got underway, Fulbright and Kahin began corresponding and had several face-to-face meetings to discuss the situation in Vietnam. (Kahin to Fulbright, Aug. 20, 1971, Box 10, July–Sept. '71, Marcy Papers.)

20. *Congressional Record,* Senate, June 29, 1961, 11703–11705.

21. Ibid.

22. Johnson and Gwertzman, *Fulbright,* 55–65, 77–86.

23. Fulbright to N. P. Talburt, Dec. 12, 1950, BCN 46, F10, Fulbright Papers.

24. *Congressional Record,* Senate, Jan. 22, 1951, 520–22.

25. Fulbright to C. N. Bellingrath, Mar. 6, 1945, BCN43, F34, Fulbright Papers.

26. Although Fulbright put his name to the infamous document, he was personally responsible for toning down the extreme original version written by Strom Thurmond (D-S.C.) and Sam Ervin (D-N.C.). See Ervin draft and Holland, Fulbright, et al., draft, 1956 Southern Manifesto, Papers of Richard Russell, University of Georgia, Athens; and Jack Yingling, interview with author, Savannah, Ga., 1988. For a brief survey of Fulbright's early legislative career, see Johnson and Gwertzman, *Fulbright,* 89–127.

27. Mike Manatos to Larry O'Brien, Oct. 1, 1963, Box 18, Papers of Lawrence F. O'Brien, JFK Library.

28. *Congressional Record,* Senate, Dec. 6, 1963, 23726–28.

29. Ibid., July 23, 1964, 16764.

30. Convinced that Fulbright had led the Democratic Party into the "soft on Communism" trap that had been set ever since the fall of China in 1949, Republican politicians and conservative columnists lined up to attack old myths and new realities. Senator Strom Thurmond (D-S.C.), William Miller, chairman of the GOP national committee, and John Tower, the former political science teacher from Wichita Falls and newly elected Republican senator from Texas, all charged Fulbright with "appeasement." Tower accused the chairman of the SFRC of urging "an even softer line towards international communism than we now have." ("Tower Says Fulbright Urges 'Even Softer Line' on Reds," *New York Tribune,* Apr. 5, 1964.) Thurmond inserted in the *Congressional Record* an article on the Fulbright speech by labor leader George Meany entitled "A Return to Appeasement." See *Congressional Record,* Senate, May 8, 1964, 10438–39. "This is a trial balloon which the Johnson administration is sending up to prepare public opinion for the acceptance of a foreign policy that could lead only to disaster for the United States and other free nations," Miller declared. "The course Senator Fulbright advocates is the same road which Neville Chamberlain traveled in the 1930s." (Ned Curran, "Critics Claim Fulbright Hit at LBJ Policy," *Arkansas Gazette,* Mar. 26, 1964.) Old myths and new realities were reminiscent of the 1930s, declared columnist David Lawrence, when the cry was heard, "'you can do business with Hitler'." (David Lawrence, "'You Can Do Business With Hitler'," Apr. 1964, *Washington Post.*)

31. The president was, for example, an enthusiastic supporter of the Alliance for Progress. "We must find ways to expand education, health, and low-cost housing facilities," he told Thomas Mann in appointing him assistant secretary of state for Latin American affairs. "We must find ways to help governments increase revenues by tax reforms and, at the same time, maintain an adequate and sustained rate of economic growth; we must find ways to bring about land reform, and at the same time, to increase agricultural production. Job opportunities must be expanded and educational and health facilities and low-cost housing must be provided. Social justice is a goal for which we must constantly strive." (LBJ to Thomas Mann, Dec. 15, 1963, Series 1, Box 2:4, Fulbright Papers. See also Turner, *Johnson's Dual War.*)

32. See, for example, "Meeting with Foreign Policy Advisers on Vietnam, May 16, 1965," Meeting Notes File, Box 1, Johnson Papers.

33. Eric F. Goldman, *The Tragedy of Lyndon Johnson* (New York: Knopf, 1969), 60–63.

34. Harriman to Johnson, Nov. 19, 1964, Box 439, W. Averell Harriman Papers, Library of Congress, Washington, D.C.

35. Rusk, Harriman, and Acheson's liberal views on race relations are well known. See, for example, "Memo of Remarks Made by Dean Acheson in Telephone Conversation, July 22, 1957," Famous Names, Box 1, Senate Papers, Johnson Papers.

36. See *Congressional Record,* Senate, Jan. 21, 1964, 893.

37. Ibid., June 29, 1961, 11703–11705.

38. McGeorge Bundy, interview with author, New York, 1991.

39. Quoted in Turner, *Johnson's Dual War,* 53.

40. Frank Valeo, who accompanied Johnson on the trip, recalled him standing up in his open boat in the Mekong River and surveying the river banks teeming with poverty and human misery saying with an enraptured look on his face, "Goddamn it, there is so much to be done here!" (Frank Valeo, interview with author, Washington, D.C., 1991.)

41. This, of course, is the justification that Johnson himself gave for his escalation of the war in Vietnam. Nonetheless, a number of historians have accepted the argument that Johnson was preoccupied with domestic policy and that he saw the war in Southeast Asia as the price he would have to pay for getting his ambitious domestic programs through Congress.

42. "Meeting between President, Rusk, McNamara, Ball, Bundy, McCone, and Lodge," Nov. 24, 1963, Meeting Note File, Box 1, Johnson Papers.

43. Quoted in George C. Herring, *America's Longest War: The United States and Vietnam, 1950–1975,* 2d ed. (New York: Knopf, 1986), 158.

44. Marcy to Fulbright, Aug. 17, 1965, Series 48:1, Box 16:2, Fulbright Papers. Marcy believed Rusk was the chief purveyor of American exceptionalism. No longer the impotent bureaucrat of Marcy's earlier imaginings, Rusk had become in his mind one of the chief villains of the escalation drama. He wrote Chalmers Roberts: "Rusk tends to be a missionary and Fulbright a historian-philosopher. Rusk wants to force change or use force to keep change within control. Fulbright tends more to see change as an evolutionary process." See Carl Marcy, interview with Donald Ritchie, *Oral History Interviews* (Senate Historical Office, Washington, D.C.), 186. Neither Marcy nor Fulbright could ever forget that Rusk's chief backer for the secretary of state position was Henry Luce.

45. Memorandum on Vietnam, Dec. 22, 1964, Box 4, Folder Oct.–Dec. '64, Marcy Papers.

46. Berman, *Fulbright and Vietnam,* 36.

47. UPI 195, Apr. 27, 1966, Series 47:1, Box 7:4, Fulbright Papers.

48. Berman, *Fulbright and Vietnam,* 55.

49. *Congressional Record,* Senate, Mar. 25, 1966, 6750–53.

50. J. William Fulbright, "The Price of Empire," in Johnson and Gwertzman, *Fulbright,* 304–11.

51. Berman, *Fulbright and Vietnam,* 64.

52. McGovern interview.

53. "Were I to vote now and express my judgment on the merits of the [foreign aid] bill before the Senate," he wrote President Kennedy in 1961, "I would vote to reduce the military program and to reorient the economic programs drastically. . . . I would move rapidly away from support of such regimes as that in Korea, putting those funds instead into priority areas where we might expect some degree of self-sufficiency and reliable political maturity within the next five years." (Marcy

to Fulbright, June 26, 1961, Box 1, Folder Misc. 1961–62, Marcy Papers.) However, he went on to assure the young chief executive that he would support the 1962 aid bill in the knowledge that the administration was new and inexperienced and in the hope that it would consider reforming the program along the lines he had suggested.

54. With Fulbright spearheading the effort, foreign aid reached a post–Marshall Plan high in 1961–62 of $4.8 billion. With the Arkansan wielding the knife, foreign assistance reached an all-time postwar low of $1.8 billion in 1969. These amounts are exclusive of aid to South Vietnam.

55. David Bell to Johnson, May 27, 1966, WHCF, Box 4, Johnson Papers.

56. UPI 13, Aug. 30, 1966, Series 78:3, Box 33:2, Fulbright Papers.

57. *Congressional Record,* Senate, Aug. 29, 1966. 21104–21107.

58. Ibid., May 17, 1966, 10807.

59. Dean Rusk, interview with author, Athens, Ga., 1988; and Harry McPherson, interview with author, Washington, D.C., 1990.

60. "Meeting in Cabinet Room, Feb. 26, 1966," Meeting Notes File, Box 2, Johnson Papers.

61. Quoted in Berman, *Fulbright and Vietnam,* 70.

62. "Meeting of the President with the Senate Committee Chairmen, July 25, 1967," Tom Johnson Notes, Box 1, Johnson Papers.

63. Ibid.

64. Berman, *Fulbright and Vietnam,* 84.

65. *Congressional Record,* Senate, July 31, 1967, 20702–20707.

66. Ibid., Apr. 29, 1964, 9596.

67. Ibid., Mar. 25, 1966, 6750–53.

68. Allen J. Matusow, *The Unraveling of America: A History of Liberalism in the 1960s* (New York: Harper and Row, 1984), 310.

69. Ibid.

70. Gillon, *Politics and Vision,* 177–96.

CHAPTER EIGHT

The Strategic Defense Initiative and the Technological Sublime

Fear, Science, and the Cold War

RACHEL L. HOLLOWAY

In 1990 Robert L. Scott wrote, "In the world of Cold War rhetoric, all science is military science."[1] All science, in Cold War rhetoric, is also political science. Scientists and engineers played critical roles as they argued for and against policies that proposed technological innovation as the answer to growing external threats. The decisions to build and use the atomic bomb, to develop the hydrogen bomb, to reduce nuclear testing, to limit defensive weapons, and ultimately to pursue a third generation of defensive nuclear weapons all split the scientific community. These controversies highlighted the nation's dependence on the capabilities and the *willingness* of scientists to apply their intellectual skill to the demands of national security during the Cold War.

Cold War rhetoric offered no escape from a dependence on science. It created a worldview based on fear of Soviet nuclear attack balanced by a belief in the deterrent power of a U.S. military response. As a result, the strategy of mutual assured destruction (MAD) was built on a fundamental belief in the ability of American science and technology to provide instruments of deterrence equal to or greater than the Soviet Union's. Whenever scientists signaled doubts about the possibility of technological response or indicated that they were reluctant to participate in American efforts to build more sophisticated and powerful weaponry to counter a growing Soviet threat, a fundamental premise of Cold War rhetoric was shaken. Such controversy required a rhetorical solution, a purification of science, as a means to eliminate and overcome those counter forces that would erode public confidence in American superiority.

Ronald Reagan faced such a challenge in the mid 1980s. On March 23, 1983, Reagan called on America's scientific community "to turn their great talents now to the cause of mankind and world peace, to give us the means of rendering these nuclear weapons impotent and obsolete."[2] He proposed what would become the Strategic Defense Initiative (SDI), a program of research focused on new technologies designed to intercept and destroy enemy missiles before they reached American soil. For Reagan's vision to quiet public fears and thus to gain public support for his administration's policies, the fundamental question of "could it be done?" first had to be answered.

Many public critics immediately rejected Reagan's vision. The *New York Times* called Reagan's vision "science fiction."[3] Senator Edward Kennedy (D-Massachusetts) called the plan "a Star Wars scheme."[4] The Democratic response to Reagan's March 23, 1983, speech accused him of attempting to distract the public with talk of "Buck Rogers' weapons."[5]

Scientists also quickly lined up in opposition. Former Defense Department technical advisers accused Reagan of holding out an attractive vision as likely as "a fountain of youth or a universal cure for cancer."[6] Jerome Weisner, former president of the Massachusetts Institute of Technology (MIT), said: "Most technical people doubt that antimissile devices in space will work. But even if they do, it's wishful thinking to believe that they would provide impenetrable defenses."[7] Noted scientists such as Nobel Prize winners Hans Bethe and Isidor I. Rabi, key figures in the postwar science community, signed a petition with fifteen others calling for a ban on all weapons in outer space.[8] In the early years of the SDI program, more than half the academics in science and engineering departments boycotted SDI research, despite the millions of dollars of research money that could secure an academic career.[9]

Despite the vigorous denunciation of Reagan's vision by scientists, the majority of Americans supported it by the end of 1985. Several scholars have analyzed the strategies of Reagan's "Star Wars" speech and its implications for technical reasoning in public debate.[10] Rebecca Bjork has detailed the broader rhetorical strategies that led to support for SDI.[11] Others have detailed the history of SDI, its foundations in earlier anti–ballistic missile (ABM) defense debates, and its implications for nuclear policy and the Cold War.[12] None, however, specifically answer the question: "How did Reagan rhetorically frame SDI to overcome the explicit opposition of scientists?" It is my contention that Reagan simultaneously rejected scientific criticism from influential scientists while maintaining the efficacy of science through a rhetoric of the technological sublime. By splitting the scientific community rhetorically into those who were living in a past of "expertise" and those with the courage and vision to create a future transformed by defensive weapons, Reagan reaffirmed American belief in technical solutions to problems. In so doing, he capitalized on a generational shift in the scientific establishment to build support for a third generation of nuclear weapons and to open the possibility of an end to nuclear stalemate.

To analyze Reagan's strategies, I first review the literature on fear appeals as a theoretical explanation for the persistence of faith in technology in Cold War rhetoric. Next, I analyze the scientists' challenges to the efficacy of Reagan's proposal and the counter arguments offered in response by scientists who supported SDI. I then analyze the frame created by Reagan's rhetoric for the understanding and interpretation of SDI. Finally, I note some of the consequences of this discourse in the larger context of Cold War rhetoric and contemporary political discourse.

Fear in the Nuclear Age

Fear is a powerful motivator. Fundamental to human experience, fear impels us to action; we stand and fight with heightened strength or run with amazing speed. Which reaction individuals choose depends on their analysis of the situation and the available responses.

People follow a two-step process in their responses to messages designed to induce fear. They first analyze the threat. If the threat reaches a threshold level, the listener evaluates the recommended response against the perceived strength of the threat.[13]

This first stage involves two variables: perceived severity and perceived susceptibility. Before people will respond to a fear appeal, they must first believe that the threat is intense enough to require a response. They must also believe that they are personally susceptible to that threat. If the perceived threat fails to reach a threshold level, the listener generally will ignore a fear appeal, will not consider a recommended response, and will make no attitude, intention, or behavior changes.[14]

The threat posed by nuclear weapons and the Soviet Union during the Cold War was a constant source of fear and rhetorical maneuvering. Political leaders could preserve the status quo and public quiescence by convincing constituents that negotiation backed by military strength created a tenuous balance between the superpowers and thus reduced the immediate threat. Or, to support change, politicians might attempt to heighten a sense of threat with descriptions of increasingly powerful nuclear weapons and evidence of Soviet intentions to launch a first strike. In either case, because citizens had little opportunity to test their leaders' claims, the argument's persuasiveness formed the basis for audience reactions.

When leaders use rhetoric to raise a sense of severe threat and induce fear, listeners respond in one of two ways: They will either attempt to control their fear or they will attempt to control the danger. The path taken results from the evaluation of the recommended response against the strength of the perceived threat. Efficacy is the key to the listener's response to fear.

Efficacy involves two judgments. First, the recommended response must be effective in reducing the identified threat (response efficacy) and the individuals must believe the response meets standards of feasibility and practicality—especially in terms of their own ability to carry out the response (self-efficacy). As long as the perceived efficacy of the recommended response is higher than the perceived threat, individuals will accept fear-arousing messages and develop cognitive responses to fear. While threat and fear trigger action, Kim Witte notes that "efficacy determines exactly what those actions will be."[15]

Throughout the Cold War, perceptions of American military superiority, belief in negotiation and treaties as a means to forestall Soviet aggression and beliefs about Soviet motivation all combined in estimates of efficacy, both individual and national.

Immediately following World War II graphic depictions of nuclear holocaust filled the media. Scientists, religious, and political leaders hoped fear would bring social change. One 1945 commentator wrote, "Fear may do what sheer morality could never do."[16] The atomic bomb was "the good news of damnation" that would frighten people into the renunciation of all war.[17] However, Soviet nuclear capability and rejection of international control brought an end to this early cycle, and Americans embraced nuclear military strength as the response.

As a result, a belief in the efficacy of American science and technology became the cornerstone of American security. Building bigger and better bombs would protect the United States. The reliance on science meant giving up a belief in personal action. "Starting with Hiroshima," Robert J. Lifton and Greg Mitchell wrote, "officials advised Americans to leave all problems surrounding the bomb to political, scientific, and military leaders—the nuclear priesthood."[18] Secrecy throughout the Cold War required citizens to place their faith in their leaders and in America's technological supremacy. The arms race and its principle of deterrence offered a sufficient, if not complete, response to control the danger of nuclear war.

A second wave of fear emerged in the late 1950s and early 1960s when the effects of radioactive fallout fed a national movement against nuclear testing and renewed interest in civil defense. This time the fear was close to home and real rather than merely the promise of what could happen. When the United States, Soviet Union, and Great Britain signed a limited nuclear test ban treaty, talk and activism about nuclear issues dropped dramatically.[19] In 1959, 64 percent of Americans listed nuclear war as the nation's most urgent problem. However, by 1964 only 16 percent held the issue at the forefront of political life, and soon it dropped from national opinion surveys altogether.[20]

Throughout the late 1960s and early 1970s, the fear of nuclear war dissipated. Paul Boyer suggests that an illusion of diminished risk, a loss of immediacy, and the promise of beneficial uses of atomic energy all combined to reduce fear during this period.[21] Another possible explanation was that the response to the fear, the strategy of mutual assured destruction, was identified as an effective response to the situation. A final possible explanation was that public attention was so absorbed in the Vietnam War that nuclear issues fell into the background.

A new era of nuclear fear emerged in the late 1970s and early 1980s. The breakdown of arms control talks, a growing anti–nuclear power movement in the United States, the so-called Window of Vulnerability created by the Committee on the Present Danger, heightened nuclear weapons protests in Europe, and the policies of the Reagan administration again made fear of nuclear war a motivating political force in the United States. Significant increases in defense spending, statements about the possibility of limited nuclear war, development of elaborate civil defense plans, and Reagan's increasingly ideological rhetoric, culminating in his "Evil Empire" speech, heightened anxiety in America.[22]

Antinuclear advocates contributed to the increasing level of fear. The Physicians for Social Responsibility dropped symbolic bombs on America's cities. The Union of Concerned Scientists (UCS) and the National Committee for a Sane Nuclear Policy (SANE) painted bleak pictures of nuclear destruction. More than half of American adults watched the made-for-television movie *The Day After* in 1983 and vicariously experienced a nuclear attack on Kansas City. The threat entered American living rooms, theaters, classrooms, and colleges.[23]

Once again Americans looked for a way to control the nuclear threat. This time they found it in the nuclear weapons freeze movement. By 1982, 72 percent of Americans supported a nuclear freeze in some form.[24] More than seven hundred thousand antinuclear demonstrators marched in New York City in support, and more than forty-five thousand workers were organized nationwide. American support for a nuclear freeze grew despite significant reservations about the potential effectiveness of such a policy.[25]

Americans acknowledged that the efficacy of a nuclear freeze fell short of addressing the threat directly. They did not trust the Soviet Union, and they understood that a freeze on production would not reduce the threat of existing nuclear weapons.[26] Nevertheless, many believed a halt to escalation might eventually lead to the elimination of nuclear weapons. But that possibility was a distant promise, one that American citizens had little hope of securing.

Reagan's answer, "peace through strength," called for continued deterrence while seeking arms control. As he struggled to justify increased defense spending, he recognized the need for a response that released Americans from the fear of the nuclear age. "What if free people could live secure in the knowledge that their security did not rest upon the threat of instant U.S. retaliation to deter a Soviet attack, that we could intercept and destroy strategic ballistic missiles before they reached our own soil or that of our allies?" he asked.[27]

As a response to nuclear fear, Reagan's vision was hopeful. If the United States could create a defense against nuclear weapons, make them "impotent and obsolete," then the very technology that had created the danger in the first place could eliminate both the threat and the public's fear. As *Newsweek* magazine suggested, "the allure is clear: weapons that kill weapons instead of people."[28]

In turning to science for an answer to the nuclear dilemma, Reagan empowered the scientific community in the political debate. The efficacy of his proposal was in their hands. The question "could it be built?" was the foundation of Reagan's vision. Only the scientists could answer his call. Although political, economic, and military arguments would be central to the multiyear debate, without a belief that SDI could become a reality through the work of American scientists and engineers, Reagan's vision, no matter how appealing, would falter.

Efficacy and the Strategic Defense Initiative

White House scientific advisers, impaneled immediately after Reagan's speech, reported optimistically on the proposal. The Defensive Technologies Study, also called the Fletcher Panel, concluded that a multitiered ballistic missile defense system could work. It predicted that an engineering validation phase would be possible in the early 1990s, with potential deployment by 2000.[29]

Edward Teller, the most passionate advocate for SDI and the X-ray laser technology on which it was based, immediately supported the president. Called an "old lion" by *Time,* the father of the hydrogen bomb and founder of the Lawrence Livermore Laboratory, Teller was given credit for persuading Reagan to support SDI.[30] Writing for the *New York Times,* Teller compared Reagan's announcement to Roosevelt's decision to launch the Manhattan Project: "Today, a wide range of good and ingenious technical plans, ranging from simple to extraordinarily complex, challenge the widespread opinion that practical defense cannot be obtained." Teller asserted that "Reagan's recent action may save us from a future war and provide the needed basis for a stable, lasting peace."[31]

Despite Teller's optimism, articles in the popular press presaged what would be a contentious and sometimes personal scientific debate. Cover stories in both *Time* and *Newsweek* following Reagan's speech reported the support of Teller and others, but devoted equal space to eminent scientists such as Hans Bethe, Wolfgang Panofsky, Jeremy Stone, and Carl Sagan—all of whom considered the plan economically unsound, technically infeasible, morally and politically suspect, and, at its worst, a "cruel hoax."[32] In a side bar article that explained the scientific basis for SDI technology, Robert McCrory, director of the Laboratory for Laser Energetics at the University of Rochester, offered little support for SDI, saying, "The theoretical physics for all this is pretty sparse."[33] Victor Weisskopf, an MIT professor and contemporary of Edward Teller, called Reagan's proposal a "pipe dream."[34] However, after recounting the obstacles, the article ended on an optimistic note, citing McCrory again: "If the potential is there, we must in our own interests pursue it, if only to find out what our adversaries may be doing."[35] *Newsweek* ended its analysis with similar skepticism, reporting: "The space technology Reagan hopes will obviate the MAD policies that now govern the debate is still 30 years—and perhaps as many as seven administrations—away. One president with a vision cannot change the world's nuclear calculus overnight."[36]

Scientists Subvert the Efficacy of SDI

The tensions between scientific possibility, economic feasibility, and political advisability characterized the ongoing debate. The most important challenge to SDI came from physicists Hans Bethe, Richard L. Garwin, Kurt Gottfried, and Henry W. Kendall. Their argument, primarily a technical one, was presented first in *Scientific American* and later republished as a book by the UCS. They argued that Reagan's plan exhibited "faith in radical solutions," a combination of novel political moves and revolutionary technological advances.[37]

The scientists' assessment began with an analysis of a presumed attack by the Soviet Union. They estimated that a nationwide defense would have to intercept and destroy virtually all of ten thousand or so nuclear warheads. They then carefully described the launch and flight of each of these missiles, both land-based intercontinental ballistic missiles and the possible use of submarine-launched ballistic missiles. They explained the shrinking window of the boost phase, a critical time for ABM defense, and built a sense of urgency as some missiles penetrated the first defense and created a "threat cloud."[38]

Having built the threat, they described possible responses. They explained the United States would need both space-based weapons and weapons that would "pop up" at the time of attack. They analyzed the time needed to launch a counterattack and the impossible weight-to-payload ratios required to respond. They reported the incredible power requirements of X-ray lasers: "300 1,000-megawatt power plants or more than 60 percent of the current electrical generating capacity of the entire U.S."[39] The power supply alone, they said, would cost $100 billion. They argued that the weapons would be highly vulnerable, would stress the limits of software development, and, in many cases, could not be tested at all. They concluded, in concurrence with a report from the Congressional Office of Technology Assessment, that "the prospect that emerging 'Star Wars' technologies when further developed, will provide a perfect or near-perfect defense system . . . is so remote that it should not serve as the basis of public expectation or national policy."[40] The Strategic Defense Initiative's efficacy, according to these experts, was nil, and efforts to develop a Star Wars defense should be abandoned.

Scientists Support Efficacy of SDI

Robert Jastrow, professor of earth sciences at Dartmouth University and founder of the Goddard Institute for Space Studies, defended SDI by directly attacking the UCS's analysis. He asserted that Bethe and others had made basic calculation errors, mistakes so obvious that he was able to correct them without a computer: "So I got hold of a polar-projection map of the northern hemisphere and a piece of celluloid. I marked the positions of the North Pole and the Soviet missile fields on the celluloid, stuck a pin through the North Pole, and rotated the celluloid around the Pole to imitate the rotation of the earth carrying the missile fields with it. Then I played with the map, the moving celluloid and different kinds of satellite orbits for a day or two, to get a feel for the problem."[41] He then checked his calculations with friends at the Lawrence Livermore Laboratory and found that the UCS calculations were exaggerated by twenty-five times. He noted similar problems throughout the data, offering alternative calculations that made Reagan's recommended course of research both technically and economically reasonable. Jastrow subtly undercut the credibility of the anti-SDI scientists without a direct attack.

Jastrow offered two explanations for the flawed data. First, he believed

SDI's critics were blinded by their political judgments. Because they opposed the president's recommendation on political grounds as "destabilizing," when their calculations bore out the position, they failed to check them carefully. He asserted that "their rational judgments can be clouded by their ideological preconceptions."[42]

What was more troubling for Jastrow, and supported his suggestion of political motivation, was how the UCS corrected errors once they were identified: "A UCS spokesman admitted his organization's rather large error in congressional testimony some months ago. But when he made the admission he did not say: 'We have made a mistake by a factor of more than a thousand, and the correct weight of the accelerator for this Neutral Particle beam is not 40,000 tons, but closer to 25 tons.' He said, 'We proposed to increase the area of the beam and accelerator, noting that would make the accelerator unacceptably massive for orbital deployment. Our colleagues have pointed out that the area could be increased after the beam leaves the small accelerator.' That was all he said about the mistake in his testimony."[43] Jastrow left the impression that the UCS was circulating data that it knew to be wrong in order to serve political motives. Rather than providing technical information to political leaders, Jastrow suggested, the scientists had used their expertise to shape policy. In accounting for their actions through political motivation, Jastrow avoided attacking science itself. Only these *particular* scientists were blinded by their ideology.

A second explanation for the flawed data, however, spoke directly to the scientific expertise of SDI opponents. Jastrow suggested that these scientists had moved outside their areas of expertise. He quoted the explanation of Dr. Lowell Wood, whom he called "one of the most brilliant of the younger generation of defense scientists," in reference to Hans Bethe's criticism of SDI: "Is Hans Bethe a good physicist? Yes, he's one of the best alive. Is he a rocket engineer? No. Is he a military-systems engineer? No. Is he a general? No. Everybody around here respects Hans Bethe enormously as a physicist. But weapons are my profession. He dabbles as a military systems analyst."[44] Hans Bethe, Nobel Prize winner, was not only outside his field, but Jastrow intimated he was from another time. The "younger generation" was taking the lead.

Jastrow reiterated the generational divide in what appeared to be a statement of sadness: "When I was a graduate student in theoretical physics, we revered some of the men who have lent their names to the report by the UCS. They are among the giants of 20th Century physics—the golden era in our profession. Yet these scientists have given their endorsement to badly flawed calculations that create a misleading impression in the minds of Congress and the public on the technical feasibility of a proposal aimed at protecting the United States from destruction."[45] In Jastrow's view, SDI's opponents were working against the nation's best interests.

Technical disagreements were couched in attributions of political motive throughout the debate. When Hans Bethe was asked about Edward Teller's unwavering support of SDI, Bethe said, "It's political for Edward, and he cannot change."[46] When Teller was asked about Bethe, he responded: "the arguments about SDI are primarily political and philosophical, not technical. We are under a propaganda attack from the Soviet Union, aided by misinformation from our own media and many of our own scientists."[47] Each side discounted the other as politically motivated and the public had little way to discern the difference.

The scientists' battle raged throughout 1984 as the administration reported preliminary successes in research. By 1985, petitions calling the SDI program "technically dubious and politically unwise" and "unworkable and dangerous" circulated among physicists, starting at the University of Illinois and at Cornell.[48] A petition circulated at 110 research universities eventually was signed by more than thirty-nine hundred faculty members, including Manhattan Project scientists Bethe and MIT's Philip Morrison. Organizers estimated that more than half the faculty at 120 university science and engineering departments in the country pledged not to accept SDI funds.[49]

Even scientists within the program attempted to lower expectations for building a leak-proof defense. The Strategic Defense Initiative's chief scientist, Gerold Yonas, said, "Nobody believes in a 100% leak-proof defense. Nobody believes in 100% anything that's ever worked on military systems." Lawrence Livermore Laboratory's assistant director for arms control supported his analysis: "I think that that's something that very few scientists think is going to be possible."[50] Computer scientist David L. Parnas resigned as a consultant to the SDI organization after saying that most of the money allocated would be wasted. "It is our duty," he wrote, "as scientists and engineers, to reply that we have no technological magic that will accomplish [making nuclear weapons impotent and obsolete]. The President and the public should know that."[51]

Of course, millions of new dollars for research were flowing to the weapons laboratories, if not to reluctant university scientists. Work on SDI would proceed in secret. But the public belief in the practicality of those expenditures could be severely shaken by the scientists' negative public evaluations of Reagan's plan. Reagan needed to counter the experts to preserve the efficacy of his vision. The divided reactions of the scientific community left Reagan room to reframe the scientific basis for his vision.

Reagan and the Technological Sublime

The technological sublime, a vision that merges technological mastery of the environment with religious fervor and nationalism, has surfaced repeatedly throughout American history. Cultural critics, philosophers, and intellectual historians, led by Emile Durkheim and Immanuel Kant, have identified a unique American conceptualization of the sublime experience that follows several steps. An observer encounters some objective of overwhelming magnitude and is struck by awe and amazement at the incomprehensible vastness of the object or by terror at the power of an overwhelming force. This observer is struck by her weakness and insignificance in the face of the sublime object but then as she comprehends it, she moves past feelings of awe to a heightened sense of her ability to master emotion with reason, to comprehend the incomprehensible and come to terms with its power.[52] In the aftermath of a sublime experience, individuals become aware of "our superiority over nature within, and thus also over nature without us."[53]

In American culture, the sublime, first experienced in response to the American landscape, took on religious overtones. As Americans contemplated the Grand Canyon, Niagara Falls, the Rocky Mountains, or the vastness of the Great Plains, they interpreted their experience in religious terms, as the reward given by God to a chosen people. David Nye notes that the religious reaction was "woven together with the nationalistic language of exceptionalism" so that these natural wonders became "a sign of a special relationship, or a covenant, between America and the Almighty."[54]

As Americans tamed and used the nation's natural resources, they began to merge natural and technological wonders. Nye argues that the popular sublime in America took on a unique character and became an integral part of American identity: "The American public celebrated the fact that a spectacular sight was the biggest waterfall, the longest railway bridge, or the grandest canyon, and they did so with a touch of pride that Europe boasted no such wonders. Natural places and great public works become icons of American greatness."[55]

Nye interprets America's technological prowess as proof of the superiority of democracy. The young nation's great public works demonstrated what "the capabilities of a free people, whose energies, undirected by absolute authority, have accomplished."[56] Americans celebrated canals, roadways, railroads, telegraphs, skyscrapers, and eventually a vast military arsenal. A belief in American technological know-how was part of American character.

Nuclear weapons, however, were the culmination and perhaps the end of the technological sublime. While such weapons demonstrated the ability of human beings to "harness the power of nature," they simultaneously gave humanity the ability to annihilate nature and all humanity with it. Nye argues that the classic form of the technological sublime broke down "not because the objects of our contemplation have ceased to be fearful but because terror has become their principal characteristic."[57] In Nye's analysis, nuclear weapons cannot produce a sublime experience: "Even the older technological sublime had always proved ephemeral—the railroad, bridge, and the light bulb, which once seemed sublime, soon became commonplace. But the Bomb could not become commonplace despite the government's best public relations efforts to domesticate it, nor could it be effectively surpassed by greater weapons that might diminish it through force of contrast. To anyone who contemplates them, nuclear weapons can only be a permanent, invisible terror that offers no moral enlightenment."[58]

Although Nye made this claim in 1994, it seems counter to the rhetorical and political evidence of the early 1980s. Reagan did, in fact, contemplate nuclear weapons as a means for moral enlightenment and movement along America's destined path. As *Time* noted: "Reagan now suggests that we slowly start investigating whether in the next century technology may offer a solution to our security that does not rest on the prospect of mass and mutual death. It is the product of Ronald Reagan's peculiar knack for asking an obvious question, one that has moral as well as political dimensions and one that the experts had assumed had been answered, or found unanswerable, or found not worth asking, long ago."[59] Reagan not only asked the question but also provided the answer. In so doing, he reinvigorated the technological sublime as the way for Americans to experience superiority, security, and hope in the 1980s.

While SDI remained an issue after Reagan's announcement in 1983 and as a campaign issue in 1984, the controversy over SDI escalated as Reagan began his second term. In his second inaugural and State of the Union addresses, Reagan created a rhetorical frame for SDI that characterized his vision for American nuclear policy. Consistent with his Star Wars speech, Reagan placed the goals of SDI within a broader notion of American destiny, an unequivocal expression of the American sublime. He called for a second revolution in America, one tied to technological progress: "My fellow citizens, this nation is poised for greatness. The time has come to proceed toward a great new challenge—a second American Revolution of hope and opportunity; a revolution carrying us to new heights of progress by pushing back frontiers of knowledge and space; a revolution of spirit that taps the soul of America, enabling us to summon greater strength than we've ever known, and a revolution that carries beyond our shores the golden promise of human freedom in a world of peace."[60]

Reagan called this "an age of marvels, technological marvels," especially in the realm of space: "America is today on the edge of vast new frontiers. The world already marvels at American aircraft and space technology. . . . Our space shuttle missions now are all but routine. . . . Americans are preparing themselves for great strides forward. Our technological advances of the last four decades are only the foundation for a new era that is almost beyond imagination."[61]

Reagan demarcated time and signaled a new beginning, a sense of wonder at the advances that were possible. He offered a vision of "a second transformation, a quantum technological leap that's making possible still greater prosperity and individual fulfillment than we've ever known."[62]

This future was an extension of the American tradition in Reagan's worldview. It was part of the American character: "The story of American technology is long and proud. It might be said to have begun with the blacksmith at his bellows, hammering out fine tools, and the Yankee craftsman using simple wood planes, saws, and mallets to fashion the fastest sailing ships on the ocean. And then came the railroad men, driving spikes across our country. And today the story continues with the workers who built the computer in a child's room; the engineers who designed the communications satellite that silently rotates with the Earth, shining in the sunlight against the blackness of space; and the men and women of skill and determination who helped to put American footprints on the Moon."[63] The technological march forward certainly could encompass the "quantum leap" needed for the success of SDI. Hard work and American "know how" would make it happen.

But the scientists who were discounting the feasibility of SDI had been part of the historic march forward. Esteemed scientists, critical members of the Manhattan Project, and national scientific advisers were calling SDI a "pipe dream." Reagan had to differentiate the scientists who wished to live in the past from those with the vision to move forward. Attitude, not ability, was the key. The only limit on American technological progress was an unwillingness to dream. Those who suggested we could not make the discoveries necessary to reach our goals were the only barrier to success: "Let us begin by challenging our conventional wisdom. There are no constraints on the human mind, no walls around the human spirit, no barriers to our progress except those we ourselves erect."[64]

What had to be acknowledged was our limited ability to know what might be. To support his point, Reagan listed *unanticipated* technological breakthroughs: "Day by day, we're shattering accepted notions of what is possible. When I was growing up, we failed to see how a new thing called radio would transform our marketplace. Well, today, many have not yet seen how advances in technology are transforming our lives. In the late 1950s workers at the AT&T semiconductor plant in Pennsylvania produced five transistors a day for $7.50 apiece. They now produce over a million for less than a penny apiece. New laser techniques could revolutionize heart bypass surgery. . . . We stand on the threshold of a great ability to produce more, do more, be more."[65] Looking forward and moving forward into the unknown were depicted as part of the American experience.

Freedom also was an essential element in American progress. The United States was "fertile soil" for the talents of scientists as opposed to "places where repression stifles creativity, chokes off opportunity for expression and development." Indeed, Americans had always been able to do what the Soviets could not, according to Reagan: "Things that are today beyond the imagination of dictators and tyrants will be conceived of and made reality by free men and women. This we can count on."[66]

In Reagan's revolution, technological breakthroughs were an expression of freedom. Moreover, technological progress could secure freedom as well: "Technological advances, like developing a space shield, offer us new options. Yet we should never forget that our independence and freedom ultimately depend on our courage, determination, and strength of character. There's no limit to what free men and women can do, and there's no limit to how far Americans can go."[67]

The fear of what free people could do was what drove the Soviets to develop their own missile defense. Moreover, the threat that the Soviets might beat the United States to such a defense lurked in the background: "We keep hearing some self-declared experts and some of those blame-America-first crowd saying that our SDI concept is unfeasible and a waste of money. Well, if that's true, why are the Soviets so upset about it? As a matter of fact, why are they investing so many rubles of their own in the same technologies?"[68]

In another interview, Reagan said: "And it reminds me of that wonderful cartoon, not too long ago, where the man was sitting watching the TV screen and from the TV the voice was coming out saying that it would never work, that it would never work, that it was too expensive, that you couldn't do it. And his wife was just leaving the room, passing through behind him, and she said,

'Well, then why don't the Russians want us to have it?'"[69] Because of the secrecy that pervaded the Cold War, Soviet reactions were valuable evidence to reinforce a belief in the capacity of the American military-industrial complex to invent and produce defensive weapons.

Furthermore, given the Soviet perception, why would an American scientist not want to aid in this effort? Reagan noted: "Let history record that in our day America's best scientific minds sought to develop technology that helped mankind ease away from the nuclear parapet. Let us move on to a happier chapter in the history of man. And I would think any scientist would be proud to help turn that page."[70] Although Reagan said he did not wish to ascribe motives to the scientists who opposed the effort, by claiming he was not ascribing motives, he in fact did. While American scientists had the "ability," they did not have the "will" required for America's contemporary problems. In language far less explicit but reminiscent of an earlier era, Reagan implied that to resist his call was unpatriotic or even un-American.

In a series of speeches delivered in Europe during the summer of 1985, Reagan reinforced the need for a courageous spirit in the face of criticism. He used a less-than-subtle analogy to Columbus's voyage to America to differentiate "will" from "ability": "Yet it's not so much the voyage but rather the decision to make the voyage that we should commemorate. The skills of the captains and sailors, although vital to success, were less significant than the genius of Columbus and the vision of Queen Isabella. Though besieged with serious challenges, the Spanish throne overcame the doubters and cynics and thus opened a golden age for Spain and a new chapter in human history."[71] Earlier in the year, Reagan said: "Anything is possible in America if we have the faith, the will, and the heart. History is asking us once again to be a force for good in the world. Let us begin in unity, with justice and love."[72]

Indeed, Reagan showed a clear impatience for "experts" who rejected innovative approaches to problems. Quoting Arthur C. Clarke, a distinguished author of science and fiction, Reagan said: "ideas often have three stages of reaction: First, 'it's crazy and don't waste my time.' Second, 'It's possible, but it's not worth doing.' And finally, 'I've always said it was a good idea'." What many American scientists lacked, said Reagan, was vision: "If we put our trust in experts and rely on their knowledge to shape our destiny, then we condemn ourselves to live in the past. For how can they be experts in what hasn't been invented yet, what doesn't yet exist? In 1899, the head of the United States Patent Bureau advised our then President to abolish that office because, he said, 'Everything that can be invented has been invented.' Well at one point, Thomas

Watson, the man behind IBM, which is today one of the largest manufacturers of computers in the world, is reported to have said, quote, 'I think there is a world market for about five computers.'"[73]

Robert McFarlane attached the president's analysis directly to SDI in another forum: "Admiral William Leahy, Chief of Staff to President Truman, warned in 1945 that: The [atomic] bomb will never go off, and I speak as an expert in explosives. . . . One scientist argued in 1932 that, 'There is not the slightest indication that [nuclear] energy will ever be obtainable. It would mean that the atom would have to be shattered at will.' That scientist was Albert Einstein." The conclusion: "With these and many more examples, one cannot blithely accept the word of some self-anointed 'experts' who tell us how a strategic defense can never work, can never be cost effective, can never be stabilizing."[74] Reagan's critics, he added, were caught in the past: "Now my point here is not to question the motives of others. But it's difficult to understand how critics can object to exploring the possibility of moving away from exclusive reliance upon nuclear weapons. The truth is, I believe that they find it difficult to embrace any idea that breaks with the past, that breaks with consensus thinking and the common establishment wisdom. In short, they find it difficult and frightening to alter the status quo."[75]

Finally, Reagan joined the analysis offered by Jastrow. This new time required new scientists—those prepared to become experts through innovation. The so-called experts who were arguing against Reagan's initiative were of the previous generation, and Reagan needed scientists ready to revolutionize thinking about nuclear weapons: "In Dr. Goddard's case, the *New York Times* claiming rockets would never work in the vacuum of space ridiculed his effort. 'He only seems to lack the knowledge ladled out daily in high schools,' the *Times* editorialized. But due to the efforts of Dr. Goddard and other individuals of vision and tenacity, America is now on the edge of a new era. By standing on the shoulders of giants like Robert Goddard, this generation is moving forward to harness the enormity of space in the preservation of peace, in increasing our economic well-being, and in expanding the horizons of human freedom beyond the greatest dreams of our Founding Fathers."[76]

Depiction of the "Star Warriors" in the media supported Reagan's optimistic characterization of American science. *Newsweek* wrote: "Here is the greatest technological challenge in the world today, out of which may come the next generation of Nobel Prize winners."[77] The scientists were young and the atmosphere at the national laboratories was "grad school writ large—cubicle walls covered with posters, 10-speed bikes in the corners."[78] Attitude was not a problem with these scientists. The typical Star Wars scientist displayed the "arrogance of a fighter-jock." "To almost everyone else," reported *Newsweek,* "including Ronald Reagan, Star Wars is an abstraction—a promise of a distant millennium when nuclear weapons will no longer exist, a piece on the global chessboard, a budget line. To scientists, it is as real as lightning."[79] Such scientists were self-assured in their ability to meet Reagan's challenge: "To kill flying kerosene cans that bring hydrogen bombs is not much more difficult at the end of the twentieth century, than dynamiting fish," said Lowell Wood, a project group director at the Lawrence Livermore Laboratory.[80] In the *Bulletin of the Atomic Scientists,* the scientists were described as "intellectual test pilots" with the "right stuff" ethic of science combined with "the glamour of space, the thrill of inventing new kinds of nuclear weapons, and youthful idealism."[81] A sense of efficacy was ever present. As one scientist said: "We can try to negotiate treaties and things like that. But one thing I can do personally, without having to wait for arms control, is to develop the technology to eliminate them myself, to eliminate offensive nuclear weapons."[82] Rather than rejecting the Star Wars label, they embraced it, naming one project within SDI the "Jedi Concept."

The new generation had arrived. Reagan reflected their excitement and connection to Star Wars: "The Strategic Defense Initiative has been labeled 'Star Wars,' but it isn't about war; it's about peace. It isn't about retaliation; it's about prevention; It isn't about fear; it's about hope. And in that struggle, if you'll pardon my stealing a film line: The force is with us."[83] In Reagan's discourse, the "force" or American spirit tied to a God-given mission and superior ability had always been with us. What was needed were new Jedi knights willing to seek out the force again and to use it to reach the nation's destiny of leading the world to freedom, the freedom of democracy and freedom from nuclear fear.

Consequences of Reagan's Reinvigoration of the Technological Sublime

Despite challenges from almost every type of expert, the American people accepted Reagan's vision. Between January and December, 1985—the height of scientific opposition to Star Wars—among Americans who reported following SDI discussions "very or fairly closely," those who wanted to see the United States go ahead with SDI research increased from 52 to 61 percent.[84] Those in favor believed the system would increase the likelihood of reaching a nuclear arms agreement with the Soviet Union and would improve the chances for peace.[85] By recasting the efficacy of SDI as part of a history of unanticipated technological breakthroughs that were part of America's character and tradition, Reagan provided the public with a way to believe in his vision.

Despite the rejection of Reagan's plan by many scientists, the public still believed it was technically possible to build a space shield for the United States. One explanation for the rejection of scientific "naysayers" was the need within the Cold War worldview for scientists to play the role of mystical leaders. Ira Chernus notes that "we still see our nuclear scientists as wizards. With few exceptions, the scientists play the role we would have them play and reinforce our assumption that they do have magical wisdom."[86] However, when scientists refuse to play the role, Americans have two options: reject their belief that science and technology can secure a brighter future or find a way to discount the scientists who subvert the image.

In this case, enough prominent scientists supported the president to lend credibility to his case. Moreover, a new generation of scientists with the "right stuff" offered the possibility of continued national efficacy based in science. The on-going distrust of the Soviet Union and of nuclear weapons required more than continued MAD policies. Edward Linenthal believed the hope inspired by SDI was ultimately unbeatable: "Living with nuclear weapons, even in greatly reduced numbers, might be a rational response to the dilemmas of the time, but it could not match SDI as a hopeful response to deeply held fears."[87]

Reagan's vision was effective enough to obtain a significant level of funding for scientists and defense contractors. In 1985 alone $180 million in SDI research funding was awarded to twenty universities.[88] The nation's scientific laboratories, Los Alamos and Lawrence Livermore, flourished. Political action committees representing sixteen defense contractors targeted key legislators in 1983–84 with more than $3 million in campaign contributions.[89]

Apparently the Soviet Union also was convinced the United States could build a credible defense and that it would need to increase its offensive and defensive weapons development as a result. Former British prime minister Margaret Thatcher credits the pressure created by SDI as a key factor in the end of the Cold War.[90] By the time the program was ended in 1993, the price tag for the United States was somewhere between the government's estimate of $33.5 billion and the Congressional Research Service's estimate of $70.7 billion.[91]

Not surprisingly, since the end of the Cold War, arguments for funding for defensive technologies have continued, ranging from building a defense against comets that might enter the Earth's atmosphere to the need to counter new threats from rogue nations, terrorists, and threats from China and North

Korea.[92] Powerful lobbying forces, working with Republicans to revive the program through the "Contract with America" in 1994, succeeded in part.[93] The Clinton administration continued a modest variation of SDI research through the Ballistic Missile Defense Organization. However, more recent nuclear development activities in Pakistan, Iran, Iraq, India, and North Korea renewed the debate about missile defense, prompting Congress to appoint the Commission to Assess the Ballistic Missile Threat to the United States in 1997. Chaired by former defense secretary Donald H. Rumsfeld, the commission's analysis, delivered on July 15, 1998, reported that the threat posed by emerging capabilities in North Korea, Iran, or Iraq was "broader, more mature, and evolving more rapidly than has been reported in estimates and reports by the intelligence community."[94] Further evidence that China had secured U.S. advanced missile technology generated additional support for the National Missile Defense Act of 1999. In March, 1999, this commitment to install a national missile defense system "as soon as technologically feasible" was passed in the Senate by a 97–3 margin and in the House by 317–105.[95]

Despite bipartisan support, feasibility was, and still is, the issue. Throughout the 1990s the efficacy of the missile defense was raised over and over again. In 1992, William J. Broad's *Teller's War: The Top-Secret Story Behind the Star Wars Deception* suggested that Edward Teller intentionally misrepresented research to increase and continue funding for SDI.[96] Broad's charges were fueled further by reports that SDI scientists had rigged tests and faked data to mislead Congress and the Soviet Union. Whistleblowers inside the SDI program reported similar exaggerations and deceptions.[97]

In 1993, former national security adviser Robert McFarlane and former defense secretary Caspar Weinberger denied the charges.[98] Defense Secretary Les Aspin investigated charges of deception and reported that "the experiment was not rigged and deception did not take place."[99] However, Aspin also reported that military technicians had developed but never employed a system of deception in the tests to fool the Soviets.

Similar mixed reports characterized the debate in 1999. Less than a week after Congress supported national missile defense the Pentagon reported a successful test of a component of the theater high-altitude area defense system. The attacking missile achieved sixteen of seventeen objectives, Defense spokesmen said. A month later, they offered a more refined analysis. The final count was "2 of 4 main goals" achieved, eliminating fourteen of the claimed successes.[100] While some Boeing officials touted a "major breakthrough on the kill vehicle," other program officials more cautiously noted that, "the program has still not hit anything."[101] Congress called for deployment as soon as the system was technically feasible, yet technical feasibility is far from certain. As John Pike, a space specialist with the Federation of American Scientists said, "They can't get it to work, but the political momentum is probably irresistible."[102]

The efficacy of science is still the crux of the issue. If scientists cannot build it, we must find another way. And if they succeed in building it, will we ask yet again if we want what their genius has wrought? To accomplish its objectives, a strategic missile defense cannot be controlled by human intelligence. Computers must time and activate the split-second response and pinpoint targeting mechanisms. There is no room for human error. If we want the technological fix, we must live with the mistrust and fear the technology itself creates.

Renewed fear of autonomous technology may be the ultimate legacy of the technological secrecy throughout the Cold War and its somewhat modified version for the post–Cold War world. Just as popular culture expressed a romantic vision of good triumphing over technological evil in the *Star Wars* trilogy, that same culture expresses anxiety about technology in the late 1990s.[103] On a recent episode of television's *The X-Files,* for example, agents Scully and Mulder discover that a computer genius has created an evil artificial intelligence and set it loose on the Internet. Because its creators have a "kill switch," a computer virus designed to destroy the artificial intelligence, the computer takes control of military satellites and uses particle beams to kill them. Ironically, agents Scully and Mulder get into an argument over the possibility of such weaponry. Scully, the scientist, says the United States does not have such military capabilities. Agent Mulder says Brilliant Pebbles, one of the Star Wars projects funded during the Bush administration, was working on just such technology. The argument ends as a second "bolt from the blue" destroys its target.

We cannot return to Eden. President Dwight Eisenhower warned us to beware the military-industrial complex and the scientific-technological elite, and we should remain alert, because we cannot seem to conceive of life with them or without them.

Notes

1. Robert L. Scott, "Cold War and Rhetoric: Conceptually and Critically," in *Cold War Rhetoric: Strategy, Metaphor, and Ideology,* by Martin J. Medhurst, Robert L. Ivie, Philip Wander, and Robert L. Scott (East Lansing: Michigan State University Press, 1997), 12.

2. Ronald W. Reagan, "Address to the Nation on Defense and National Security," in *Public Papers of the Presidents of the United States* (hereafter *Public Papers*), *1983* (Washington, D.C.: GPO, 1983), 443.

3. "Nuclear Facts, Science Fictions," *New York Times,* Mar. 27, 1983, D18.

4. Lou Cannon, "President Seeks Futuristic Defense Against Missiles," *Washington Post*, Mar. 24, 1983, A1.

5. Francis X. Clines, "Democrats Assert Reagan Is Using 'Star Wars' Scare to Hide Blunders," *New York Times*, Mar. 24, 1983, A9.

6. George W. Rathjens and Jack Ruina, "100% Defense? Hardly," *New York Times*, Mar. 27, 1983, D19.

7. Ibid.

8. Ibid.

9. Rosy Nimroody, *Star Wars: The Economic Fallout* (Cambridge: Ballinger, 1988), 89.

10. Janice Hocker Rushing, "Ronald Reagan's 'Star Wars' Address: Mythic Containment of Technical Reasoning," *Quarterly Journal of Speech* 72 (1986): 415–33; G. Thomas Goodnight, "Ronald Reagan's Re-formulation of the Rhetoric of War: Analysis of the 'Zero Option,' 'Evil Empire,' and 'Star Wars' Addresses," *Quarterly Journal of Speech* 72 (1986): 390–414; Kenneth S. Zagacki and Andrew King, "Reagan, Romance, and Technology: A Critique of 'Star Wars,'" *Communication Studies* 40 (1989): 1–12.

11. Rebecca S. Bjork, *The Strategic Defense Initiative: Symbolic Containment of the Nuclear Threat* (Albany: State University of New York Press, 1992).

12. B. Bruce Biggs, *The Shield of Faith: A Chronicle of Strategic Defense from Zeppelins to Star Wars* (New York: Simon and Schuster, 1988); Gregg Herken, *Cardinal Choices: Presidential Science Advising from the Atomic Bomb to SDI* (New York: Oxford University Press, 1992); Nimroody, *Star Wars*.

13. Kim Witte, "Fear as Motivator, Fear as Inhibitor: Using the Extended Parallel Process Model to Explain Fear Appeal Successes and Failures," in *Handbook of Communication And Emotion: Research, Theory, Applications, and Contexts*, ed. Peter A. Andersen and Laura K. Guerrero (New York: Academic Press, 1998), 424–48.

14. Ibid., 428.

15. Ibid., 441–42.

16. Quoted in Paul Boyer, *By the Bomb's Early Light: American Thought and Culture at the Dawn of the Atomic Age* (New York: Pantheon, 1985), 69.

17. Ibid.

18. Robert Jay Lifton and Greg Mitchell, *Hiroshima in America: Fifty Years of Denial* (New York: Putnam, 1995), 335.

19. Boyer, *By the Bomb's Early Light*, 355.

20. Ibid.

21. Ibid., 357–58.

22. Ibid., 360–62; Bjork, *Strategic Defense Initiative*, 14–15; Edward Tabor Linenthal, *Symbolic Defense: The Cultural Significance of the Strategic Defense Initiative* (Chicago: University of Illinois Press, 1989), 114–16.

23. J. Michael Hogan, *The Nuclear Freeze Campaign: Rhetoric and Foreign Policy in the Telepolitical Age* (East Lansing: Michigan State University Press, 1994), 48–51.

24. Ibid., 175.

25. Bjork, *Strategic Defense Initiative*, 50–60.

26. "U.S.-Soviet Nuclear Arms Gap Seen Closing," *The Gallup Report* 208 (1983): 10–11.

27. Reagan, *Public Papers, 1983*, 443.

28. Michael A. Lerner, "A 'Star Wars' Defense," *Newsweek*, Apr. 4, 1983, 18.

29. Gary L. Guertner and Donald M. Snow, *The Last Frontier: An Analysis of the Strategic Defense Initiative* (Lexington, Mass.: Lexington Books, 1986), 20.

30. "The Old Lion Still Roars," *Time,* Apr. 4, 1983, 22.

31. Edward Teller, "Reagan's Courage," *New York Times,* Mar. 30, 1983, 31-A.

32. Walter Isaacson, "Reagan for the Defense," *Time,* Apr. 4, 1983, 18–19.

33. Frederic Golden, "High Tech on the High Frontier," *Time,* Apr. 4, 1983, 22.

34. Ibid.

35. Ibid.

36. Michael Reese, "Rethinking the Unthinkable," *Newsweek,* Apr. 4, 1983, 18.

37. Hans Bethe, Richard L. Garwin, Kurt Gottfried, and Henry W. Kendall, "Space-Based Ballistic Missile Defense," in *The Star Wars Debate,* ed. Steven Anzovin (New York: Wilson, 1986), 52–73.

38. Ibid., 58–61.

39. Ibid., 64.

40. Ibid., 72.

41. Robert Jastrow, "The War against Star Wars," in *Star Wars Debate,* ed. Anzovin, 79.

42. Ibid, 90.

43. Ibid, 84.

44. Ibid, 86.

45. Ibid, 85.

46. Robert Sheer, "Scientists Split Over 'Star Wars,'" *Los Angeles Times,* Sept. 24, 1985, 1-A.

47. Ibid.

48. Kim McDonald, "Opposition to Reagan's 'Star Wars' Grows Among Research Scientists; Many Spurn Funds from Pentagon," *Chronicle of Higher Education,* July 24, 1985, 21.

49. Nimroody, *Star Wars,* 89–91.

50. Robert Scheer, "Scientists Scramble to Fulfill Plan," *Los Angeles Times,* Sept. 22, 1985, A14.

51. Ibid.

52. David E. Nye, *American Technological Sublime* (Cambridge: Massachusetts Institute of Technology Press, 1994), 7–10.

53. Ibid., 16.

54. Ibid., 22.

55. Ibid., 36.

56. Ibid.

57. Ibid., 253.

58. Ibid.

59. Isaacson, "Reagan for the Defense," 13.

60. Reagan, *Public Papers, 1983,* 458–59.

61. Ronald W. Reagan, "Remarks at a Fundraising Luncheon for Senator Slade Gorton in Seattle, Washington, Dec. 2, 1985," in *Public Papers, 1985* (Washington, D.C.: GPO, 1985), 1428.

62. Ronald W. Reagan, "Remarks at the Presentation Ceremony for the National Technology Awards, Feb. 19, 1985," in *Public Papers, 1985,* 184.

63. Ibid.

64. Reagan, "Address Before a Joint Session of the Congress on the State of the Union, Feb. 6, 1985," in *Public Papers, 1985,* 132.

65. Ibid.

66. Reagan, "Toast at the State Dinner in Madrid, Spain, May 7, 1985," in *Pulbic Papers, 1985,* 579.

67. Reagan, "Radio Address to the Nation on Soviet Strategic Defense Programs, Oct. 12, 1985," in *Public Papers, 1985,* 1240.

68. Reagan, "Remarks at a California Republican Party Fundraising Dinner in Los Angeles, Aug. 22, 1985," in *Public Papers, 1985,* 1005.

69. Reagan, "Interview with Morton Kondracke and Richard H. Smith of Newsweek Magazine, Mar. 4, 1985," in *Public Papers, 1985,* 260.

70. Reagan, "Remarks at the National Space Club Luncheon, Mar. 19, 1985," in *Public Papers, 1985,* 364.

71. Reagan, "Toast at the State Dinner in Madrid, Spain, May 7, 1985," in *Public Papers, 1985,* 580.

72. Reagan, "Address Before a Joint Session of the Congress on the State of the Union, Feb. 6, 1985," in *Public Papers, 1985,* 134.

73. Reagan, "Remarks to Community Leaders in Madrid, Spain, May 7, 1985," in *Public Papers, 1985,* 578.

74. Robert D. McFarlane, *Department of State Bulletin* 85 (1985): 42.

75. Reagan, "Remarks at the Annual Dinner of the Conservative Political Action Conference, Mar. 1, 1985," in *Public Papers, 1985,* 227.

76. Reagan, "Remarks at the National Space Club Luncheon, Mar. 29, 1985," in *Public Papers, 1985,* 364.

77. Jerry Adler and Gerald L. Lubenow, "The Star Warriors," *Newsweek,* June 17, 1985, 34.

78. Ibid., 36.

79. Ibid., 35.

80. Ibid., 38.

81. Alan P. Lightman, "Lost in Space," *Bulletin of the Atomic Scientists* 40 (1984): 2.

82. Ibid.

83. Reagan, "Remarks at the National Space Club Luncheon, Mar. 29, 1985," in *Public Papers, 1985,* 366.

84. "Americans Rate Gorbachev's Nuclear Arms Reduction Proposals," *The Gallup Report* 243 (1985): 4.

85. Ibid.

86. Ira Chernus, *Dr. Strangegod: On the Symbolic Meaning of Nuclear Weapons* (Columbia: University of South Carolina Press, 1986), 16.

87. Linenthal, *Symbolic Defense,* 89–90.

88. Nimroody, *Star Wars,* 86.

89. Ibid., 98–99.

90. Holger Jensen, "Thatcher says 'star wars' key to ending Cold War," *Rocky Mountain News,* Oct. 10, 1995, A6.

91. Victoria Griffith, "Heavenly inspiration—The US Star Wars Initiative Has Led to a Wide Range of Discoveries," *Financial Times,* July 30, 1993, 15; Jonathan Landay, "Pentagon Hit for Hiding Spending on 'Star Wars,'" *Christian Science Monitor,* Sept. 5, 1995, 3.

92. Robert L. Park, "Star Warriors on Sky Patrol," *New York Times,* Mar. 25, 1992, A23.

93. "SDI Contractors donated heavily to Congressmen," *Chicago Tribune,* Feb. 1, 1995, A4.

94. Richard L. Garwin, "What We Did: Report by the commission to Assess the Ballistic Missile Threat to the United States," *Bulletin of the Atomic Scientists* 54 (1998) 40.

95. Eric Schmitt, "House Joins Senate in Voting for a System to Defend Against Missiles," *New York Times,* Mar. 19, 1999, A14.

96. William J. Broad, *Teller's War: The Top Secret Story Behind the Star Wars Deception* (New York: Simon and Schuster, 1992).

97. William J. Broad, "Beyond the Bomb: Turmoil in the Labs." *New York Times,* Oct. 9, 1988, F23.

98. Cal Thomas, "SDI Revisionism," *Times-Picayune,* Aug. 27, 1993, B7.

99. Richard A. Serrano, "Aspin Denies 'Star Wars' Tests Were Rigged," *Los Angeles Times,* Sept. 10, 1993, A22.

100. William J. Broad, "Missile Test Success! Next Time We'll Hit the Target," *New York Times,* Apr. 18, 1999, D5.

101. Paul Richter, "Deployment of U.S. Missile Shield Looks Ever Likelier," *Los Angeles Times,* Mar. 21, 1999, A1.

102. Ibid.

103. For an overview of nuclear issues as revealed in mass culture, see Paul Boyer and Eric Idsvoog, "Nuclear Menace in the mass Culture of the Late Cold-War Era and Beyond," in *Fallout: A Historian Reflects on America's Half-Century Encounter with Nuclear Weapons* (Columbus: Ohio State University Press, 1998), 199–225.

CHAPTER NINE

"By Helping Others, We Help Ourselves"

The Cold War Rhetoric of American Foreign Policy

ROBERT J. MCMAHON

In December, 1992, on the campus of Texas A&M University, President George Bush celebrated, in rather grandiloquent terms, the Cold War victory of the United States and "the forces of freedom." That victory had been won, Bush declared, "against an alien ideology that cast its shadow over every American. Today, by the grit of our people and the grace of God, the cold war is over. Freedom has carried the day." Rapidly approaching the final weeks of his presidency, Bush spent the remainder of his address recalling the foreign policy achievements of his administration—and his generation—and reflecting even more broadly on "America's purpose in the world." The president offered what he described as a "simple" thesis. "Amid the triumph and the tumult of the recent past," Bush stated, "one truth rings out more clearly than ever: America remains today what Lincoln said it was more than a century ago, 'the last best hope of man on Earth.'" It continued to serve, he said, "as a beacon for all the peoples of the world."[1]

There was nothing particularly novel about Bush's depiction of the United States as the world's selfless guardian of peace, freedom, and democracy. Quite the contrary, American leaders have, since the foundation of the republic, been drawing attention to what they have judged to be the uniqueness of America's civilization, history, character, and driving forces. They have habitually claimed that U.S. foreign policy aimed to defend the peace and to carry the blessings of freedom to other peoples. Many American statesmen have even found divine sanction for the conceit that the United States had a global mission to share its superior values, institutions, and culture with others. The United States was "the world's best hope," Thomas Jefferson proclaimed in his 1801 inaugural address, and the "last, best hope of earth" in Abraham Lincoln's famous rephrasing. Just before America's entry into World War I, Woodrow Wilson articulated that missionary imperative with even greater fervor: "We created this nation not just to serve ourselves, but to serve mankind." And, in a similar vein, at the height of the Cold War Harry S. Truman publicly professed his conviction "that God has created us and brought us to our present position of great power and strength for some great purpose."[2]

To Jefferson, Lincoln, Wilson, Truman, and virtually all other national leaders, the United States was not just another nation among nations. It was unique, special, anointed. America's relationship with the world beyond its borders consequently encompassed far more than the pursuit of narrow, national advantage. The "city upon a hill" was destined not just to take its place within the world, but to transform that world—to lead by the power of its righteousness and by the righteousness of its power. In keeping with so grandiose and noble a self-image, American statesmen have consistently downplayed any exclusively national interests undergirding U.S. actions. They have instead highlighted the selflessness of American motives and the universality of U.S. objectives.

Their country's engagement with the world, presidents have invariably insisted, advanced universalistic goals: peace, freedom, democracy, individual liberty, social justice, and material betterment. That U.S. national interests happened to coincide with the promotion of such exalted goals abroad simply confirmed their nation's special purpose—what scholars have labeled the doctrine of "American exceptionalism." Ever since the era of the founding fathers, the nation's statesmen have simply taken for granted that what was best for the United States was best for the world as a whole. They have frequently and unabashedly made exactly such a connection in their public proclamations about America's role in the world.[3]

This essay focuses on the rhetoric that American presidents employed throughout the Cold War era to explain and defend American foreign policy. I argue that U.S. chief executives have always depicted the United States as the noble and courageous guardian not just of America's interests, but of the world's. Since "interests," by their very nature, connote needs that might conceivably conflict with those of others, U.S. leaders have shrewdly presented their nation's interests as utopian objectives completely in harmony with the needs of all other members of the international community. Each of America's Cold War presidents adopted a similar strategy. By making U.S. interests appear so generous, so universal, so obviously beneficial to all people of good will, they implied (and sometimes directly stated) that any nation or group that would oppose such objectives was, by definition, evil.

Of course, if the United States was purely seeking to do good in the world, a potential problem loomed: How could American leaders convince fellow citizens that such a Pollyannaish foreign policy was worthy of support? Why expend American resources and sacrifice American lives just to help others? Cold War presidents characteristically strove to resolve that dilemma by positing a direct connection between America's defense of peace and freedom abroad—the most ubiquitous Cold War metaphor for the nation's global role—and the potential loss of American security and liberty if such a course were not pursued. In other words, America's idealism blended indistinguishably into America's self-interest. But it was the least selfish brand of self-interest imaginable, according to this linguistic construct, for America's self-interest was presented simply as a natural function of its magnanimous defense of peace and freedom. This conflation of idealism with self-interest is justified, in large part, through the conception of global interdependence emphasized by every Cold War chief executive. Since the loss of peace or freedom anywhere will endanger peace and freedom everywhere, according to this logic, the United States *must* act as global guardian for the sake of its own welfare and security. Idealism and realism, at least in this vision, meld. Harry S. Truman employed these basic rhetorical strategies throughout his presidency. In his landmark speech of March 12, 1947, in which he requested congressional support for a U.S. aid package to beleaguered regimes in Greece and Turkey, Truman placed the United States squarely on the side of peace, freedom, and justice. In one of that speech's most famous passages, he contrasted America's values and institutions with those of its unnamed adversary: "One way of life is based upon the will of the majority, and is distinguished by free institutions, representative government, free elections, guarantees of individual liberty, freedom of speech and religion, and freedom from political oppression. The second way of life is based upon the will of a minority forcibly imposed upon the majority. It relies upon terror and oppression, a controlled press and radio, fixed elections, and the suppression of personal freedoms."

What, then, were the principal goals of American policy? Essentially, according to Truman, the United States stood for the promotion of peace and freedom across the globe. This utopian and seemingly selfless objective, as Truman strove to make clear, was actually grounded solidly in national self-interest. After all, how could he gain congressional support for a $400 million aid request if such a request was based solely on the pressing needs of foreign peoples, no matter how desperate their plight? Humanitarianism offers a powerful appeal, to be sure, but such an appeal has limits. Truman thus emphasized that America's defense of peace and freedom in Greece, Turkey, and elsewhere contributed significantly to its own security. "This is no more than a frank recognition," he explained, "that totalitarian regimes imposed upon free peoples, by direct or indirect aggression, undermine the foundations of international peace and hence the security of the United States."

In other words, the interconnectedness of world affairs brought a happy conjunction between doing right in the world and doing right by the citizens of the United States. Truman powerfully reemphasized that link in his closing remarks. "The free peoples of the world look to us for support in maintaining their freedoms," the president insisted. "If we falter in our leadership, we may endanger the peace of the world—and we shall surely endanger the welfare of this Nation."[4]

Those themes reappear in virtually all of Truman's major public speeches dealing with foreign affairs. In his January, 1948, State of the Union address, for example, the president described America's primary foreign policy goal as the achievement of "world peace based on principles of freedom and justice and equality of all nations." Lest his listeners think that it was purely a selfless, missionary impulse that was driving the United States to assume new burdens and obligations, Truman stressed the profound lessons of two world wars. Those conflicts "have taught us that we cannot isolate ourselves from the rest of the world," he intoned solemnly. "We have learned that the loss of freedom in any area of the world means a loss of freedom to ourselves—that the loss of independence by any nation adds directly to the insecurity of the United States and all free nations." The speech offered high-sounding ideals aplenty—"Above all else, we are striving to achieve a concord among the peoples of the world based upon the dignity of the individual and the brotherhood of man"—but they were ideals organically connected to the needs of the United States. Moreover, Truman's rhetoric pointed to an absence of choice. To do anything less than it was presently doing to preserve peace and freedom would jeopardize the physical safety of the American homeland and compromise fundamental national values.[5] What responsible national leader could dare countenance such dire risks?

Equally crucial to Truman's rhetorical strategy, and to that of so many of his successors, was his liberal sprinkling of religious imagery throughout his public addresses. The president typically found divine sanction for the current course of action being followed by the United States. "Steadfast in our faith in the Almighty," he proclaimed in his January, 1949, inaugural address, "we will advance toward a world where man's freedom is secure. . . . With God's help, the future of mankind will be assured in a world of justice, harmony, and peace."[6] Similarly, in his State of the Union speech that same month, Truman declared that "the strength of the Nation . . . must continue to be used unselfishly in the struggle for world peace and the betterment of mankind the world over." He implored "Almighty God" for help to enable the country "to perform the great tasks which He now sets before us." The United States was not just asking for God's help, in this construction it was performing God's work.[7]

The search for a more peaceful, free, just, and prosperous world, in short, was part of a divinely sanctioned mission. The fact that that mission also promoted the interests of the United States, since it aimed to defend, at one and the same time, the security and freedoms of the American people, appears almost incidental in Truman's rhetoric—even if never lost from sight. This conflating of the interests of the United States with America's divinely anointed responsibility to better the lot of the world's people is well in evidence in a major address Truman delivered after the dispatch of U.S. combat forces to Korea in June, 1950. After praising the outmatched South Koreans for making "a brave fight for their liberty," Truman emphasized that the North Korean attack constituted "a direct challenge to the efforts of the free nations to build the kind of world in which men can live in freedom and peace." By rising to the defense of South Korea, Americans were thus also protecting their own freedom—and the world's. "We know the cost of freedom is high," he said. "But we are determined to preserve our freedom—no matter the cost." Note the emphasis on "our."

With the following, stirring conclusion to his call to arms, Truman attempted to bind those different strands together: "Our country stands before the world as an example of how free men, under God, can build a community of neighbors, working together for the good of all. That is the goal we seek not only for ourselves, but for all people. We believe that freedom and peace are essential if men are to live as our Creator intended us to live." The United States was not just defending South Koreans for their own sake, then, but for America's—*and* for the sake of the international community as a whole. The latter role, moreover, Truman's rhetoric suggested, was one in which God had directly anointed Americans to serve, presumably as his earthly surrogates.[8] It was a remarkable vision, yet one that resonated powerfully with a people accustomed to thinking about themselves as paragons of selfless virtue. Had they not already saved the world from the twin scourges of German and Japanese barbarism? Who could doubt the purity of America's motives, other than those whose own motives were highly suspect?

The images evoked in Truman's public messages echo throughout the Cold War era. His successor, Dwight D. Eisenhower, repeatedly invoked the metaphor of freedom in his public explanations of America's Cold War foreign policy. In his 1953 inaugural address, Eisenhower described the global situation starkly as one in which "Freedom is pitted against slavery; lightness against the dark." It was Manichaeanism in its most extreme form. Eisenhower believed America's "moral strength" and its global leadership derived from the status of Americans as "free men." This special status conferred upon Americans an obligation to serve, protect, and lead the peoples of the world, all the while defending peace and freedom. As Eisenhower put it: "Knowing that only a United States that is strong and immensely productive can help defend freedom in the world, we view our Nation's strength and security as a trust upon which rests the hope of free men everywhere." The reasoning, such as it was, was circular: Americans were strong because they were productive, productive because they were free, and free because they were strong. That combination of strength, productivity, and freedom combined to catapult the United States into its present position of global leadership—the leader, that is, of the fittingly named "Free World."

Yet, lest it appear that some mystical impulse of selfless religiosity alone was impelling America to assume the role of global sentinel for peace and freedom, Eisenhower reminded his fellow citizens that their own welfare and security were on the line as well. Referring to what he called a "basic law of interdependence," the president noted that this operated in both the realms of international economics and world politics. Speaking with greater frankness than most U.S. leaders have—then or since—about America's economic needs, he put it thusly: "No free people can for long cling to any privilege or enjoy any safety in economic solitude. For all our own material might, even we need markets in the world for the surpluses of our farms and our factories. Equally, we need for these same farms and factories vital materials and products of distant lands." Drawing a direct connection between material deprivation and threats to global peace and prosperity, he added that "the impoverishment of any single people in the world means danger to the well-being of all other peoples." Similarly, he proclaimed the "defense of freedom, like freedom itself, to be one and indivisible." By protecting freedom elsewhere, according to this logic, Americans helped guarantee their own freedom.[9]

In his second inaugural address, in January, 1957, Eisenhower again emphasized the theme of interdependence: "No nation can [any] longer be a fortress, lone and strong and safe. And any people, seeking such shelter for themselves, can now build only their own prison." To reject America's role of global defender of peace and freedom thus would be not just an act of crass ungenerosity, an act at odds with the nation's noblest, historic traditions, it would constitute a shortsighted blunder of suicidal proportions. Ironically, then, the United States had no choice but to act as global steward. No matter how selfless such a role might seem, it was actually dictated by the security and welfare needs of the American people.[10]

The foreign policy exhortations of John F. Kennedy and Lyndon B. Johnson were invariably cut from the same cloth as those of Truman and Eisenhower. Kennedy, of course, is perhaps best remembered for the stirring, idealistic rhetoric that formed so central an aspect of his presidency. That rhetoric added little, however, to the image of America as global defender of peace and freedom presented so assiduously by his predecessors. Take the obvious example of Kennedy's renowned inaugural address in January, 1961. Probably its most memorable and oft-quoted line is: "Let every nation know, whether it wishes us well or ill, that we shall pay any price, bear any burden, meet any hardship, support any friend, oppose any foe, in order to assure the survival and success of liberty." Although later commentators have appropriately called attention to the overblown—and dangerous—nature of so expansive a pledge, it bears emphasizing that Kennedy's attempt to frame American foreign policy in terms of a messianic mission to protect and transform humankind hardly constituted a new vision.

As had Truman and Eisenhower before him, Kennedy turned the burdens of power into a challenge—and a privilege. Moreover, just as they had, he portrayed the United States as responding to a divine calling as well. "In the long history of the world," the new president observed near the end of his inaugural address, "only a few generations have been granted the role of defending freedom in its hour of maximum danger." Could any of his listeners have doubted that Kennedy was referring here to the divinity as having done the granting? Or question the underlying, if unstated, assumption that Americans were God's chosen people? "The energy, the faith, the devotion which we bring to this endeavor will light our country and all who serve it," he proclaimed, "and the glow from that fire can truly light the world." As if to ensure that the conflation of America's global responsibility with God's divine plan was not missed by any of his countrymen and women, Kennedy concluded with the following flourish: "Let us go forth to lead the land we love, asking His blessing and His help, but knowing that here on earth God's work must surely be our own."[11]

Although less fondly remembered for the rousing power of his rhetoric than his more charismatic predecessor, and possessed of a much flatter style of delivery, Lyndon B. Johnson actually made some of the most grandiose presidential speeches of the entire Cold War era. On April 20, 1964, for example, Johnson delivered a major foreign policy address that again nicely melded America's global idealism with its national self-interest—a tradition by then quite familiar to the American public. Striking a chord common to every other presidential rhetorician of the postwar period, Johnson insisted upon the purity of American motives and foreswore any selfish or expansive ambitions on the part of the United States. "We seek to add no territory to our dominion," he said, "no satellites to our orbit, no slavish followers to our policies." As evidence, he cited the fact that "for a century our own frontiers have stood quiet and stood unarmed." But, Johnson added, Americans had learned through the painful crucible of two world wars "that our own freedom depends upon the freedom of others, that our own protection requires that we help protect others, that we draw increased strength from the strength of others." Turning directly to Asia, where he faced his most immediate, and most daunting, foreign policy crisis, the president called "the independence of Asian nations . . . a link in our own freedom."[12]

Johnson further elaborated on those themes and extended those images in his January, 1965, State of the Union message. "Our own freedom and growth have never been the final goal of the American dream," Johnson claimed, finding his most idealistic voice. "We were never meant to be an oasis of liberty and abundance in a worldwide desert of disappointed dreams. Our Nation was created to help strike away the chains of ignorance and misery and tyranny wherever they keep man less than God means him to be." Later in that same speech, Johnson explained America's stake in external affairs in the language of realism: "Our own security is tied to the peace of Asia. To ignore aggression now would only increase the danger of a much larger war." Not to stand up for freedom in South Vietnam, in other words, would in the long run endanger the United States. How, under such circumstances, could anyone oppose the necessity for military intervention in Southeast Asia?

In sum, once again a president managed cleverly to merge quite separate propositions. Johnson was saying that on one hand the United States must stand up for peace and freedom abroad because it was the right thing to do. It formed an essential part of America's divinely ordained mission to effect a humanitarian transformation of the earth. Idealism triumphant, as it were. On the other hand, he was arguing that Americans must stand up for peace and freedom abroad because if they did not do so, their own welfare and security would surely be jeopardized. That was realism triumphant. They were quite distinct lines of argument, of course. Yet in this speech, as in so many other postwar presidential speeches, the two propositions were woven into a seamless web: idealistic realism presumably meant realistic idealism. Since what was best for the United States was so obviously what was best for the rest of the world, Americans were in the enviable position of doing right by others by doing what was best for themselves.

Still, Johnson and other U.S. chief executives have generally preferred to close major public addresses with rhetorical flourishes that highlighted the magnanimous rather than the self-interested dimension of U.S. actions. Johnson thus ended this speech with the insistence that "We seek not to extend the power of America but the progress of humanity. We seek not to dominate others but to strengthen the freedom of all people." America's global goals, in his rendering, were as simple—and unopposable—as they were straightforward. "We seek peace," Johnson implored in his most reasonable voice. "We seek freedom. We seek to enrich the life of man. For that is the world in which we will flourish and that is the world that we mean for all men to ultimately have." Who could possibly oppose such goals? Who stood against peace? Against freedom? Against the enrichment of man? Any who did were, by definition, the enemies of humankind: the forces of darkness who craved to enslave rather than liberate, who were animated not by the true faith that made Americans God's chosen people but by the false appeals of godless communism.[13]

Yes, the United States did have its own interests, Johnson admitted. The "touchstone" of American policy in Vietnam and elsewhere, he declaimed in his January, 1966, State of the Union address, "is the interest of the United States—the welfare and freedom of the people of the United States." But that interest could only be upheld, he quickly added, if Americans recognized their vulnerability to the threats always lurking on a shrinking planet marked by interdependence among no longer distant peoples. "In a world that has grown small and dangerous, pursuit of narrow aims could bring decay and even disaster," Johnson warned. "An America that is mighty beyond description—yet living in a hostile or despairing world—would be neither safe nor free to build a civilization to liberate the spirit of man."[14]

Such soaring presidential rhetoric survived the national soul-searching and self-doubt occasioned by the Vietnam debacle and Watergate scandals that did so much to diminish the presidency throughout the 1970s. Richard M. Nixon, Gerald R. Ford, and Jimmy Carter suddenly began emphasizing limits—the limits imposed on American power and on American resources—along with the need to share global responsibilities with like-minded allies and friends. There was no longer any talk of paying any price or bearing any burden. But the principal emphases of the past remained intact. Americans still stood for peace and freedom, the United States remained a force for good in the world, and the nation retained solemn obligations and responsibilities that did not fall on the shoulders of lesser—and less blessed—nations. By helping others, moreover, the United States was helping itself.

Americans, declared Richard Nixon in 1972, were an "influence for good in the world." He characterized the United States as a force for "justice, stability, progress, and peace."[15] On May 22, 1977, in the first major foreign policy speech of his presidency, Jimmy Carter cautioned his audience that "a peaceful world cannot long exist one-third rich and two-thirds hungry." Americans consequently needed to play an active role in ameliorating conditions of hunger and poverty lest those conditions breed conflict that would inevitably engulf America's own shores. One must do good for others, in this familiar trope, in order to protect oneself. Lest there be any doubt about where Carter stood in the idealist-realist continuum, he proclaimed toward the end of his Notre Dame University address: "Our policy is designed to serve mankind." It was a direct, if unacknowledged, borrowing from Woodrow Wilson.[16]

When the Soviet Union invaded Afghanistan during his final, crisis-filled year in office, reigniting the Cold War, Carter returned to the theme of freedom's indivisibility. "History teaches perhaps very few clear lessons," he said in attempting to explain his administration's firm response. "But surely one such lesson learned by the world at great cost is that aggression, unopposed, becomes a contagious disease." By acting to deter aggression, then, the United States could simultaneously preserve the peace, keep faith with its messianic mission, and ensure America's own security.[17]

The Cold War rhetoric of peace and freedom reached its apotheosis during Ronald Reagan's presidency. Although renowned as one of the most stirring rhetoricians of the modern American presidency, and appropriately so, Reagan, it bears emphasizing, actually added little to the vocabulary of the past. His speeches reinforced old themes far more than they blazed new ones.

Like his predecessors, Reagan ritualistically identified the United States with the grandest aspirations of the world's peoples. He frequently cast the United States in its familiar role of selfless steward of the world's fortunes. "I believe we are destined to be the beacon of hope for all mankind," he proclaimed in February, 1982, upon unveiling the Caribbean basin initiative.[18] "With God's help, we can make it so." United States policy rests on "a simple premise," he explained during a major address to the nation on Central America in May, 1984. "We do not start wars. We will never be the aggressor. We maintain our strength in order to deter and defend against aggression, to preserve freedom and peace. We help our friends defend themselves."[19] Similarly, in his January, 1983, State of the Union address, Reagan explained the basis for America's international role in terms of its values—values that had universal appeal: "America's leadership in the world came to us because of our strength and because of the values which guide us as a society: free elections, a free press, freedom of religious choice, free trade unions, and above all, freedom of the individual and rejection of the arbitrary power of the state. These values are the bedrock of our strength. They unite us in a stewardship of peace and freedom with our allies and friends in NATO, in Asia, in Latin America, and elsewhere."[20]

Reagan often invoked the language of his predecessors so as to connect his own frequently controversial foreign policies with the great undertakings of the past. In his January, 1985, State of the Union speech, for example, Reagan approvingly quoted Truman's description of the United States as the world's best hope for forging a path to peace and human progress. Then, offering his own gloss on that identification, he added: "Our mission is to nourish and defend freedom and democracy and to communicate these ideals everywhere we can. America's economic success is freedom's success; it can be repeated a hundred times in a hundred different nations."[21] Most remarkably, in an April, 1983, address to Congress on Latin American policy, he lifted several paragraphs verbatim from the famous Truman Doctrine speech of March, 1947. That speech, alluded to above, remains notorious for its Manichaen contrast between the forces of light and the forces of darkness. Yet Reagan called Truman's stark words "as apt today as they were in 1947."[22] The "great communicator" reached back much farther into the American past for one of his favorite and oft-cited images: John Winthrop's conception of America as a "city upon a hill." The United States, Reagan remarked in July, 1985, was for millions throughout the world "a symbol that is loved, a country that remains a shining city on a hill."[23]

But if Reagan proved especially fond of idealistic imagery that depicted the United States as the world's protector and transformer, he made sure, as had earlier occupants of the Oval Office, that listeners made the necessary connection between America's seemingly selfless mission and its unsentimental defense of its own interests. In his various appeals for aid to the Nicaraguan Contras, Reagan emphasized that it was the security and welfare of Americans, first and foremost, which was at stake. "If we cannot defend ourselves there," he warned in one speech, "we cannot expect to prevail elsewhere. Our credibility would collapse, our alliances would crumble, and the safety of our homeland would be put in jeopardy." Thus, the United States had "a vital interest, a moral duty, and a solemn responsibility" to take firm action. Note the way in which he effortlessly conflated national security needs with the quite distinct notion of moral duty.[24] On other occasions, Reagan framed external threats in terms of the indivisibility of peace, freedom, and prosperity in an increasingly interdependent, and hence vulnerable, world—another familiar rhetorical ploy. "Clearly our world is shrinking," he observed on one occasion. "We cannot pretend otherwise if we wish to protect our freedom, our economic vitality, and our precious way of life." It was crucial to understand, Reagan noted on another occasion, "that freedom is never more than one generation away from extinction."[25] The selfless actions of the United States thus derived as much from hard-headed realism as from utopian magnanimity. Or, as Reagan himself put it in a State of the Union address: "We're realists," but "we're also idealists."[26] In this, as in so many other ways, Reagan articulated a view of the United States that echoed throughout the Cold War era—and whose roots were firmly planted long before that era. George Bush showed himself the proud heir to that rhetorical tradition during the remarkable Texas A&M University speech with which this chapter began. His comments also offer a fitting close as they exemplify each of the major themes I have emphasized. "The leadership, the power, and yes, the conscience of the United States of America, all are essential for a peaceful, prosperous international order," he stated, "just as such an order is essential for us." Conflating America's global mission with its own national interests, Bush proudly reviewed his country's accomplishments throughout the previous half-century. "The American people demonstrated," he boasted, "that they would shoulder whatever defense burden, make whatever sacrifice was needed to assure our freedom and protect our allies and interests."

With a post–Cold War world dawning, Bush called upon Americans to seize "a unique opportunity to see the principles for which America has stood for two centuries, democracy, free enterprise, and the rule of law, spread more widely than ever before in human history. It is a hope that embodies our country's tradition of idealism, which has made us unique among nations and uniquely successful. And our vision is not mere utopianism. The advance of democratic ideals reflects a hard-nosed sense of our own, of American self-interest." Democratic governments tend to be peaceful governments, he stressed, and free markets contribute not just to global trade expansion but to American prosperity: "In short, by helping others, we help ourselves."[27]

Notes

1. George H. W. Bush, "Speech at Texas A&M University, Dec. 15, 1992," in *Public Papers of the Presidents of the United States* (hereafter *Public Papers*), *1992–93* (Washington, D.C.: GPO, 1992), 2:2189–90.

2. For the Jefferson quote, see Reginald Horsman, *The Diplomacy of the New Republic, 1776–1815* (Arlington Heights, Ill.: Harlan Davidson, 1985), 82. For the Lincoln quote, see Tony Smith, *America's Mission: The United States and the Worldwide Struggle for Democracy in the Twentieth Century* (Princeton, N.J.: Princeton University Press, 1994), 22. For the Wilson quote, see Arthur

Link, *Woodrow Wilson: Revolution, War, and Peace* (Arlington Heights, Ill.: Harlan Davidson, 1979), 7. For the Truman quote, see Walter McDougall, *Promised Land, Crusader State: the American Encounter with the World Since 1776* (Boston: Houghton Mifflin, 1997), 169.

3. For an elaboration of this theme, see especially Michael H. Hunt, *Ideology and U.S. Foreign Policy* (New Haven, Conn.: Yale University Press, 1987).

4. Harry S. Truman, "Special Message to the Congress on Greece and Turkey: The Truman Doctrine, Mar. 12, 1947," in *Public Papers, 1947* (Washington, D.C.: GPO, 1963), 176–80.

5. Harry S. Truman, "Annual Message to the Congress on the State of the Union," Jan. 7, 1948, in *Public Papers, 1947*, 7–8.

6. Harry S. Truman, "Inaugural Address," Jan. 20, 1949, in *Inaugural Addresses of the Presidents of the United States* (Washington, D.C.: GPO, 1989), 285–91.

7. Harry S. Truman, "Annual Message to the Congress on the State of the Union, Jan. 5, 1949," in *Public Papers, 1949* (Washington, D.C.: GPO, 1964), 1–7.

8. Harry S. Truman, "Radio and Television Address to the American People on the Situation in Korea," July 19, 1950, in *Public Papers, 1950*, 537–42.

9. Dwight D. Eisenhower, "Inaugural Address," Jan. 20, 1953, in *Inaugural Addresses*, 296–99.

10. Dwight D. Eisenhower, "Inaugural Address," Jan. 21, 1957, in *Inaugural Addresses*, 303.

11. John F. Kennedy, "Inaugural Address, Jan. 20, 1961," in *Public Papers, 1961* (Washington, D.C.: GPO, 1962), 1–3.

12. Lyndon B. Johnson, "Remarks on Foreign Affairs at the Associated Press Luncheon in New York City, April 20, 1964," in *Public Papers, 1963–64*, vol. 1 (Washington, D.C.: GPO, 1965), 493–500, 498.

13. Lyndon B. Johnson, "Annual Message to the Congress on the State of the Union, January 4, 1965," in *Public Papers, 1965*, vol. 2 (Washington, D.C.: GPO, 1966), 1–9.

14. Lyndon B. Johnson, "Annual Message to the Congress on the State of the Union, January 12, 1966," in *Public Papers, 1966*, vol. 1 (Washington, D.C.: GPO, 1967), 3–12.

15. Richard M. Nixon, "Address on the State of the Union Delivered Before a Joint Session of the Congress, January 20, 1972," in *Public Papers, 1972* (Washington, D.C.: GPO, 1974), 47.

16. Jimmy Carter, "University of Notre Dame: Address at Commencement Exercises of the University, May 22, 1977," in *Public Papers, 1977*, vol. 1 (Washington, D.C.: GPO, 1977), 954–62.

17. Jimmy Carter, "Soviet Invasion of Afghanistan: Address to the Nation, January 4, 1980," in *Public Papers, 1980–81*, vol. 1 (Washington, D.C.: GPO, 1981), 21–24.

18. Ronald W. Reagan, "Remarks on the Caribbean Basin Initiative to the Permanent Council of the Organization of American States, February 24, 1982," in *Public Papers, 1982*, vol. 1 (Washington, D.C.: GPO, 1983), 215.

19. Ronald W. Reagan, "Address to the Nation on United States Policy in Central America, May 9, 1984," in *Public Papers, 1984*, vol. 1 (Washington, D.C.: GPO, 1986), 659–60.

20. Ronald W. Reagan, "Address Before a Joint Session of the Congress on the State of the Union, January 25, 1983," in *Public Papers, 1983*, vol. 1 (Washington, D.C.: GPO, 1984), 108–109.

21. Ronald W. Reagan, "Address Before a Joint Session of the Congress on the State of the Union, February 6, 1985," in *Public Papers, 1985*, vol. 1 (Washington, D.C.: GPO, 1988), 134–35.

22. Ronald W. Reagan, "Address Before a Joint Session of the Congress on Latin America," Apr. 27, 1983, in *Public Papers, 1983*, 1:604–605.

23. Ronald W. Reagan, "Remarks at the Annual Convention of the American Bar Association," July 8, 1985, in *Public Papers, 1985*, 2:900.

24. Ronald W. Reagan, "Address Before a Joint Session of the Congress on Latin America," Apr. 27, 1983, in *Public Papers, 1983*, 1:604–605.

25. Ronald W. Reagan, "Address to the Nation on United States Policy in Central America," May 9, 1984, in *Public Papers, 1984,* 1:659–60.

26. Ronald W. Reagan, "Address Before a Joint Session of the Congress on the State of the Union," Jan. 25, 1983, in *Public Papers, 1983,* 1:109.

27. Bush, "Speech at Texas A&M University," 2:2189–90.

CHAPTER TEN

A New Democratic World Order?

ROBERT L. IVIE

Drawing lessons from the Cold War is a precarious but unavoidable preoccupation of our times. The meaning we give to the experience guides our interpretation of current challenges and shapes the policies we formulate in charting a course toward a more democratic world order of peace and prosperity, security and justice, freedom, human rights, and international cooperation. Perhaps the greatest imperative of interpretation is to avoid the risk of Cold War rhetorical continuities prevailing in new circumstances over unprecedented opportunities for democratic transformation. Democracy, after all, is a potent symbol of American identity, mission, and exceptionalism in this, the American century. It represents a Wilsonian ideal of world order that sustained the United States through two world wars and four decades of Cold War hostilities, eventually prevailing over totalitarian world orders of German Nazism and Soviet Communism. This development has been interpreted famously (many have said infamously) by Francis Fukuyama as the "end of history," the final triumph of liberal representative democracy over its ideological rivals.[1] The rhetoric of democracy, laden with such associations, is a powerful vehicle for carrying the legacy of America's global struggle and enlarged fear of hostile aliens into present representations of post–Cold War provocations, opportunities, and responsibilities. As John Lewis Gaddis has observed, Americans are peculiarly prone to the "curious myopia" that nations possessing different forms of government are hostile to the United States, an ideological litmus test that has caused "repeated misunderstandings, and often gross exaggerations of the dangers the nation actually faced."[2] Ideological homogeneity and global democratization as measures of national security pose a conundrum, then, for U.S. foreign policy in a world now challenged by the centrifugal forces of nationalism, ethnicity, religion, and economic disparity.

Indeed, Gaddis argues that the preeminent challenge of the post–Cold War environment is "the contest between forces of integration and fragmentation" that the United States must learn to balance against each other more than states or ideologies. Even as the United States anticipates one secure democratic world connected peacefully by global communications in an open market economy, the quest for freedom and power reasserts itself locally in the form of divisive regional struggles and disintegrative issues over protectionism, aggression, civil war, terrorism, and racial, ethnic, linguistic, and religious self-determination. "The end of the Cold War," Gaddis concludes, "brings not an end to threats, but rather a diffusion of them" along with the "dangerous conviction" that "only the United States has the will and the capacity to take the lead in policing (or nannying) the world." The more widely the United States projects its interests, the more threats and risks it incurs and the greater the temptation becomes to succumb to "paranoia." Accordingly, a judicious "middle ground" must be found of maintaining a "healthy skepticism" toward global integration even while resisting unbridled fragmentation.[3]

Order is a problematic term in the current discourse of foreign affairs, including the language of American leadership and democratic peace, which requires close monitoring if we hope to negotiate a middle ground to avoid the mistake of triumphalism and its abiding culture of fear. It is a term that defines the phrase "New World Order" more than any other to project the discourse of the Cold War onto present articulations of democratic aspirations. Accordingly, my purpose is to examine the rhetoric of a new democratic world order for vestiges of the recent past that inhibit suitable adaptations to present circumstances. My hope is that we can avoid what Roger Burbach has called "the tragedy of American democracy," with the nation caught in a "fundamental dilemma" between declaring support for democracy and using it as an ideological tool primarily to advance U.S. economic interests abroad.[4] The rhetorical tendency, of course, is to subordinate the term *democracy* to the purposes of liberalism and thus to the interests of the state in promoting and protecting private enterprise. However, the expectations generated by this response to world Communism's demise cannot be met, and indeed may exacerbate international tensions and the nation's chronic sense of insecurity, unless the facade of democracy can somehow be transformed into a meaningful commitment. Order, for now at least, is the reigning symbol of the new age in which democracy—a term of awe, of both approach and avoidance—connotes disorder and chaos within American political culture more than trust in the rule of the people. The question is: Can we overcome the rhetorical legacy of the Cold War (and before) to constitute a more democratic world order?

The Cold War Crusade for Democracy

For Tony Smith, the decisive moment for the fate of democracy was the "defeat of fascism in 1945 and the American-sponsored conversion of Germany and Japan to democracy and a much greater degree of economic liberalism." Those were the "glory days," the "moment of triumph," he argues, "of American liberal democratic internationalism," that is, the realization of tenets by Franklin Roosevelt and Harry Truman that had been brought to the fore of the national agenda in this century by Woodrow Wilson. Thus, when William Clinton, like his immediate predecessors, makes democratization the linchpin of his foreign policy, he perpetuates a twentieth-century tradition of linking American national security to the hegemony of one form of government. Although the classic period of the Cold War focused on containing Communism, even when that meant supporting non-Communist authoritarian regimes as a tactical measure, the leitmotiv of American foreign policy remained constant throughout even the Vietnam debacle. This resulted in what Tony Smith acknowledges to be "a bid for international hegemony," that is, "a form of anti-imperialist imperialism, aiming to structure other countries economically, socially, and politically so that they would presumably be part of a peaceful world order congenial to American interests" and security. "The dominant logic of American foreign policy," Smith continues, "was dictated by concerns for national security; and the dominant way Washington saw to assure this security in terms of the construction of a stable world order congenial to America's way of life was that democratic governments be promoted worldwide."[5]

Even the promotion of human rights abroad, as illustrated in Jimmy Carter's response to post-Vietnam malaise, remained true to Cold War objectives while advancing traditional Wilsonian principles within a rhetoric of ideological conversion. Breaking with Henry Kissinger's increasingly criticized version of amoral realism, Carter censured the Soviet Union for its ill treatment of dissidents, put South Africa on notice for its apartheid policy, and distanced the United States from repressive military regimes. The soul of his foreign policy was a crusade for human rights consistent with the predilections of a born-again Christian while aimed at containing Soviet expansion and insuring national security.[6] In fact, the continuity between Carter's and his predecessors' images of U.S.-Soviet relations was sufficient to renew the quest for security in terms that reinforced a cycle of fear.

The source of Carter's rhetorical continuity with, and extension of, other Cold War presidents was the conceptual metaphor guiding his particular construction of how to achieve peace and security. Truman had promoted visions of disease, fire, and flood to evoke a sense of emergency in postwar Greece, Turkey, and Western Europe that inaugurated the containment doctrine. Eisenhower in turn relied on an image of Soviet brutality blocking the road to true peace in his campaign to legitimize a perilous crusade of nuclear deterrence. But Carter's rhetorical signature was religious imagery, often thoroughly secularized.[7] Intently against making any bargains with the devil, Carter's rhetorical ministry was devoted to achieving peace and freedom by converting the Soviets through moral suasion and, when that failed, by punishing the Communist infidels for their transgressions. The president himself, Gaddis Smith's claim to the contrary, never underwent a personal conversion from a pre-Afghanistan "philosophy of repentance" to a post-Afghanistan commitment to Cold War realism.[8] His goal was to persuade the Soviets, whom he knew to be evil, to repent and convert to the ways of freedom—a goal he maintained until it became apparent they were beyond repentance and still continuing their evil ways.

If freedom could not be worshiped universally, Carter assumed, it was vulnerable everywhere and would have to be defended wherever it came under attack. The vehicles of Carter's religious imagery expressed a "quiet confidence" that "democracy works" and that "democracy's example will be compelling" without succumbing to the "tempt[ation] to employ improper tactics" akin to the "flawed and erroneous principles" of the Communist adversary. The fire of Communism would be quenched with the water of renewed faith in democracy by a "politically awakening world."[9]

As circumstances unfolded, the president concluded that the Soviets remained immune to moral suasion and unwilling to convert to the democratic faith. Thus, after Afghanistan, he no longer spoke of converting the enemy but of punishing the Soviets for their transgressions. The Soviet Union's decision to use military force "to subjugate the fiercely independent and deeply religious people of Afghanistan," Carter told Americans in his 1980 State of the Union address, would be "costly to every political and economic relationship it values."[10] The Soviets had proven by their behavior that they remained infidels against all religious peoples, Muslims as well as Christians.

Carter had never believed in a détente that meant cooperating or coexisting with the Soviets in an undemocratic world, any more than he would ever accommodate to evil. His confidence in the nation's quest for a moral peace merely added to the heavy burden of national insecurity by a people already unable to accommodate themselves to an imperfect peace in a world of conflicted motives. Carter, as characterized by a senior aide, was a "Christian warrior" who sought to make American power an instrument of moral suasion.[11]

Confident of democracy's superiority and Communism's ultimate demise, he set out to transform and convert the Soviets to democratic ways through a rhetorical ministry of candid persuasion, negotiation, and cooperation while at the same time preaching the sermon of human rights. He understood himself to be in a "struggle with evil" and believed that peace ultimately depended on fulfilling the world's spiritual requirement for freedom.[12] Power was exercised on behalf of a moral agenda. Having reinforced the premise that peace would be achieved through strength, Carter's moral quest paved the way for Ronald Reagan's crusade against Communism, giving the nation one less reason to support anything short of total security backed by military might and realized in ideological hegemony.[13] As Barry Gills and others have observed, "The Carter administration policy on human rights can be viewed as the direct predecessor of the more overt U.S. policy of democratisation that followed under President Reagan."[14]

Ronald Reagan announced his administration's "crusade for democracy" in 1982 while addressing the British Parliament, a crusade that economically subordinated the Third World through "austerity measures, debt servicing, privatisation, economic liberalisation and structural adjustment, promoted by the U.S. via the IMF, the World Bank, and the Group of Seven Industrialised Countries."[15] Simultaneously, the Reagan administration began abandoning beleaguered dictatorial regimes in the Philippines, Chile, Haiti, and Paraguay in order to forestall revolutionary movements in those countries while also attempting to overthrow revolutionary regimes in Angola, Afghanistan, and Nicaragua. The purported purpose was to establish new democratic governments by supporting "freedom fighters" and funding the National Endowment for Democracy while contesting the Soviet Union's "evil empire."[16] Reagan's foreign policy, more aggressively Wilsonian than that of any of his predecessors, was based on the premise that the best hope for peace was a world of democratic nations. In his words, "History has shown that democratic nations do not start wars."[17]

George Bush, who inherited Reagan's crusade, witnessed the break up of the Soviet Empire and announced the emergence of a new world order in which "great nations of the world are moving toward democracy through the door of freedom . . . [and] toward free markets through the door to prosperity."[18] A new world order such as Wilsonianism, Amos Perlmutter has argued, "is mission oriented, seeking stability in the name of a hegemonial ideology that is intended to dominate the world system."[19] Thus, "beyond containment lies democracy," proclaimed Bush's secretary of state, James Baker. America's mission, he told the World Affairs Council in 1990, was the "promotion and consolidation of democracy."[20] And when the Bush administration failed to pursue this mission with sufficient fervor, it caught a blast of criticism from challenger Bill Clinton, who proclaimed national security required an American-led global alliance to secure "democracy's triumph around the world."[21] Yet, as Perlmutter notes, the melting of the Soviet glacier has resulted in the growth of very little democratic grass where tribal, nationalistic, and ethnic forces have trampled the ground. The present trend, he believes, is actually against a new world order that would ensure peace and security. "The world is not ready for democracy," in Perlmutter's judgment, nor is democracy necessary for international order and national tranquillity.[22] Nevertheless, the quest for a new democratic world order remains unabated in President Clinton's foreign policy rhetoric.

Clinton's Fearful Quest for a Democratic Order

Clinton's rhetoric of a democratic world order is important to examine not only for its perpetuation of Cold War themes, but also for the imagery in which they are embedded, revealing strong overtones of national insecurity and vulnerability that drive the desire to dominate others. His message is that the United States must grasp this fleeting moment of opportunity, building on the great victories of World War II and the Cold War, to lead a bold adventure of securing democracy and prosperity in the global village, all the while recognizing the substantial threats facing America, including the risks of extending freedom and democracy to the world. Everything about this message conveys the sense of tenuous times, fragility, instability, uncertainty, the compensatory need for control, and thus the fear of democracy itself. The president's words are a national repository of democratic anxiety.

Clinton's myriad variations on the theme of democracy's endangerment and fragility range from allusions to epidemic, plague, purgation, nurturing, and renewal through suggestions of instability, engulfment, containment, storms, darkness, crime, and chaos to invocations of bold journeys, marching, frontier spirit, and civil courage. Such imagery permeates his foreign policy discourse from the beginning of his first term to the present, effectively recovering the narrative of the Cold War as the tragic plot line of America's heroic mission in a new world. The prevailing threat and unspoken implication of heroic courage throughout Clinton's text is one of ultimate defeat and democracy's failure to secure the peace. Thus, we might reasonably ask if democratic hubris is America's tragic flaw—if that, indeed, is the unintended lesson of the president's rhetoric. His actual words are revealing.[23]

Clinton's first inaugural address on January 20, 1993, devoted to "celebrat[ing] the mystery of American renewal," was uttered in "the depth of winter" in hopes of "forc[ing] the spring," a "spring reborn in the world's oldest democracy, that brings forth the vision and courage to reinvent America." The nation's founders knew, he continued, "that America, to endure, would have to change." Each generation must learn to "march to the music" of the nation's "timeless . . . mission," and "today, a generation raised in the shadows of the Cold War assumes new responsibilities in a world warmed by the sunshine of freedom but threatened still by ancient hatreds and new plagues." The nation's economy, although the world's strongest, has been weakened in an age of global communications and commerce that are among the profound and powerful forces "shaking and remaking our world" and raising the "urgent question" of "whether we can make change our friend and not our enemy." Ominously, the nation has "drifted" in the face of "fearsome" challenges, and "drifting has eroded our resources, fractured our economy, and shaken our confidence." Americans, always "a restless, questing, hopeful people," must now recover "the vision and will of those who came before" them to rebuild the "pillars" of their history and "foundations" of their nation, to make democracy the "engine" of their own "renewal." To "renew America," Clinton proclaimed, "we must revitalize our democracy," meeting challenges abroad as well as at home, for "there is no longer division between what is foreign and what is domestic." The world's problems affect us all, and "the new world is more free but less stable" than its passing predecessor, for "communism's collapse has called forth old animosities and new dangers." The United States, therefore, must "work to shape change, lest it engulf us."[24]

The "imperative of American leadership," the president told an American University audience one month later, was to meet "the great challenge of this day" in "the face of global change" now that "democracy is on the march everywhere in the world" following the end of the Cold War. But, he reported, people across America were "raising central questions about our place and our prospects in this new world we have done so much to make," this "new global economy, still recovering from the after-effects of the Cold War," in which the prosperity of the whole world depends upon insuring America's prosperity. Government must break free of "the death grip of gridlock," avoid "repeat[ing] the mistakes of the 1920s or the 1930s by turning inward," and follow the example of "the successes of the 1940s and the 1950s by reaching outward." The world "remains a dangerous place" of "ethnic hatreds, religious strife, the proliferation of weapons of mass destruction, [and] the violation of human rights flagrantly." Even though "democracy is on the march in many places in the world," it "has been thwarted in many places, too." American leadership thus is crucial to fostering "the world's new and emerging democracies" upon which U.S. security and prosperity depends. "If we could make a garden of democracy and prosperity and free enterprise in every part of this globe," Clinton proclaimed to the applause of his audience, "the world would be a safer and a better and a more prosperous place for the United States and for all of you to raise your children in." But, he quickly cautioned, "democracy's prospects are dimmed" by slow global growth and trade barriers. We must "strengthen the bonds of commerce" if we "believe in the bonds of democracy." Moreover, to overcome the perils facing Russia's fledgling democracy, the United States should be willing to invest at least a tiny fraction of the trillions of dollars it spent to ensure Communism's defeat in the Cold War. We can never forget that the global economy is "unruly," a veritable "bucking bronco that often lands with its feet on different sides of old lines, and sometimes with its whole body on us." We must "harness the whole horse" if we are "to ride the bronco into the next century" and continue to expand "the frontiers of democracy."[25]

In April, Clinton spoke to the American Society of Newspaper Editors about the nation's purposes in the world, continuing to juxtapose promise with risk and the constant threat of failure in assuming "the ennobling burdens of democracy." Following the collapse of the Soviet Empire, the world now faced "the proliferation of demonic weapons" and "resurgent ethnic conflict," undermining U.S. security in a "global village" where "there is no clear dividing line between domestic and foreign policy." Thus, U.S. policy must focus on "relations within nations," that is, on "a nation's form of governance, economic structure, and ethnic tolerance" that influence how it treats its neighbors, because "democracies are far less likely to wage war on other nations than dictatorships." We must learn, he observed, from the "triumph of Truman's era" that "we cannot stop investing in peace now that we have obtained it." In particular, "the danger is clear if Russia's reforms turn sour—if it reverts to authoritarianism or disintegrates into chaos." The hope is that "Russia's transition can continue to be peaceful" and its progress toward democracy and free markets will not be "thwarted."[26]

In July, the president took his message to Seoul, declaring that "Korea proves that democracy and human rights are not western imports" but instead are "universal aspirations" that "flow from the internal spirit of human beings." The "struggle for freedom and democracy" as the "guardian of our security" is a "marathon," a race nations must somehow run together but are not sure to win.[27] At the United Nations in September, Clinton observed that Boris Yeltsin was "leading his nation on its bold democratic journey" in a "new era of peril and opportunity." The "habits of democracy are the habits of peace," the president proclaimed, but "as we work toward this vision we must confront the storm clouds that may overwhelm our work and darken the march toward freedom," for "the end of the Cold War did not bring us to the millennium of peace. And, indeed, it simply removed the lid from many cauldrons of ethnic, religious, and territorial animosity." Thus, the challenge is to "ensure that the tide of freedom and democracy is not pushed back by the fierce winds" of ethnic hatred and dangerous weapons.[28]

Clinton's theme in the May, 1994, CNN telecast of a "global forum" with the president continued to stress "an era of change and opportunity and peril [in which] America must be willing to assume the obligations and the risks of leadership." The world's "oldest democracy," a "unique nation," he said, must remain the "beacon of strength and freedom and hope," continuing its "most daring experiment in forging different races, religions and cultures into a single people, . . . promoting the spread of democracy abroad," and confronting "an epidemic of humanitarian catastrophes" in this "pivotal moment" for expanding "the frontiers of freedom."[29] In July, while visiting Poland, Clinton warned of "oppression's fatal grip" and against "would-be dictators and fiery demagogues [who] live among us in the East and in the West, promoting ethnic and racial hatred, promoting religious divisions and anti-Semitism and aggressive nationalism." The president called upon his audience to "sustain the civil courage" it takes to stay on track with "free markets and democracy [which] remain the only proven path to prosperity and to peace."[30]

Back at the United Nations in September, 1994, Clinton pushed hard and explicitly on the theme of democracy's fragility. Telling the members of the General Assembly they were meeting in a "time of great hope," he observed nevertheless that the world faced a contest "as old as history" between "freedom and tyranny." It was this generation's task to "secure the peace" and to assume the "sacred mission" of building a new world that is more democratic and prosperous, for "terrible examples of chaos, repression and tyranny . . . mark our times" and challenge "the very institutions of fragile democracy."[31] Thus, as he told the nation in October, America was working for "a post–Cold War world of democracy and prosperity."[32]

The theme of a struggle for American leadership against the forces of isolationism punctuated Clinton's address on March 1, 1995, at the Nixon Center in Washington, D.C. There he argued that the idea of an open society remains as much under attack today as it was previously by fascism and then Communism and thus that democracy still must be "nurtured" with investment and support given to "fledgling democracies." Democracy is a "trend," not an inevitability, nor will it be easy to "establish or shore up fragile democracies," he stressed.[33] In May, the president visited Moscow State University, urging faith in their "young, fragile democracy" but observing as well that "the more open and flexible our societies are, the more our people are able to move freely without restraint, the greater we are exposed to [new security] threats," such as the bombing of the World Trade Center, the tragedy of Oklahoma City, bombings in the streets of Israel, the gas attack in a Tokyo subway, and the problem of organized crime. It is a point he reiterated as recently as his State of the Union address on January 27, 1998.[34] Democracy itself, and the free flow of information it permits, seemingly is a source of insecurity about which we must become increasingly vigilant. Thus, as Clinton stressed in October, 1995, the United States must "continue to bear the responsibility of the world's leadership." It is "our special obligation to lead" the "construction of a post–Cold War world" in the "cause of democracy, freedom, security and prosperity" and in a "Technology Age that can mean simply breaking open a vial of sarin gas in a Tokyo subway. It can mean hooking into the Internet and learning how to build a bomb that will blow up a federal building in the heart of America. These forces, just as surely as fascism and communism, would spread darkness over light, disintegration over integration, chaos over community."[35] In his second inaugural address the president declared that "America stands alone as the world's indispensable nation," that the "world's greatest democracy will lead a whole world of democracies," sustaining its "journey" and striving to keep an "old democracy forever young."[36]

Clinton's Democratic Peace

Besides the pervasive theme of democracy's fragility, Clinton's rhetoric features the motif of a democratic peace—that is, the premise that peace and security depend on spreading democracy globally. This amounts to another extension of Cold War discourse into a fragmented world where the meaning of liberal democratic internationalism—America's Wilsonian vision of world order—is sufficiently obtuse to disguise the fact that democracy is a contested term. In Clinton's rhetoric, which is typical of his Cold War predecessors, democracy equals capitalism and vice versa. It is an equation that enables the guardian of world order to legitimize its economic agenda of world capitalism under the sign of a quest for democracy.[37] Moreover, the vagueness of the meaning of democracy as the key term in the logic of a democratic peace—the claim that democratic nations do not attack one another—undermines the premise that democracy is rapidly spreading throughout the world and thus the conclusion that peace is at hand. This is not to argue against the notable increase in the number of liberal democratic states. Instead, it is to emphasize (a) that this trend represents only one relatively weak variation on the theme of democracy, (b) that the extension of liberal democratic regimes has not necessarily improved the general quality of political and material lives, and (c) that any increase in the number of democratic states has not corresponded to an increase in the democratic practices among and between nations.[38] Furthermore, as democratic theorists have argued, "the theorem of 'peace among democracies' is a dangerous one" because it "almost suggests that by using any means to force autocratic regimes into submission, including war, the best of all possible worlds can be achieved," thus lending "ideological ammunition to the strongest states . . . to defend their interests in the international realm regardless of the interests of weaker parties."[39]

Bruce Russett, author of *Grasping the Democratic Peace: Principles for a Post–Cold War World,* makes the strongest argument for the theory that democracies do not fight each other. This norm developed toward the end of the nineteenth century, became harder to ignore in the 1970s, when there were nearly three dozen democracies in the international arena, and was widely recognized by the end of the 1980s. The empirical argument, in his words, is "extremely robust, in that by various criteria of war and militarized diplomatic disputes, and various measures of democracy, the relative rarity of violent conflict between democracies still holds up." This does not mean, Russett emphasizes, that democracies are peaceful in their relations with nondemocratic states or that they are less likely to experience civil war. The standard of what counts as a democracy, however, is quite low, including only the criteria of "a voting franchise for a substantial fraction of citizens, a government brought to power in contested elections, and an executive either popularly elected or responsible to an elected legislature." No provision is made for civil liberties or even economic liberty as defining qualities of democracy in this line of argument, but a "stability" factor is included so that no fledgling democratic states are counted when they engage in wars against other democracies. Moreover, Russett's discussion of marginal cases of democratic nations fighting one another reveals that a key factor is whether one nation sees the other as democratic or not. That was the case in the Spanish-American War of 1898, when U.S. decision makers and the American public were persuaded that they represented the forces of liberty while Spain, which practiced universal male suffrage and had a bicameral legislature with an executive accountable in some degree to it, was represented as the tyrant.[40]

Russett acknowledges that at best the research establishes an empirical relationship of democracies remaining at peace with one another, which does not yield a compelling case without a strong theoretical explanation. Furthermore, he dismisses the theoretical account that democratic cultures are inherently more peaceful, noting that democracies are no less war-prone than nondemocracies and that they have been strongly predisposed to imperialism. A better account, he believes, is that powerful norms within democracies operate as restraints on violence against other states that are perceived as sharing those same norms of legitimate decision making. As Russett explains, "By this hypothesis, the *culture, perceptions, and practices* that permit compromise and the peaceful resolution of conflicts without the threat of violence within countries come to apply across national boundaries toward other democratic countries." Self-governing people, that is, do not believe other self-governing people are easily misled by self-serving elites into aggressive acts toward others, and when democracies do fight each other it is usually because at least one of them is politically unstable.[41]

This theory leaves the notion of a democratic peace on shaky grounds. First, the empirical argument, perhaps the soundest element of the theory, depends on a flexible definition of democracy, sometimes excluding civil liberties and sometimes requiring a condition of stability. Second, wars between democracies are dismissed as a function of political instability, which is a function of perception. One person's instability may be another person's idea of democratic practice. Third, the theory accepts that democratic regimes are prone to frequent violent conflicts with nondemocratic nations, both empirically and because theoretically democratic culture requires a reciprocity of norms in order to feel secure toward another country, and thus they feel vulnerable to aggression from nondemocratic regimes. Finally, democratic nations cannot feel secure, according to this theory of a democratic peace, until the unlikely time when all nations become stable democracies. Even Russett acknowledges the problems entailed in at least some of these four reservations. He notes, for instance, that when one democracy threatens or uses force against another, its case for war will emphasize the instability of the targeted regime, and, of course, a case is even easier to make when the opponent is characterized as hostile to democracy. The theory could also have the unfortunate consequence, he acknowledges, of encouraging wars against authoritarian regimes, the great majority of which are not aggressive, for the purpose of creating a peaceful democratic world order. "A crusade for democracy," Russett feels compelled to warn, "is not in order" and in fact is a dangerous way to deal with even "the most odious dictators."[42]

All of this should be cause for concern when we consider the Clinton administration's rhetorical emphasis on achieving national security through a democratic peace while at the same time stressing the fragility of fledgling democracies and the continuing threat of totalitarianism, dictatorship, and authoritarianism. Of particular concern is the claim that "the growth of cooperation between the United States and the Russian Federation . . . is rooted in democracy"—which of course is a weak foundation for a relationship in which one of the partners is the oldest democracy in the world and the other is characterized as a "young, fragile democracy."[43] Indeed, the proposition of a peaceful democratic world order is a dangerous source of national insecurity and a strong invitation to war. Moreover, it focuses attention on achieving order and away from enriching democratic practice itself, which within the American tradition of liberal democratic internationalism is a thin concept at best reflecting a basic distrust of the democrats.[44]

The question we must ask, then, is whether the United States can break its Cold War habit of using democracy as an ideological tool that perpetuates a crusading sense of national insecurity and begin to develop a more robust democratic culture that promotes responsible international participation without requiring global domination. How might the nation transform its understanding of democracy to more readily balance the post–Cold War forces of integration and fragmentation?

Reconstituting Democracy

The problem indicated by the question of reconstituting democracy is not subject to a quick or easy fix, nor is it my purpose here to offer a definitive solution. The cultural, rhetorical, and institutional dimensions of the problem, however, point to the direction we might take in search of answers, where opportunities for democratic transformation most likely exist, before the post–Cold War enthusiasm for a more democratic world dissolves into fear of international disorder. In particular, we need to attend to the nation's tradition of liberal democracy and ask how its frail republican constitution might develop into a robust democratic disposition. America, as Benjamin Barber, David Held, and others have argued, has a long but thin democratic legacy. This is increasingly problematic in an era that has made democracy the basic standard of political legitimacy.[45] "While we cannot do without democracy," Held maintains, "it is increasingly bankrupt in its traditional shape and, thus, needs fundamental reform."[46] Within this tradition of thin, liberal representative democracy, the people are marginalized by overdeveloped institutions of elite representation that act as a disincentive for participatory politics. Individual rights, in particular property rights, the marketplace, economic growth, and social stability, are given priority over the rule of the people.[47] Accordingly, the historically contested premise that democracy and free-market capitalism are compatible has been maintained, albeit with increasing difficulty, only by diminishing the vitality of democracy while protecting economic interests.[48]

According to republican liberalism's prevailing logic, which equates direct democracy with demagoguery rather than rational deliberation, exercising democracy vigorously increases the risk of mobocracy and democratic distemper. Where democracy promotes popular rule, liberalism concerns itself with the proper limits and scope of political power, conflating power with reason in order to control the outcome of political decisions while attempting to contain the democratic impulse enough to make it safe to practice. As Russell Hanson has observed, democracy possessed little normative value in the founding years of the American republic because it referred to the rule of the commoners, who ostensibly lacked sufficient virtue to protect individual liberty, minority interests, and the accumulation of personal property or to look after the commonweal. Such virtue was considered imperative to protect the nation against the internal threat of faction and external threat of invasion. Federalists chastised democratic societies in the United States with colorful phrases such as a "hateful synagogue of anarchy," "odious conclave of tumult," and "frightful cathedral of discord." They strongly preferred republicanism over "democratic distemper," "popular passions," and the "prejudices" of "mob rule." In nineteenth-century America, republican forces attempted to discipline the popular impulse through a regime of political party rule, believing party regularity to be the vessel of civic virtue "essential to the health of the republic."[49] Influenced by Progressive Era reforms, democratic virtue in the twentieth century became a function of managerial and administrative expertise, developing increasingly into a greater reliance on experts equipped to look after the common good.

Historically, then, Americans have placed neither unqualified trust nor collective faith in democracy despite its status as a god term of national ideals and mission. It inspires more awe than faith or trust, engendering feelings of fear and dread combined with wonder and veneration and fraught with ambivalence, ambiguity, and a chronic sense of insecurity. The paradox of American political consciousness is that it predisposes the nation to fear its own demise by depicting unfettered democracy as a dangerous disease of illiberal rule while rendering suspect any explicit repudiation of egalitarian ideals. Such paradoxical danger is a function, rhetorically at least, of representing democracy as a political disease. Unable to resolve this conflicted trope domestically, the country has sought its redemption and security in a vision of democratic peace realized globally as an end of history and confirmation of national virtue. Its historic mission as a beacon of liberty has evolved into a manifest destiny to expand the domain of liberal democratic rule across the continent and into a global order. Spreading democracy globally, however, has not resolved the problem of transforming an image of popular distemper into a healthy vehicle of international peace and security. The concept of democracy as presently constituted remains a calcified discourse that reinforces national anxieties in a decidedly risky world and perpetuates a war mentality by chronically exaggerating perceptions of national peril.[50] In short, an excess of liberalism has diminished the nation's confidence in its democratic imagination and undermined its ability to respond comfortably to popular movements.

This legacy of anemic, thin democracy, which Barber labels "the politics of zookeeping," renders democracy fragile and weak out of distrust for its devotion to liberty and doubts over its ability to secure freedom and justice, containing it like a deadly virus and reserving the sturdiest cages for the people. Barber traces this fear of an outbreak of democratic distemper to a deficient model of political reasoning, which I argue elsewhere is grounded in an antirhetorical and unrealistic conception of public deliberation. In a thin democracy where citizens are deemed the irrational and threatening Other—an Other that must be contained domestically and globally in order to secure the peace and insure prosperity—diversity and difference are equated with error, disorder, and danger rather than taken as normal, healthy signs of articulating interests, addressing audiences, developing strategies of identification, and transacting agreements through public persuasion. Rhetoric thus exercises democracy and strengthens it by courting and befriending the otherwise threatening Other wherever and whenever possible.[51] It values agonistic politics over antagonistic relations.[52]

Consistent with the rhetorical enactment of democratic culture, an extension of democratic institutions would help to redress the traditional imbalance of liberalism in American politics and foreign affairs. Held's recent work on "cosmopolitan democracy" is illustrative of the possibilities of institutional change along these lines. Again, my purpose is only to indicate directions for further exploration and development of a more robust democratic constitution, not to argue for a specific solution at this time. As Held himself underscores, the cosmopolitan model of democracy represents a program of "possible transformations"—a "direction of possible change with clear points of orientation"—not a plan that can be realized immediately, nor one with all the possibilities worked out and all possible objections answered.[53]

Held's model responds to the conditions of globalization that have eroded and crossed national barriers to create interconnections among diverse peoples at several levels of governance, and it aims to maximize the degree to which the people affected by a policy decision participate in its formulation and deliberation. Moreover, it recognizes that the "dynamics and logic of the inter-state system would still represent an immensely powerful force in global affairs" even if more regional parliaments were created and strengthened, international referendums were conducted on transnational issues, and participatory democracy was intensified at local levels to complement representative deliberative bodies at the global level. A democratic world order organized vertically and horizontally into a cosmopolitan community to accommodate "diverse and distinct domains of authority" and respect a plurality of identities would not presume the integration of cultural and political diversities into a single consensus of beliefs and values but would rely on a robust and continuing democratic practice to deliberate competing narratives and address conflicted values.[54] These are the kinds of practices that have to be considered and confronted, Held concludes, if the new emerging world order is actually going to become democratic.[55]

Under present circumstances, the challenge of balancing the post–Cold War forces of integration and fragmentation will be difficult to meet. Reconstituting America's democratic disposition into a robust commitment might very well be a key to achieving such a balance, whereas the liberal appropriation of democracy is becoming increasingly problematic and quite possibly self-defeating by repeating the myth of democracy's fragility and perpetuating the cycle of national paranoia. The unfortunate legacy of Cold War discourse as illustrated in President Clinton's foreign policy addresses is a republic of fear holding fast to a vision of the new world order that is more democratic in name than practice. That legacy need not prevail, however, if we explore ways of rhetorically enacting a strong and healthy democratic culture.

Notes

1. See Francis Fukuyama, *The End of History and the Last Man* (New York: Avon, 1992). For a current and trenchant discussion of the Wilsonian democratic world order and its Nazi and Communist ideological challengers, see Amos Perlmutter, *Making the World Safe for Democracy: A Century of Wilsonianism and its Totalitarian Challengers* (Chapel Hill: University of North Carolina Press, 1997).

2. John Lewis Gaddis, *The United States and the End of the Cold War: Implications, Reconsiderations, Provocations* (New York: Oxford University Press, 1992), 13–14.

3. Ibid., 196, 208–209, 212, 215–16.

4. Roger Burbach, "The Tragedy of American Democracy," in *Low Intensity Democracy: Political Power in the New World Order,* ed. Barry Gills, Joel Rocamora, and Richard Wilson (London: Pluto, 1993), 101.

5. Tony Smith, *The United States and the Worldwide Struggle for Democracy in the Twentieth Century* (Princeton, N.J.: Princeton University Press, 1995), 10, 143–44, 181–84.

6. Ibid., 239–42.

7. See Robert L. Ivie, "Eisenhower as Cold Warrior," in *Eisenhower's War of Words: Rhetoric and Leadership,* ed. Martin J. Medhurst (East Lansing: Michigan State University Press, 1994), 7–25; Dan F. Hahn, "The Rhetoric of Jimmy Carter, 1976–1980," *Presidential Studies Quarterly* 14 (1984): 280; Robert L. Ivie, "Fire, Flood, and Red Fever: Motivating Metaphors of Global Emergency in the Truman Doctrine Speech," *Presidential Studies Quarterly* 29 (1999): 570–91; and Robert L. Ivie, "Dwight D. Eisenhower's 'Chance for Peace": Quest or Crusade?" *Rhetoric and Public Affairs* 1 (1998): 227–43.

8. Gaddis Smith, *Morality, Reason, and Power: American Diplomacy in the Carter Years* (New York: Hill and Wang, 1986), 47–48.

9. Quotations from Carter's speech at Notre Dame University, May 22, 1977, are taken from the text released by the White House following the commencement address, a copy of which was located in "SP 3-37 1/20/77—1/20/81," Box SP-21, WHCF, Subject File—Speeches, Jimmy Carter Library, Atlanta, Ga. (hereafter Carter Library).

10. Speaking Draft, State of the Union, Jan. 23, 1980, "1/23/80 (Material for State of the Union Address) (1)," Box 166, Handwriting File, Carter Library.

11. Erwin C. Hargrove, *Jimmy Carter as President: Leadership and the Politics of the Public Good* (Baton Rouge: Louisiana State University Press, 1988), 112.

12. Jimmy Carter, *Keeping Faith: Memoirs of a President* (Toronto: Bantam, 1982), 142–46.

13. For a more extensive analysis of Carter's Cold War discourse on these themes, see Robert L. Ivie, "From Conversion to Punishment: Jimmy Carter's Rhetorical Ministry Before and After Afghanistan" (paper delivered at the Seventy-seventh Annual Meeting of the National Communication Association, Atlanta, Oct. 31, 1991).

14. Barry Gills, Joel Rocamora, and Richard Wilson, "Low Intensity Democracy," in *Low Intensity Democracy,* ed. Gills et al., 8.

15. Ibid., 9–10.

16. Burbach, "Tragedy of American Democracy," 101–104.

17. Smith, *United States and the Worldwide Struggle,* 268–71.

18. Quoted ibid., 313.

19. Perlmutter, *Making the World Safe,* 9. Perlmutter observes specifically about President Bush that he "coined the phrase 'new' world order to define the post Cold War era. By this he meant the end of totalitarianism and the spread of democracy and free markets to the former Soviet Empire. It was actually a disguise for American hegemonial conduct in international politics" (161).

20. Quoted in Burbach, "Tragedy of American Democracy," 100.

21. Quoted in Smith, *United States and the Worldwide Struggle,* 320.

22. Perlmutter, *Making the World Safe,* 162, 164–65.

23. The set of Clinton addresses examined here was compiled by accessing the White House Virtual Library (http://www.whitehouse.gov/WH/html/library.html) and asking for all of Clinton's presidential texts (through Dec. 31, 1997) including the term "democracy" in them. From that set, forty were selected for closer examination (distributed fairly equally over the five years from 1993 through 1997) because of the extent to which they were devoted to foreign policy questions

and democracy themes. Of those forty, thirteen proved most revealing and thus are cited in the analysis that follows.

24. William J. Clinton, "Inaugural Speech," Jan. 20, 1993, White House Virtual Library, Internet, Dec. 24, 1997.

25. William J. Clinton, "Remarks by the President at American University Centennial Celebration," Feb. 26, 1993.

26. William J. Clinton, "Prepared Remarks of President William J. Clinton to the American Society of Newspaper Editors, 'A Strategic Alliance with Russian Reform,'" Apr. 1, 1993.

27. William J. Clinton, "Remarks by the President in Address to the National Assembly of the Republic of Korea," July 10, 1993.

28. William J. Clinton, "Address by the President to the 48th Session of the United Nations General Assembly," Sept. 27, 1993.

29. William J. Clinton, "Remarks by the President in CNN Telecast of 'A Global Forum with President Clinton,'" May 3, 1994.

30. William J. Clinton, "Remarks by the President to the Sejm," July 7, 1994.

31. William J. Clinton, "Address by the President at the 49th Session of the U.N. General Assembly," Sept. 26, 1994.

32. William J. Clinton, "Remarks by the President in Address to the Nation," Oct. 10 1994.

33. William J. Clinton, "President William Jefferson Clinton Address to the Nixon Center for Peace and Freedom Policy Conference," Mar. 1, 1995.

34. William J. Clinton, "Remarks by the President to Students of Moscow State University," May 10, 1995.

35. William J. Clinton, "Remarks by the President in Freedom House Speech," Oct. 6, 1995.

36. William J. Clinton, "Inaugural Address of President William J. Clinton," Jan. 20, 1997.

37. See Gills et al., "Low Intensity Democracy," 6–7, on this point, as well as Noam Chomsky, "The Struggle for Democracy in the New World Order," in *Low Intensity Democracy,* ed. Gills et al., 80–99.

38. On this point, see Daniele Archibugi and David Held, "Editors' Introduction," *Cosmopolitan Democracy: An Agenda for a New World Order,* ed. Daniele Archibugi and David Held (Cambridge: Polity, 1995), 3–4.

39. Ibid., 11–12.

40. Bruce Russett, *Grasping the Democratic Peace: Principles for a Post–Cold War World* (Princeton, N.J.: Princeton University Press, 1993), 5, 10–11, 14–15, 19.

41. Ibid., 30–31.

42. Ibid., 123, 126, 135–36.

43. William J. Clinton, "Address to the 49th U.N. General Assembly," and William J. Clinton, "Remarks to Students of Moscow State University."

44. For a discussion of thin democracy and the prevalence of liberalism over democracy in American political culture, see Benjamin Barber, *Strong Democracy: Participatory Politics for a New Age* (Berkeley: University of California Press, 1984); and Russell L. Hanson, *The Democratic Imagination in America: Conversations with Our Past* (Princeton, N.J.: Princeton University Press, 1985).

45. Barber, *Strong Democracy,* 3–25; David Held, *Models of Democracy,* 2d ed. (Stanford, Calif.: Stanford University Press, 1996), xi, 254; Hanson, *Democratic Imagination,* 5, 13–19. Douglas Lummis, *Radical Democracy* (Ithaca, N.Y.: Cornell University Press, 1996), 111–42, discusses the larger context of the problem in Western culture as "democracy's flawed tradition."

46. David Held, "Democracy and the New International Order," in *Cosmopolitan Democracy,* ed. Archibugi and Held, 96–97.

47. Burbach, "Tragedy of American Democracy," 120; see also Norberto Bobbio, *Liberalism and Democracy* (London: Verso, 1990).

48. Burbach, "Tragedy of American Democracy," 101, 117–19.

49. Hanson, *Democratic Imagination,* 84, 114, 116.

50. For a discussion of America's war mentality, see Michael S. Sherry, *In the Shadow of War: The United States Since the 1930s* (New Haven, Conn.: Yale University Press, 1995).

51. Barber, *Strong Democracy,* xvii, xx, xxiii, 20–21, 36–37, 151, 160, 162. 167, 177, 189; Robert L. Ivie, "Democratic Deliberation in a Rhetorical Republic," *Quarterly Journal of Speech* 84 (1998): 491–505.

52. Archibugi and Held, "Editors' Introduction,"10; Lawrence J. Hatab, *A Nietzschean Defense of Democracy: An Experiment in Postmodern Politics* (Chicago: Open Court, 1995), 78–93, 108, 158–73, 191, 199, 220.

53. Held, "Democracy and the New International Order," 110–12.

54. Ibid., 106–108, 112, 115–16.

55. For an elaboration of the cosmopolitan model, see David Held, *Democracy and the Global Order: From the Modern State to Cosmopolitan Governance* (Stanford, Calif.: Stanford University Press, 1995).

Afterword

Rhetorical Perspectives on the Cold War

MARTIN J. MEDHURST

As these essays demonstrate, rhetoric and history are inextricably intertwined. The exigencies of history are the motive forces that call rhetoric into being. If there were not problems that needed to be addressed—things that needed changing—there would be no need for rhetoric. But in the real world, people and situations are forever changing and ideas are forever in need of being modified, altered, tweaked, or improved. The dominant means by which such changes are effected is rhetorical discourse.

Of course not all changes are improvements, and not all rhetoric is successful. And even that locution—"successful rhetoric"—presupposes someone's intentions, standards, and interpretations. Successful according to whom? By what measures? According to whose theory or critical stance? As these essays make clear, rhetoric is a complicated business, particularly when practiced within the conceptual framework of something as multifaceted as the Cold War.

Yet that is precisely why rhetoric and history must be studied together, because both are complicated matters that directly impinge upon one another. To try to study history apart from the influential discourses that helped to constitute that history is to ignore one crucial component of historical causation. It is to assume that humans really do not matter, that some determining force or cause—biological, psychological, economic, or cosmological—has foreordained the human condition, and nothing can be done to change the world as we know it.

To try to study rhetoric apart from history is equally unsatisfying. Poetry can be practiced in a vacuum; self-expression needs no audience. But rhetoric is a form of discourse that is both weighted and addressed—it bears both the conditions of its making and the vicissitudes of its reception. It is never wholly under the control of any one person or group, and therefore possesses a power (*dynamis*) of its own, a power that operates from history and in history to make history.

As the essays in this book demonstrate, there is more than one way to conceptualize rhetoric and its influence on human decision making. For Norman Graebner, rhetoric is a verbal formulation that masks reality, a sort of false consciousness that operates through myth, ideology, and the calcification of belief into doctrine. For Frank Costigliola, rhetoric is best understood as strategic language choices that are utilized to accomplish the speaker's—in this case Joseph Stalin's—goals. For Robert P. Newman, rhetoric is a form of dialectical exchange, a sort of debate whereby historical actors use argument and counterargument to forge yet more rhetoric, such as the persuasive document NSC-68. For Shawn Parry-Giles and J. Michael Hogan, rhetoric is the theoretical basis of state-sponsored propaganda, where rhetoric is not merely verbal discourse, but pamphlets and polls, broadcasts and balloons, deception and the management of mass perceptions. For H. W. Brands, Randall Bennett Woods, and Rachel L. Holloway, rhetoric is the public presentation of an ideological stance—a liberal stance in the cases of Eisenhower, Johnson, and Fulbright, and a conservative stance in the case of Reagan. For Robert J. McMahon, rhetoric is the purveyor of myth, not in the sense of falsehood or deception, but myth as narrative—the story we tell to ourselves about ourselves. And for Robert L. Ivie, rhetoric—which is a dominant factor in the production and reproduction of political culture—is turned back on itself as a mode of critique and cultural analysis.

All of these senses of rhetoric are useful, the more so when we can clearly see both the similarities and the differences in their understandings and uses of various rhetorical traditions. As dissimilar as some of those approaches are, they all share certain basic building blocks. For example, all involve one or more *speakers* or *writers* who embody and give expression to motives and purposes. Speakers possess various levels of talent and natural abilities. So do writers. Personality factors such as beliefs, attitudes, and values shape the mind and hence the discourse, as does the communicator's training, formal or informal, in the art and practice of rhetoric. To relate the speaker and her or his historical and rhetorical situation to the message produced, much as Costigliola does in his essay, is one form of rhetorical analysis.

Messages are, of course, the heart of rhetorical criticism. The *message*, whether embodied in a speech, letter, radio or television broadcast, coded signal, handshake, or diplomatic document, is subject to various types and levels of analysis. Some rhetorical critics focus on language choices, others look at the argumentative form of the message. Some examine particular images—metaphors, similes, analogies and the like—to discern how those figures function conceptually and argumentatively in the discourse. Some look to the developmental history of the message, examining speech drafts or working notes or planning session minutes. In all instances, the emphasis is not merely on what the message is, but rather on what it does in the overall situation. How the message functions to bring about change is a central question.

In rhetorical studies, messages become important only in relationship to *audiences.* Rhetorical critics are never satisfied with understanding just the internal dynamics of the message, important as those dynamics may be, but strive always to relate the internal form to one or more external exigence—and that always involves an audience, often multiple audiences. Before one can assess the potential effectiveness of any given message, one must know both the characteristics of that message and the beliefs, values, and expectations of those to whom the message is sent. Messages mean very little in isolation. Certainly speakers and writers intend to convey specific ideas, and if they are talented speakers or writers they can construct their messages in such a way as to invite particular interpretations. Yet, in the final analysis, it is the audience, collectively and individually, that attributes meaning to a message. And how do audience members do that? They assimilate what they read or hear into the conceptual framework that they already possess. Costigliola's chapter is a prime example of the American audience hearing and understanding what it had been prepared to hear and understand. The very same message was interpreted quite differently inside the Soviet Union by the Russian peoples. Did Americans misinterpret Stalin's speech? Possibly. Yet it is also possible that Stalin intended his speech to be heard by multiple audiences and intended that different audiences understand the speech in different ways. Astute speakers have long understood that messages can be prepared in such a way as to convey different ideas to different audiences simultaneously.[1] It thus behooves the critic to examine the speaker/message/audience relationship very closely.

Speakers, messages, and audiences never exist in a vacuum. All are creatures of the geography they occupy, the ideologies they espouse, the political systems they work within, and the historical moment that they appear upon the world's stage. In short, they exist within a specific *context.* Here is where rhetorical analysis and historical investigation necessarily overlap. One cannot understand any rhetorical transaction without thoroughly understanding the contextual factors that give meaning to the exchange. There are linguistic contexts (the language system within which the message is formulated), geographical contexts (the place where the message originates and the place where it is received), ideological contexts (the specialized meanings of terms within a doctrinal or ideological system), sociological contexts (the group norms that function as message filters), and psychological contexts (the individual personality traits, talents, motives, and drives by which the message is produced on one end—and assimilated and judged on the other). Failure to understand how these contextual factors affect both the production of the message by the speaker or writer and the reception and interpretation of the message by one or more audiences is sure to result in misunderstanding. Perhaps that is why one prominent rhetorical theorist, the late I. A. Richards, defined rhetoric as the study of "misunderstanding and its remedies."[2]

When we stop to consider that rhetorical messages are regularly delivered through *channels* as diverse as face-to-face conversation (Reagan and Gorbachev at Reykjavik), small group interaction (diplomats around the conference table), public speech (Clinton delivering the State of the Union address in front of Congress), and mass communication (from international broadcasting to Internet web sites), it is clear that analysis of such messages is anything but simple. However, by combining the methods of the rhetorical critic with the tools of historiography, much can be learned. In the final analysis that is the message of this book.

The Cold War has been examined from many different perspectives. This book is the first attempt to bring the insights of both rhetoric and history to bear on specific texts and practices of that long twilight struggle between the United States and the Soviet Union. Such an approach to scholarship seems natural when one pauses to consider that "the Cold War era is a rich amalgam of personalities, crises, manifestoes, and various attempts at symbolic inducement, often on a worldwide scale."[3] As archives continue to be opened, both in the former Soviet Union and throughout Eastern Europe, more will be learned about the struggle we called the Cold War. The analytical perspectives of both historians and rhetoricians have much to offer in the quest to discover what "really" happened.

Notes

1. For a rhetorical analysis that examines a Cold War message sent simultaneously to three different audiences see Martin J. Medhurst, "Eisenhower's 'Atoms for Peace' Speech: A Case Study in

the Strategic Use of Language," *Communication Monographs* 54 (1987): 204–20. This article is reprinted in Martin J. Medhurst, Robert L. Ivie, Philip Wander, and Robert L. Scott, *Cold War Rhetoric: Strategy, Metaphor, and Ideology* (East Lansing: Michigan State University Press, 1997), 29–50.

2. I. A. Richards, *The Philosophy of Rhetoric* (New York: Oxford University Press, 1965), 3.

3. Martin J. Medhurst, "Eisenhower and the Crusade for Freedom: The Rhetorical Origins of a Cold War Campaign," *Presidential Studies Quarterly* 27 (1997): 646–61.

Contributors

H. W. Brands, the Thomas Professor in the Department of History at Texas A&M University, is the author of several books on U.S. history, including *The Devil We Knew; What America Owes the World;* and *TR.*

Frank Costigliola, professor of history at the University of Connecticut, is the author of *Awkward Dominion: American Political, Economic, and Cultural Relations with Europe, 1919–1933* and *The Cold Alliance: France and the United States since World War II.* He is currently working on a book on the impact of emotion and cultural difference on the formation of the Cold War.

Norman A. Graebner, the Randolph P. Compton Professor of History and Public Affairs Emeritus at the University of Virginia, is the author or editor of some twenty books, including *Empire on the Pacific; Manifest Destiny; Ideas and Diplomacy;* and *America As a World Power.*

J. Michael Hogan, professor and graduate officer in the Department of Speech Communication at the Pennsylvania State University, is the author of *The Panama Canal in American Politics* and *The Nuclear Freeze Campaign* and the editor of *Rhetoric and Community.*

Rachel L. Holloway, associate professor of communication studies at Virginia Tech University, is the author of *In the Matter of J. Robert Oppenheimer: Politics, Rhetoric, and Self Defense* and the coeditor of *The Clinton Presidency: Images, Issues, and Communication Strategies.*

Robert L. Ivie, professor and department chair of communication and culture at Indiana University, is the coauthor of *Cold War Rhetoric: Strategy, Metaphor, and Ideology* and is currently working on a book manuscript entitled *Democracy in a Republic of Fear.*

Robert J. McMahon, professor of history at the University of Florida, has written widely on the history of America foreign relations, especially the Cold War and Vietnam War eras. His books include *The Cold War on the Pe-*

riphery: The United States, India, and Pakistan and *The Limits of Empire: The United States and Southeast Asia since World War II.*

Martin J. Medhurst, professor of speech communication and coordinator of the program in presidential rhetoric at Texas A&M University, is the author or editor of eight books, including *Dwight D. Eisenhower: Strategic Communicator; Eisenhower's War of Words: Rhetoric and Leadership;* and *Beyond the Rhetorical Presidency.*

Robert P. Newman, adjunct professor of communication studies and associate of the Obermann Center for Advanced Studies at the University of Iowa, is the author of five books, including *Owen Lattimore and the "Loss" of China,* which earned Pulitzer and National Book Award nominations and was a finalist in the *Los Angeles Times Book Prize* competition, and *Truman and the Hiroshima Cult,* which won the Diamond Jubilee Book Award of the National Communication Association.

Shawn J. Parry-Giles, assistant professor of communication and adjunct assistant professor of women's studies at the University of Maryland, is the author of numerous articles appearing in such outlets as the *Quarterly Journal of Speech; Political Communication;* and *Presidential Studies Quarterly.*

Randall Bennett Woods, Cooper Distinguished Professor of History at the University of Arkansas, is the author or coauthor of seven books, including *Fulbright: A Biography; The Dawning of the Cold War: The United States' Quest for Order;* and *A Changing of the Guard: Anglo-American Relations, 1941–1946.* He is currently working on a one-volume biography of Lyndon B. Johnson.

Index